A General Introduction
to the Bible

A General Introduction to the Bible

NORMAN L. GEISLER

and

WILLIAM E. NIX

Foreword by
SAMUEL J. SCHULTZ

MOODY PRESS • CHICAGO

Library of Congress Catalog Card Number: 68-18890

ISBN: 0-8024-2915-7

A MOODY PRESS BOOK

———————

Sixth Printing, 1973

To Our Wives,
BARBARA and EULAINE,
who have been
constant sources of encouragement
and assistance

FOREWORD

This general introduction to the Bible is timely and significant. Numerous are the questions currently being asked concerning the origin and transmission of the Bible. It is to these inquiries and related problems that the authors of this volume devote their research and scholarship in the following pages.

Never before has any generation had available so many versions of the Scriptures. Faced with a variation of translations the average reader of the Bible rightfully raises questions concerning the origin, authority and canonicity of the books that constitute the Bible as well as the accuracy with which they have been transmitted throughout the centuries.

What distinguished the Bible from other ancient literature? If the books of the Bible were produced only by the initiative and ability of the authors, then their writings would be primarily human productions. If these books were dictated by God—and I know of no biblical scholar who maintains this view—then they would be primarily divine products. A recognition of both the human and divine aspects in the writing of the Scriptures is essential for regarding the Bible as unique in being a human-divine product.

When were the books of the Bible recognized as authoritative, and by whom? Did the Israelites and the Christian church declare the books of the Bible authoritative or did they recognize them as divinely inspired and on that basis regard them as valuable and authoritative?

How were the books of the Bible transmitted? Did scribes correct and change the Scriptures or did they transmit them with care and accuracy? How reliable are our present versions when compared with the oldest manuscripts of the Scriptures available to modern scholarship?

Why do some Bibles include the Apocrypha and others omit them? On what basis do the limits of the canon vary?

The authors of this book are to be commended for their consideration of these questions so frequently discussed in regard to the Bible.

Refreshingly significant is the attitude reflected throughout these pages expressed in the assertion that "Christ is the key to canonicity." Modern scholarship that gives serious consideration to the attitude and teaching of Jesus concerning these problems related to the Bible deserves commendation.

SAMUEL J. SCHULTZ
Professor of Bible and Theology
Wheaton College

PREFACE

This book on General Biblical Introduction covers the three main areas of the general field: Inspiration, Canonization and Transmission of the biblical text. It is not concerned as such with the problems of authorship, date and purpose of the individual books of the Bible, as these are the subjects of Special Biblical Introduction. This work is designed to give a general survey of the process of the transmission of the Bible from God to man. It expounds the claim that God inspired the biblical books, that men of God wrote them, and that the Fathers (Hebrew and Christian) collected and transmitted them to future generations. The bulk of the material considered here deals with the transmission of the Bible from the earliest centuries to the present time. It attempts to answer in the affirmative the all-important question: Is the Bible used today (and the Hebrew and Greek texts upon which it is based) a faithful representation of the text as originally written by the authors of the Old and New Testaments?

The Bible quotations used in this book are from the Authorized King James Version, the American Standard Version of 1901, and, unless otherwise stated, the Revised Standard Version.

CONTENTS

ILLUSTRATIONS

Part One

INSPIRATION
OF THE BIBLE

1

STRUCTURE AND DIVISIONS OF THE BIBLE

THE BIBLE AND ITS TESTAMENTS: DEFINITIONS

MEANING OF "BIBLE"

The word *Bible* can rightfully claim to be the great-grandson of the Greek word *biblos*, which was the name given to the outer coat of a papyrus reed in Egypt during the eleventh century B.C. The plural form of biblos is *biblia*, and by the second century A.D. Christians were using this latter word to describe their writings. Biblia gave birth to the Latin word of the same spelling, *biblia*, which was in turn transliterated into the Old French *biblia* by the same process. The modern English word *Bible* is derived from the Old French, with the Anglicized ending. This word is the product of four stages of transliteration and transmission.

MEANING OF "TESTAMENT"

Next to the fact that the Bible is a biblos, or one book, the most obvious fact is that it is divided into two parts called Testaments. The Hebrew word for testament is *berith*, meaning "covenant, compact or arrangement between two parties." The Greek word *diathēkē* is often translated "testament" in the Authorized Version.[1] This is a poor translation, and is one of the corrections made in the American Standard Version of the Bible and retained by the Revised Standard Version, which regularly translates it as "covenant."[2] The Greek version of the Old Testament, the Septuagint (LXX), translates the Hebrew word *berith* as *diathēkē*, thus showing the derivation of the

[1]Thirteen of the thirty-three times *diathēkē* occurs in the New Testament, it is translated "testament" in the Authorized Version. Cf. *Englishman's Greek Concordance*, p. 144. Technically, however, the English term "testament" requires action on the part of one person only (the one making the testament or will). The heir's agreement is not necessary to the disposition of the testament. This is not true of a covenant.

[2]Except in Heb. 9:16-17, where the context indicates that the wider sense of *diathēkē* is demanded, viz., "will," or "testament." Cf. preface of ASV.

17

Greek term. The Old Testament was first called *the* covenant in Moses' day (Exodus 24:8). Later, Jeremiah announced that God would make a "new covenant" with His people (Jer. 31:31 ff.), which Jesus claimed to do at the Last Supper (Matt. 26:28; cf. I Cor. 11:23-25; Heb. 8:6-8). Hence, it is for Christians that the former part of the Bible is called the *Old* Covenant (Testament), and the latter is called the *New* Covenant.[3]

The relationship between the two covenants is well summarized by the famous statement of St. Augustine: ". . . the Old Testament revealed in the New, the New veiled in the Old . . . ."[4] Or, as another has put it, "The New is in the Old contained, and the Old is in the New explained."[5] For the Christian, Christ is the theme of both covenants (cf. Heb. 10:7; Luke 24:27, 44; John 5:39), as may be seen from the accompanying chart.

In the Old Testament Christ is:	In the New Testament Christ is:
in shadow	in substance
in pictures	in person
in type	in truth
in ritual	in reality
latent	patent
prophesied	present
implicitly revealed	explicitly revealed

THE BIBLE AND ITS ANCIENT FORMS

Hebrew Form

Probably the earliest division of the Hebrew Bible was twofold: the Law and the Prophets. This is the most common distinction in the New Testament and is confirmed as well by Jewish usage and the Dead Sea Scrolls.[6] However, from less ancient times the Jewish Bible was divided into three sections totaling twenty-four books (twenty-two books if Ruth is attached to Judges, and Lamentations is attached to Jeremiah). Nonetheless, this Old Testament contains all thirty-nine of the books of the Protestant Old Testament in Eng-

---

[3]Cf. Heb. 8:13: "In that he saith, A new *covenant,* he hath made the first old" (AV, italics added).
[4]Augustine, *Expositions on the Book of Psalms,* Ps. 106:31 in Philip Schaff (ed.), *Nicene and Post-Nicene Fathers* (2d series), Vol. VIII, col. 2, p. 531.
[5]W. Graham Scroggie, *Know Your Bible,* I, 12.
[6]R. Laird Harris, *Inspiration and Canonicity of the Bible,* pp. 146 ff.

lish. The basic difference is in the fact that the books are grouped differently.

THE HEBREW OLD TESTAMENT ARRANGEMENT*		
The Law (Torah)	The Prophets (Nebhiim)	The Writings (Kethubhim)

1. Genesis
2. Exodus
3. Leviticus
4. Numbers
5. Deuteronomy
	A. Former Prophets:
	  1. Joshua
	  2. Judges
	  3. Samuel
	  4. Kings
	B. Latter Prophets:
	  1. Isaiah
	  2. Jeremiah
	  3. Ezekiel
	  4. The Twelve
		A. Poetical Books:
		  1. Psalms
		  2. Proverbs
		  3. Job
		B. Five Rolls (Megilloth):
		  1. Song of Songs
		  2. Ruth
		  3. Lamentations
		  4. Esther
		  5. Ecclesiastes
		C. Historical Books:
		  1. Daniel
		  2. Ezra-Nehemiah
		  3. Chronicles

*This is the arrangement in modern Jewish editions of the Old Testament. Cf. *The Holy Scriptures, According to the Masoretic Text;* and Rudolf Kittel and Paul E. Kahle (eds.), *Biblia Hebraica.*

Such a threefold division is suggested by the statement of Jesus in Luke 24:44: "Everything written about me in the law of Moses and the prophets and the psalms must be fulfilled."[7] Philo, the Jewish philosopher at Alexandria, alluded to a threefold division of the Old Testament, and Flavius Josephus divided the twenty-two books of the Hebrew Scriptures into three sections, saying that these twenty-two books "contain the records of all the past; . . . five belong to Moses, . . . the prophets, who were after Moses, wrote down what was done in their times in thirteen books. The remaining four books contain hymns to God, and precepts for the conduct of human life."[8]

Perhaps the earliest testimony to a threefold division, however, comes from the prologue to Ecclesiasticus which reads, ". . . my grandfather Jesus, after devoting himself especially to the reading of the law and the prophets and the other books of our fathers . . . ."[9]

[7]Psalms was the first and largest book in this portion of the Hebrew Scriptures, and may have become the unofficial nomenclature for the entire section; hence, it could be used here as a reference to the section as a whole.
[8]Josephus, *Against Apion,* William Whiston (trans.), I, 8.
[9]"The Prologue of the Wisdom of Jesus the Son of Sirach," The Apocrypha (RSV), p. 110.

The modern threefold division, with eleven books in the Writings, stems from the Mishnah (Baba Bathra tractate), which in its present form dates from the fifth century A.D.

It is possible that this threefold division is based on the official status of the writers in a descending order: Moses the lawgiver appeared first, with his five books; next came the prophets, with their eight books; finally, the nonprophets, or wise men, kings and princes, appear with their books. In light of this, it would seem that the older breakdown of books was twenty-two rather than twenty-four. The books of Ruth and Lamentations were probably written by the authors of Judges and Jeremiah respectively, and only later removed from their original position to form, with Ecclesiastes, Esther and Song of Songs, the five books to be read during the festal year.[10] This feature would also leave a more symmetrical arrangement of books in the canon, with three books in each of the three subsections of the Kethubhim, namely, the poetical, five rolls, and historical. At least the overall number (twenty-two) would thus correspond with Josephus' count, as well as the number of letters in the Hebrew alphabet, indicating that the leaders of Israel considered twenty-two books to be a complete collection, as twenty-two letters formed the complete Hebrew alphabet.

GREEK FORM

The Hebrew Scriptures were translated into Greek at Alexandria, Egypt (c. 280-150 B.C.). This translation, known as the Septuagint (LXX), introduced some basic changes in the format of the books: some of the books were reclassified, others regrouped, and some were renamed (see the chart at the end of this chapter). The Alexandrian tradition divided the Old Testament according to subject matter, which is the basis of the modern classification of five books of Law, twelve books of History, five books of Poetry, and seventeen books of Prophecy. The accompanying chart illustrates this breakdown, indicating a different total than the Hebrew.

To this arrangement, the early Christian Fathers added the books of the New Testament, which were classified in four groups: Gospels (four books), History (one book), Epistles (twenty-one books),

---

[10]This is the general consensus, as held by Joseph Angus, *The Bible Handbook*, Samuel G. Green (rev.); Edward J. Young, *Introduction to the Old Testament; The Jewish Encyclopedia; et al.*

and Prophecy (one book). Further, the twenty-one Epistles were subdivided into the Pauline (thirteen)[11] and the General (eight).

The Law (Pentateuch)—5 books	Poetry—5 books
1. Genesis	1. Job
2. Exodus	2. Psalms
3. Leviticus	3. Proverbs
4. Numbers	4. Ecclesiastes
5. Deuteronomy	5. Song of Solomon

History—12 books	Prophets—17 books	
	A. Major	B. Minor
1. Joshua	1. Isaiah	1. Hosea
2. Judges	2. Jeremiah	2. Joel
3. Ruth	3. Lamentations	3. Amos
4. I Samuel	4. Ezekiel	4. Obadiah
5. II Samuel	5. Daniel	5. Jonah
6. I Kings		6. Micah
7. II Kings		7. Nahum
8. I Chronicles		8. Habakkuk
9. II Chronicles		9. Zephaniah
10. Ezra		10. Haggai
11. Nehemiah		11. Zechariah
12. Esther		12. Malachi

The order of these books varies in the early canonical lists, but the grouping of the books remains the same throughout.[12]

Latin Form

The grouping of books in the Latin Bible follows that of the Septuagint (LXX), or Greek version. Jerome, who translated the Latin Vulgate (c. 383-405), was familiar with the Hebrew division, but Christendom had come to favor (or be associated with) the Greek version; thus it was only natural for him to adopt its fourfold classification. In fact, any other classification would no doubt have been unacceptable to Latin Christians.[13]

[11]In the Eastern Church, the tendency was to classify them as fourteen Pauline Epistles (including Hebrews) and seven General; the Western Church, on the other hand, tended to follow the classification as presented above.

[12]For example, the Gospels were sometimes placed in other sequences, and on some occasions the General Epistles appeared before the Pauline. Cf. B. F. Westcott, *On the Canon of the New Testament;* also see his *The Bible in the Church,* Appendix B.

[13]For a brief discussion of the acceptance of the LXX by Christians, and the rejection of it by Jews, see F. F. Bruce, *The Books and the Parchments,* rev. ed., pp. 150-52.

THE BIBLE IN ITS MODERN FORM

THE HISTORICAL REASON FOR THE STRUCTURE OF THE ENGLISH BIBLE

After the Vulgate had reigned for a thousand years as the standard Bible of Christendom, it was to be expected that Wycliffe's first English Bible would follow the timeworn divisions of its Latin precursor. As a matter of fact, this fourfold division of the Old Testament, and the similar division of the New Testament, has been the standard ever since. As a result, the divisions of the modern English Bible follow a *topical* rather than an *official* order (i.e., by rank or office of the writer), in contrast to the Hebrew Bible. Yet, within this overall topical structure, there is a semichronological listing of the books from Genesis through Revelation.

THE TOPICAL REASON FOR THE STRUCTURE OF THE ENGLISH BIBLE

Since the present structure of the English Bible has been subject to several historical variations, it would be too much to assume that it is God-given. The order as we have it is not, however, purely arbitrary. In fact, the order shows evidence of being purposefully directed, at least insofar as it falls into meaningful categories, because it presents the historical unfolding of the drama of redemptive revelation.

Since redemption and revelation center about the person of Jesus Christ, it may be observed that the several sections of Scriptures form a Christocentric structure (Luke 24:27, 44; John 5:39; Heb. 10:7). That is, Christ is not only the theme of both Testaments of the Bible, as mentioned above, but He may also be seen as the subject in the sequence of each of the eight sections of the Scriptures.[14]

Section	Name	Christocentric Aspect	Viewpoint
1	Law	Foundation for Christ	Downward Look
2	History	Preparation for Christ	Outward Look
3	Poetry	Aspiration for Christ	Upward Look
4	Prophecy	Expectation of Christ	Forward Look
5	Gospels	Manifestation of Christ	Downward Look
6	Acts	Propagation of Christ	Outward Look
7	Epistles	Interpretation and Application of Christ	Upward Look
8	Revelation	Consummation in Christ	Forward Look

[14]It should be noted that a similar Christocentric structure has been presented in many works, e.g., Norman L. Geisler, *Christ: The Theme of the Bible;* W. Graham Scroggie, *Know....*

In the Old Testament, the books of the Law lay the foundation for Christ in that they reveal how God chose (Genesis), redeemed (Exodus), sanctified (Leviticus), guided (Numbers), and instructed (Deuteronomy) the Hebrew nation, through whom He was to bless all nations (Gen. 12:1-3). The Historical books illustrate how this nation was being prepared to carry out its redemptive mission. In order for the chosen nation to be fully prepared for this task, it had to conquer its land (Joshua—Ruth), to be established under its first king, Saul (I Samuel), and later to expand its empire under David and Solomon (II Samuel—I Kings 10). After Solomon's reign, the kingdom was divided (I Kings 11 ff.), and later deported to Assyria (721 B.C.) and Babylonia (586 B.C., II Kings). However, redemptive hopes were not lost, for God protected and preserved His people (Esther) so He could cause them to return (Ezra), and their holy city to be rebuilt (Nehemiah).

While in the Law the foundation is laid for Christ, and in the Historical books the nation takes root in preparation for Christ, in the Poetical books the people look up in aspiration for Christ and, finally, in the Prophetical books they look forward in expectation of Christ. Or, in other words, the Law views the moral life of Israel, History records their national life, Poetry reveals their spiritual life, and Prophecy depicts their prophetical or Messianic life and expectations.

The Gospels of the New Testament bring this prophetic expectation to a historical manifestation in Christ. Here the promised Saviour becomes present; the concealed becomes revealed; the Logos enters the cosmos (John 1:1, 14), as Christ is made manifest in the flesh. The Gospels give a fourfold manifestation of Christ: He is seen in His sovereignty (Matthew), ministry (Mark), humanity (Luke), and deity (John). This manifestation was limited in Jesus' day, for the most part, "to the lost sheep of the house of Israel" (Matt. 10:6). After Christ died and rose again, the disciples were commissioned to carry the account of this manifestation "to the end of the earth" as told in the book of Acts. Here is recorded propagation of faith in Christ as He had commanded: "And you shall be my witnesses in Jerusalem and in all Judea and Samaria and to the end of the earth" (Acts 1:8).

The Gospels give the manifestation of Christ, Acts the propagation of faith in Him, and the Epistles the interpretation of His person and work. The Gospels and Acts record the deeds of Christ and

His disciples, but the Epistles reveal His doctrine as it was taught by the apostles. The former give the historic foundation for New Testament Christianity; the latter give the didactic interpretation and application of it.

The climactic chapter of this Christocentric revelation comes in the final book of the New Testament, Revelation, where all things are brought to a consummation in Christ. The "Paradise Lost" of Genesis becomes the "Paradise Regained" of Revelation. Whereas the gate to the tree of life is closed in Genesis, it is opened forevermore in Revelation. All things are to be summed up in Him (Col. 2:9), for all things were made by Him, redemption was accomplished through Him, and it is only fitting that all things should be consummated in Him (Eph. 1:10).

SUMMARY AND CONCLUSION

The Bible is a biblos, a single book. It has two Testaments, better called covenants or agreements between God and His people. These two parts of the Bible are inseparably related; the New Testament is in the Old concealed, and the Old is in the New revealed.

Down through the centuries the Bible has been subdivided into sections, and has had several different arrangements of its books. The Hebrew Bible came to have a threefold division (Law, Prophets and Writings), so categorized according to the official position of the writer. However, beginning with the Septuagint, and continuing in the Latin and modern English translations, the Old Testament has been given a fourfold topical structure. The New Testament was also given a fourfold topical arrangement of Gospels, Acts, Epistles and Revelation.

When viewed carefully, these sections of the Bible are obviously not arbitrarily put together. Instead, they form a meaningful and purposeful whole, as they convey the progressive unfolding of the theme of the Bible in the person of Christ. The Law gives the *foundation* for Christ, History shows the *preparation* for Him. In Poetry there is an *aspiration* for Christ and in Prophecy an *expectation* of Him. The Gospels of the New Testament record the historical *manifestation* of Christ, the Acts relate the *propagation* of Christ, the Epistles give the *interpretation* of Him, and in Revelation is found the *consummation* of all things in Christ.

A COMPARATIVE CHART OF THE NAMES OF
THE OLD TESTAMENT BOOKS

ENGLISH	LATIN	GREEK	HEBREW (WITH TRANSLATION)
Genesis	Genesis	Genesis	B⁼r'ēshîth (In [the] beginning)
Exodus	Exodus	Exodos	Sh⁼mōth (Names)
Leviticus	Leviticus	Leuitikos	Wayyigrā (And he called)
Numbers	Numeri	Arithmoi	B⁼mîdbar (In the wilderness)
Deuteronomy	Deuteronomium	Deuteronomion touto	D⁼vārîm (Words); 'Elleh ha-Dĕbārîm (These are the words)
Joshua	Iosua	Iesous Neue	Y⁼hôshūa' (Joshua)
Judges	Iudicum	Kritai	Shōphêtîm (Judges)
Ruth	Ruth	Routh	Rūt (Ruth)
I Samuel	Regum I	Basileion A	Sh⁼mû-'ēl A (Asked [heard] of God)
II Samuel	Regum II	Basileion B	Sh⁼mû-'ēl B (Asked [heard] of God)
I Kings	Regum III	Basileion Γ	M⁼lchîm A (Kings; kingdoms)
II Kings	Regum IV	Basileion D	M⁼lchîm B (Kings; kingdoms)
I Chronicles	Paralipomenom I	Paraleipomenon A	Dibrê hayyāmîm A (The affairs [words] of the days)
II Chronicles	Paralipomenom II	Paraleipomenon B	Dibrê hayyāmîm B (The affairs [words] of the days)
Ezra	Esdras I	Esdras	Edsra (Ezra)
Nehemiah	Esdras II	Neemias	Nêh⁼mîah (Nehemiah)
Esther	Esther	Esther	Hadassah (Myrtle)
Job	Iob	Iob	'Iyyôb (Job)
Psalms	Psalmi	Psâlterion	T⁼hillîm (Praises)
Proverbs	Proverbia	Paroimia	Mish⁼lê (Proverbs; parables)
Ecclesiastes	Ecclesiastes	Ekklesiastes	Qōhelet (One who assembles)
Song of Solomon	Canticum Canticorum	Asma	Shîr hash-shirîm (Song of songs)
Isaiah	Iësaias	Esaias	Y⁼sha'-yāhû (Jehovah is salvation)
Jeremiah	Ieremias	Ieremias	Yirm⁼yāhû (Jehovah will raise or lift up)
Lamentations	Threnorum	Threnoi	'êkâ (Ah, how! Alas!)
Ezekiel	Ezechiel	Iesekiel	Y⁼hezqēl (God strengthens)
Daniel	Daniel	Daniel	Daniêl (God is my judge)
Hosea	'Osee	'Osee	Hosh⁼a (Salvation)
Joel	Ioel	Ioel	Yô'êl (Jehovah is God)
Amos	Amos	Amos	Amos (Burden)
Obadiah	Abdias	Obdiou	'ôbedyâ (Servant [worshiper] of Jehovah)
Jonah	Ionas	Ionas	Yônah (Dove)
Micah	Michaeas	Michaias	Mîkāyāhû (Who is like Jehovah?)
Nahum	Nahum	Naoum	Nāhûm (Consolation; consoler)
Habakkuk	Habacuc	Ambakoum	H⁼bâkûk (Embrace; embracer)
Zephaniah	Sophonias	Sophonias	S⁼panyâ (Jehovah hides; Jehovah has hidden)
Haggai	Aggeus	Aggaios	Hâggai (Festive; festal)
Zechariah	Zacharias	Zecharias	Z⁼chârîah (God remembers)
Malachi	Malachias	Malachias	Malachiah (The messenger of Jehovah)

2

DEFINITION OF INSPIRATION

The most basic question about the nature of the Bible centers in its claim to be "inspired," or to be the "Word of God." Just what is meant by and what is included in this claim is the subject of the first link and, in that sense, the most important link in the chain of communication "from God to us."

INSPIRATION DEFINED

The starting point in the discussion of inspiration is the claim of the Scriptures themselves. It is only proper that the Bible should be permitted to witness about its own nature. Once the claim is understood clearly, the character and credentials should be checked carefully; but the Scriptures should not be denied the opportunity to testify on their own behalf.[1] The starting point for such an examination then is the claim of inspiration as it is asserted by the Bible, and the procedure will be to study that claim in the light of the phenomena of Scripture.

BIBLICAL DESCRIPTIONS OF INSPIRATION

Two prominent New Testament passages set the stage for the discussion of inspiration:

1. "All scripture is inspired by God and profitable for teaching, for reproof, for correction, and for training in righteousness" (II Tim. 3:16).[2] This is the only occurrence of the word *theopneustos* ("God-breathed") in the New Testament. The parallel Hebrew word for inspiration, *neshamah,* also occurs only once in the Bible. This occurrence reads: "But it is the spirit in a man,

---

[1]It is sometimes thought that this is *petitio principii,* or arguing in a circle. Actually it is not, since we first ask only what the Bible claims about itself, and then whether or not this is true. The latter is properly a question of apologetics and not of biblical introduction; nevertheless, it will be treated briefly in chapter 9.

[2]Note that the RSV correctly renders this verse, as does the AV. The ASV incorrectly reads, "Every scripture inspired of God is also profitable . . ." but has the correct rendering in the margin.

the *breath* of the Almighty, that makes him understand" (Job 32:8). Closely allied to this verse is another New Testament statement: "For what person knows a man's thoughts except the spirit of the man which is in him? . . . And we impart this in words not taught by human wisdom but taught by the Spirit, interpreting spiritual truths to those who possess the Spirit" (I Cor. 2:11, 13). In both of these passages the emphasis is upon the *man*, whereas II Timothy 3:16 lays stress upon the *message*, or writing.

2. "No prophecy ever came by the impulse of man, but men moved by the Holy Spirit spoke from God" (II Peter 1:21). So, in literal biblical terminology, inspiration is the process by which Spirit-moved writers recorded God-breathed writings. Hence, when inspiration is viewed as a total process, it includes both the writer and the writings; but, when it is seen as a product (as in II Tim. 3:16), it relates only to the writings (*graphē*). This picture is well summarized in Hebrews 1:1: "God spoke of old *to* our fathers *by* the prophets," to which II Timothy 3:16 would add the thought "*in* their writings" (emphasis supplied).

The whole process of inspiration begins with the matter of divine revelation.

1. First, God spoke *to* the prophets. This was done "in many and various ways" (Heb. 1:1).

   a. God sometimes spoke to the prophets by angels, as He did to Abraham in Genesis 18, and to Lot in Genesis 19.

   b. God also spoke to the prophets in dreams (Dan. 7:1; cf. Num. 12:6).

   c. Sometimes God used visions, as He did with Isaiah and Ezekiel (Isa. 1:1; Ezek. 1:1; 8:3; 11:24; 43:3; cf. Hosea 12:10).

   d. On occasion God used miracles to speak to the prophets, for instance, Moses and the burning bush (Exodus 3:2); Gideon's enterprise (Judges 6:37); and Jonah's experiences (Jonah 1:1; 4:6 ff.).

   e. Even nature was used to speak to the psalmist (Ps. 19:1).

   f. Sometimes God spoke in an audible voice (I Sam. 3).

   g. No doubt the most common method God used was the inner voice of the individual's conscience and communion with God. This is probably what is often meant when the prophets write, "And the word of the Lord came unto me saying. . . ."

h. The priests determined the will of God by means of the Urim and Thummim (Exodus 28:30; Num. 27:21).

i. Even the lot was designated as a means by which God indicated His will (Prov. 16:33).

j. Finally, some of the prophets received a revelation from the study of other prophetic writings (cf. Dan. 9:1-2).

2. God not only spoke to the prophets in various ways, but He spoke through the prophets. That is, the prophets' message was God's message; their voices were God's voice. God was saying what they were saying; or, to put it more precisely, they were saying what God wanted said.

a. This is verified in a general way by II Peter 1:21 and Hebrews 1:1, which indicate that the oral message of the prophets came from God; it was God's word given through the prophets' mouths. This is what David said in II Samuel 23:2: "The Spirit of the LORD speaks by me, his word is upon my tongue." Jeremiah also cites God as saying, "Behold, I have put my words in thy mouth" (Jer. 1:9).

b. This is borne out in particular by the prophetic formulas, as each prophet introduced his oral message by statements such as "Thus saith the LORD," "The word of the LORD," "The LORD spoke" (see chaps. 4-6).

Theological Definition of Inspiration

From this biblical description of the total process of inspiration, the necessary constituents of a theological definition of inspiration may be derived. There are three:

1. *God's causality.* The prime mover in inspiration is God: "No prophecy ever came by the impulse of man, but men moved by the Holy Spirit spoke from God" (II Peter 1:21). In other words, God *moved* and the prophet *mouthed* these truths; God *revealed* and man *recorded* His word. The Bible is God's word in the sense that it originates with Him and is authorized by Him, even though it is articulated by men.

2. The *prophetic agency.* The prophet played an important role in the overall process of inspiration; he was the means through which God spoke. The word of God was written by men of God. God used persons to convey His propositions. God prepared the

prophets by training, experience, gifts of grace and, if need be, by direct revelation, to utter His word. "By it [inspiration], the Spirit of God, flowing confluently with the providentially and graciously determined work of men, spontaneously producing under the Divine directions the writings appointed them, gives the product a Divine quality unattainable by human powers alone."[3] In inspiration, then, God is the efficient cause, and the prophets are the instrumental causes.

3. The final product of God's causality and the prophetic agency is *scriptural authority,* that is, a divinely authoritative book. God moved the prophets in such a way as to breathe out (literally, "spirate") their writings. In other words, God spoke to the prophets and is speaking through their writings. The cause of inspiration is God, the means is the men of God, and the end result is the word of God in the language of men.

Therefore, a working definition of inspiration is suggested. Inspiration is that mysterious process by which the divine causality worked through the human prophets without destroying their individual personalities and styles, to produce divinely authoritative writings.

INSPIRATION DISTINGUISHED FROM REVELATION AND ILLUMINATION

REVELATION CONCERNS THE ORIGIN AND GIVING OF TRUTH (I Cor. 2:10)[4]

In order to refine the concept of inspiration, one must contrast it with two other closely associated concepts: revelation and illumination. The Hebrew word for revelation, *galah,* "to uncover," and the Greek word, *apocalypto,* "to unveil," are roughly identical in meaning. In this connection, both refer to a *divine disclosure.* Sometimes this may be a disclosure of a person (as in Christ, the Living Word of God, cf. Gal. 1:16), while at other times it may be of *propositions* (as in Scripture, the *written* Word of God, cf. Rom. 3:2). In the ultimate sense, only God can give a revelation or disclosure of truth; man at best can only have an interpretation or discovery of that truth.

---

[3]Benjamin B. Warfield, *Inspiration and Authority of the Bible,* pp. 154-60.
[4]Cf. Merrill F. Unger, *Introductory Guide to the Old Testament,* 2d ed., pp. 22-25.

Inspiration Relates to the Reception and Recording of Truth (II Peter 1:20-21)

God revealed truth to men who received and recorded it. Inspiration is the means God used to achieve His revelation in the Bible. Inspiration involves man in an active sense, whereas revelation is solely the activity of God. In inspiration, the prophet received from God what he in turn related to others. Inspiration then includes both the person of the prophet and the product of his pen.

Illumination Focuses on the Apprehension and Understanding of Truth (I Cor. 2:13-14)

Whereas revelation is an objective disclosure, and inspiration is a subjective discovery of the truth God is communicating, illumination emphasizes the apprehension and understanding of truth. In revelation God unveils the truth; in illumination man understands it; nonetheless, both are acts of God. Even though these three concepts are interrelated in the total process of God's communication, they are quite distinguishable. They form three necessary links in the chain "from God to us": (1) revelation is the fact of divine communication, (2) inspiration is the means of divine communication, and (3) illumination is the gift of understanding that divine communication.

INSPIRATION DISCUSSED

What Is Inspired, the Writer or His Writings?

Although the biblical concept of inspiration has been outlined in general, several important questions must be discussed about inspiration in particular. Is it the writers, their ideas, their writings, or a combination of these which is inspired? As was mentioned above, inspiration certainly includes the man and his ideas, but it must not exclude his writings. James Orr feels that "Inspiration belongs primarily to the person and to the book only as it is the product of the inspired person."[5] Other theologians would reverse this opinion, asserting, "Properly speaking, inspiration pertains to the holy Scriptures themselves. It may be said, however, that the writers too were inspired by God."[6] Regardless of which position is primary, it must be held that the person as well as his pen is under the direction of the Holy Spirit in the total process of inspiration. Nevertheless, the

[5]James Orr, *Revelation and Inspiration,* p. 162.
[6]Robert Preus, *Inspiration of Scripture,* p. 22.

New Testament reserves the word "inspiration" only for the product of that process, that is, the writings, or *graphē* (II Tim. 3:16).[7]

That inspiration of necessity involves the very words of Scripture may be seen for two reasons: (1) Linguistically, words are necessary for the full expression of thought.[8] If God in any meaningful sense expressed Himself to the prophets, He had to use words. Words are the "clothes of ideas," and a naked thought is a very nebulous entity at best. The desire for clarity in revelation would scarcely be consonant with the ambiguity of unsymbolized ideas. In fact, an idea without a symbol to express it is an unexpressed idea, and an unexpressed idea is scarcely a revelation or communication. (2) Biblically, it is the repeated claim that "words" are God-given. Observe how many times Jesus and the apostles used the phrase "it is written" or similar expressions.[9] The Bible literally abounds with the assertions that God gave the *very words* of the prophets.[10] Moses was told, "I will be with your mouth and teach you what you shall speak" (Exodus 4:12). God charged Ezekiel saying, "And you shall speak my words to them" (Ezek. 2:7). Of the Decalogue it is said, "And God spoke all these words" (Exodus 20:1). Paul claimed to speak "In words . . . taught by the Spirit" (I Cor. 2:13). These references serve to illustrate the idea of the claim that the very words of the Bible were God-given.

WHAT IS INSPIRED, THE AUTOGRAPHS[11] OR THE COPIES?

If every word of the Bible is inspired, does every copy, translation or version of the Scriptures necessarily have to be inspired too? There are some who think so. But, here again, two extremes must be avoided.

On the one hand, some claim that every translation is inspired in the same sense as the original. This extreme position was held by the Jewish philosopher Philo in the first century of the present era. He said of the Greek translation of the Hebrew Old Testament, known as the Septuagint, that the translators "under inspiration, wrote, not each several scribe something different, but the same word for word, as though dictated to each by an invisible prompter."[12]

---

[7]B. B. Warfield, "Inspiration," *International Standard Bible Encyclopaedia*, rev. ed., James Orr (ed.).
[8]See Ronald Nash, *New Evangelicalism*, p. 42.
[9]See chap. 6.
[10]See chap. 5.
[11]An autograph is usually an original, or author's, manuscript; it may have been written by either the author himself or a secretary.
[12]Philo, *Life of Moses*, F. H. Carlson (trans.), II, 37.

More recently, D. M. Beegle reflected a similar view when he wrote, "There is no evidence to show that the apostles denied the inspiration of the LXX. . . . The correct inference, therefore, is that in spite of some mistakes, all reasonably accurate translations of Scripture are inspired."[13] This position, as can be seen, necessitates the recognition of errors (errancy) in inspiration, since some errors of copyists have obviously crept into the Scriptures.[14]

Only the autographs are inspired, not the translations. If only the errorless autographs were God-breathed, and the translators were not preserved from error, how can there be certainty about any passage of Scripture? Perhaps the very passage which comes under question is a mistaken transcription or copy. The delicate art of textual criticism (see chap. 26) treats this problem, by showing the accuracy of the copies of the originals. To borrow this conclusion in advance, the copies are known to be accurate and sufficient in all matters except minor details. The resultant situation, then, exists that while only the autographs are inspired, it may nevertheless be said that all good copies or translations are *adequate.*

Some have objected to what they consider a retreat to "inerrant autographs" from errant copies, as if the doctrine of inspiration were created to protect the errancy of the Bible, as they chide that no one in modern times has ever seen these "infallible originals." While it may be true that no one in modern times has ever seen an infallible original, it is also true that no one has ever seen a fallible one either. In light of this situation, it is well to note that the pursuit of the original renderings is at least an *objective science* (textual criticism) rather than a *subjective guess.*

Just why God did not see fit to preserve the autographs is not known, although man's tendency to worship religious relics is certainly a possible determining factor. An excellent example of this tendency may be seen in II Kings 18:4, where the brazen serpent made by Moses was later worshiped by the Israelites. Furthermore, just exactly why God did not preserve the copyists from errors, as He did the writers of the autographs, is not known. The net result, however, has proved to be profitable insofar as it has occasioned the very worthwhile study of textual criticism. Another valuable side

[13]Dewey M. Beegle, *Inspiration of Scripture,* pp. 38-40.
[14]For example, II Kings 8:26 gives 22 as the age of Ahaziah, whereas II Chron. 22:2 gives 42. The latter cannot be correct, or he would have been older than his father. Nevertheless, the best available *copies* of the originals render II Chron. 22:2 as "42 years." According to II Chron. 9:25, Solomon had 4,000 horses, but I Kings 4:26 says 40,000; some copyists must have added an extra "zero" by mistake in the Kings passage.

effect of not preserving all the copies from error is that it serves as a warning to biblical scholars not to esteem paleographic, numeric, or other trivia over the essential message of the Scriptures.[15]

While the autographs were actually inspired, good copies are virtually inspired. In seeking to avoid the two extremes of either an unattainable original or a fallible one, it must be asserted that a good copy or translation of the autographs is *for all practical purposes* the inspired word of God. It may not suit the scholar who, for technical purposes of theological precision, wants both the correct text and the exact term in the original language, but it certainly does suit the preacher and layman who desire to know "What saith the Lord" in matters of faith and practice. Inasmuch as it is only what the Bible teaches (and the primary teaching of the Bible is doctrinal), and no major doctrine rests on any one minor detail, then a good translation will not fail to capture the overall teaching of the original. In this sense, then, the translation will have virtual inspiration, although actual inspiration is reserved for the autographs.

How Much of the Autographs Is Inspired?

Another question to be asked concerns the degree of inspiration. Are all sections of the Bible equally inspired, or are some parts of Scripture more inspired than others? The question itself confuses the issue, and fails to distinguish between truth and the relative value of truth under varied conditions. Just because a given passage, at certain times and under stated circumstances, is more "inspiring" to a particular person does not thereby mean that it is more inspired than other passages. Inspiration merely vouches for the truth of the record, no matter how valuable that particular record may be to the individual's edification, or even to the overall picture of redemption. The overall value may be judged by the principle of progressive revelation,[16] but this is not to be confused with a notion of varying degrees of inspiration. The record is either true or false; inspired or not inspired; of God or not of God. If the various passages are true, they are equally true, and not more or less true. It is a record completely true in the context for which God intended it. While it may not be the "whole" truth from the vantage point of the full and ultimate revelation, it is nonetheless a true record of "all" the truth which God wanted to reveal at that particular time in His progressive revelation of truth. Take, for example, the case of the parent who

[15]Cf. J. W. Haley, *Alleged Discrepancies of the Bible*, pp. 30-40.
[16]Cf. Bernard Ramm, *Protestant Biblical Interpretation*, rev. ed., pp. 111-13.

at one time says to his small child, "You aren't supposed to eat your cake with your fingers, use your spoon." Then, the same parent may say to the same child some years later, "You aren't supposed to use your spoon to eat your cake, use your fork." What the parent said is not contradictory, it is merely a progressive revelation of the truth as it is adapted to the maturing level of the child. Thus, one may observe that the final command to the child was "truer" in the sense that it is at a higher level. However, the doctrine of inspiration, on the other hand, merely asserts that the records of what the parent said on both occasions are equally true statements.

How Does Inspiration Operate?

One final question on the nature of inspiration deals with the means or process. What means did God's causality employ to produce scriptural authority without interfering with the personality, freedom and individuality of the prophetic agents? Or, how did God produce an infallible book through fallible men? A frank and forthright answer, and yet often very reluctantly given by biblical scholars, is "We don't know." It must be asserted *that* God inspired the Scriptures even though it cannot be ascertained exactly *how* He did it.

Some attempted explanations. Several solutions have been suggested for this problem, all of which have their own inherent difficulties.

1. One suggestion is that God dictated the words to the prophets who acted as recording secretaries.[17] Although this may explain how every word was inspired, it would not explain how or why so many distinctly individual traits of the various human writers are so apparent in the Scriptures, nor why the biblical writers themselves claimed to have used human sources for some of their information.[18] Mechanical word-for-word dictation may account for *some* of Scripture (e.g., the Ten Commandments or some prophecies), but it certainly does not account for *all* of it.

2. Another view is that God produced much of the truth of Scripture by His providential control over natural processes, and that He could have produced it all in this manner. Kenneth Kantzer writes,

     . . . no theist who believes in God's providential control of the

---

[17]See chap. 3.
[18]See chap. 4.

universe can possibly use this objection [viz., that "divine inspiration must necessarily negate the freedom and humanity of the Biblical writers"] against the inspiration of the Bible. The God of Romans 8:28, who works all things together for good, including the sinful acts of wicked men, could certainly have worked through the will and personality of His prophets to secure the divine Word which He wished to convey through them.[19]

While it may not be disputed that God could, and perhaps even did, secure the truth of the inspired record through General Providence, it must not be supposed that this gives a scientific explanation of the *modus operandi* of inspiration. The truth of the matter is that it is not known how General Providence works, as Kantzer admits, "The mechanics of inspiration are left unexplained."[20]

The nature of the problem. The problem of the means of inspiration falls within the category of a theological "mystery." Two sides of the overall picture are given to man in the Bible, and it is asserted that they are both true. No one can show that they are contradictory, nor can anyone show exactly how they are complementary. They are not contrary to reason, but they are beyond finite reasoning. The reason both sides of inspiration are given is that man may have the "whole" truth, and not just one "part" or side of it. It is like a two-sided coin which an infinite God may comprehend completely at once, but which a finite man must apprehend partially, one side at a time. If it be admitted that the words of the Bible are truly God's, yet distinctly man's, there would seem to be no way of denying that the process is a mystery without eventuating in one of the two extremities.

Two extremes to avoid. If the human nature of the Bible be emphasized on the one hand, the divine may be compromised on the other. If the divine be emphasized, the human is in danger of being relegated to the hypothetical. In one case the divine nature is taken seriously, and the human is viewed only incidentally. In the other extreme, the human is so prominent that the divine is obscured. The difficulty is not with the revelation of both sides of the truth, it is with their reconciliation. In this connection it is well to remember that man's inability to understand a mystery does not render ineffective God's ability to accomplish one. It must then be held that, by the activity of the Holy Spirit and through the instrumentality of the

19*The Word for This Century*, ed. Merrill C. Tenney, p. 46.
20*Ibid.*

prophets, the infallibility of the Scriptures was effected (John 10:35), even though this is admittedly a great mystery.

A close parallel. The inspiration of the Bible is not the only enigma before man, but the other major credal statements are also kinds of "distilled mysteries."[21] In fact, the incarnation of Christ affords an excellent illustration of the divine and human sides of Scripture. Both the Saviour and the Scriptures have heavenly and earthly natures. In both the human side is perfect, as is the divine. Just as it is unorthodox to try to explain away the divine nature of Christ in order to understand His human nature (as did the Arians),[22] or to sacrifice His true human nature in order to *explain* His divine nature (as did the Docetics),[23] so it is wrong to deny that the words of Scripture are *both* divine and human in their nature. The mistake is in trying to explain the inexplicable, and in trying to fathom the unfathomable.

In the whole question of the *modus operandi* of inspiration, a balance must be sought between the two extremes of divine dictation and human fallibility. Such a balance must guarantee the final product (the words of the Bible) and still guard the freedom and humanity of the authors.

SUMMARY AND CONCLUSION

Inspiration is the mysterious process by which divine causality on the prophetic agency resulted in scriptural authority, the Bible. Revelation is the *fact* of divine communication, inspiration is the *means* by which that communication is brought to the written record, and illumination is the *understanding* of that communication. The total process of inspiration includes both the writer and the writing, although the product of inspiration is the authoritative writing and not the man. It is only the autographs (original writings) that are *actually* inspired, although accurate copies or translations may be said to be *virtually* inspired, inasmuch as they correctly reproduce the original. There are no degrees of inspiration; all the Bible is equally inspired, that is, equally authoritative and true. The means or process of inspiration is a mystery of the providence of God, but the result of this process is a *verbal* (the words), *plenary* (extending to all parts equally), *inerrant* (errorless), and *authoritative* record.

[21]Cf. Vernon Grounds, "Postulate of Paradox," *Bulletin of the Evangelical Theological Society*, Vol. VII, No. 1 (1964), pp. 3-22.

[22]Their error led to a call for the Council of Nicea (I), A.D. 325, where Arianism was condemned.

[23]Their argument was that Christ did not actually die on the cross, but that He only "appeared" to die.

3

SEVERAL THEORIES OF INSPIRATION
AND REVELATION

The history of the Bible is that of a chain which extends from God to man; it includes revelation, inspiration and transmission. That there is such a chain is the evident claim of Scripture, as is seen in the following chapters. Nonetheless, just how and where this appeared, that is, the exact process and place of revelation, have been the subjects of much debate. The general area in which the debate centers is the method or *modus operandi* of revelation, while the locus or place of revelation is the particular area of debate as related to the Bible. Three basic views emerge from this debate, and they follow along the theological party lines of Liberalism, Neoorthodoxy, and Conservatism.

SOME LIBERAL[1] VIEWS: THE BIBLE CONTAINS
THE WORD OF GOD

Basically and briefly the Liberal view states that the Bible *contains* the word of God, along with varied admixtures of the words of men. In other words, within the Bible one may find the word of God by rational and moral reflection, but he is not to equate the words of the Bible with the word of God. Accordingly, the Bible is not completely the word of God, nor is the word of God complete in the Bible. There are revelations of God elsewhere than the Bible for faith and practice, and all that the Bible teaches is not a worthy standard for faith and practice.

THE RIGHT WING: THE ILLUMINATION VIEW

On the right wing of the Liberal camp is the view that revelation is to be found from place to place within the Bible, wherein God granted to pious men of old a deep religious insight into His truth,

[1]Liberal is used here in the sense of "Modernist" theology rather than its literal meaning: generous, broad-minded.

37

with varied degrees of understanding.[2] This they recorded in their religious lore. Thus God's words are contained within the Bible in the sense that these men were *illuminated* by God to understand His will in a manner much akin to the insights into the pious life and divine truth that Christians today receive from God. Saintly men of all ages have shared in this common process of "inspiration," which was varied only in degree and depth.

THE LEFT WING: THE INTUITION VIEW

On the left wing of Liberalism is a much more general view of inspiration. This view holds that the writers were inspired only in the sense that from time to time their natural religious insight and genius were deepened and heightened to discover "divine truths" for their own day. The Bible itself, however, is only a kind of religious scratch pad of the scribes. It is a necklace of pearls strung out at random amid many less valuable and some even undesirable stones, or as Van Loon states,

> The Old Testament was a national Jewish scrapbook. It contained stories and legends and genealogies and love poems and songs, classified and arranged and re-classified and re-arranged without any regard for chronological order or literary perfection.[3]

Emphasis in this view is laid upon man's *discovery* of the gems of godly genius, and not upon God's disclosure of divine doctrine. It is human *intuition* rather than divine revelation.

SOME OBJECTIONS TO THE LIBERAL VIEW

Basically, the Liberal view is weakened by its narrow naturalistic presupposition. It is assumed that man is the most active, if not the only, agent actively involved in the process of the discovery of divine truth. While this is no doubt an assumption to be expected from a materialistic or atheistic perspective, it is hardly to be anticipated from theistic and theological friends of the Bible. At best the position has a deistic connotation: there is a God who did create the world, but from that beginning, man is on his own. Philosophically, it would seem that the a priori probability for God's interest and activity in the world is greater than His disinterest and inactivity. Unless God is presumed to be either impotent or malicious, it would seem to follow that His desire to communicate to His creatures

---

[2]L. Harold DeWolf, *The Case for Theology in Liberal Perspective*, pp. 54-59.
[3]Henrik W. Van Loon, *Story of the Bible*, p. 227.

would transcend all other motives that would send Him on an eternal vacation from human truth-involvement. At least historically and biblically Christianity has taught that God is omnipotent and self-revealing.

Another objection to the Liberal view of inspiration is that it is *rationalistic* and *man-centered*. It makes human reason or feeling the final judge of determining which part of the Bible is divine, and which part is human. It places into the hands of finite, feeble and fallible man the power to determine what and where God is speaking. Man is granted power *over* infinite truth rather than taking a place *under* it. This produces a situation in which it is impossible to know what is of God and what is not, since certainty and unanimity of human thought and feeling are virtually impossible attainments for the human race. Thus, God's word is left either in the cold calculating clutches of rationalism, or it is lost in the dismal dungeon of subjectivism. In either case, the objective word of God is lost in the subjective world of man.

Finally, the Liberal view is not biblical. It exists in obvious neglect of what the Bible says about itself. Unless it is argued that the Bible is not the most basic and essential document to Christianity,[4] it would seem that no greater charge could be issued against a view that claims to be Christian than that it is simply *not* what the Bible teaches. That the Bible does indeed emphatically teach that God is the source of the truth and message of the whole Bible is shown in full in chapters 5-8. Briefly, some of the more important supporting Scripture passages are: Hebrews 1:1; Matthew 5:18; II Timothy 3:16; II Peter 1:20; John 14:26; 16:13. In these passages there is an explicit claim for the inspiration of the whole Old Testament, and an implicit claim for the inspiration of the entire New Testament, as being God's Word.

SOME NEOORTHODOX VIEWS: THE BIBLE BECOMES THE WORD OF GOD

The untenability of the Liberal position has a manifest reactionary verification in the twentieth century move back toward orthodoxy known as Neoorthodoxy, or New Reformation theology.[5] Liberalism had accepted the effects of a destructive higher criticism,[6] which

---

[4]Which view is decisively exposed by J. Gresham Machen in *Christianity and Liberalism.*
[5]See William Hordern, *The Case for New Reformation Theology.*
[6]See Glossary.

reduced the Bible to a religious scrapbook. Karl Barth, a German pastor and theologian, had accepted and preached these views, accompanied by their optimism of human perfectibility. His hopes, however, were shattered by World War I and, with heavy heart, he returned to the great Reformers, Luther and Calvin, and to the "thus saith the Lord" of the biblical message. He began to preach a divine revelation and an authoritative Bible. It worked! His own life was renewed and his congregation was transformed. Thus was born, in the first third of the twentieth century, the movement known popularly today as Neoorthodoxy.[7]

THE RIGHT WING: THE EXISTENTIAL[8] VIEW

Pragmatically, the Bible had proven to be the locus of revelation for Barth. Academically, however, he had embraced the Liberal adjunct of higher criticism. To him there were no doubt many human errors and imperfections in the biblical record, even in the autographs. How then could the Bible be God's perfect Word when it was really, in many places, a record of man's erring words? The answer was simple and forthright: the Bible *becomes* the Word of God when He chooses to use this imperfect channel to confront man with His perfect word. For Barth, the Bible and the Bible alone uniquely reveals God to man—not in *propositions* about God, but as a means of a *personal encounter* by God with man in an act of revelation. In this existential experience, crisis encounter, the meaningless ink blots on the pages leap from the Bible to speak to man concretely and meaningfully. At this "moment of meaning," the Bible *becomes* the Word of God to the individual.

How can it be that the Bible at such a moment can be both man's errors and God's truth? Just as the dog can clearly recognize the voice of his master through the scratched and imperfect record on the old victrola, so the Bible can transmit the word of God through its imperfect record.[9] Emil Brunner, who was also associated with this conservative wing of Neoorthodoxy, reiterated the same view most clearly when he wrote, "I myself am an adherent of a rather radical school of Biblical criticism which for example does not accept the

---

[7]Karl Barth is rightly viewed as the father of Neoorthodoxy, although he borrowed much from Sören Kierkegaard who might be considered the grandfather of the movement.

[8]Existentialism is derived from the verb "to exist," or from the noun "existence," and is a philosophy that stresses the subjectivity, individuality and freedom of the finite creature.

[9]*Church Dogmatics*, G. T. Thompson (trans.), Vol. I, Part II, pp. 592, 595.

Gospel of John as an historical source and finds much to be objected to in many parts of the Synoptics. . . ."[10] For Brunner, to consider the Bible objectively and propositionally to be the word of God is "Bibliolatry." It is setting up a Protestant "paper pope." The Bible itself is not a revelation to Brunner. It is, rather, a *record* of revelation that was received personally, individually and existentially by other men, and that can *become* a revelation to us if we receive it in the same way.

THE LEFT WING: THE DEMYTHOLOGIZING VIEW

On the other wing of the Neoorthodox movement, men like Rudolf Bultmann and Shubert Ogden have attempted to explain just how it is that the biblical exegete can discover or uncover this revelation. Their answer is found in their principle of demythology:[11] The Bible must be stripped of culture in order to get at the core of truth. It must be divested of religious myth in order to get at the real message of God's self-giving love in Christ. One must look through and beyond the historical record with all its myth and error to the superhistorical. Events such as the fall, the crucifixion, and the resurrection of Christ are "real" and "true," but not necessarily the objects of verifiable and factual history. Hence, the Bible *becomes* a revelation when, by the proper (demythological) interpretation, one is confronted with absolute love as set forth in the "myth" of God's selfless love in Christ.

SOME OBJECTIONS TO THE NEOORTHODOX VIEW

In the first place, the Neoorthodox view, like the Liberal, is naturalistic. Although it is historically a move back toward orthodoxy, it never quite arrives. Nor does it entirely leave the Liberal position on higher criticism. Inspiration and errancy are made bedfellows contrary to the classical tradition of Christianity. While it cannot be contended that human language is an absolutely perfect means of communication, nor that the authors were themselves infallible, nevertheless it must be held that the writing was errorless and that the language was adequate in the conveyance of divine revelation. In no meaningful sense may God's authorship cover the whole of Scripture and, at the same time, the errors in Scripture. As Edward John Carnell has aptly put it, "If Christ blundered on the data of simple history, how can he suddenly become an authority when he

---

[10]Emil Brunner, *Theology of Crisis*, p. 41.
[11]See Rudolf K. Bultmann, *Jesus Christ and Mythology*, pp. 32-34, 45.

switches to revelation-history?"[12] Or, as Robert Mounce points out, "If he [Gospel writer] is wrong in an area where we can check him (history), how can we rely upon his accuracy in an area where no checks are possible (doctrine)? The whole thing stands or falls together."[13]

Again, the Neoorthodox position on the locus of revelation is too subjective. Only at those moments and in those verses in which the individual hears the voice of God is the Bible considered to be the word of God. What about the passages that do not speak, or those that speak at one time but at another time are voiceless? This existentialism is even more subjective than Liberalism, which at least attempted to generalize and objectify sections of the Bible containing the word of God. If the Bible only *becomes* the Word of God occasionally and subjectively, then what has become of the Word of God objectively? There is in this view a basic confusion with that which has been traditionally called *revelation* and the process of *illumination*. There is no distinction made between God's objective disclosure and man's subjective discovery by God's help. The Bible is not merely God's Word when man hears or understands it; it is God speaking whether man is listening or not.

Perhaps the most inexcusable mistake for a biblical theologian to make about the Bible is not to consider first what the Bible says about itself. In this respect, Neoorthodoxy is certainly unbiblical. It has been alleged that revelation is not propositional but personal; that revelation is not found in facts but in acts; not in verbal expressions but in experiences. Although it cannot be denied that God has revealed Himself in acts and deeds (e.g., the plagues in Egypt, the deeds of Christ), it must not be asserted that God can only reveal Himself in this manner. Why is it that God could not also reveal Himself through words and propositions if He should so choose? Indeed, this is the unmistakably clear claim of the Bible as to exactly what God did do. The classical text, and the only place the word "inspiration" is used in the New Testament, says that God breathed *the writings* (*pasa graphē Theopneustos,* II Tim. 3:16), speaking of the objective words. Jesus declared repeatedly that God's voice was to be heard in "that which *has been and remains written.*"[14] In the Old Testament, God spoke to Israel through the *written commandments* (Ex-

---

[12]Edward John Carnell, "The Problem of Religious Authority," *His* (Feb., 1950), p. 8.

[13]*Can I Trust My Bible?* A symposium, p. 174.

[14]The proper rendition of the Greek perfect tense. The same phrase occurs seventy-three times in the Gospels alone. Cf. Matt. 4:4; 21:13; 26:24.

odus 31:18), the *writings of Moses* (Exodus 24:3-4), and the *words of David* (II Sam. 23:2). David made the pattern of the temple clear to the people, "by the writing from the hand of the LORD" (I Chron. 28:19). Furthermore, Jesus equated *the propositional writings of the Old Testament* as a whole with the word of God (Matt. 5:17; 15:3-4; John 10:35); the New Testament is also considered a propositional revelation.[15]

SOME CONSERVATIVE VIEWS: THE BIBLE IS THE WORD OF GOD

While the Liberal contends that the Bible merely *contains* God's word, and the Neoorthodox asserts that the Scriptures *become* God's word in an existential "moment of meaning," the orthodox, or Conservative, position is that the Bible *is* the Word of God. It holds the Bible to be God's objective revelation whether or not man has a subjective illumination of it. The Bible is God's word in the same sense that *The Critique of Pure Reason* is the objective declaration of Immanuel Kant, whether or not one has understood it or, for that matter, has even read it. It is written, Kant has spoken and *is* speaking. So it is with the Bible and God. The Bible is written, God has spoken and is speaking through it.

THE RIGHT WING: THE VERBAL DICTATION VIEW

On the right wing of Conservatism is Fundamentalism that is accused (rightly or wrongly) of teaching mechanical inspiration, or verbal dictation. Every word of the Bible was given, according to this view, to the prophet who served as a secretary for the dictation of God, much as Moses may have done on Mount Sinai (Exodus 24:4; 34:27). Although it is difficult to find any theologian who actually claims to hold this "wooden" view of inspiration for the entire Bible, the illustration of Moses is sometimes cited as the *modus operandi* of inspiration, and if this were carried out logically it would amount to mechanical dictation.[16] Fortunately, most proponents of this view do not carry it out logically. Nevertheless, their theological enemies do accuse them of holding to a verbal dictation.[17]

[15]That the written word of God as a whole claims to be the objective word of God will be fully discussed in chaps. 5-8.
[16]Cf. John R. Rice, *Twelve Tremendous Themes*, pp. 8, 11.
[17]A verbal dictation view is held by Muslims, who believe that the Koran was given by dictation from Gabriel to Muhammad out of the eternal book in heaven. See *The Glorious Koran*, an explanatory translation by M. M. Pickthall, Surah II, pp. 97-98. A mechanical verbal dictation view may also be found in Occultism and Spiritism.

THE LEFT WING: THE INSPIRED CONCEPT VIEW

The dangers of the dictation view have sent many Conservatives seeking a more sensible solution to the problem of inspiration.[18] Some writers have suggested that it is *not the words* but the *thoughts* or *ideas* that God inspired. To them, God gave the thought and the prophet was "free" to record it "in his own words."[19] By this method they are able to explain the obvious *personality* and *literary* differences reflected in Scripture (which only the uninformed, ill-advised, or unwilling fail to see), and at the same time maintain that the Bible is God's word because the real meaning, or the message, came from God. Thus, the biblical author gave expression to "God's word" in his own words and way, in what has been called "dynamic" inspiration.

SOME OBJECTIONS TO THESE CONSERVATIVE VIEWS

The Mechanical Dictation View. Objections to this concept are appropriate and relevant even if no one actually claims to hold this view, because some theologians do come dangerously close to it and do teach it indirectly and implicitly. This view does not accord with the teaching of the Bible, which says that God used human agents not as passive receptors but as active contributors in the writing of Scripture (cf. Rom. 16:26; Heb. 1:1). The Bible states that God used *the words of men*; in one place the words of a man are *his own* and, in another, they are called *God's* (cf. Matt. 19:4-5; Acts 3:25; I Cor. 6:16).[20] The prophets were free moral agents actively contributing their own personality and literary ability to the record. They were not religious robots, nor were they divine teletypes typing out the message from headquarters.

The Bible not only teaches that the writers were not robots or teletypes, but the very nature of the Bible indicates that they were not. Dictation does not square with the phenomena or facts of Scripture. Only the most casual reader who is completely unfamiliar with the original languages could possibly miss the distinct and characteristic styles of the various writers. Differences of vocabulary, syntax, interests and human objectives are very observable from book to book, unmistakably marking it as the product of human

[18]Recently a group known as Neo-Evangelicals has been active in attempting to restate and redefine the doctrine of inspiration in an attempt to do just this; see Edward John Carnell, *The Case for Orthodox Theology;* and Ronald Nash, *The New Evangelicalism.*

[19]See Augustus H. Strong, *Systematic Theology,* I, 216.

[20]For a more complete list, see chap. 4.

writers. A mechanical view of dictation to man in a vacuum simply does not accord with the actual facts of Scripture or of human personality.

The Dynamic View. The initial difficulty with the dynamic view, which localizes inspiration in the concepts or ideas, is that it is too concessive to be orthodox. It explains the Bible's humanity but in so doing it weakens its divinity. If the writers were free to express God's ideas in their own way, how could the final product be God's? What assurance is there that they did not distort it, or that they expressed it correctly? How can the final product be infallible or authoritative if there was no divine control over the actual composition? The mechanical view *deifies* the human aspect of the Bible, and the dynamic view *humanizes* the divine. The first is a sort of bibliological Docetism, while the latter is a bibliological Arianism.[21]

The essential objection to the inspired concept theory is that it is *linguistically impossible*. It is problematic whether or not there is any such thing as a "pure thought" impression, and it is certain that there is no such thing as a full thought expression without some sort of symbolization or language. Symbolization is absolutely essential to the fullest expression of thoughts.[22] In order for God to give full expression of His thoughts to man, He had to use man's symbols or language.

Since "pure thought" must be expressed in human symbols for man to understand it, the available alternatives must be ascertained. Hypothetically, there are three basic alternatives available with respect to the locus of revelation and the words of the Bible. The first alternative is that God inspired written words distinct from human thought. This would be nonsense, and nobody seriously adheres to this position. God is attempting to communicate, not confound, and communication is a mind-to-mind or heart-to-heart process. "Thoughtless words," words without meaning, are just that—meaningless words. Certainly God ought not be charged with such mockery.

A second alternative is that God inspired "pure thought" apart from words. This is basically the dynamic view, and it too is untenable, although it carries a certain believable appeal. Words are the clothes of concepts, and "naked notions" are nonentities when one

[21]Docetism was a heresy in the early church that believed that Christ was *really* God and only *apparently* man. Arians believed that Christ was genuinely human but *not actually* and fully God.

[22]Nash, p. 42.

is giving expression to his thoughts. God could not symbolize for man what He meant without using symbols and particularly symbols that the given man understood. So God limited Himself in His revelation to the cognitions, concepts and culture of the agent to whom and through whom He was communicating. God gave the idea, yet it was given *in man's words*. The idea was first given to man mentally, and then graphically.

THE BASIC BIBLICAL VIEW:[23] THE VERBAL PLENARY INSPIRATION VIEW

The third alternative, and the one that is biblical, is that all the words (verbal) which are written are God-breathed (*pasa graphē Theopneustos;* II Tim. 3:16). God gave full (plenary) expression to His thought in the words of the biblical record. He guided in the very choice of words used within the personality and the cultural complex of the writers so that, in some inscrutable manner, the Bible is the word of God while being the words of men.

Where, then, is the locus or place of revelation? It is in the *words* of Peter, Paul and the other biblical writers. What is it that is inspired? It is the *words* of Scripture. How, then, is inspiration to be defined? Inspiration is that mysterious process by which the guidance of God on the human prophets invests their writings with divine authority. It is the process by which *Spirit-moved men* (II Peter 1:20-21) produce *Spirit-breathed writings* (II Tim. 3:16).

SUMMARY AND CONCLUSION

Basically, there are three major views about the place of the Bible in God's revelation. The Liberal view is that the Bible *contains* the word of God, along with the words and errors of men. This view is based upon a naturalistic premise, it makes human reason and feeling the final judge of revelation, and it does not take seriously what the Bible has to say about itself. The Neoorthodox view is that the Bible *becomes* the word of God in an existential experience, when its message becomes meaningful to the individual. This position is too subjective, it is also based on a naturalistic premise, and it furthermore ignores the fact that the Bible is not only a record of personal revelations but that it is itself a propositional revelation. Among

[23]This is the view which has been held by classical orthodoxy (see chap. 8), historical Fundamentalism (e.g., Benjamin B. Warfield, *The Inspiration and Authority of the Bible;* J. Gresham Machen, *Christianity and Liberalism*), and contemporary Evangelicalism (e.g., G. C. Berkouwer, "General and Special Divine Revelation," in *Revelation and the Bible,* Carl F. H. Henry [ed.]; Charles C. Ryrie, *Biblical Theology of the New Testament*).

the Conservatives, or orthodox, there are two extremes in the contention that the Bible *is* the Word of God. On the one hand, those on the right wing approach a rigid "wooden" view of mechanical dictation, where God supposedly recited the revelation word by word to secretarial scribes. On the other hand are those attempting to evade the mechanical snare by contending for a "dynamic" process, who view God as giving the idea or thought to a man who "freely" expresses it in "his own words." The first Conservative view is impersonal and does not accord with either the teaching or the facts of Scripture. The latter Conservative view is too concessive, as it weakens the authority and infallibility of the Bible. Finally, the true biblical position is not an either/or issue as to thought or words, it is a both/and proposition: God directed the expression of the writers' thoughts without disturbing the free exercise of the writers' personalities. The end product is as authoritative as if it were mechanically dictated, but as writer-orientated as if it were humanly created. The *means* is dynamic, and the *end result* is authoritative and canonic Scripture.

4

SCRIPTURAL CLAIM FOR INSPIRATION IN GENERAL

THE CLAIM FOR INSPIRATION

In order to understand what is meant by inspiration as a whole, the biblical claim must be examined and compared with the character and contents of the Bible. The fact of inspiration as claimed in the Bible must be understood in the light of the phenomena of inspiration. What the Bible says about itself can best be conceived by what the Bible shows in itself. In order to demonstrate the divine authority of the Scriptures, it must be shown that the Bible has a divine *claim* corroborated by a divine *character* and supported by substantial *credentials*. For the present, however, discussion is limited to the general claim and character of inspiration (chap. 9 deals with the credentials, or evidences, of inspiration).

Some Biblical Declarations About Inspiration

It is sometimes objected that it is a "circular argument" to refer to biblical passages in support of biblical claims. But this objection is unfounded for several reasons. (1) *Practically*, there is no better place to begin than with what is self-claimed. (2) *Legally*, a man can testify in his own behalf in a court of law. Why should not the Bible be permitted to witness in its own behalf? (3) *Logically*, the claim is not being used to *support* itself, but as a point of departure to *study* itself.

The claim for inspiration within the Bible itself includes several pertinent characteristics.

It is verbal. The classical text for inspiration in the Bible (II Tim. 3:16) affirms that the *writings* are inspired. Inspiration extends to the very *words* of Scripture. "Moses *wrote* all the *words* of the Lord" (Exodus 24:4). Isaiah was told to "take a large tablet and *write*" (Isa. 8:1) and to "inscribe it in a *book*, that it may be for the time to come as a witness for ever" (Isa. 30:8).[1] The distinct claim of the New Testament is that what had been written by the prophets is God's word; for example, the gospel of Mark introduces the prophet's word by the statement "It is written."[2]

Some have denied that the Bible actually claims to be verbally inspired by saying, "We need to remind ourselves that the verbal plenary formulation is, after all, only a doctrine—a non-Biblical doctrine at that."[3] However, in the light of the repeated general and specific claims that the *words* of the prophets are God's words, it would be a more consistent view simply to admit that the Bible does claim "verbal inspiration" for itself, whether or not this claim is accepted. The evidence that *the very words* of the Bible are God-given may be briefly summarized as follows:

1. This is the claim of the classical text (II Tim. 3:16).

2. It is the emphatic testimony of Paul that he spoke in "*words* . . . taught by the Spirit*" (I Cor. 2:13).

3. It is evident from the repeated formula "It is *written.*"

4. Jesus said that that which was *written* in the whole Old Testament spoke of Him (Luke 24:27, 44; John 5:39; Heb. 10:7).

5. The New Testament constantly equates the word of God with the *Scripture* (*writings*) of the Old Testament (cf. Matt. 21:42; Rom. 15:4; II Peter 3:16).

6. Jesus indicated that not even the smallest part of a *Hebrew word* or letter could be broken (Matt. 5:18).

7. The New Testament refers to the *written record* as the "oracles of God" (Rom. 3:2; Heb. 5:12).

8. Occasionally the writers were even told to "diminish not *a word*" (Jer. 26:2, AV), and John even pronounced an anathema upon all who would add to or subtract from the "*words* of the prophecy of this book" (Rev. 22:18-19).

9. The *very words* uttered by men in the Old Testament were considered to be God's words by the New Testament writers, as the accompanying chart illustrates. It may be an academic option to deny that the Bible claims "verbal inspiration" for itself, but it it clearly not a biblical possibility.

[1]See also chaps. 2-3 for more references.
[2]See chap. 6 for elaboration of this point.
[3]Dewey M. Beegle, *The Inspiration of Scripture*, p. 187.

Old Testament Designation	New Testament Designation
The psalmist said (Ps. 95:7)	The Holy Spirit says (Heb. 3:7)
The psalmist said (Ps. 45:6)	God said (Heb. 1:8)
The psalmist said (Ps. 102:25, 27)	God said (Heb. 1:10-12)
Isaiah said (Isa. 7:14)	The Lord spoke by the prophet (Matt. 1:22-23)
Hosea said (Hosea 11:1)	The Lord spoke by the prophet (Matt. 2:15)
Narrator's comment in Genesis (Gen. 2:24)	God said (Matt. 19:3-6)
Eliphaz' words (Job 5:13)	God's Word (I Cor. 3:19)

It is unbreakable. Another biblical claim for inspiration is that the written word is unbreakable or *infallible.* Jesus said to the Jews, to whom He had quoted from Psalm 82, "Scripture cannot be broken" (John 10:35). Edward J. Young has put it,

> The force of his argument is very clear, and it may be para-phrased as follows: "what is stated in this verse from the psalms is true because this verse belongs to that body of writings known as Scripture, and the Scripture possesses an authority so absolute in character that *it cannot be broken.*" When Christ here em-ploys the word Scripture, he has in mind, therefore, not a par-ticular verse in the psalms, but rather the entire group of writings of which this one verse is a part.[4]

For Jesus, then, inspiration meant a divinely authoritative and *un-breakable writing.*

It is irrevocable. Another claim for inspired writings is that their message is irrevocable. The Bible states, "For truly, I say to you, till heaven and earth pass away, not an iota, not a dot, will pass from the law until all is accomplished" (Matt. 5:18). Again, "But it is easier for heaven and earth to pass away, than for one dot [smallest part of a letter] of the law to become void" (Luke 16:17). This claim is unequivocal; the message of the written word, including the smallest letters, must be fulfilled. In a similar claim, Jesus included the whole Old Testament, section by section, as He said, "Everything written about me in the law of Moses and the prophets and the psalms *must be fulfilled*" (Luke 24:44). Peter added these words, "Brethren, the

---

[4]E. J. Young, "The Authority of the Old Testament," *The Infallible Word,* a sym-posium, N. B. Stonehouse and Paul Woolley (eds.), p. 55.

scripture had to be fulfilled, which the Holy Spirit spoke beforehand" (Acts 1:16).

It has final authority. The biblical writers and Jesus Himself claim that the written word is the *final arbitrator* in matters of faith and practice. Jesus quoted the Old Testament Scriptures with finality when resisting the tempter (Matt. 4:4, 7, 10). He used the Old Testament decisively to settle the question about the resurrection in His answer to the Pharisees (Matt. 21:42), and in vindicating His authority to cleanse the temple (Mark 11:17). Paul used the Scriptures as the basis for his *arguments* with the Jews (Acts 17:2). Peter declared of the Scriptures that "the ignorant and unstable twist them to their own destruction" (II Peter 3:16). In fact, the finality which is based on the verbal inerrancy of the Old Testament as the word of God "is demonstrated by New Testament arguments which rest on a small historical detail (Heb. 7:4-10), a word or phrase (Acts 15:13-17), or even the difference between the singular and the plural (Gal. 3:16)."[5]

It is plenary (full, complete, extending to every part). It is the claim of II Timothy 3:16 that *all* of Scripture (i.e., the whole Old Testament) is inspired and not just part of it. That inspiration extends universally to all of Scripture is borne out by the use of the inclusive phrases "it is written," "the Scriptures," "the law and the prophets," "the word of God" (cf. Mark 7:13; see chap. 6 for a more complete elaboration of this point). Jesus referred to all sections of the Hebrew canon as predictive of Himself (Luke 24:27, 44), and Peter considered the Old Testament as a whole to be "prophetic writing" (II Peter 1:20-21) given by the "Spirit of Christ" (I Peter 1:10-11).

Some Logical Deductions About Inspiration

While it must be recognized that much of what has been claimed refers *explicitly* only to the Old Testament Scriptures, nevertheless, logically and *implicitly* the New Testament is included within this same claim of inspiration.

1. *The New Testament is "Scripture."* Stated in logical or syllogistic form, this argument is as follows:

All "Scripture" is inspired (II Tim. 3:16).

---

[5]John A. Witmer, "The Biblical Evidence for the Verbal-Plenary Inspiration of the Bible," *Bibliotheca Sacra*, Vol. CXXI, No. 483 (1964), p. 250.

The New Testament is also "Scripture" (I Tim. 5:18;
II Peter 3:16).

Therefore, the New Testament is inspired.

The use of the word Scripture has a distinct and technical sense
in the New Testament, as may be readily seen by its specialized application. The term is reserved in its definitive and articular sense
for only the authoritative and canonical books of Holy Writ. For
the devout although converted Jews who wrote the books of the New
Testament to describe any other books by this technical word
amounts to claiming inspiration for them. As a matter of fact, this is
precisely what Peter does claim for Paul's epistles when he writes,
"So also our beloved brother Paul wrote to you . . . speaking of this
as he does in all his letters . . . which the ignorant and unstable twist
to their own destruction, as they do the *other scriptures*" (II Peter
3:15-16). Here Paul's writings are considered Scripture in the same
sense as the Old Testament writings referred to earlier in the same
passage (cf. II Peter 3:5, 7-8). While this passage does not claim
that all the New Testament books are Scripture, it does include many
of them. In I Timothy 5:18 the Apostle Paul quotes from Luke,
placing it on the same level with Scripture, and under the same introduction "for the scripture says" (with reference to Luke 10:7).
Certainly if Paul's and Luke's writings were considered Scripture,
then the epistles of the apostles of Jesus, and particularly those of
the "inner circle" (Peter and John), which traditionally comprise
most of the remainder of the New Testament, cannot logically be
excluded from the category of inspired Scripture.

2. *The New Testament is "prophetic writing."* Another logical deduction about inspiration substantiates the foregoing. According to
II Peter 1:20-21, no prophetic utterances (and writings) ever come
by any other means than the moving of the Holy Spirit. Since the
New Testament writings are considered to be "prophetic writings"
too, it would follow that they must be included within the group of
Spirit-moved utterances. Jesus promised to give His disciples a Spirit-
directed ministry (John 14:26; 16:13) and the New Testament
church claimed this prophetic gift (cf. Eph. 4:11; I Cor. 14:31-32).
Like their Old Testament counterparts, the New Testament prophets
exercised their ministry both orally (cf. Agabus, Acts 11:28) and in
writing. John, the author of the book of Revelation, classified himself with his "brethren the [Old Testament] prophets" (Rev. 22:9).
By direct inference, therefore, his writing claimed to be a prophetic

writing. Indeed, this is what John himself said when he wrote, "I warn every one who hears the *words of the prophecy of this book:* if any one adds to them, God will add to him the plagues described in this book" (Rev. 22:18). Paul also considered his writings to be prophetic. In Ephesians 3:3-5 he speaks of his revelation and mystery "which was not made known to the sons of men in other generations as it has now [in Paul's time] been revealed to his holy apostles and prophets[6] by the Spirit." Apostles and prophets are classed together, as are their revelations and writings, as Paul declared: "The mystery was made known to me by revelation, as I have written briefly. When you read this you can perceive my insight into the mystery of Christ."

To summarize, then, it is suggested that:

All "prophetic writings" are inspired (II Peter 1:20-21).
The New Testament is "prophetic writing" (Rev. 22:18; Eph. 3:5).
Therefore, the New Testament is inspired.

3. *The whole Bible is inerrant.* Still another deduction to be drawn from inspiration is the fact that the Bible is inerrant (errorless). Even though it may be technically correct that "the Bible itself, in advancing its own claim of inspiration, says nothing precisely about its inerrancy,"[7] it is as necessary and logical a deduction as is the "Trinity," about which nothing is "precisely" stated in the Bible. Logically, if the words of Scripture are God's and God cannot err, then it follows that there are no errors in the Scriptures. Formally presented, the argument is as follows:

Whatever God utters is errorless (inerrant).
The words of the Bible are God's utterances.
Therefore, the words of the Bible are errorless (inerrant).

[6]In fact, the very prophets spoken of here may be New Testament prophets, upon the foundation of whose teaching the New Testament church is built (cf. Eph. 2:20; Acts 2:42). Commenting on the "prophets" of Eph. 2:20, Charles J. Ellicott wrote, "In spite of much ancient and valuable authority, it seems impossible to take the 'prophets' of this verse to be the prophets of the Old Testament. The order of the two words and the comparison of chaps. 3:5 and 4:11, appear to be decisive—to say nothing of the emphasis on the present, in contrast with the past, which runs through the whole chapter." See *Ellicott's Commentary,* VIII, 30. The same conclusion is stated by S. D F. Salmond in *The Expositor's Greek Testament,* ed. Robert Nicoll, III, 299. He comments, "Hence the *prophetai* are to be understood as *Christian* prophets, of whom large mention is made in the Book of Acts and the Epistles—the N.T. prophets who in this same Epistle (3:5) are designated as *Christ's* prophets and are named (4:11) among the gifts of the ascended Lord to His Church."
[7]Everett F. Harrison, "The Phenomena of Scripture," *Revelation and the Bible,* Carl F. H. Henry (ed.), p. 238.

John A. Witmer correctly observed this matter, when he stated,

> Logic likewise demands that the divine perfections or inerrancy
> and infallibility be recognized as inhering in the "God-breathed"
> Scripture. This, in effect, the Bible does; for it speaks of itself as
> "perfect" (Psalm 19:7), "pure" (Psalm 19:8; 119:140), "true"
> (Psalm 19:9; 119:43, 142, 160; John 17:17; James 1:18), and "eter-
> nally enduring" (Psalm 19:9; 119:89, 144, 160; Isaiah 40:8;
> Matthew 24:34; I Peter 1:23, 25).[8]

THE CHARACTER AND CONTENT OF INSPIRATION

THE NATURE OF INSPIRATION

When careful examination is made of the *phenomena* of Scripture
in the light of the fact that it *claims* to be inspired, it becomes apparent that what the Bible *means* by what it *says* about itself is what
is manifest by those phenomena. That is, the claim for inspiration
must be understood in light of the phenomena of Scripture. Hence,
attention must be centered on the *practical manifestations* of the
theological declaration of inspiration. Such an examination reveals
that whatever is meant by inspiration, it certainly *does not exclude*
the following factors:

The use of variety of expression. Since God said the same thing in
different ways, or at least from different viewpoints, at different
times, inspiration cannot be meant to exclude a diversity of expression. The four Gospels relate the same story in different ways to
different groups of people; and sometimes even quote Christ as saying the same thing with different words. Compare, for example,
Peter's famous confession at Caesarea Philippi:

Matthew records it:	"You are the Christ, the Son of the living God" (16:16).
Mark records it:	"You are the Christ" (8:29).
Luke records it:	"The Christ of God" (9:20).

Even the Decalogue, "written by the finger of God" (Deut. 9:10),
is stated with variations the second time that God gave it (cf. Exodus
20:8-11 with Deut. 5:12-15).[9] There are many variations between

---

[8]Witmer, p. 246.

[9]For example, Exodus gives "creation" as the reason for rest on the Sabbath, and
Deuteronomy gives "redemption" as the reason.

the books of Kings and Chronicles in their description of identical events, yet there is no contradiction in the story they tell.

If such important utterances as Peter's confession of Christ and the inscription on the cross (cf. Matt. 27:37; Mark 15:26; Luke 23:38; John 19:19) and such permanent and special laws as the one "written with the finger of God" can be stated in different ways, then there should be no problem in extending to the rest of Scripture a diversity of expression within the concept of a verbal inspiration.

The use of individuality and personalities. Inspiration apparently does not exclude the use of different personalities, with their own literary styles and idiosyncrasies in recording the written word of God. To observe this, one need only compare the powerful style of Isaiah with the mournful tone of Jeremiah in the Old Testament. In the New Testament, Luke manifests a marked medical interest,[10] James is distinctly practical, Paul is theological and polemical, and John has an obvious simplicity. God has communicated through a multiplicity of human personalities, with their respective literary characteristics. The traditional biblical authors include a lawgiver (Moses), a general (Joshua), prophets (Samuel, Isaiah, *et al.*), kings (Solomon and David), a musician (Asaph), a herdsman (Amos), a prince and statesman (Daniel), a priest (Ezra), a tax collector (Matthew), a physician (Luke), a scholar (Paul), fishermen (Peter and John). With such a variety of occupations represented by biblical writers, it is only natural that their personal interests and differences should be reflected in their writings.

The use of nonbiblical documents. Undoubtedly the doctrine of inspiration does not mean to exclude the use of human documents as a source of divine truth, since the use of such is exactly what the Bible does claim. Luke confessed that his gospel was based on the research he had done in the written sources of his day (cf. Luke 1:1-4). The writer of Joshua used the Book of Jasher for his famous quotation about the sun standing still (Joshua 10:13). The Apostle Paul quoted unhesitatingly from a heathen poet (Acts 17:28) in his well-known Mars Hill address. Jude cited a noncanonical book about the prophecy of Enoch (v. 14). This use of nonbiblical sources should not be thought incongruous with inspiration, since it is to be remembered that "all truth is God's truth." The God who "commanded the light to shine out of darkness" (II Cor. 4:6) is able to speak truth through a pagan prophet (Num. 24:17), an unwitting

[10]Cf. W. M. Ramsay, *St. Paul the Traveller and the Roman Citizen*, pp. 38-39.

high priest (John 11:50), and even a stubborn donkey (Num. 22:28).

The use of nonscientific language. Inspiration certainly does not necessitate the use of scholarly, technical and scientific language. The Bible is written for the common men of every generation, and it therefore uses their common everyday language. The use of phenomenal, nonscientific language is not *unscientific*, it is merely *prescientific*. The Scriptures were recorded in *ancient* times by ancient standards, and it would be anachronistic to superimpose *modern* scientific standards upon them. It is no more unscientific to speak of the "sun standing still" (Joshua 10:12) than it is to refer to the "sun rising" (Joshua 1:16). Even the most brilliant modern scientists may speak phenomenally of "the beautiful sun*set*." The Scriptures say that the Queen of Sheba came "from the end of the earth." Since "the end of the earth" was only several hundred miles away, in Arabia,[11] it is apparent that this is another example of the use of phenomenal language. In like manner, on the day of Pentecost there were people "from every nation under heaven" (Acts 2:5). However, these nations are enumerated in verses 9-11 and do not include literally all the world, for some geographical areas are definitely excluded (e.g., North and South America). Thus, universal language used in a *geographical*[12] sense is apparently to be taken phenomenally, meaning "the then-known world."[13] The Bible was written to a nonscientific people in a prescientific age, and it is unreasonable for one to say that it is scientifically *incorrect;* it is merely scientifically *imprecise* by modern standards. But, in sacrificing precision, it has gained a perfection by its universality and simplicity of style.

The use of a variety of literary devices. Finally, it should not be thought that an "inspired" book must have been written in one and only one literary mold. Man is not limited in his modes of expression, and there is no reason to suppose that God can only speak in one manner (e.g., literally). It is better to refer to the grammatical or *normal* meaning of biblical words than to insist on their literal meaning in all cases.[14] The Bible reveals a number of literary devices, and

[11]Emil G. Kraeling, *Rand McNally Bible Atlas,* p. 231, map IV.
[12]Universal language used in a *generic* sense, as in Rom. 3:23, is different. Language used generically includes all who participate in the common nature or name.
[13]Cf. Bernard Ramm, *Protestant Biblical Interpretation,* rev. ed., pp. 134 ff.
[14]E. R. Craven stated this point quite well when he wrote, "*Normal* is used instead of *literal* . . . as more expressive of the correct idea. No terms could have been chosen more unfit to designate the two great schools of prophetical exegetes than *literal* and *spiritual*. These terms are not antithetical. . . . They are positively misleading and confusing" (*A Commentary on the Holy Scriptures.* Revelation. Philip Schaff [trans. and ed.], p. 98 n.*).

there are times when the normal sense of a passage may be entirely metaphorical (e.g., Ps. 91:4; John 15:5). Several whole books are written in *poetic* style (e.g., Job, Psalms, Proverbs). The synoptic gospels are filled with *parables*. In Galatians 4, Paul uses an example of an *allegory*. The New Testament abounds with *metaphors* (e.g., II Cor. 3:2-3; James 3:6) and *similes* (cf. Matt. 20:1; James 1:6); *hyperboles* may also be found (e.g., Col. 1:23; John 21:25; II Cor. 3:2). And Jesus Himself used the device of *satire* (cf. Matt. 19:24 with 23:24). In a word, then, the *claim* for inspiration, as understood in the light of the *character* of the inspired record itself, reveals that "inspiration" must not be viewed as a mechanical or wooden process. It is, rather, a *dynamic* and *personal* process which results in a divine and authoritative record.

WHAT IS THE EXTENT OF INSPIRATION?

Since inspiration includes the very written words of Scripture, and all parts of Scripture are equally inspired, it may legitimately be asked whether this inspiration preserves every part of the Bible from error. If every word is equally inspired, does it follow that every word is true? And furthermore, does inspiration extend to matters of history and science, or only to spiritual matters? Several factors need to be considered at this point.

Inspiration necessitates the truthfulness of only what the Bible teaches. Not everything the Bible *contains* is true; only what the Bible *teaches* is true. The whole record is under *inspiration,* but only what is taught in it is a *revelation.* The Bible teaches only *truth* (John 17:17), but it contains some *lies,* for example, Satan's lie (Gen. 3:4) and Rahab's lie (Joshua 2:4). Inspiration covers the Bible fully and completely in the sense that it records accurately and truthfully even the lies and errors of sinful beings. The truth of Scripture is not to be found in what the Bible *says,* but in what it *means,* in other words, in what it *reveals,* not what it *records.* Unless this distinction is held, it may be concluded that the Bible teaches immorality, because it narrates David's sin (II Sam. 11:4); that it promotes polygamy, because it records Solomon's (I Kings 11:3); or that it asserts atheism, because it quotes the fool as saying, "There is no God" (Ps. 14:1). In each case the interpreter of Scripture must seek the *commitment of the writer* of the particular passage in question. The important thing for the interpreter to keep in mind is not what the writer seems to say, not what he refers to, nor even whom he quotes, but what he is *really attempting to teach* by way of all his devices. Admittedly, this is not always easy to discover, as anyone knows who has tried to apply this principle to the discourses of Job's friends, the apparent skepticism of the "man under the sun" in Ecclesiastes, or even to Stephen's speech in Acts 7. Was what they said *really true,* or is the Bible merely rendering a *true record* of what they said, whether it was all true, partly true, or completely false? The basic question is: Did the biblical writer approve or commend what he recorded for his readers, or merely record it to illustrate what he really approved? In each case the commitment of the author must be sought, however difficult this may be.

Inspiration does not necessitate the truthfulness of biblical illustrations. Whatever interpretation be taken of the foregoing passages, there can be no doubt that on occasion the Bible contains *illustrations* of truth which are themselves not true. For instance, inspiration does not guarantee the truth of every aspect of a *parable;* it guarantees only the *point* the parable makes. This may be seen in the parable in Luke 18, where Jesus illustrates truth about God by using an unjust judge. It would be a gross error to make this parable "walk on all four." The point of the parable is not to demonstrate the nature of God, it is rather to indicate the results of persistent prayer.

This raises another very important question: How far may this principle of illustration of truth extend? Does it include historical matters? In other words, could the writers be using a historical framework to convey suprahistorical truth without intending to teach the historicity of an event at all? For example, was Jesus really teaching the historicity of Elijah and the widow when He said,

> But in truth, I tell you, there were many widows in Israel in the days of Elijah, when the heaven was shut up for three years and six months, when there came a great famine over all the land; and Elijah was sent to none of them but only to Zarephath, in the land of Sidon, to a woman who was a widow (Luke 4:25-26).

Or was He merely meaning to say, "As you commonly believe by your tradition . . ."? In order to answer this question properly, another must be addressed.

Inspiration necessitates inerrancy in historical and factual matters. Since the Bible is inerrant (errorless) in what it teaches, the preliminary question to be answered is: Does the Bible *ever teach* historical or factual matters? In answer to this question, it should be admitted that the primary and explicit claim for what the Bible teaches is in regard to matters of "faith and practice." Inspiration primarily covers *doctrine and deed* (II Tim. 3:16), *things to be believed* (John 20:31), *words of the Law* (Deut. 29:29), and matters of *life and godliness* (II Peter 1:3). However, some of these things have direct *historical and factual connections and implications*. As a result, there must be a recognition that the historical and factual are not only implicitly contained in the spiritual and doctrinal teachings, but often they are *inseparably connected* with them. Several reasons for this conclusion are:

1. Archaeology has confirmed much of biblical history as actual history (see p. 122).

2. There is no distinguishable difference between the narration and the description of events that have not been confirmed (e.g., the creation of Adam or the resurrection of Christ) and those that have been confirmed (e.g., Nebuchadnezzar's conquest of Jerusalem).

3. Further, it is impossible to demythologize, or strip the historical from the spiritual (e.g., the life of Christ), without making the Man and His message as mythical as the so-called "myth" or manner through which it is being presented.

4. Finally, many of the disputable passages have had their historicity directly verified by Christ, including Adam (Matt. 19:4), Cain and Abel (Luke 11:51), Noah (Luke 17:26), Lot (Luke 17:28), and even Jonah (Matt. 12:40). The very integrity of Jesus hinges upon the reality of these people and the historicity of their lives.

Inspiration does not include accommodation to error. Some have attempted to account for the supposed historical assertions and yet spare Jesus' integrity by proposing an accommodation theory.[15] Briefly, this theory states that Jesus, in His reference to the Old Testament, accommodates His teaching to the prejudices and erroneous views of His day. It holds that He did not actually mean that Jonah was *really* in the "whale." It claims that Jesus' purpose was

---

[15]Johann Salomo Semler (1725-91), "the father of German Rationalism," seems to have been the first to suggest this view. Cf. Milton S. Terry, *Biblical Hermeneutics*, p. 166.

not to question the historical truth, nor to establish critical theories, but to preach spiritual and moral values.

There are several significant fallacies in the accommodation view which should be noted in passing.[16]

1. *Accommodation is confused with adaptation.* There is a legitimate kind of adaptation of infinite truth into finite terminology by the use of anthropomorphisms (picturing God with human characteristics such as hands and arms), but this *adaptation is necessary for human understanding* rather than an *accommodation to human errors.*[17]

2. *Accommodation is confused with progressive revelation.* It is true that God adapted His revelation to the cultural immaturity of its day, but He never compromised it to the falsehoods of that day. There is a difference between not telling small children *all* about sex and telling them the "stork story." The former is truth *appropriate* for the circumstances, whereas the latter is a fabrication.

3. *Accommodation destroys the basis for objective meaning.* If truth were conveyed through myths and not via objectifiable or historical situations in the Bible, there would be nothing but a subjective or mystical basis for the meaning of the Bible. For if there is no factual basis for the historical references of the Bible, then how can it be known if there is any actual basis for its theological assertions? As Jesus said, "If I have told you earthly things and you do not believe, how can you believe if I tell you heavenly things?" (John 3:12).

4. *Accommodation opens the door to agnosticism.* If Jesus accommodated so completely and conveniently to current ideas, how can it ever be known with certainty just what He actually believed? "If such a principle be admitted into our exposition of the Bible, we at once lose our moorings, and drift out upon the sea of conjecture and uncertainty."[18]

5. *The character of Jesus as we know it could hardly be considered one of accommodation to prevailing opinion and error.* Actually, just the opposite is true. Jesus did not hesitate to rebuke the

---

[16]For a pointed and incisive refutation of the accommodation theory see Thomas Horne, *An Introduction to the Critical Study and Knowledge of the Holy Scriptures* (8th ed.), I, 324.

[17]See article on "Accommodation" in *Baker's Dictionary of Theology* for four legitimate kinds of accommodation.

[18]Terry, p. 167.

Jews of His day for exalting their traditions "above God's commandments" (Matt. 15:1-3), nor was He reticent to assert His own authority above rabbinical opinion. Six times He affirmed, "You have heard that it was said to the men of old . . . but I say unto you" (Matt. 5:21, 27, 31, 33, 38, 43). In fact, Jesus gave one of the most scathing religious denunciations in recorded history against the prevailing religious views of His day (cf. Matt. 23:16-27). His words and attitude are hardly features of accommodation. They are rather aspects of a clear condemnation of all the prevalent false ideas.

6. The telling "objection to this kind of interpretation is that it necessarily impugns the veracity of the sacred writers, and of Christ Himself."[19] That He who was "the truth" and who spoke no falsehood, should accommodate Himself to error is not only a demonstration of poor hermeneutics, but it is reflective of a low view of the nature of Christ.

Summarily, there is a vast difference between a legitimate adaptation of infinite truth to finite understanding, and an illegitimate accommodation of truth to human errors. Inspiration vouches for the veracity of whatever the Bible teaches, and the Bible does teach historical and factual matters as well as theological truths. Therefore, it teaches these factual matters simply but never incorrectly.

SUMMARY AND CONCLUSION

The Bible makes an explicit claim for itself in the matter of inspiration for the Old Testament; it logically claims the same inspiration for the New Testament. Some necessary deductions from inspiration must include the infallibility and inerrancy of the written record. However, when the claim for inspiration is studied in the light of its character of phenomena, it is clear that inspiration includes a diversity of expression, the instrumentality of human personalities, the use of source documents, nonscientific language and a variety of literary devices. Inspiration also extends equally to every part of Scripture and guarantees a true record of all that it contains, although it does not necessarily make the claim that everything said in the record is true. A distinction is to be made between what the Bible teaches and what it records or contains. The Bible contains a true record of some lies and errors, but what it teaches is true and errorless (inerrant).

[19]Ibid.

5

SPECIFIC CLAIMS OF INSPIRATION
IN THE OLD TESTAMENT

The discussion to this point has centered around a few major texts which claim inspiration *for* the Bible. Now attention must be given to the specific claims *of* each section and book of the Bible individually. Is the specific claim *in* these books the same as the claim *for* them by other books? To answer this question fully, the next four chapters will discuss, in order, (1) the claim of inspiration *in* the Old Testament, (2) the claim *for* the Old Testament (*in* the New Testament), (3) the claim *in* the New Testament, and (4) the claim of inspiration *for* the New Testament (*in* the Church Fathers). The present chapter is concerned with carefully examining what the Old Testament claims in and of itself.

THE CLAIM FOR INSPIRATION IN EACH BOOK
OF THE OLD TESTAMENT

AN EXAMINATION OF THE CLAIM FOR INSPIRATION

A brief examination of each of the books of the Old Testament will help to confirm in detail the thesis that each of the individual sections is divinely authoritative. It should be noted that every book of the Old Testament does not have an explicit and unequivocal claim to divine inspiration. Nevertheless, it can be demonstrated that most of them do have such a distinct claim, and that the remainder have either an implicit claim or a character which serves as an implicit claim to inspiration.

Genesis. In Genesis God spoke to the patriarchs (cf. Gen. 12, 26, 46) and they made records in a permanent "family album" of divine dealings under the title "This is the book of the generation of . . ." (Gen. 5:1; 10:1, 10).

Exodus. In Exodus the record reads, "And God spoke all these words" (Exodus 20:1). Moses said to the people, "These are the things which the Lord has commanded you to do" (Exodus 35:1). "And the tables were the work of God, and the writing was the writing of God" (Exodus 32:16).

Leviticus. The introduction to Leviticus says, "The Lord called Moses, and spoke to him from the tent of meeting, saying, . . ." (Lev. 1:1). "The Lord said to Moses" is found repeatedly (cf. 4:1; 5:14; 6:1, 8).

Numbers. This book repeatedly records, "The Lord spoke to Moses" (Num. 1:1; see 2:1; 4:1; 5:1; 6:1; 8:1), and it closes by saying, "These are the commandments and the ordinances which the Lord commanded by Moses to the people of Israel" (Num. 36:13).

Deuteronomy. In Deuteronomy, Moses' speeches are regarded as God's word, saying, "You shall not add to the word which I command you, nor take from it" (Deut. 4:2); it even sets forth tests of truth for divine utterances: "When a prophet speaks in the name of the Lord, if the word does not come to pass or come true, that is a word which the Lord has not spoken" (Deut. 18:22).

1. *Michelangelo's "Moses" (Metropolitan Museum of Art)*

Joshua. In this book, Joshua relates how "after the death of Moses . . . the LORD said to Joshua, 'This day I will begin to exalt you in the sight of all Israel, that they may know that, as I was with Moses, so I will be with you'" (Joshua 1:1–3:7). "And Joshua wrote these words in the book of the law of God" (Joshua 24:26).

Judges. After the death of Joshua, the book of Judges reveals that "the LORD said, . . ." (Judges 1:2), and again, later, God spoke to Gideon (Judges 6:25). The angel of the Lord appeared with a message on several occasions (cf. Judges 2, 5, 6, 13).

Ruth. This book was probably appended to the book of Judges in its original position (see chaps. 1, 12), and, as a result, needs no explicit reference to God speaking. However, this book does give a record of divine activity, as it records an important link in the Messianic chain, namely, the ancestors of David the king, Boaz and Ruth (Ruth 4:21).

I and II Samuel. The books of I and II Samuel, which were originally one book, have many references to the voice of God. Through Samuel, the traditional author of the book, these books record, "Then the LORD said to Samuel" (I Sam. 3:11). "And the word of Samuel came to all Israel" (I Sam. 4:1). Then I Chronicles 29:29 adds, "The acts of King David, from first to last, are written in the Chronicles of . . . Gad the seer" (possibly II Sam.). This support would make the books prophetic, and hence authoritative.

I and II Kings. Formerly one book, I and II Kings have no explicit claim to inspiration. Tradition ascribes these books to Jeremiah the prophet, which would automatically make them prophetic. The emphasis on the divine ministry of the prophets, and the prophetic viewpoint of the books of Kings, would confirm the traditional view that some prophet wrote these books. Hence, they too would be divinely authoritative.

I and II Chronicles. These books lack an overt claim to inspiration, but they do present an authoritative history of Israel, Judah and the temple from the priestly point of view. The books *assume* authority rather than stating or claiming it. And since the books are descriptive rather than didactic, there is no need for an explicit reference to their message as being a "thus *saith* the Lord." There is, however, an implicit, yet clear, "thus *did* the Lord," which is even more discernible than in Kings.

Ezra-Nehemiah. Continuing the temple-centered history of Judah, Ezra-Nehemiah declares definitely that God was responsible for the restoration of the deported nation. While the book makes no explicit claim for its inspiration, there is again the clear assumption that it is a record of God's *deeds*, and such a record is no less authoritative than a record of God's words.

Esther. The book of Esther also fits into this same category. Even though the name of God is absent from the book (except in acrostic form),[1] nonetheless, the presence of God is certainly evident as He protects and preserves His people. The book implicitly claims to be a *true record* of God's providence over His people, which is all that inspiration means.

Job. In Job, not only does the author claim to give a view into the very council chamber of heaven (Job 1-2), but he records the actual words of God which were spoken out of the whirlwind (Job 38:1 ff.). Between chapters 2 and 38, an accurate record of what Job and his friends said is presented.[2]

Psalms. A book addressed primarily *to* God, Psalms can hardly be expected to say "God said," or "Thus saith the Lord." There is, however, within the very selection and structure of the psalms, a divine approval of the theology and truth which is reflected in the varied spiritual experiences of the psalmists. It is apparent that God moved particular men to record their select experiences, with His approbation, for future generations. The last five psalms sum up the divine exhortation "Praise the LORD." This is a book in which *God declares how men should praise Him.* In fact, II Samuel 23:1-2 says that David, who wrote many of the psalms, was Spirit-directed in his utterances.

Proverbs. This book is introduced as "The proverbs of Solomon" (1:1). That Solomon claims these words of wisdom to be the word of God is evident when he writes: "Have not I written unto thee of excellent things of counsels and knowledge, to make thee know the certainty of the words of truth, that thou mayest carry back words of truth to them that send thee?" (Prov. 22:20-21, ASV). It will be remembered that Solomon's wisdom was God-given for this very purpose—to help his people (cf. I Kings 3:9 ff.). Chapter 25 and the following chapters are "proverbs of Solomon, which . . . Hezekiah king of Judah copied out" (25:1) but are nonetheless Solomon's. Chapters 30 and 31 each claim in the first verse to be an "oracle". (ASV) or "prophecy" (AV) from God (cf. II Chron. 9:29).

[1]W. Graham Scroggie, *Know Your Bible,* I, 96.
[2]It is interesting to note that the New Testament quotes from this section using the formula "It is written." Cf. I Cor. 3:19, as it cites Job 5:13.

Ecclesiastes. This book has clear and authoritative exhortations (cf. 11:19; 12:1, 12) which lead to this definite conclusion: "All has been heard. Fear God, and keep his commandments; for this is the whole duty of man" (12:13). That is, the teaching of this book claims to be the word from God on the subject.

Song of Solomon. Although it has no explicit claim for its divine inspiration, this book was thought to be inspired by the Jews on the grounds that it gave a picture of the Lord's love for Israel. Others have suggested that it is God's word about the sanctity of marriage.[3] Whatever the interpretation, the implication is that the book is a revelation from God about the intimacy and purity of love (whether human or divine).

The Prophets. The prophetical books may be summarily treated, since the record is replete with distinctive claims as to the divine origin of the individual messages. Isaiah 1:1-2: "The vision of Isaiah . . . for the LORD has spoken." Jeremiah (and Lamentations, which was originally appended to it) 1:1-2: "The words of Jeremiah, . . . to whom the word of the LORD came." Ezekiel 1:3: "The word of the LORD came to Ezekiel." Daniel received visions and dreams (e.g., Dan. 7:1) as well as angelic messages from God (e.g., 9:21 ff.). Hosea through Malachi were all one book in the Hebrew Bible (The Twelve), but each one has an explicit claim, as Amos 1:3 and the opening verse in each of the following books indicate: Hosea, Joel, Obadiah, Jonah, Micah, Nahum, Habakkuk, Zephaniah, Haggai, Zechariah, Malachi.

AN EXPLANATION OF BOOKS WHICH LACK EXPLICIT CLAIM FOR INSPIRATION

The vast majority of the books of the Old Testament (about twenty-six of thirty-nine) have an explicit claim that they are God's words to men, but some do not have such clear statements as to their origin. Several reasons may be proffered in the clarification of this important matter.

They are all part of a given section. Every book is included within the organic unity of a section (Pentateuch, Prophets, Writings) in which there is distinct and indisputable claim for inspiration, a fact which thereby speaks for every book within that section. As a result, each individual book does not need to state its own case; the claim has already been made for it by the *claim* made for the section as a whole, and *confirmed* by the fact that later biblical books

[3]Edward J. Young, *An Introduction to the Old Testament*, p. 355.

refer to the authority of that particular section as a whole. Of course, it is to be assumed that unless a book had an implicit claim to inspiration of its own it would never have been included in the canon from the beginning. This, however, is a matter of canonization, and is considered more fully in chapter 13.

Another reason may be found in their nature. It is only the historical and poetical books that do not contain direct statements as to their divine origin; all of the didactic books do have an explicit "thus saith the Lord." The obvious reason that the historical and poetical books do not is that they are not presented as divine truth addressed "from God to man," but "from man to God" (Poetry); or, to put it another way, they present "what God *showed*" (History) rather than "what God *said*" (Law and Prophets). Nonetheless, there is an implicit didactic, or "thus saith the Lord," even in the historical and poetical books. History is what God said in the concrete events of national life. Poetry is what God said in the hearts and aspirations of individuals within the nation. Both are what God said, just as much so as the explicit record which He spoke through the Law and the other didactic writings.

Traditional writers of these books were men accredited of God with prophetic ministries. Solomon, who is credited by Jewish tradition with writing Song of Solomon, Proverbs and Ecclesiastes, had God-given wisdom (I Kings 4:29). Furthermore, he fulfilled the qualification for a prophet laid down in Numbers 12:6: one to whom God spoke in visions or dreams (cf. I Kings 11:9). David is credited with writing nearly half of the psalms. And although the psalms themselves do not lay direct claim to divine inspiration, David's testimony of his own ministry is recorded in II Samuel 23:2: "The Spirit of the LORD speaks by me, his word is upon my tongue." Jeremiah, the traditional author of I and II Kings, has well-known prophetic credentials (cf. Jer. 1:4, 17). Chronicles and Ezra-Nehemiah are attributed to Ezra the priest, who functioned with all the authority of a prophet interpreting the law of Moses and instituting civil and religious reforms thereupon (cf. Jer. 1:10, 13). So then, either the books of the Old Testament testify for themselves or the men who are believed to have written them, almost without exception,[4] claim them to be the authoritative word of God.

---

[4]The book of Esther does not have an explicit claim to inspiration and its author is unknown. Esther or any other book of undetermined authorship raises questions about its authority. See the discussion on Esther and these other Old Testament books of questioned authority in chap. 13.

THE CLAIM OF INSPIRATION IN THE LAW
AND PROPHETS

As is shown later (chap. 13), the earliest and most basic division of the Old Testament Scriptures was that of Law and Prophets, that is, the five books of Moses and then all of the prophetic writings which came after them. The New Testament refers about a dozen times to this twofold division (cf. Matt. 5:17; 7:12) and only once suggests a threefold division (Luke 24:44). However, in this same chapter, Jesus refers to the "law and the prophets" as being "all the scriptures" (Luke 24:27). Within the Old Testament itself there is a basic, twofold division between the law of Moses and all the prophets who came after him (Neh. 9:14, 26 and Dan. 9:2, 11). This same twofold distinction is carried on in the period between the Old and New Testaments and in the Qumran community (see chap. 12). A consideration of these two divisions of the Hebrew Old Testament will reveal what each claimed for itself and what one claimed for the other as regards the matter of divine inspiration.

THE LAW

The first and most important section of the Old Testament is the Torah, or Law of Moses. The claim for inspiration in this section of the Bible is very distinct, as has already been seen from the previous examination of the individual books of the Law.

The claim in the Law for inspiration. The books of Exodus (32:16), Leviticus (1:1), Numbers (1:1), and Deuteronomy (31:26) all make an explicit claim to inspiration. Genesis alone has no such direct claim. However, since Genesis too was considered to be part of the "book of Moses" (cf. Neh. 13:1; II Chron. 35:12), it is safe to assume that it too possessed the same divine authority. Whatever holds for one book, holds for all of them. In other words, a claim by or for one book in this canonical section is thereby a claim for all of them since they were all unified under a title such as *the* book of Moses or *the* Law of Moses.

The claim for the Law. Throughout the remainder of the Old Testament, in an unbroken succession, the law of Moses was enjoined on the people as the law of God; Moses' voice was heeded as God's. Joshua began his ministry as Moses' successor by saying, "This book of the law shall not depart out of your mouth, . . . that you may be careful to do according to all that is written in it" (Joshua 1:8). In Judges 3:4, God tested Israel to know whether they "would obey the commandments of the Lord, which he commanded their fathers by Moses." "And Samuel said to the people, 'The Lord is witness, who appointed Moses and Aaron and brought your fathers up out of . . . Egypt. But they forgot the Lord their God'" (I Sam. 12:6, 9). In Josiah's day, "Hilkiah the priest found the book of the law of the Lord given through Moses" (II Chron. 34:14). In exile, Daniel recognized Moses' law as God's word, saying, "And the curse and oath which are written in the law of Moses the servant of God have been poured out upon us, because we have sinned against him. He [God] has confirmed his words, which he spoke against us" (Dan. 9:11-12). Even in postexilic times, the revival under Nehemiah came as a result of obedience to Moses' law (cf. Ezra 6:18; Neh. 13:1).

The Prophets

The next section of the Hebrew Scripture was known as "The Prophets." This section literally abounds with claims of its divine inspiration.

The claim in the Prophets. The characteristic "thus saith the Lord" and similar expressions are found here and in other parts of the Old Testament some 3,808 times.[5] A sample survey finds Isaiah proclaiming, "Hear, O heavens, and give ear, O earth; for the Lord has spoken" (Isa. 1:2). Jeremiah wrote, "And the word of the Lord came to me, saying, . . ." (Jer. 1:11). "The word of the Lord came to Ezekiel" (Ezek. 1:3). Similar statements are found throughout the twelve "minor" prophets (cf. Hosea 1:1-2; Joel 1:1).

The claim for the Prophets. Some references in the later prophets reveal a high regard for the utterances of earlier prophets. God spoke to Daniel through the writings of Jeremiah (cf. Dan. 9:2 with Jer. 25:11). Ezra likewise recognized the divine authority in Jeremiah's writings (Ezra 1:1), as well as in those of Haggai and Zechariah (Ezra 5:1). One of the strongest passages is found in one of the last of the Old Testament prophets, Zechariah. He speaks of "the law and the words which the Lord of hosts had sent by his Spirit through the former prophets" (Zech. 7:12). In a similar passage in the last historical book of the Old Testament, Nehemiah writes, "Many years thou [God] didst bear with them, and didst warn them by the Spirit through thy prophets" (Neh. 9:30). These examples confirm the high regard that the latter prophets had for the writings of their predecessors; they considered them to be the word of God, given by the Spirit of God for the good of Israel.

[5]William Evans, *The Great Doctrines of the Bible,* p. 203.

THE CLAIM FOR INSPIRATION IN THE OLD TESTAMENT
AS A WHOLE

Throughout the foregoing discussion runs the concept that a writing was considered the word of God if it was written by a prophet of God. In order, therefore, to see that the Old Testament as a whole claims to be the word of God, it must be determined what is meant by a prophet and a prophetic utterance.

The Function of a Prophet

A prophetic utterance, of course, is that which comes from a prophet in the exercise of his prophetic ministry. Hence, the nature of the prophetic gift becomes crucial in the understanding of the authoritative character of the Old Testament Scriptures which were written as a result of this prophetic gift.

Names given to a prophet. First, a brief examination of the names given to a prophet will help to reveal the character and origin of his ministry. He is called:

1. a man of God (I Kings 12:22), meaning that he was chosen by God

2. a servant of the Lord (I Kings 14:18), indicating that he was to be faithful to God

3. a messenger of the Lord (Isa. 42:19), showing that he was sent by God

4. a seer (*Ro'eh*) or beholder (*Hozeh*) (Isa. 30:9-10), revealing that his insight was from God

5. a man of the Spirit (Hosea 9:7; cf. Micah 3:8), telling that he spoke by the Spirit of God

6. a watchman (Ezek. 3:17), relating his alertness for God

7. a prophet (which he is most commonly called), marking him as a spokesman for God

In summary, all of the prophetic titles refer essentially to the same function, that of a man receiving a revelation from God and relating it to men.

Nature of his office. This same conclusion is substantiated by an examination of the nature of the prophetic office. The etymology of the word "prophet" (*nabhi*) is obscure,[6] but the nature of the prophetic office is clearly defined throughout the Old Testament. The prophet was one who felt as Amos, "The Lord God hath spoken; who can but prophesy?" (Amos 3:8) or even as the Prophet Balaam who said, "I could not go beyond the command of the Lord my God, to do less or more" (Num. 22:18).

Not only was a prophet one who felt the constraint to relate faithfully the command of the Lord, but he was indeed the very mouthpiece of God to men. The Lord said to Moses, "See, I make you as God to Pharaoh; and Aaron your brother shall be your prophet" (Exodus 7:1). In accordance with this, Aaron spoke "all the words which the Lord had spoken to Moses" (Exodus 4:30). In Deuteronomy 18:18 God defines a prophet in these words: "I will put my words in his mouth, and he shall speak to them all that I command him." Moses was told, "You shall not add to the word which I command you, nor take from it" (Deut. 4:2). Micaiah the prophet confirmed the same: "As the Lord lives, what the Lord says to me, that I will speak" (I Kings 22:14). The nature of the prophetic ministry, then, was to be the voice of God to men. And this voice of God had to be heeded; the prophets demanded that the nation give obedience to their message as to God Himself (cf. Isa. 8:5; Jer. 3:6; Ezek. 21:1; Amos 3:1).

Thus, the Old Testament concept of a prophet was one who served as a mouthpiece of God. Aaron was to be a "prophet" for Moses, and Moses was told, "He shall be a mouth for you, and you shall be to him as God" (Exodus 4:16). Edward J. Young summarized well the nature of the Old Testament prophet when he wrote, "We conclude, then, that upon the basis of the Old Testament usage, the *nabhi* was a speaker who declared the word that God had given him."[7]

The Whole Old Testament Is a "Prophetic Utterance"

Not only were the prophets the voice of God in what they *said* but in what they *wrote* as well. Moses was commanded, "Write these words" (Exodus 34:27). The Lord ordered Jeremiah to "take another scroll and write on it all the former words that were in the first scroll" (Jer. 36:28). Isaiah testified that the Lord said to him: "Take a

---

[6]It is variously derived from root words meaning (1) to bubble forth, (2) to speak, (3) to announce, (4) ecstatic behavior, (5) a speaker, (6) a called one. See Edward J. Young, *My Servants the Prophets*, pp. 56-57.

[7]*Ibid.*, p. 60.

large tablet and write upon it" (Isa. 8:1). And again, God told him:
"Go, write it before them on a tablet, and inscribe it in a book that
it may be for the time to come as a witness for ever" (Isa. 30:8). A
similar command was given to Habakkuk: "Write the vision; make
it plain upon tablets, so he may run who reads it" (Hab. 2:2). There
can be little doubt, then, that the prophets did write, and what they
wrote was the word of God just as much as what they spoke was the
word of God. This being the case, it remains only to discover whether
the Old Testament was the work of the prophets in order to establish
it, in its entirety, as the Word of God.

Besides the fact that the New Testament repeatedly refers to all
of the Old Testament as Law and Prophets (cf. Luke 16:31; 24:27),
there are several lines of evidence within the Old Testament that all
of the books were written by prophets (whether recognized as such
by their office or only by their spiritual gift).

1. Moses was a prophet (Deut. 34:10). Moreover, he was a medi-
   ator and lawgiver with whom God spoke "face to face" (Exodus
   33:11) and "mouth to mouth" (Num. 12:8). Hence, his books
   were prophetic beyond question.

2. All of the second division of the Old Testament known as Prophets, and divided into "former" and "latter" prophets in the Hebrew Bible, is considered to be written by prophets, as the name
   of this section suggests (cf. Zech. 7:7, 12; Neh. 9:30).

3. Even if it be agreed that the Hebrew canon was originally divided into three sections—the Law, Prophets and Writings[8]—the
   latter being written by men who did not hold the prophetic
   office but who possessed a prophetic gift[9]—nevertheless, the books
   classed in this third section were still prophetic utterances. In
   fact, Daniel, whose book is found in the Writings, is called by
   Jesus "Daniel the prophet" (Matt. 24:15). Solomon, whose books
   appear among the Writings, was a prophet by definition, since
   he had visions from the Lord (Num. 12:6; cf. I Kings 11:9).
   David, who wrote many of the psalms, is called a prophet in Acts
   2:30. David's testimony of himself was: "The Spirit of the LORD
   speaks by me" (II Sam. 23:2; cf. I Chron. 28:19). If there is a

[8]See chap. 12 where this position is discussed.
[9]Edward J. Young and Merrill F. Unger follow W. H. Green, A General Introduction
to the Old Testament, p. 85, in making this distinction as the basis for classification
of the third section of the Old Testament, viz., the Writings.

distinction between the prophetic office and gift, it in no way affects the prophetic function which was possessed by all of the Old Testament writers.

The Whole Old Testament Is the Word of God

To summarize the foregoing discussion, it may be contended that:

All "prophetic utterances" are the word of God.

All the Old Testament Scriptures are "prophetic utterances."

Therefore, all the Old Testament is the word of God.

In other words, if the whole Old Testament is a prophetic writing, as it claims to be and the New Testament says it is (cf. II Peter 1:20), and if all "prophetic writing" comes from God, then it follows that the whole Old Testament is the word of God.

SUMMARY AND CONCLUSION

An examination of each book of the Old Testament reveals either a direct or an indirect claim to be the word of God. The claim in the historical and poetical books is usually indirect because they are not a record of what God *said* but what He *did* in Israel's national life (History) and in their individual lives (Poetry). Further, the Old Testament was originally divided into two sections: the Law and the Prophets. Each of these sections was considered a unit; hence, the claim that holds for the section as a whole, holds for every book in that section. On this basis, all of the books, Law and Prophets, are seen to claim divine authority. Finally, the Old Testament as a whole claims to be a "prophetic utterance," even the books which were sometimes classified as "writings." Since a "prophetic utterance" means to utter the word of God, it follows that the Old Testament as a whole lays claim to be the divinely inspired Word of God, since the whole claims to be a prophetic utterance.

6

SUPPORTING CLAIMS FOR THE INSPIRATION OF THE OLD TESTAMENT

Not only does the Old Testament claim inspiration for itself, but this claim is overwhelmingly supported by the New Testament use of the Old Testament. A careful examination of the New Testament writings reveals that the whole Old Testament is substantiated in its claim to authenticity and authority by New Testament references to sections and books of the Old Testament.

NEW TESTAMENT REFERENCES TO THE OLD TESTAMENT AS A WHOLE

The New Testament has varied descriptions of the Old Testament as a whole. Each declares in its own way the divine origin of the entire canon of Hebrew Scriptures.

SCRIPTURE

The New Testament uses the term Scripture in a technical sense. It occurs some fifty times, and in most cases it refers unmistakably to the Old Testament as a whole. To first century Christians, the word Scripture meant primarily the sacred canon of the Old Testament,[1] which is called "sacred Scriptures" (II Tim. 3:15, Berkeley) or "holy scriptures" (Rom. 1:2). These they acknowledged to be "inspired of God" (II Tim. 3:16, Berkeley) and the rule for faith and practice (v. 17; cf. Rom. 15:4). Several New Testament passages may be cited to illustrate this point.

1. In Matthew 21:42, Jesus charged the Pharisees saying, "Have you never read in the *scriptures* . . . ?" This question implied that they were ignorant of their own sacred authority, the Old Testament.

---

[1]Even in the first century, however, Christians applied the term Scripture to the books of the New Testament as well, the beginning of which may be seen in II Peter 3:16 and I Tim. 5:18. See the article on "Scripture" in *The New Bible Dictionary*, pp. 1151 ff.

2. In Matthew 22:29, Jesus answered the Sadducees in like manner, saying, "You are wrong, because you know neither the *scriptures* nor the power of God."

3. On the eve of His betrayal, in Matthew 26:54, 56 (NASB), Jesus referred to the Old Testament Scriptures as He said, "But all this has taken place that the Scriptures of the prophets may be fulfilled."

4. Luke 24 is a crucial passage in the present discussion, for Jesus not only opened to the disciples *"the scriptures"* (v. 32), but the Scriptures are described as everything written about Christ "in the law of Moses and the prophets and the psalms" (v. 44). Earlier in this same chapter, while relating Christ's exposition of the Old Testament Law and Prophets, Luke calls these "all the scriptures" (v. 27).

5. John 2:22*b* states that after Jesus was raised from the dead, the disciples "believed the *scripture* and the word which Jesus had spoken."

6. In John 5:39, Jesus said of the Jews: "You search the *scriptures*, . . . it is they that bear witness to me."

7. Several times in the gospel of John the word Scripture (singular) is used without citing a specific passage from the Old Testament, for example, "As the *scripture* has said" (John 7:38; cf. 7:42; 19:36; 20:9). This statement is somewhat akin to the current expression, "The Bible says."

8. In John 10:35, another crucial passage, Jesus asserted that *"scripture* cannot be broken," showing that He considered the sacred Scriptures to be infallible.

9. In Acts, the words Scripture and Scriptures were used in the same manner as they were by Jesus. The Apostle Paul "argued with them [the Jews] from the *scriptures*" (Acts 17:2). The Bereans "searched the *scriptures* daily" (Acts 17:11, AV). Apollos, who was called "an eloquent man, well versed in the scriptures," ministered to the Jews, "showing by the *scriptures* that the Christ was Jesus" (Acts 18:28).

10. Paul repeatedly used the word Scripture(s) to refer to the entire authoritative canon of the Old Testament. In Romans he

wrote that God had promised the gospel "through his prophets in the *holy scriptures*" (Rom. 1:2). The expression, "What saith the *scriptures?*" occurs several times in this same epistle (cf. 4:3; 9:17; 10:11; 11:2). In Romans 15:4, he said that whatever was written in former days in the Scriptures was for the believer's admonition. He also spoke of the "scriptures of the prophets" (Rom. 16:26, ASV). In his other epistles the Apostle Paul said that Christ had died and arisen "in accordance with the *scriptures*" (I Cor. 15:3-4); that the *"scripture"* foresaw that God would justify the Gentiles (Gal. 3:8); that "the *scripture* consigned all things to sin" (Gal. 3:22). He also asked, "What does the *scripture* say?" (Gal. 4:30); made the statement, 'The *scripture* says" (I Tim. 5:18); and declared that "all *scripture* is inspired of God" (II Tim. 3:16).

11. The Apostle Peter added to this picture, as he wrote that "*scripture*" did not come "by the impulse of man, but men moved by the Holy Spirit spoke from God" (II Peter 1:20-21; see 3:16).

12. In a number of New Testament passages the word "scripture" (singular) refers to a particular section or quotation from the Old Testament: Luke 4:21; John 13:18; 17:12; 19:24, 28, 37; Acts 1:16; 8:32, 35; James 2:8, 23; 4:5; I Peter 2:6.

In summary, Jesus and the New Testament writers referred to the complete Hebrew canon of their day, including the Law and Prophets (or, the Law, Prophets and Psalms), as inspired, unbreakable, authoritative in disputes, prophetic of Christ, given by the Holy Spirit through the prophets and, in effect, *the very word of God.*

IT IS WRITTEN

Other captions closely allied to the word Scriptures (*graphē*) are forms of the verb "to write" (*graphō*) and "it is written" (*gegraptai*). These expressions occur about ninety-two times in the New Testament in direct reference to the Old Testament.[2] While the vast majority of these references are to specific passages in the Old Testament, in terms of quotations or paraphrases, some of them are more general in scope, for example, "How *is it written* of the Son of man, that he should suffer many things and be treated with contempt?" (Mark 9:12). Other examples of this usage would include, "For the Son of man goes as *it is written* of him" (Mark 14:21); "*Every-*

[2]*Englishman's Greek Concordance*, 9th ed., pp. 127-28.

thing that is written of the Son of man by the prophets will be accomplished" (Luke 18:31); and other statements such as those in Luke 21:22; 24:44; John 1:45. Furthermore, all of these passages—whether specific quotations or general references—imply an authoritative collection of writings. The expression "it is written" either directly implies or specifically refers to the authoritative writings—sacred Scripture—of the Jewish Old Testament. These references actually mean "It is written in *the* writings [Scriptures]."

THAT IT MIGHT BE FULFILLED

Another expression that either implies or applies to the whole Old Testament is "That it might be fulfilled." This statement is found thirty-three times in the New Testament.[3] Like the clause "It is written," this statement usually refers to a given passage in the Old Testament, but it is sometimes used in a general sense to apply to the entire Hebrew canon, for example, in Matthew 5:17, Jesus said, "I have come not to abolish them [the Law and the Prophets] *but to fulfil them.*" So it is in Luke 24:44, where Jesus said that the Law, Prophets and Psalms *"must be fulfilled,"* and in Luke 21:22, He foretells the time when history will *"fulfil all that is written."* In specific instances, this introduction applies to Old Testament predictions which must come to pass, for example, Luke 4:21, "Today this scripture *has been fulfilled* in your hearing." However, there are times when the expression refers to the preparatory nature of the whole Old Testament, which awaited completion in Christ (see Matt. 5:17).[4] In the latter cases, there is a direct acknowledgment of the inspiration of the entire Old Testament; whereas, in the former cases, there is implicit recognition of this fact. In either case, the formula "that it might be fulfilled," as used in reference to the Old Testament, implies a direct acknowledgment of the prophetic nature of those writings, and prophetic writings were considered to have been divine and authoritative (cf. II Peter 1:20-21).[5]

THE LAW

Although the term "Law" was often reserved for the first five books of the Hebrew canon, as a shortened form of the expression "the law of Moses," it was sometimes used to refer to the Old Testa-

---

[3]*Ibid.*, p. 630.
[4]Robert D. Culver, "The Old Testament as Messianic Prophecy," *Bulletin of the Evangelical Theological Society,* Vol. VII, No. 3 (1964), pp. 91-97.
[5]See also chap. 5.

ment as a whole. In fact, the use of the word "Law" for other than the Mosaic writings demonstrates that they too were considered to have equal authority with the great lawgiver's writings. Matthew 5:18 used "law" in parallel reference to "law and prophets" (v. 17). In John 10:34, Jesus said to the Jews, "Is it not written in *your law* . . .?" just prior to quoting Psalm 82:6. Similarly, John 12:34 used "the law"; John 15:25, "their law"; "your . . . law" appears in John 18:31; and Acts 25:8 refers to "the law of the Jews." Paul's epistles made broad usage of the term "law," as he applied it to the Gentiles, who "do not have the law" (Rom. 2:14), spoke of the "works of the law" (Rom. 3:20), wrote of the "righteousness . . . based on the law" (Rom. 10:5), and cited Isaiah 28:11-12, after the introduction "In the law it is written" (I Cor. 14:21). Thus, by extension, the term "law," which originally denoted the God-given books of Moses, came to be applied to the remainder of the Old Testament by both the Jews and the New Testament writers. Hence, the whole Old Testament was variously called by the authoritative titles "the Law," "the Law of the Jews," and even "the Law of God" (cf. Rom. 7:22).

THE LAW AND THE PROPHETS

Other than the word Scriptures, the most common description of the Old Testament is "the law and the prophets." This is what Jesus called the Old Testament on two occasions during His Sermon on the Mount (Matt. 5:17; 7:12). Sometimes the parallel "Moses and the prophets" was used (cf. Luke 16:29, 31; 24:27; Acts 26:22). The canonical breadth of the title is revealed in Luke 16:16, which states, "The law and the prophets were until John." In other words, the Law and Prophets included all God's written revelation to the time of John the Baptist. Further, it was "the law and the prophets" that were read in the synagogues (Acts 13:15). Paul, in his defense before Felix, asserted that he worshiped "the God of our fathers, believing everything laid down by the law or written in the prophets" (Acts 24:14). The apostle's point here was that he believed and practiced the whole of God's revelation to Israel, and the phrase "the law and the prophets" describes the totality of that revelation.

WORD OF GOD

Another expression which reflects the totality and authority of the Old Testament Scriptures is "the word of God." It is used several times in the New Testament. In Mark 7:13, Jesus charged that the Pharisees made void "the word of God" through their tradition. John 10:35 uses "the word of God" as a parallel to the "scripture," which cannot be broken. Referring to the Old Testament, Paul said, "Not as though the word of God had failed" (Rom. 9:6). There are numerous other New Testament references to "the word of God," most of which are not positively identifiable with the Old Testament. However, many references may be applied to the present discussion. In II Corinthians 4:2, Paul records the Christians' refusal to "tamper with *God's word*"; the writer of Hebrews states that "the word of God is living and active" (4:12); and Revelation 1:2 tells of John "who bore witness to the *word of God* and to the testimony of Jesus."

ORACLES OF GOD

Closely allied with the foregoing descriptions of the Old Testament is the expression, "the oracles of God." Romans 3:2 indicates that the Jews were "entrusted with the *oracles* of God." Hebrews 5:12 also refers to the Old Testament by this introduction, as it states the "need [for] some one to teach . . . again the first principles of God's word" (Greek: *oracles*) before the readers could go on into perfection in Christ. In these references, the Old Testament as a whole is viewed as the voice of God, a divine oration.

From Abel to Zechariah

On one occasion Jesus used still another phrase that includes the totality of the Old Testament, when He accused the Jews of the guilt of "all the righteous blood shed on earth, from the blood of innocent Abel to the blood of Zechariah" (Matt. 23:35; cf. Gen. 4:8; II Chron. 24:20-22). Since Genesis records Abel's death and II Chronicles, the last book in the Hebrew canon, records Zechariah's death, the phrase "from Abel to Zechariah" is somewhat akin to the current expression "from Genesis to Revelation."

Previous discussion (chap. 1) has indicated that the Hebrew canon contained twenty-two (or twenty-four) books in New Testament times. Jesus and the apostles referred to this collection of books by various titles, all of which are reducible to the simple formula "the inspired word of God."

NEW TESTAMENT REFERENCES TO SECTIONS
OF THE OLD TESTAMENT

As has been previously stated, the Hebrew Old Testament has two sections. A brief survey of the New Testament references to these sections further confirms the authoritative nature of the Old Testament.

REFERENCES TO BOTH SECTIONS

The whole Old Testament was divided into two basic sections: the Law and the Prophets. The phrase combining both of these together, namely, "the Law and the Prophets" or "Moses and the Prophets" occurs twelve times in the New Testament (see Matt. 5:17; 7:12; 11:13; 22:40; Luke 16:16, 29, 31; 24:27; Acts 13:15; 24:14; 26:22; Rom. 3:21). That these two sections encompass the whole Old Testament is obvious from several passages. In Luke 24:27 they are called "all the scriptures" by Jesus. In Matthew 11:13, Jesus said, "For all the prophets and the law prophesied until John" (cf. Luke 16:16), which engulfs the entire time span of God's revelation through Old Testament prophets. Further, the other passages reveal that it was the foundation of moral and religious belief—that final authority to which appeal is made in all such matters. In brief, these two sections were the whole written Word of God for Jesus and the Jews of His day.

REFERENCES TO INDIVIDUAL SECTIONS

There are also numerous separate references to the Law and to the Prophets.

The Law. This section of the Old Testament is variously referred to as "the law" (Matt. 12:5; 22:40); "the law of Moses" (Acts 13:39; Heb. 10:28); "Moses" (II Cor. 3:15); "the book of Moses" (Mark 12:26); and "the book of the law" (Gal. 3:10). Each reference is a direct appeal to the divine authority of Moses' writings. That the New Testament considered the law of Moses in its entirety to be the inspired word of God is beyond question.

The Prophets. This section is usually called "the prophets" (cf. Luke 18:31; John 1:45), but it is also labeled "the scriptures of the prophets" (Matt. 26:56) and "the book of the prophets" (Acts 7:42). In each case the reference is clearly to the books or writings of the prophets, and the appeal to them is to a group or collection of books that serve as a divine authority in matters moral and theological.

The most common description of the Old Testament is "the Law and the Prophets." Sometimes the New Testament refers to one or the other of these two sections. In any case, whether as a whole or individually, the Old Testament canon with both of its sections and all of its books, known and used by Jesus and the first century church, was considered to be the inspired word of God.

NEW TESTAMENT REFERENCES TO THE INDIVIDUAL OLD TESTAMENT BOOKS

There are many references to the authority of the Old Testament as a whole, but the particular references to the individual books and events of the Old Testament are even more illuminating in their bearing on authority and authenticity, because of their specific and definitive nature. As a result, the following discussion will be treated under these two heads.

NEW TESTAMENT REFERENCES TO THE AUTHORITY OF OLD TESTAMENT BOOKS

Not only does the New Testament lend support to the claim of inspiration of the Old Testament as a whole, and for each of its two sections, but it provides a direct confirmation for the authority of most of the individual books of the Old Testament, as may be seen in the following sample survey.

Genesis. The book of Genesis is authoritatively quoted by Jesus in Matthew 19:4-5 (cf. Gen. 1:27; 2:24), as He says, "Have you not read that he who made them from the beginning made them male and female, and said, 'For this reason a man shall leave his father and mother and be joined to his wife, and the two shall become one'?" Here the assertion is made that God said what is written in Genesis. Romans 4:3 refers to Genesis 15:6, saying, "For what does the scripture say?"

Exodus. Jesus quotes Exodus 16:4, 15 in John 6:31, "As it is written, 'He gave them bread from heaven to eat'"; "Honor your father and mother" is from Exodus 21:12 and is cited in Ephesians 6:1 as authority.

Leviticus. This book was referred to by Jesus when He commanded the cleansed leper, "Go, show yourself to the priest, and offer the gift that Moses commanded" (Matt. 8:4; cf. Lev. 14:2). Leviticus 20:9 is cited in Mark 7:10: "He who speaks evil of father or mother, let him surely die," although this passage is also found in Exodus 21:17.

Numbers. Although not quoted, Numbers 12:7 is alluded to authoritatively in Hebrews 3:5: "Now Moses was faithful in all God's house." While this is not a direct quote, it is a clear reference to the teaching of Numbers. Paul in I Corinthians 10:5-11 refers to the events of Numbers as things written for the admonition of New Testament believers (see v. 11).

Deuteronomy. This is one of the most often quoted Old Testament books. For example, this may be seen from the three quotations used by Jesus when He resisted the tempter in Matthew 4:4, 7, 10: "Man shall not live by bread alone" (cf. Deut. 8:3); "You shall not tempt the Lord your God" (cf. Deut. 6:16); and "You shall worship the Lord your God and him only shall you serve" (cf. Deut. 6:13).

Joshua. Joshua 1:5 is quoted as God's word of promise in Hebrews 13:5: "I will never fail you or forsake you."

Judges (Ruth). Although these books are not directly cited in the New Testament, several of their personages are authenticated (see Heb. 11:32).

I and II Samuel. These books are referred to in Matthew 12:3-4, when Jesus said to the Pharisees, "Have you not read what David did, when he was hungry, and those who were with him: how he entered the house of God and ate the bread of the Presence . . .?" (I Sam. 21:1-6).

I and II Kings. These are quoted in Romans 11:4: "I have kept for myself seven thousand men who have not bowed the knee to Baal" (cf. I Kings 19:18, where God replied to Elijah).

I and II Chronicles. Although these books are not quoted in the New Testament, events from them are authenticated (see discussion below).

Ezra-Nehemiah. There is one quotation in the New Testament, in John 6:31, from Nehemiah 9:15: "He gave them bread from heaven to eat" (however, there are similar passages from which this quotation may have been adopted; cf. Ps. 78:24; 105:40).

Esther. This book is neither clearly quoted nor alluded to in terms of a teaching or an event in the New Testament. There is a possible literary dependence on Esther 5:3 in Mark 6:23, in the phrase "even half of my kingdom." Revelation 11:10 refers to those who "make merry and exchange presents," as was done in Esther 9:22 during the Feast of Purim. Then, too, some have felt that John 5:1, "a feast of the Jews," may have been this same Feast of Purim mentioned in Esther. In any event, there is no unquestioned reference to the authoritative teaching of the book of Esther in the New Testament.

Job. Job 5:12 is distinctly quoted by I Corinthians 3:19: "For it is written, 'He catches the wise in their craftiness.'"

Psalms. This is another book frequently quoted by the New Testament writers. It was one of Jesus' favorite books. Compare Matthew 21:42: "Have you never read in the scriptures: 'The very stone which the builders rejected . . .'?" (Ps. 118:22-23), and Hebrews 1:6: "Let all God's angels worship him" (Ps. 97:7).

Proverbs. Proverbs 3:34 is clearly cited in James 4:6: "God opposes the proud, but gives grace to the humble" (cf. 25:6; Lk. 14:8).

Ecclesiastes. This book is not directly quoted in the New Testament, although there are a number of passages which have a close *doctrinal dependency* on its teachings. The accompanying chart is indicative of this fact.

What we sow we reap.	Eccles. 11:1, cf. Gal. 6:7 ff.
Avoid lusts of youth.	Eccles. 11:10, cf. II Tim. 2:22
Death is divinely appointed.	Eccles. 3:2, cf. Heb. 9:27
Love of money is evil.	Eccles. 5:10, cf. I Tim. 6:10
Do not be wordy in prayer.	Eccles. 5:2, cf. Matt. 6:7

If these New Testament passages are doctrinally dependent on the teaching of Ecclesiastes, then the New Testament confirms the inspiration, or authority, of the book.

Song of Solomon. This book is not referred to directly by the New Testament. There is at least one possible example of borrowing a descriptive phrase from this book, which is *literary dependence.* In John 4:10, the reference to "living water" indicates possible literary dependence on Song of Solomon 4:15. It should be remembered, however, that literary dependence alone is not a sufficient argument for the authority of this book.

Isaiah. This book has numerous New Testament quotations. John the Baptist introduced Jesus by citing Isaiah 40:3: "Prepare the way of the LORD." Paul prefaced his quote of Isaiah 6:9-10 with the words "The Holy Spirit was right in saying . . ." (Acts 28:25). Jesus read from Isaiah 61:1-2 in His hometown synagogue, saying, "The Spirit of the Lord is upon me . . ." (Luke 4:18-19).

Jeremiah. Jeremiah 31:15 is quoted in Matthew 2:17-18 and the new covenant of Jeremiah 31:31-34 is quoted twice in Hebrews (cf. 8:8-12 and 10:15-17).

Lamentations. Lamentations 3:30 is alluded to in Matthew 27:30: "And they spat upon him, and took the reed and struck him on the head."

Ezekiel. This book is not clearly cited by the New Testament, but Jesus' question to Nicodemus in John 3:10 implies that Nicodemus should have known about the new birth on the basis of Ezekiel 36:25 ff. In addition, there are these possible allusions: John 7:38, "As the scripture has said, 'Out of his heart shall flow rivers of living water,' " is very similar to Ezekiel 47:1, although it may refer to Isaiah 58:11. Ezekiel 18:20, "The soul that sins shall die," may be reflected in Romans 6:23, "The wages of sin is death." Revelation 4:7 is undoubtedly taken from Ezekiel 1:10.

Daniel. This book is clearly quoted in Matthew 24:15 (cf. Dan. 9:27; 11:31; 12:11): "So when you see the desolating sacrilege spoken of by the prophet Daniel. . . ." Further, Matthew 24:21 and 30 are taken directly from Daniel 12:1 and 7:13 respectively.

The Twelve. This is quoted several times in the New Testament. Habakkuk 2:4: "The just shall live by . . . faith" (AV) is quoted three times in the New Testament (Rom. 1:17; Gal. 3:11; Heb. 10:38). Hebrews 12:26 is a clear quotation of Haggai 2:6, "Yet once more I will shake not only the earth but also the heaven." Zechariah 13:7 is quoted in Matthew 26:31 as follows, "For it is written, 'I will strike the shepherd, and the sheep of the flock will be scattered.' "

In summary, of the twenty-two books of the Hebrew Old Testament, as many as eighteen of them (all but Judges, Chronicles, Esther and Song of Solomon) are quoted or referred to as authoritative.[6] There are New Testament teachings which are directly dependent upon the teachings of these Old Testament books. It should

---

[6]Roger Nicol has broken this down into 231 quotations, 19 paraphrases, and 45 additional items which have no direct formula (e.g., "It is written"), for a total of 295 citations, about 4.4 percent of the New Testament (approximately one verse of every 22.5). Allusions range from 613 to 4,105, depending on the criteria used. Cf. Carl F. H. Henry (ed.), *Revelation and the Bible*, p. 137.

be pointed out that the absence of reference to a specific Old Testament book does not mean that particular book lacks authority; instead, it indicates that the New Testament writers had no occasion to refer to it. This is not difficult to understand when a person is asked to recall the last time he quoted from Esther or Judges. Some books, by their didactic or devotional nature, lend more readily to quotation and, hence, they are quoted more often; those that lack a didactic nature are not often used in this manner.

NEW TESTAMENT REFERENCES TO THE AUTHENTICITY OF OLD TESTAMENT BOOKS

Some of the Old Testament books which have no distinct reference to their authority do, however, have clear commitments to their *authenticity*. The accompanying list indicates some of the more important people and events of the Old Testament (which thereby verifies the authenticity of the books that record them).

1.	Creation of the universe (Gen. 1)	John 1:3; Col. 1:16
2.	Creation of Adam and Eve (Gen. 1-2)	I Tim. 2:13-14
3.	Marriage of Adam and Eve (Gen. 1-2)	I Tim. 2:13
4.	Temptation of the woman (Gen. 3)	I Tim. 2:14
5.	Disobedience and sin of Adam (Gen. 3)	Rom. 5:12; I Cor. 15:22
6.	Sacrifices of Abel and Cain (Gen. 4)	Heb. 11:4
7.	Murder of Abel by Cain (Gen. 4)	I John 3:12
8.	Birth of Seth (Gen. 4)	Luke 3:38
9.	Translation of Enoch (Gen. 5)	Heb. 11:5
10.	Marriage before the flood (Gen. 6)	Luke 17:27
11.	The flood and destruction of man (Gen. 7)	Matt. 24:39
12.	Preservation of Noah and his family (Gen. 8-9)	II Peter 2:5
13.	Genealogy of Shem (Gen. 10)	Luke 3:35-36
14.	Birth of Abraham (Gen. 11)	Luke 3:34
15.	Call of Abraham (Gen. 12-13)	Heb. 11:8
16.	Tithes to Melchizedek (Gen. 14)	Heb. 7:1-3
17.	Justification of Abraham (Gen. 15)	Rom. 4:3
18.	Ishmael (Gen. 16)	Gal. 4:21-24
19.	Promise of Isaac (Gen. 17)	Heb. 11:18
20.	Lot and Sodom (Gen. 18-19)	Luke 17:29
21.	Birth of Isaac (Gen. 21)	Acts 7:9-10
22.	Offering of Isaac (Gen. 22)	Heb. 11:17
23.	The burning bush (Exodus 3:6)	Luke 20:32

24. Exodus through the Red Sea (Exodus 14:22)   I Cor. 10:1-2
25. Provision of water and manna (Exodus   I Cor. 10:3-5
    16:4; 17:6)
26. Lifting up serpent in wilderness (Num. 21:9)   John 3:14
27. Fall of Jericho (Joshua 6:22-25)   Heb. 11:30
28. Miracles of Elijah (I Kings 17:1; 18:1)   James 5:17
29. Jonah in the great fish (Jonah 2)   Matt. 12:40
30. Three Hebrew children in furnace (Dan. 3)   Heb. 11:34
31. Daniel in lion's den (Dan. 6)   Heb. 11:33
32. Slaying of Zechariah (II Chron.   Matt. 23:35
    24:20-22)

In this sample survey, several things should be noted. (1) Most of
the controversial passages of the Old Testament are referred to,
for example, the creation, fall, flood, miracles of Moses and Elijah,
and Jonah in the great fish. These are not just alluded to, they are
authenticated as historical events by the New Testament.[7] If these
major miraculous events are authentic, there is no difficulty in accepting the rest of the events of the Old Testament. (2)' Virtually
every one of the first twenty-two chapters of Genesis, and each of
those prior to Abraham (i.e., chaps. 1-11), has either a person or
an event that is confirmed by an authoritative New Testament quotation or reference. If these people and events are authentic, then it
may be argued a fortiori that the rest of the Old Testament is authentic. (3) Whereas there are direct quotations or references confirming the *authority* of eighteen of the twenty-two books of the
Hebrew Old Testament, events from two of the remaining books
have their *authenticity* confirmed by the New Testament. Several
of the Judges are referred to in Hebrews 11:32, as well as events
from Chronicles (cf. Matt. 23:35). Thus, only Esther and Song of
Solomon are without any direct confirmation as to their authority or
authenticity.

SUMMARY AND CONCLUSION

The claim for inspiration by the Old Testament is supported in
three ways in the New Testament. First, there are many terms
in the New Testament, such as Scripture, Word of God, Law and
Prophets, which are used to refer authoritatively to the Old Testament as a whole. Second, both of the sections of the Hebrew canon

[7]The New Testament writers were not accommodating themselves to accepted
"myths" of their day. Cf. chap. 4, for objections to this accommodation theory.

(Law and Prophets) are viewed as authoritative units by the New Testament. Finally, of the twenty-two books in the Hebrew canon, eighteen are quoted or referred to by the New Testament, thus confirming their authority. Two others have their authenticity confirmed, which brings the total to twenty of the twenty-two books having their authority and/or authenticity directly affirmed by the New Testament. As a result, at least twenty of the twenty-two books of the Hebrew canon have their claim for inspiration confirmed individually by the New Testament writers, who regard the record of events or teachings therein as authentic and/or divine in origin.

7

SPECIFIC CLAIM OF INSPIRATION
IN THE NEW TESTAMENT

Now that the claim in and for the inspiration of the Old Testament has been examined, a similar examination of the New Testament claim is needed in order to complete the proposition that the Bible as a whole, and the whole Bible, claims to be the authoritative Word of God. The testimony of the New Testament to its own inspiration begins with the words of Christ, the central figure of the New Testament.

THE NEW TESTAMENT WRITERS WERE
SPIRIT-DIRECTED

In a real sense, Christ is the key to the inspiration and canonization of the Scriptures. It was He who confirmed the inspiration of the Hebrew canon of the Old Testament; and it was He who promised that the Holy Spirit would direct the apostles into "all truth," the fulfillment resulting in the New Testament.

JESUS PROMISED THAT THE NEW TESTAMENT WRITERS WOULD BE
SPIRIT-DIRECTED

Jesus Himself did not commit His teaching to writing, but on several occasions during His earthly ministry He promised that the apostles would be directed by the Holy Spirit in the utterance and propagation of His teaching. This promise was fulfilled during the life of Christ and extended as well into the postresurrection and post-Pentecostal ministries of the apostles.

Guidance in preaching. First, Jesus promised the guidance of the Holy Spirit in what the apostles would *speak about Him.*

1. When the twelve were first commissioned to preach "the kingdom of heaven" (Matt. 10:7), Jesus promised them, saying, "When they deliver you up, do not be anxious how you are to speak

or what you are to say; for what you are to say will be given to you in that hour; for it is not you who speak, but the Spirit of your Father speaking through you" (Matt. 10:19-20; cf. Luke 12:11-12).

2. The same promise was also given to the seventy when Jesus authorized them to preach "the kingdom of God" (Luke 10:9), with this added confirmation: "He who hears you hears me, and he who rejects you rejects me, and he who rejects me rejects him who sent me" (Luke 10:16).

3. In the Mount Olivet Discourse, Jesus reiterated the same promise of Spirit-directed utterances for those called on to give an account for their faith in the hour of trial, saying, "And when they bring you to trial and deliver you up, do not be anxious beforehand what you are to say; but say whatever is given you in that hour, for it is not you who speak, but the Holy Spirit" (Mark 13:11).

4. Later, after the Last Supper, Jesus further elaborated this promise to the eleven, saying, "But the Counselor, the Holy Spirit, whom the Father will send in my name, he will teach you all things, and bring to your remembrance all that I have said to you" (John 14:26). At that same time He also told them, "When the Spirit of truth comes, he will guide you into all the truth" (John 16:13).

5. The Great Commission of Christ provides the same promise, as it states "that repentance and forgiveness of sins should be preached in his name to all nations, beginning from Jerusalem. You are witnesses of these things" (Luke 24:47-48). The disciples were further told, "And behold, I send the promise of my Father upon you; but stay in the city, until you are clothed with power from on high" (Luke 24:49). This very commission was recorded by Matthew in the following words, "And lo, I am with you always, to the close of the age" (Matt. 28:20). Thus, the apostles were again promised the presence of God in and through their preaching and teaching.

6. Just prior to His ascension, Jesus answered the disciples' inquiry about the future with the promise "But you shall receive power when the Holy Spirit has come upon you; and you shall be my witnesses in Jerusalem and in all Judea and Samaria and to the

end of the earth" (Acts 1:8). That the Holy Spirit would empower them in their *witness* about Christ was their assurance.

Guidance in teaching. Not only were the apostles promised the guidance of the Spirit in what they spoke about Jesus, but they were also promised that they were to be guided by the Spirit in what they *taught about Him.*

1. According to Matthew's account of the Great Commission, the guidance of the Holy Spirit was to extend to what the disciples taught about Christ, as it stated, "Go therefore and make disciples of all nations, baptizing them in the name of the Father and of the Son and of the Holy Spirit, teaching them to observe all that I have commanded you; and lo, I am with you always, to the close of the age" (Matt. 28:19-20).

2. The promise that the Holy Spirit would bring "all things" to their remembrance and lead them into "all the truth" (John 14:26; 16:13) obviously applies to the fullness of apostolic teaching as well as preaching.

3. Further confirmation of this fact is directly implied in the book of Acts, which was the record of what Jesus "began to do and teach" (Acts 1:1-2). Properly speaking then, Acts is the book of the acts of the Holy Spirit through the works and *words* of the apostles.

4. A very practical manifestation of this teaching ministry of the Holy Spirit through the apostles is that the first church continued in "the apostles' teaching" (Acts 2:42). Apostolic preaching (Acts 2, 4, 10) and teaching (Acts 2:42; 6:4) were the foundation stones of the early church. It is in this sense that the church was "built upon the foundation of the apostles and prophets, Christ Jesus himself being the chief cornerstone" (Eph. 2:20), that is, it is built upon their teaching which, as Jesus repeatedly promised, was the result of the ministry of the Holy Spirit through them.

Briefly, Jesus promised that the Spirit of truth (John 15:26) would guide the apostles in the teaching of "all things," or "all the truth" (obviously meaning all truth necessary for faith and practice; cf. John 20:31; 21:25). Now there is no more reason to believe that the guidance of the Holy Spirit was limited to their verbal teaching than there is to believe that the Old Testament prophets were

Spirit-directed only in what they spoke (see chaps. 5-6). In fact, in direct continuity with the promise of Christ, virtually every New Testament writer claimed that his *writing* was divinely authoritative. Furthermore, when knowledge of the apostolic teaching is traced to its original documentary record, the pursuit ends in one, and only one, definite document, that is, the New Testament. Thus, the New Testament is the only primary source for study of the Spirit-directed teaching of the apostles, which teaching was promised by Christ in the Gospels. Formally stated, this argument takes the following form:

> Whatever the apostles taught doctrinally and officially was Spirit-directed teaching.

> The New Testament is what the apostles taught doctrinally and officially.

> Therefore, the New Testament is Spirit-directed teaching.

THE NEW TESTAMENT WRITERS CLAIM THAT THEY WERE SPIRIT-DIRECTED

In full consciousness and fulfillment of Jesus' oft-repeated promise to guide them unto "all the truth," the apostles claimed divine authority for what they taught orally and in their writings.

New Testament writers compared their message to Old Testament prophets. Remembering how highly esteemed were the Old Testament prophets, and how divinely authoritative their writings were considered,[1] then the comparison of the New Testament message to the Old Testament Scriptures amounts to a claim for the same *authority and inspiration.* Such is the case in Hebrews 1:1-2 which declares that "God spoke of old to our fathers by the prophets; but in these last days he has spoken to us by a Son," and adds that the message "was declared at first by the Lord, and it was attested to us by those who heard him" (Heb. 2:3). In other words, the message of Christ as given by His disciples is God's voice today just as much as the message of the prophets was in time past.

New Testament writers claimed their message was the foundation of the church. According to Ephesians 2:20, the church is "built upon the foundation of the apostles and prophets." In Acts 2:42 the first church "devoted themselves to the apostles' teaching and fellowship." The authority of apostolic teaching, then, is seen not

[1] See chaps. 5-6 for a more detailed comparison.

only by its equality with the prophets, but by its fundamentality to the church. Since the New Testament is what the "apostles and prophets" taught, and what they taught is the foundation of the church, then it would follow that the New Testament is the authoritative foundation of the church.

New Testament writers claimed their message was authoritative for the church. Throughout Acts the pronouncements of the "apostles and prophets" were final (cf. 21:11). By their voice the church was born (Acts 2); miracles were performed (Acts 3); rulers were restricted (Acts 4); the disobedient were judged (Acts 5); the Holy Spirit was given to the Samaritans (Acts 8) and the Gentiles (Acts 10). Thus, in accordance with the promise of Jesus that His disciples would be Spirit-directed in what they spoke and taught, the New Testament writers considered their pronouncements and teachings to be equally authoritative with the Old Testament prophets, as well as fundamental to and authoritative for the New Testament church.

THE NEW TESTAMENT WRITINGS ARE
SPIRIT-DIRECTED

The assumption that there is a valid connection between apostolic teaching and the New Testament writings is abundantly substantiated by both general and specific reference in the New Testament.

GENERAL CLAIM THAT THE WHOLE NEW TESTAMENT
Is SPIRIT-DIRECTED

Outstanding passages. There are two outstanding passages which bear on this point, and several others which lend their support. In II Peter 1:20-21, it is made clear that all *prophetic Scripture*[2] comes as men are "moved by the Holy Spirit." The reference here is to the Old Testament writings which have already been seen to be the unbreakable oracles of God (cf. Rom. 3:2; Heb. 5:12). However, since New Testament writers also claimed to be giving prophetic utterances and writings, then it follows that they considered their writings to be just as Spirit-directed as the Old Testament writings. Some of the New Testament writers make a direct claim that their writings are prophetic. In Revelation 22 John is classed with the Old Testament prophets (v. 9) and concludes by saying, "I warn every one who hears the words of the prophecy of this book" (v. 18). The

[2]See chap. 4 where this point is elaborated.

Apostle Paul classes his revelation of the mystery of Christ as even superior to that of the Old Testament (cf. Eph. 3:5). The writer of Hebrews also classes his book in line with the revelation through the Old Testament prophets, saying, "God spoke of old to our fathers by the prophets; but in these last days he has spoken to us by a Son" (1:1), to whose message one must take heed because "it was declared at first by the Lord, and it was attested to us by those who heard him [viz., the apostles], while God also bore witness by . . . gifts of the Holy Spirit" (2:3-4). Hence, the ministry and writings of the New Testament writers are no less prophetic than those of their Old Testament counterparts.

New Testament books considered to be Scripture.[3] Peter refers to Paul's writings as "scripture" (II Peter 3:16), and I Timothy 5:18 quotes from Luke 10:7 and Deuteronomy 25:4 under the one phrase "for the scripture says." If the writings of Luke, who was not an apostle, are quoted as "scripture" and Peter, who incidentally was rebuked by Paul (Gal. 2:11), considered Paul's books to be "scripture," then it is not difficult to conceive how the New Testament as a whole would be considered to be "scripture." And, since II Timothy 3:16 declares that "all scripture is inspired by God," it would follow that the New Testament as a whole is inspired by God too.

Specific claims. There are specific claims of apostolic authority in the New Testament that admit of a wide application. Paul told his sons in the faith to "command" his teachings (I Tim. 4:11) "with all authority" (Titus 2:15), and hinged his authority and even the veracity of the gospel itself, on his apostleship (Gal. 1:1, 12). On another occasion Paul wrote, "If anyone refuses to obey what I say in this letter, note that man, and have nothing to do with him" (II Thess. 3:14). Likewise, Peter reminded the believers of apostolic authority, saying, "Remember . . . the commandment of the Lord and Savior through your apostles" (II Peter 3:2). In effect, the authority of an apostle was the authority of Christ, and the only credential necessary to commend the authority of any particular writing was its apostolicity (see chap. 14).

Books were to be circulated. One final consideration that manifests the high regard for New Testament writings by the first century church is the fact that the books were commanded to be *circulated, read in the churches and collected.* It is obvious that Peter had a collection of Paul's books (II Peter 3:15-16), and Paul dis-

[3]See chap. 4 for discussion.

tinctly enjoined the Colossians to read and circulate their epistle (Col. 4:16). The Thessalonians, too, were charged to read their epistle (I Thess. 5:27). Such regard shows that the books had for them not only a spiritual value but a divine origin (cf. the Jews who read and preserved God's Word, Deut. 31:26).

In general, then, the New Testament writings as a whole claim to be "scripture," "prophetic writings," authoritative and divine, which is the same as saying they are inspired of God.

SPECIFIC CLAIMS THAT NEW TESTAMENT BOOKS ARE SPIRIT-BREATHED

Not only did Jesus promise divine guidance, and the New Testament as a whole claim to be the product of that guidance, but each individual New Testament book contains a claim to substantiate that position. A brief survey will suffice to support this point.

Matthew. This gospel begins, "The book of the genealogy of Jesus Christ," which, by linking Christ's lineage to the record of the Old Testament, is a tacit acknowledgment that this book is a continuation of Messianic truth. In fact, there is implied in the repeated assertion that Christ is the fulfillment of Old Testament prophecy (cf. Matt. 5:17-18, 21) that this book is an authoritative account of that fulfillment in Christ. The author closes his book with the command of Christ to teach the truth of Christ to all nations (28:18-20), which by implication is precisely what the book of Matthew is professing to do (cf. 10:7).

Mark. This gospel is entitled "The beginning of the gospel of Jesus Christ, the Son of God. As it is written in Isaiah the prophet." Like Matthew, there is no explicit claim to authority; it is merely assumed throughout (cf. 13:11).

Luke. This book has a statement about its own character. In his writing, Luke claims that it is an authentic "narrative of the things which have been accomplished [by God through Christ]" that Theophilus "may know the truth concerning the things of which" he had "been informed" (1:1, 4).

John. In this book, John is likewise clear about the nature of his gospel, saying that it is written that "you may believe that Jesus is the Christ, the Son of God, and that believing you may have life in his name" (20:31). He further adds, "This is the disciple who is bearing witness to these things, and who has written these things; and we know that his testimony is true" (21:24; cf. 14:26, 16:13).

Acts. This book is a continuation of Luke and of what Jesus "began to do and teach" (1:1); that is, it claims to be an authentic record of the teaching (and working) of Christ through the apostles.

Romans. This book claims to be the work of an apostle of Jesus Christ (1:1). In 9:1 Paul says, "I am speaking the truth in Christ, I am not lying; my conscience bears me witness in the Holy Spirit." The final appeal of the epistle is not to accept any other doctrine than that which they have been taught, which would include, of course, the great teachings of this doctrinal book (16:17).

I Corinthians. This book contains what "God has revealed . . . through the Spirit" (2:10; cf. also 7:40). Besides making authoritative pronouncements on morals (5:1-3) and doctrine (15:15), Paul asserts, "What I am writing to you is a command of the Lord" (14:37).

II Corinthians. This book is introduced by an apostle of God (1:1), who strongly contests for his own authority (10:8) and declares his lofty revelations from God (12:1-4).

Galatians. This book states the case for its author's divine authority as strongly as any book in the New Testament: "Paul an apostle—not from men nor through man, but through Jesus Christ and God the Father" (1:1) it begins. "For I did not receive it from man, nor was I taught it, but it came through a revelation of Jesus Christ" (1:12), and "even if we, or an angel from heaven, should preach to you a gospel contrary to that which we preached to you, let him be accursed" (1:8).

Ephesians. This book, along with the claim to be written by an apostle (1:1), declares itself to be a revelation of the mystery of God showing "how the mystery was made known [to Paul] . . . by revelation" (3:3). Those who read it can gain "insight into the mystery of Christ" (3:4).

Philippians. This book not only comes as from an apostle, and with the standard greetings "from God our Father and the Lord Jesus Christ" (1:2), but it further enjoins the readers to follow the moral example and spiritual teaching of its author, saying, "Brethren, join in imitating me" (3:17). Again it says, "What you have learned and received and heard and seen in me, do" (4:9).

Colossians. This book also comes "from an apostle of Christ Jesus" (1:1), with greetings "from God our Father" (1:2), as an authoritative refutation of heresy (2:4, 8), with a command to be circulated and read in the churches (4:16).

I Thessalonians. In 5:27, the author charges the church "that this letter be read to all the brethren," and in 4:15 says, "For this we declare to you by the word of the Lord."

II Thessalonians. This book adds to its God-given pronouncements a warning about a false letter "purporting to be from" Paul (2:2). It closes by saying, "If anyone refuses to obey what we say in this letter, note that man, and have nothing to do with him" (3:14).

I Timothy. This book is from "Paul, an apostle of Christ Jesus by command of God" and speaks with authority saying, "Command and teach these things" (4:11).

II Timothy. This book adds, "Follow the pattern of sound words which you have heard from me" (1:13), and charges Timothy "in the presence of God and of Christ Jesus" to "preach the word" (4:1-2).

Titus. This book also claims to come from Paul "an apostle of Jesus Christ" with the injunction to "declare these things; exhort and reprove with all authority" (2:15), adding, "I desire you to insist on these things" (3:8).

Philemon. This book is brief, but it claims authority from the Apostle Paul (v. 1), brings salutation "from God our Father and the Lord Jesus Christ" (v. 3), and asserts apostolic authority (v. 8).

Hebrews. In 1:1, Hebrews introduces its message as the voice of God through Christ "in these last days," and concludes with an appeal to accept its exhortations (13:22).

James. James writes as a "servant of God" (1:1), and speaks with authority about doctrine (cf. chap. 2) and practice (chap. 3).

I Peter. This book is from "an apostle of Jesus Christ" (1:1) and claims to be an exhortation on "the true grace of God" (5:12).

II Peter. This book is from "a servant and apostle of Jesus Christ" (1:1) who is giving commandments from the Lord (3:2). He claims to "have the prophetic word made more sure" (1:19) and gives a prophetic pronouncement about the future (3:10-13).

I John. This book comes from an eyewitness (1:1) who is proclaiming Christ so that believers' "joy may be complete" (1:4) and that the reader may be assured of eternal life (5:12).

II John. In this book John purports to be writing a "commandment" (v. 5), warns against deceivers (v. 7), and claims to possess "the doctrine of Christ" (v. 9).

III John. This is written by one with apostolic authority (v. 9) and who has the "truth itself" (v. 12).

Jude. This book claims to be a record of "our common salvation" and "the faith which was once for all delivered to the saints" (v. 3).

Revelation. This book begins: "The revelation of Jesus Christ, which God gave" (1:1) through John, who considered himself to be one with the "prophets" (22:9). The book ends with the most severe warning in the Bible for anyone who "adds to" or "takes away from the words of the book of this prophecy" (22:18-19).

So, virtually every book in the New Testament contains a claim for its own authority in one manner or another. The cumulative effect of this self-testimony is an overwhelming confirmation that the New Testament writers claimed inspiration.

Sometimes I Corinthians 7:10-12 is used to deny this position, where Paul said, "To the married I give charge, not I but the Lord . . . . To the rest I say, not the Lord. . . ." It is argued that Paul is here giving his own opinion and not an authoritative pronouncement. However, it should be observed that Paul probably meant merely to say that Jesus said nothing explicitly about the subject at hand during His earthly ministry. Hence, Paul had to say, "I have no command [*epitagēn*] of the Lord, but I give my opinion . . ." (7:25). His opinion, however, was inspired. Jesus said to His disciples before His death, "I have yet many things to say to you, but you cannot bear them now. When the Spirit of truth comes, he will guide you into all the truth" (John 16:12-13). The inspired advice of Paul in I Corinthians 7 is apparently an example of the fulfillment of this promise. In fact, Paul later said in this same epistle, "What I am writing to you is a command [*entolē*] of the Lord" (I Cor. 14:37).

SUMMARY AND CONCLUSION

The claim for inspiration in the New Testament is derived from the fact that Jesus promised His disciples that He would guide them into "all the truth" by the Holy Spirit. The New Testament writers claimed the fulfillment of this promise for their oral message and for their writings. They claimed that their oral message was: (1) on the same level as the Old Testament messages of the prophets; (2) the foundation of the New Testament church; (3) authoritative for the church. They also claimed to be directed by the Holy Spirit in their writings, which they held to be: (1) prophetic; (2) sacred Scripture; (3) divinely authoritative; and (4) commanded to be read and circulated in the churches.

Furthermore, when a survey is made of all of the books of the New Testament, a claim is found in each individual book for its own divine origin and authority, either directly or indirectly. So, then, both in all of its parts and as a whole the New Testament claims to be the inspired Word of God.

8

SUPPORTING CLAIMS FOR THE INSPIRATION OF THE NEW TESTAMENT

Just as the Old Testament claim for inspiration finds support in the New Testament, so the New Testament claim for inspiration finds support in the testimony of early Christian writers, the Church Fathers. Although the testimony of the Fathers is not authoritative or inspired, yet a survey of the Fathers will reveal that the orthodox doctrine of inspiration prevailed throughout the history of the church from apostolic times to the rise of Deism and rationalism in the seventeenth and eighteenth centuries, with hardly a noteworthy voice dissenting.

THE EARLY CHURCH (c. A.D. 70-c. 350)

Even as the New Testament writers assumed the inspiration of the Old, the Church Fathers assumed the inspiration of the New. This fact is observable in the two major periods of the development of the Old Catholic Church prior to about A.D. 350.

THE APOSTOLIC AND SUBAPOSTOLIC FATHERS (c. A.D. 70-c. 150)

These writers indicate an early and widespread acceptance of the New Testament claim for inspiration. Several examples should suffice to bear witness to this conclusion.

The Epistle of Pseudo-Barnabas (c. 70-130). So designated *The Epistle of Pseudo-Barnabas* because it was falsely ascribed to Paul's first associate, this writing cites the gospel of Matthew (26:31) after stating that it is what "God saith" (5:12). The same writer refers to the gospel of Matthew (22:14) by the New Testament title "Scripture" in 4:14.

Clement of Rome. Clement wrote his epistle *Corinthians* (c. 95-97) after the pattern of the Apostle Paul. In it he quotes the synoptic gospels (Matt. 9:13; Mark 2:17; Luke 5:32) after calling them "Scripture" (chap. 2). In chapter 46, he cites Mark 9:42 after the introductory "God saith." In chapter 36 he writes, "It is written" and quotes Hebrews 1:3-7, while referring to the "gospel" in chapter 47.

Ignatius of Antioch. Ignatius (d. *c.* 110) wrote his seven epistles en route to martyrdom in Rome. Although he did not give references to particular citations from the Scriptures, he did make many loose quotations and allusions to them.

Polycarp. The disciple of John, Polycarp referred to the New Testament several times in his *Epistle to the Philippians* (*c.* 110-35). His quotation of Ephesians 4:26 is introduced by the expression "the Scripture saith" (chap. 12). In chapter 3, he introduces his quotation of Ephesians 1:3 by "the word of truth," while using the title "word of righteousness" (chap. 9) as introductory to his Hebrews 5:13 quote.

Hermas. The so-called *Shepherd of Hermas* (*c.* 115-40) follows the pattern of the Apocalypse, although no direct quotations of the New Testament appear therein.

Didache. Such is the case of the *Didache* or *Teaching of the Twelve* (*c.* 100-20), as it too makes loose quotations and allusions to the New Testament.

Papias. In about A.D. 130-40 Papias wrote five books entitled *Exposition of the Oracles of the Lord,* which included the New Testament.[1] This is precisely the title ascribed to the Old Testament by the Apostle Paul in Romans 3:2.

Epistle to Diognetus. Finally, the so-called *Epistle to Diognetus* (*c.* 150) makes loose quotations and allusions to the New Testament; however, no direct title is given to them.

The above material illustrates the early (by *c.* 150) and widespread (West and East) acceptance of the New Testament claim for inspiration. The Fathers looked upon these books with the same regard as the New Testament writers did the Old Testament Scriptures. Where no direct reference is given nor title presented, the loose quotations and allusions lend support to the esteem extended the New Testament writings. This is especially true considering the scarcity of available copies during this early period.

THE ANTE-NICENE AND NICENE FATHERS (*c.* A.D. 150-*c.* 350)

These add further support to the New Testament claims for inspiration.

---

[1]Eusebius, *Ecclesiastical History,* III, 39. Loeb ed., I, 291.

Justin Martyr (d. 165). In his first *Apology* (*c.* 150-55), Justin Martyr regarded the Gospels as the "Voice of God" (chap. 65). He further stated of the Scriptures, "We must not suppose that the language proceeds from men who were inspired, but from the Divine Word which moves them" (*Apology* I:36).

Tatian (*c.* 110-80). The disciple of Justin, Tatian refers to John 1:5 as "Scripture" in his *Apology* (chap. 13). He is also noted for his pioneer effort in writing a harmony of the Gospels, *Diatessaron* (*c.* 170).

Irenaeus (*c.* 130-202). Irenaeus referred to the New Testament in his treatise *Against Heresies,* where he stated,

> For the Lord of all gave the power of the Gospel to his apostles, through whom we have come to know the truth, that is, the teaching of the Son of God. . . . This Gospel they first preached. Afterwards, by the will of God, they handed it down to us in the Scriptures, to be "the pillar and ground" of our faith.[2]

In fact, he entitled the third book of this treatise "The Faith in Scripture and Tradition."

Clement of Alexandria (*c.* 150-215). Clement held to a rigid doctrine of inspiration, but allowed that the Greek poets were inspired by the same God in a lesser sense. In his *Stromata,* Clement notes:

> There is no discord between the Law and the Gospel, but harmony, for they both proceed from the same Author, . . . differing in name and time to suit the age and culture of their hearers . . . by a wise economy, but potentially one, . . . since faith in Christ and the knowledge . . . of the Gospel is the explanation . . . and fulfillment of the Law.[3]

He does call the gospel "Scripture" in the same sense as the Law and the Prophets, as he writes of "the Scriptures . . . in the Law, in the Prophets, and besides by the blessed Gospel . . . [which] are valid from their omnipotent authority."[4]

Tertullian (*c.* 160-220). Tertullian never wavered in his support of the doctrine of inspiration of both the Old and the New Testaments, neither as a Catholic nor as a Montanist. In fact, he maintained that the four Gospels ". . . are reared on the certain basis of Apostolic

---

[2]Irenaeus, *Against Heresies* in *The Library of Christian Classics,* V, 67.

[3]Brooke Foss Westcott, *An Introduction to the Study of the Gospels,* 7th ed., p. 439. It should be observed, however, that Clement regarded the *Shepherd* as inspired (cf. *Stromata,* IV, 15, 128).

[4]Clement of Alexandria, *Stromata* in *The Ante-Nicene Fathers,* Alexander Roberts and James Donaldson (eds.), II, 408-9.

authority, and so are inspired in a far different sense from the writings of the spiritual Christian; 'all the faithful, it is true, have the Spirit of God, but all are not Apostles' . . . ."[5]

Hippolytus (*c.* 170-236). A disciple of Irenaeus, Hippolytus exhibited the same deep sense of the spiritual meaning of Scripture as has already been traced in his immediate teacher and in earlier writers. He writes of the inspiration of the Old Testament,

> The Law and the Prophets were from God, who in giving them compelled his messenger to speak by the Holy Spirit, that receiving the inspiration of the Father's power they may announce the Father's counsel and will. In these men therefore the Word found a fitting abode and spoke of Himself; for even then He came as His own herald, shewing the Word who was about to appear in the world. . . .[6]

Of the New Testament writers, he confidently affirms:

> These blessed men . . . having been perfected by the Spirit of Prophecy, and worthily honoured by the Word Himself, were brought to an inner harmony like instruments, and having the Word within them, as it were to strike the notes, by Him they were moved, and announced that which God wished. For they did not speak of their own power (be well assured), nor proclaim that which they wished themselves, but first they were rightly endowed with wisdom by the Word, and afterwards well foretaught of the future by visions, and then, when thus assured, they spake that which was [revealed] to them alone by God.[7]

Novatian (d. *c.* 251). Novatian, the individual after whom the heretical sect was named, claimed the Old and New Testaments as authoritative Scripture in widespread references in his writings.

Origen (*c.* 185-*c.* 254). The successor of Clement at the Catechetical School in Alexandria, Origen appears to have held that both *the writer and the writing* were inspired, as he wrote, "This Spirit inspired each one of the saints, whether prophets or apostles; and there was not one Spirit in the men of the old dispensation, and another in those who were inspired at the advent of Christ. . . ."[8] His view of the authority of the Scriptures is "that the Scriptures were written by the Spirit of God, and have a meaning . . . not known to all, but

[5]Westcott, p. 434.
[6]Hippolytus, *Contra Noetum* as cited by Westcott, pp. 431-32.
[7]Hippolytus, *De AntiChristo* as cited by Westcott, p. 432.
[8]Origen, *De Principiis* in *The Ante-Nicene Fathers*, IV, 240.

to those only on whom the grace of the Holy Spirit is bestowed in the words of wisdom and knowledge."[9]

Cyprian (c. 200-58). Cyprian was bishop of one of the largest cities in the West during the persecution under Decius (A.D. 249-51). In his treatise *The Unity of the Catholic Church,* he appeals to the gospel as authoritative, referring to it as the "commandments of Christ." He also adds the Corinthian letters of Paul to his list of authorities, and appeals to Paul's Ephesian letter (4:4-6).

In the same passage, Cyprian reaffirms the inspiration of the New Testament, as he writes, "When the Holy Spirit says, in the person of the Lord. . . ."[10] Again, he adds, "The Holy Spirit warns us through the Apostle, . . ." as he cites I Corinthians 11:19.[11] This, and several other examples in his writings, leads to the conclusion that Cyprian held to the fact that both the Old and New Testaments are "Divine Scriptures."[12]

Eusebius of Caesarea (c. 263 or 265-340). As a church historian, Eusebius spent much time espousing the Old and New Testaments as inspired writings which were commented upon by the successors of the apostles. He also wrote much about the canon of the New Testament in his *Ecclesiastical History.*

Athanasius of Alexandria (c. 295-373). Known by the epithet "Father of Orthodoxy" because of his contributions against Arius at Nicea (325), Athanasius was the first to use the term "canon" in reference to the New Testament books, which he called "the fountains of salvation."[13]

Cyril of Jerusalem (c. 315-86). Cyril adds interesting light to round out the early church period. In his *Catecheses,* he informs his catechumen that he is offering a summary of "the whole doctrine of the Faith" which "has been built up strongly out of all the Scriptures"; then he proceeds to warn others not to change or contradict his teachings because of the Scripture's injunction as found in Galatians 1:8-9.[14] In his treatise *Of the Divine Scriptures,* he speaks of "the divinely-inspired Scriptures of both the Old and the New Tes-

---

[9]*Ibid.,* p. 241.
[10]Cyprian, *The Unity of the Catholic Church* in *The Library of Christian Classics,* V, 126.
[11]*Ibid.,* p. 443.
[12]Cyprian, *Epistle About Cornelius and Novatian* in *The Ante-Nicene Fathers,* V, 328.
[13]Westcott, *A General Survey of the History of the Canon of the New Testament,* 7th ed., p. 456.
[14]Cyril of Jerusalem, *Catechetical Lectures* in *The Nicene and Post-Nicene Fathers,* 2d series, VII, 32.

tament."[15] He then proceeds to list all of the books of the Hebrew Old Testament (twenty-two) and all of the books of the Christian New Testament except Revelation (twenty-six), saying, "Learn also diligently, and from the Church, what are the books of the Old Testament, and what are those of the New. And, pray, read none of the apocryphal writings."

Such evidence, coupled with the other writings of this era of church history, has led many to conclude that *virtually every Church Father enthusiastically adhered to the doctrine of the inspiration of the Old and New Testaments* alike. J. N. D. Kelly, the noted Oxford patristic scholar, affirms this position, as he writes,

> There is little need to dwell on the absolute authority accorded to the Scripture as a doctrinal norm. It was the Bible, declared Clement of Alexandria about A.D. 200, which as interpreted by the Church, was the source of Christian teaching. His greater disciple Origen was a thorough-going Biblicist who appealed again and again to Scripture as the decisive criterion of dogma . . . "The holy inspired Scriptures," wrote Athanasius a century later, "are fully sufficient" for the proclamation of the truth. . . . Later in the same century John Chrysostom bade his congregation seek no other teacher than the oracles of God. . . .[16]

THE ESTABLISHED CHURCH (from *c.* A.D. 350)

The established church period covers a much larger span of time and space, and, as a result, will necessitate an even more cursory treatment of the subject matter. This period extends to the rise of rationalism, including the medieval church, the Reformation church, and the early modern church.

The Medieval Church (*c.* 350-1400)

The medieval church may be represented by several outstanding men who had widespread influence.

Ambrose of Milan (340-97). Ambrose has the distinctive honor of guiding St. Augustine in his early Christian experience. The Bishop of Milan also did much work with the Christian Scriptures. His *Letters* give a clear insight into his view of the New Testament. In his letter to the Emperor Valentinian II, Ambrose cites Matthew 22:21 by using the familiar introductory statement "It is written"

---

[15]*Ibid.*, pp. 26-27.
[16]J. N. D. Kelly, *Early Christian Doctrines*, p. 42.

(20:19) as he proceeds to quote loosely John 6:15 and II Corinthians 12:10 (20:23).[17] He also appeals to "The Divine Scriptures . . ." (10:7) in his letter to the Emperor Gratian, where he presents his disputation with the Arians.[18]

Jerome (c. 340-420). Jerome needs only to be mentioned in passing, as he makes many references to the "Holy Scriptures" and to their authority.[19] He spent much time translating the Bible, and disputed with others over the canon of the Old Testament, while *assuming* the inspiration, canonicity and authority of the New.

Augustine (354-430). Augustine, the "Medieval Monolith," wholly endorsed the claims of the New Testament for its inspiration. An example of this view may be seen in his *Confessions*, where the reading of Romans 13:13-14 was sufficient for him to be converted. His monumental work, *The City of God*, contains much Scripture, and he indicates the authority of Scripture therein in contrast to all other writings (cf. XI, 3; XVIII, 41).

Gregory I (540-604). Gregory I, "the Great," wrote his *Commentary on Job* in which he refers to Hebrews 12:6 as "Scripture."[20] He, being the first medieval Pope, set the pace for the succeeding centuries just as he epitomized the preceding. L. Gaussen summarized the situation very well when he wrote,

> . . . that with the single exception of Theodore of Mopsuestia, (c. A.D. 400), that philosophical divine whose numerous writings were condemned for their Nestorianism in the fifth ecumenical council, . . . it has been found impossible to produce, in the long course of the *eight first centuries of Christianity*, a single doctor who has disowned the plenary inspiration of the Scriptures, unless it be in the bosom of the most violent heresies that have tormented the Christian Church; that is to say, among the Gnostics, the Manicheans, the Anomeans, and the Mahometans. . . .[21]

Anselm (1033-1109). In his famous *Cur Deus Homo?* (XXII), Anselm continued the orthodox view of inspiration when he wrote, "And the God-man himself originates the New Testament and approves the Old. And, as we must acknowledge him to be true, so no one can dissent from anything contained in these books."

[17]Ambrose, *Letters*, No. 20, as cited in *Library of Christian Classics*, V, 209-17.
[18]*Ibid.*, No. 10, pp. 184-89.
[19]Jerome, *Letters*, No. 107, as cited in *Library of Christian Classics*, V, 332-34, will suffice to support this position.
[20]Gregory the Great, *The Commentary of Job* in *Library of Christian Classics*, IX, 189.
[21]Louis Gaussen, *Theopneustia*, David Scott (trans.), pp. 139-40.

Thomas Aquinas (*c.* 1225-74). The chief spokesman of medieval Scholasticism, and the great theologian of the Roman Catholic theology, Thomas Aquinas clearly held to the orthodox doctrine of inspiration. In his *Summa Theologiae*, Aquinas twice states that "the Author of Holy Scripture is God. . . ."[22] Although he asks the question of "senses" of Scripture, he *assumes* the "inspiration" of both the Old and New Testaments.

John Wycliffe (*c.* 1320-84). Wycliffe marks a turning point in the *transmission* of the Scriptures, but not in the history of the doctrine of the *inspiration* of the Scriptures. Wycliffe is noted for his pioneer work in translation and distribution of the Scriptures, because he believed the Scriptures to be the Word of God. He felt that the Scriptures alone in the hands of the people would be sufficient for the Holy Spirit to use among them. So confident of this was he that he advocated the Scriptures as the only law of the church, and devoted his life and energies to their dissemination.

The Reformation Church (*c.* 1400-*c.* 1620)

The Reformation church followed the tradition of the fathers and doctors of the church to that time in affirming the inspiration of the Scriptures. The Reformation era actually began earlier than Luther, as evidenced by the title ascribed to Wycliffe: "The Morning Star of the Reformation."

Balthasar Hubmaier (*c.* 1480-1528). Hubmaier represents the radical wing of the Anabaptist movement. Although he had studied under John Eck and received his doctor of theology degree in the Roman Catholic Church, he opposed Catholicism, Zwingli and Luther in many areas (especially regarding infant baptism, because it lacked scriptural support). Within his own movement, "An appeal to the Word of God was the method which Hubmaier used in dealing with difficulties which threatened the Anabaptist fellowship."[23] In fact, Estep adds that Hubmaier "set forth the Reformation principle of obedience to the Bible as his personal conviction."[24]

Martin Luther (1483-1546). Luther has often been attacked for not holding to the inspiration of Scripture because of his criticism of certain books. James Orr clears the air when he writes of Luther's view of inspiration as compared to his predecessors,

[22]Thomas Aquinas, *Summa Theologiae,* Thomas Gilby (ed.), I. Q.1, a. 10. This is an excellent summary of Thomas' view on inspiration.
[23]W. R. Estep, *The Anabaptist Story,* p. 60.
[24]*Ibid.,* p. 51.

Luther's views, as his ordinary teaching and use of Scripture show, were scarcely less high; but, applying a subjective standard, his judgments on certain books, as the epistle of James, Revelation, Esther, even to the Epistle to the Hebrews, were rash and arbitrary. These judgments affected canonicity rather than inspiration.[25]

Huldreich Zwingli (1484-1531). Zwingli made constant reference to Scripture during his ministry in Zurich, where he used the biblical languages in his pulpit ministry. From his disputation with Luther and Melanchthon at Marburg in 1529, it is apparent that Zwingli differed with the other Reformers on some *interpretations* of the Scripture, as there was a *unanimity* of conviction on the *inspiration* of the Scriptures. In his *Sixty-seven Articles* (1523), Zwingli affirms his view of inspiration, as he writes in the preface,

> The articles and opinions below I, Ulrich Zwingli, confess to having preached in the worthy city of Zurich as based upon the Scriptures which are called inspired by God, and I offer to protect and conquer with the said articles, and where I have not now correctly understood said Scriptures I shall allow myself to be taught better, but only from said Scriptures.[26]

Martin Bucer (1494-1551). Bucer exerted some influence on John Calvin during the latter's stay in Strassburg. While Bucer was noted for his moderate position in other matters, he nevertheless adhered to the orthodox doctrine of inspiration.

William Tyndale (c. 1494-1536). Tyndale was the English Bible translator following in the train of Wycliffe, but he was much more of a Protestant than his precursor. His Bible translation is indicative of his view that the Scripture was inspired, and Luther's influence is also seen there. His appeal to Scripture as final authority led him to oppose the Papal claims to it.

John Calvin (1509-64). Calvin was at least a second generation Reformer, but his influence was felt by all his successors, as James Orr states,

> There is a singular breadth and modernness in Calvin's exegesis; but his faith in the entire inspiration of the Scriptures is profound and uncompromising. The ultimate guarantee of inspiration, as already seen, is found by him in the internal witness of

[25]James Orr, *Revelation and Inspiration*, p. 208.
[26]Huldreich Zwingli, *Sixty-seven Articles*, Preface, in Ray C. Petry and Clyde L. Manschreck (eds.), *A History of Christianity*, II, 67-70.

the Holy Spirit. The creeds of the Reformed Church embodied the same conceptions. [27]

John Knox (*c.* 1513-72). Knox was in exile when he studied under Calvin at Geneva. But, when he returned to Scotland, he took the Calvinistic doctrine of inspiration with him. There he was able to establish Calvinism, with its view of inspiration, as the official religion. His disciples in turn trained James VI, later James I of England, who likewise shared this high regard for Scripture.

To this point individual men have been discussed; now two church groups are to be considered in regard to their views of the doctrine of inspiration of Scripture, and especially the New Testament.

The Council of Trent (1545-63). The Council of Trent of the Roman Catholic Church made a special "Decree Concerning the Canonical Scriptures" in its fourth session, April 8, 1546. It refers to itself therein as

> . . . following the examples of the orthodox fathers, received and venerated with an equal affection of piety and reverence, all the books both of the Old and the New Testament—seeing that one God is the author of both—as also the said traditions, as well those appertaining to faith as to morals, as having been dictated, either by Christ's own word of mouth, or by the Holy Ghost, and preserved in the Catholic Church by a continuous succession.[28]

The council also asserted the inspiration of the Apocrypha (cf. chap. 13), and elevated tradition to the level of the Scriptures.

The Synod at Dort (1618-19). The Synod at Dort of the Reformed Church settled on the Calvinistic position as it pertained to the doctrine of the inspiration of Scripture. In effect, at the time of Dort, every major branch of Christianity, whether Roman Catholic, Anabaptist or Protestant, assumed the inspiration of both the Old and New Testaments. Their major differences lay in areas other than the inspiration of Scriptures, for example, the place of tradition, methods of interpretation, manner of salvation. But *all were agreed in the support of the New Testament claims for inspiration.*

THE MODERN CHURCH (*c.* 1620-*c.* 1900)

This is where the *first major deviation* from the orthodox doctrine of inspiration of the Scriptures, both the Old and the New Testaments,

---

[27]Orr, p. 207. Orr makes reference to Calvin's *Institutes of the Christian Religion,* I, 7, 4, 5.

[28]Canons and decrees of the Council of Trent, 1545-63, in Petry and Manschreck, *A History of Christianity,* II, 131.

makes its appearance. Yet, even here the *deviation is not universal.* At this juncture, the shift is made from individuals to movements, since the latter indicate the development of this deviant doctrine better than the former.

Pietism (*c.* 1635-*c.* 1725). Pietism is represented by the group at Halle, Germany. This group held to the inspiration of Scripture in the same manner as the Roman Catholic, Lutheran, Reformed and Anabaptist groups; however, their view had a *different emphasis* than did the others mentioned. Their emphasis stressed the individual's personal experience rather than the propounding of biblical doctrines. While they *adhered* to the inspiration of the Bible, they *advocated* the individual feeling as being of primary importance. Whereas this was an adequate method of avoiding cold orthodoxy, it opened the door for an equally dangerous enemy. The first generation of Pietists could recall its grounding in Scripture and validly advocate individual experience. The second generation would stress the individual experience, but often without the proper biblical basis; hence, the third generation would question the experience with no biblical basis to act as a "standard." They, in turn, would raise unanswered questions which would tend to demand an authority. If the Scriptures were neglected, human reason would be used as the demanded "standard." Thus, Pietism gave impetus to three other movements in the modern church period: Deism, skepticism, and German rationalism.

Deism (*c.* 1625-*c.* 1750). Deism was a contemporary to Pietism, and shared some common characteristics with it. This movement swept over England and into America, exerting widespread influence from there through such men as the statesman-philosopher John Locke (1632-1704) and Thomas Jefferson (1743-1826). They were a part of that movement which adhered to naturalism and free thought, as they denied the inspiration of Scripture, taught that God was merely "providentially" involved with the world, and stressed such things as the laws of nature, and natural rights. This was merely one phase of the reaction against the subjectivism of Pietism.

French Skepticism (*c.* 1725-present). This was the French counterpart to English Deism. Its chief representatives include Voltaire (1694-1788), who spent three years in England (1726-29), and Jean Jacques Rousseau (1712-78). From France skepticism moved out in a wave which affected the English, American and German theological, political and philosophical worlds. It also denied the inspiration of the Scriptures, deity of Christ, and miracles. In 1753 Jean Astruc (1684-1766), Professor of Medicine at Paris and court physician to Louis XIV, published his *Conjectures* in Brussels. In that work, Astruc attempted to reconcile some of the difficulties he found in Genesis. As a result he emphasized the distinctions between words such as Elohim, Jehovah, Jehovah Elohim, and El-Elyon, and espoused a view which would become popular among the German rationalists during the latter part of the nineteenth century. Astruc's views were first followed in principle by Eichhorn, Ilgen and others before Kuenen and Wellhausen brought the theory to its prominent position in the present day.

German Rationalism (*c.* 1725-present). This school has had unprecedented influence upon the doctrines of Christianity. However, lest it be assumed that these writers were viciously attacking Christianity, it should be stated that they were assuming the role of "the champions of the faith." Their approach to the Scriptures was an attempt to answer and counterattack the skepticism which had spread abroad from France. Several outstanding men may be called upon to bear witness to this conclusion.

1. *Johann Semler* (1725-91) is referred to as "the father of German Rationalism," as he was the first to advocate the "Accommodation Theory." This man, reared in pietistic training, arrived at the conclusion that "Revelation is in Scripture, but all Scripture is not revelation."[29]

2. *Johann Eichhorn* (1752-1827) is regarded as the founder of Old Testament criticism, as he espoused several principles which later formed a part of higher criticism.[30] He is believed to have followed Astruc's views, and he prepared the way for others to follow.

3. *Heinrich Paulus* (1761-1851) wrote *The Life of Jesus* (1828) in which he opposed all supernaturalism in the Bible. He endeavored to explain the miracles of the Bible as ordinary facts and events which had been exaggerated or misconceived, or treat the writers as sufferers of hallucinations when they intentionally recorded such things as visions and miracles. He took Eichhorn's principles and applied them to the New Testament, though he felt that he was championing the Bible's cause against skepticism.

[29]Williston Walker, *A History of the Christian Church*, p. 259.
[30]*International Standard Bible Encyclopaedia*, rev. ed. II, 751 f.

4. *Wilhelm DeWette* (1780-1849) found that Paulus' views were inadequate and cumbersome and offered the myth theory in its stead. This view was presented as an attempt to absolve the Bible writers from the charges of lunacy and imbalance by contending that metaphor and allegory were prosaically turned into fact by the writers.

5. *David F. Strauss* (1808-74) is typical of those who followed the myth theory of DeWette. Strauss transferred to the New Testament the ideas of Graf and Kuenen.

6. *Karl H. Graf* (1815-69) and *Abraham Kuenen* (1828-91) attempted to show that the Law and History of the Bible were legendary. The work of Graf, Kuenen, Strauss and others resulted in much of the Bible being regarded as a myth, but this idea gradually began to fall into disuse.

7. *Julius Wellhausen* (1844-1918) appears to have rescued the Graf-Kuenen theory from intellectual oblivion when he applied the newfound theory of evolution to the Bible. Following Kuenen, who seems to have invented the term, Wellhausen added Joshua to the Pentateuch, calling it the Hexateuch. This lead was followed by Robertson Smith, S. R. Driver and their followers. Wellhausen also raised the theory that Israel's tribal God (Jehovah) gradually gained supremacy over other gods until He became the only God, during the time of Amos and Hosea, thus showing that monotheism had evolved from polytheism. Since the time of Wellhausen, his theory has been the basis of destructive higher criticism, as it found exponents of note in England and America who desired to be known as the "mediating school," or "compromising school," between Traditionalism and skepticism. They espoused a position of antisupernaturalism in a practical denial of inspiration, but held to the word "inspiration."[31]

SUMMARY AND CONCLUSION

Just as the Old Testament claims for inspiration found support in the New, so the New Testament claims for inspiration found support in the writings of the Church Fathers. In the early church, the evidence is early and widespread for the acceptance of the New Testament claim for inspiration. In the established church, the evidence

---

[31]See chap. 3 for the Modernist view that the Bible *contains* the word of God.

is consonant with the former period. Throughout the Middle Ages and during the Reformation period, Roman Catholics and Protestants alike followed the traditional doctrine of inspiration. With the pietistic movement, the position of the Bible was weakened from within, while simultaneously it suffered attacks from without. Contemporary with Pietism came English Deism, which led Voltaire to oppose Christianity openly when he returned to France. French skepticism, in turn, led to German rationalism, which gave rise to higher criticism, a movement which, paradoxically enough, was intended to defend the Bible. Wellhausen's theory of the evolution of Scripture has influenced subsequent scholarship; but it, like its predecessors (Deism, skepticism and rationalism), is actually an intruder into the field. Thus, in the long course of the church's history it is virtually impossible to produce a noteworthy voice dissenting from the orthodox doctrine of inspiration of Scripture until the mid-seventeenth century.

9

EVIDENCES FOR THE INSPIRATION OF THE BIBLE

Technically speaking, this chapter is not part of biblical introduction, but rather of apologetics. Nevertheless, it is included here in order to complete the Bible's claim that it is inspired. It is obviously one thing *to claim* divine authority and quite another to possess the credentials *to confirm* that claim. The purpose of this chapter is to indicate that the Scriptures not only claim to be, but indeed prove to be the word of God.

THE CLAIM FOR INSPIRATION

The five preceding chapters have outlined the claim of Scripture for its divine inspiration. A brief summary of those claims is in order at this juncture, in order to crystallize that claim before the credentials are examined.

THE CLAIM FOR INSPIRATION OF THE BIBLE AS A WHOLE

The Bible's statements about its own nature are very unusual. The Bible claims to be unbreakable and indestructible as well as the verbal Word of God. Logically this claim must be applied to the whole Bible, since the descriptions are used indiscriminately. This point may be illustrated by the New Testament statement that all "prophetic writings" and all "Scripture" are inspired; whereupon it proceeds to refer to various sections of the New Testament with the same descriptions, placing them on the same level as the inspired and authoritative Old Testament.[1]

THE CLAIM FOR INSPIRATION OF THE OLD TESTAMENT

The Old Testament makes an explicit claim to be a prophetic utterance, or the voice of God. This claim applies to the Old Testament as a whole, but each of the sections also contains distinct claims to

[1]See chap. 7 for further discussion of this point.

divine revelation. In addition to these more general claims, each of the books of the Old Testament claims the same thing in one way or another, but these claims are not so dominant in the historical and poetical books as they are in the didactical books (see chap. 5).

The New Testament gives overwhelming support to the Old Testament claim for inspiration when it refers to the Old Testament as a whole under such titles as "The Law," "The Law and Prophets," "The Word of God," "The Oracles of God" and "Scripture." Furthermore, as many as eighteen of the twenty-two books of the Hebrew canon are referred to authoritatively by the New Testament writers, and two more have their authenticity confirmed (see chap. 6).

THE CLAIM FOR INSPIRATION IN THE NEW TESTAMENT

The New Testament presents a similar picture to the Old. There is a general claim that apostolic writing is "prophetic" and, as a result, "Scripture," or that it is "Spirit-directed." In addition, there is a claim in virtually every book of the New Testament for divine authority (see chap. 7).

Of course, since the New Testament completes the canon of revelation (see chap. 15), there are no subsequently inspired books to support its claim as there were to support the Old Testament. However, in an unbroken line of succession from the first century, there is abundant evidence that the Church Fathers felt the very same way about the New Testament, as they quoted authoritatively all of the twenty-seven New Testament books.

Conclusion: The claim of the Bible is clear and unequivocal with regard to its own inspiration. Not only are the Scriptures as a whole considered divinely authoritative and their teachings unbreakable, but virtually every book contains an individual claim to be God-breathed. Among the sacred writings of the great living world religions only one other book boasts of equal authority:[2] the Koran (cf. Surah 2:2, 87, 89, 101; 3:7, 23; 29:47; 41:41). But, even though this claim is unequivocal, it is (1) *fanciful*, for example, claiming to have been dictated by the angel Gabriel from an eternal book in heaven to the Prophet Muhammad who wrote it down, although he could neither read nor write (cf. Surah 7:158). (2) Its claim is also of *doubtful* authenticity, because it lacks the credentials of being God-breathed. Several features will bear out this charge: for example, it

[2]For a treatment of these sacred books see Sidney Collett, *All About the Bible*, pp. 300 ff.

has a fatalistic view of God (cf. 2:255; 3:26),[3] a sensualistic view of heaven (47:15; 77:41-43), a highly antagonistic attitude toward other religions (cf. 2:193; 8:39), and a tragic effect on society (cf. the status of women). None of these features is comparable to the elevating character of the Christian Scriptures, nor are they compatible with the claim of the Koran to be the "clear revelations" and "unassailable Scripture" of Allah (God).

The credentials of the Bible, on the other hand, are of an entirely different variety. The Bible has a sensible claim to inspiration (no mere mechanical dictation), a high moral standard, a universal appeal, and a provable character.

THE CREDENTIALS OF INSPIRATION

What are the credentials that corroborate the Bible's claim that it is God's Word? Christian apologists have suggested several lines of evidence that possess varied degrees of validity and probability, which, when taken together, form a convincing case for the inspiration of the Scriptures. They are listed here in what may be considered a descending order of importance.

THE ARGUMENT FROM THE SELF-VINDICATING AUTHORITY OF THE BIBLE

One of the most important evidences of inspiration is also the simplest and most fundamental. It is that the Bible is *its own proof*. It needs no other authority to confirm it because, in fact, there is no higher authority by which to establish it (cf. Heb. 6:18). The Scriptures may be likened unto a lion that does not need to be defended, but merely loosed so it can defend itself. To use a New Testament illustration, this type of argument, which is in a sense not really an argument at all, is portrayed by the reaction of the crowd to the authoritative teaching of Jesus, as "they were astonished at his teaching, for he taught them as one who had authority, and not as the scribes" (Mark 1:22), or, as others observed, "No man ever spoke like this man!" (John 7:46). There was a stamp of genuineness, a ring of authority, about the utterances of Christ that was so immediately recognized that their veracity was almost self-evident. So

---

[3] Also cf. the Muslim poet, Omar Khayyám, in his famous poem, *Rubaiyat*, Edward Fitzgerald (trans.), where he writes,

'Tis all a chequer-board of nights and days,
    where destiny with men for pieces plays;
Hither and thither moves and mates and slays,
    and one by one back in the closet lays.

it is with the Scriptures: they speak for themselves and are their own authority as the voice of God. To formalize this argument, the following summary is suggested:

A book that speaks with ultimate (self-vindicating) authority is God's Word.

The Bible is such a book.

Therefore, the Bible is God's Word.

THE ARGUMENT FROM THE TESTIMONY OF THE HOLY SPIRIT

Closely akin to the argument *from* the authority of the Word of God is the testimony *to* that authority by the Spirit of God. Basically, this argument is built upon the premise that God's Word is confirmed (attested) by God's Spirit. Not only does the Holy Spirit bear witness to the believer that he is a child of God (Rom. 8:16), but He also bears witness that the Bible is the Word of God (II Peter 1:20-21).[4] It is reasonable to assume that, if God's Spirit operated in the inspiration of the Bible, He would not be absent from the confirmation of the Bible. From the earliest centuries the universal consent of the church has been that the canonical books of the Bible, and those alone, have been attested by the Spirit of God (see chaps. 10, 13, 15); therefore, by the complete consent of the Christian community, the Bible has been confirmed as the Word of God. Formally stated, this argument proceeds as follows:

The book witnessed to by the Spirit of God is the Word of God.

The Bible is the book witnessed to by the Spirit of God.

Therefore, the Bible is the Word of God.

THE ARGUMENT FROM THE DYNAMIC ABILITY OF THE BIBLE

The transforming power of the Scriptures has always been one of the strongest evidences of its own divine origin. Untold thousands of individuals down through the centuries have been converted, and societal reforms have resulted from the application of biblical teachings.[5] There is an unending line of testimonials to the dynamic ability of the Word of God to do the work of God in making men into the children of God. The story of the confirmation of the super-

---

[4]This argument has been stressed in recent theology, cf. Karl Barth, *Church Dogmatics*, Vol. I, No. 2, pp. 457 ff.

[5]Kenneth Scott Latourette, *A History of Christianity*, pp. 1198-1201.

natural nature of Christian conversion has been told many times;[6] and, as any true believer can witness, the power within himself that enabled him to rise above himself came from outside himself. It came from God. Logically stated, this argument takes the following form:

> That which can effect a complete moral conversion finds its ultimate source in God.
>
> The Bible can effect a complete moral conversion.
>
> Therefore, the Bible finds its ultimate source in God.

The foregoing arguments come with greater force to Christians who have responded to the authority of Christ, have been transformed by His power, and possess His Spirit. They are subjective and personal in nature; but, in this respect, so is the Christian conversion experience. The following arguments, however, are more objective and general in nature. Both kinds of evidence are valid, and thereby contribute to the overall confirmation of the Bible as the Word of God.

THE ARGUMENT FROM THE INTEGRITY OF JESUS (AND THE GOSPEL RECORD)

The character and teachings of Christ are a matter of history. There are literally thousands of manuscript copies which confirm that the New Testament gives an accurate picture of what He did and said (cf. chap. 20). If the life and thoughts of any one figure from the first century are known to scholars today, certainly they are those of Jesus of Nazareth. Furthermore, hardly a word of criticism is ever leveled against the integrity of Christ. Certainly no word of accusation about His honesty has ever been proven. Pilate's statement has been the verdict of history, namely, "I find no crime in this man" (Luke 23:4). Since Jesus' veracity is unquestionable, it remains only to discover what He taught with authority about the Bible in order to settle the question: Is the Bible the Word of God? A survey of Jesus' view of the Old Testament reveals that He considered it to be the unbreakable Word of God (see chap. 6).[7] In other words, unless one denies the accuracy of the New Testament

---

[6]For a good defense of this point see Robert O. Ferm, *The Psychology of Christian Conversion.*

[7]See also P. C. Marvel, "Our Lord's Use of Scripture," *Revelation and the Bible,* Carl F. H. Henry (ed.).

record or the integrity of Christ, he must accept the divine authority of the Bible (at least the Old Testament), because Jesus taught it. The force of this argument cannot be evaded by saying that Jesus' view of the Bible was an accommodation (see chap. 4), nor by maintaining His integrity while denying His authority. If Jesus' authority is denied at this point, it does not hold on any point, and the whole foundation of Christian teaching falls with its Founder. This entire argument is presented in the following syllogism:

> Whatever Jesus taught theologically and categorically is true.
>
> The doctrine of the inspiration of the Bible (Old Testament) is something Jesus taught theologically and categorically.
>
> Therefore, the doctrine of inspiration of the Bible (Old Testament) is true.

THE ARGUMENT FROM THE UNITY OF THE BIBLE

One of the most often repeated arguments for the inspiration of Scripture is based on the amazing unity of the Bible. Briefly stated, this argument contends that:

> A book with amazing unity amid great diversity is best explained as a work of Deity.
>
> The Bible is such a book.
>
> Therefore, the Bible is best explained as a work of Deity.

In support of the minor premise, it has been observed that the Bible contains hundreds of themes, written in several languages, by nearly forty writers, over a period of about fifteen hundred years, in several different countries, by men of various occupations. Yet, amid all this diversity there is a sustained unity of subject, teaching, and solution to man's problem of sin. It has but one basic cause of man's woes (sin), and but one cure for sin (Christ).[8] Yet, the same universal appeal is an up-to-date solution for all of man's spiritual problems. The probability of such unity being accidental is infinitely less than that it is providential.

---

[8]For a good defense of the Christocentric unity of the Bible see Adolph Saphir, *Christ and the Scriptures*. For a classic discussion of the doctrinal unity of the Bible see James Orr, *The Problem of the Old Testament*, chap. 2.

2. *In fulfillment of prophecy (Obad. 1-4), Petra is today a deserted ruin. This is the so-called "Treasury" (Giovanni Trimboli)*

THE ARGUMENT FROM THE PROPHECY OF THE BIBLE

Perhaps as much attention has been given to this confirmation of the Bible as any other in recent years. Sometimes the argument is overstated by making every minute detail of typology and prophetic utterance directly and explicitly predictive of future events. However, the overstatement of the case in no way diminishes the strength of the passages that have repeatedly and accurately foretold the future, and which have now been confirmed as facts of history and archaeology.[9] To cite just a few examples: (1) the regathering of Israel (Isa. 11:11); (2) the destruction of Tyre (Ezek. 26); (3) the prediction of the great world kingdoms (Dan. 2 and 7); (4) even the judgment of Petra (Obad. 1-4). A higher critical view, which seeks to date these prophetic utterances after certain of the historical events portrayed in them, does not destroy the effect of these proph-

[9]See George T. B. Davis, *Bible Prophecies Fulfilled Today.*

ecies, because, even with these late dates, many other of the direct prophecies of the Old Testament are still well in advance of the occurrence of the events they predicted. For example, even if Daniel is dated at about 165 B.C., Daniel 9:24-27 is still well in advance of the coming of Jesus the Messiah. To summarize, it may be said that:

Repeated and accurate predictions of future events must be supernaturally given.

Bible prophecies have repeatedly and accurately predicted future events.

Therefore, Bible prophecies must have been supernaturally given.

The Argument from the Moral Superiority of the Bible

All truth is God's truth, and it is found in varying degrees throughout the many religious and philosophical systems in the world. However, the Bible is the *only book* which sums up the totality of this truth, and transcends it. There are flashes of high moral teaching in the Koran, Bhagavad-Gita (Hindu), Tripitaka (Buddhist), and other writings, but the floodlight of all these truths *and more* shines forth from the Bible alone. As Justin Martyr wrote, "Whatever things were rightly said among all men, are the property of us Christians. For next to God, we worship the Word who is from the unbegotten and ineffable God."[10] On a comparative level, the moral superiority of the Bible shines through with brilliance among the teachings of the world's great religions. Professor M. Monier-Williams, after having spent forty years studying the religious literature of the Orient, came to the following conclusion about them:

Pile them, if you will, on the left side of your study table; but place your own Holy Bible on the right side—all by itself, all alone—and with a wide gap between them. For, . . . there is a gulf between it and the so-called sacred books of the East which severs the one from the other utterly, hopelessly, and for ever . . . a veritable gulf which cannot be bridged over by any science of religious thought.[11]

This argument may be summarized as follows:

A book that sums up and transcends the best morality of all books of all time is best explained as God's Word.

[10]Justin Martyr, *Apology*, II.
[11]As cited by Collett, p. 315.

The Bible is such a book.

Therefore, the Bible is best explained as God's Word.

One possible evasion of this argument is that it only proves that the Bible is the best of all human books on morality. However, it must be remembered that the Bible repeatedly claims to be God's Word, and it would be morally incongruous for the very book that presents the highest morality to be itself the perpetrator of one of the world's biggest lies, namely, that it is God's Word, when in actuality it is not. If it be suggested that the writers wrongly attributed it to God, then their integrity, or authority to speak on morality, is undermined, and there is no reasonable explanation left for the Bible's superiority.

THE ARGUMENT FROM THE UNIVERSALITY OF THE BIBLE

The teachings of the Bible are the most universal in scope of any book in the world. In fact, its teachings begin with the *creation* of all things by God, indicate how all things *consist* by God, and relate how all things will be *consummated* by God. There is one unfolding drama from Genesis through Revelation.[12]

The Bible is also the most universal book in the world in terms of translation and distribution. Complete Bibles or portions have now been translated into over 1,100 languages and dialects. These languages represent about 90 percent of the world's population. The amount of Bible portions distributed annually by the combined Bible societies is phenomenal:

1963—54,123,820
1964—69,852,377
1965—76,953,369
1966—87,398,961

Normally, any book which has been translated into a half-dozen languages and printed in over a million copies is considered an all-time best seller. By adding the annual figures from all the Bible societies, it has been computed that by 1932 some 1,330,231,815 Bibles or portions had been published.[13] Counting an annual average of 30,000,000 since then, the grand total reaches over two billion. In fact, in the all-time circulation records, there are *no close seconds*. The distant seconds are books related to or dependent on the Bible,

[12]See Erich Sauer, *The Dawn of World Redemption;* also *The Triumph of the Crucified.*
[13]Hy Pickering, *One Thousand Wonderful Things About the Bible,* p. 7.

such as *Pilgrim's Progress, The Imitation of Christ,* or the works of William Shakespeare. "No other book has known anything approaching this constant circulation."[14] Briefly, then, it may be said that:

> The most universal book in the world is God's Word (if any book is).
>
> The Bible is the most universal book in the world.
>
> Therefore, the Bible is God's Word (if any book is).

The Argument from the Historicity of the Bible

No area of modern science has confirmed the historicity and authenticity of the Scriptures so much as has archaeology. The testimony of the spade has caused the reversal of many of the previously held conclusions of higher criticism about the Bible.[15] Historical confirmation of the Old Testament has come from all over the biblical world. Persons, places and events have been substantiated: from the Patriarchs to Israel in Egypt, to the conquest of Canaan, to the kingdom under Solomon, to the deportations of Israel and Judah to Assyria and Babylonia respectively.[16] In the field of New Testament studies, the evidence has also been abundant. Even a casual survey of any good book on New Testament archaeology will indicate that the accuracy of details in the events of Christ's life has been confirmed from the ruins of Palestine, as has been the case with the details about the journeys of the Apostle Paul.[17] Historical confirmation of the accuracy of the Scriptures has come from all over the biblical world. Donald J. Wiseman wrote,

> The geography of Bible lands and visible remains of antiquity were gradually recorded until today more than 25,000 sites within this region and dating to Old Testament times, in their broadest sense, have been located. . . . Among the finds are about half a million clay documents in the cuneiform script, dating from about 3300 B.C. to A.D. 50, widely used throughout the area.[18]

Yet, while archaeology itself does not directly prove the authority of the Bible, for it merely confirms its accuracy, it does confirm the

[14]S. L. Greenslade (ed.), *The Cambridge History of the Bible,* p. 479.
[15]See Nic. H. Ridderbos, "Reversal of Old Testament Criticism," and Merrill C. Tenney, "Reversal of New Testament Criticism," in Henry (ed.), *Revelation.* . . .
[16]See William F. Albright, *Recent Discoveries in Bible Lands.*
[17]See Merrill F. Unger, *Archaeology and the New Testament;* Joseph Free, *Archaeology and Bible History;* and Jack Finegan, *Light from the Ancient Past.*
[18]Donald J. Wiseman, "Archaeological Confirmation of the Old Testament" in Henry (ed.), *Revelation* . . . , pp. 301-2.

credibility of the individual writers and, as a result, enhances their integrity when they claim to speak with divine authority. In other words,

> Confirmation of the Bible's credibility is an indirect confirmation of the inspiration of the Bible.
>
> Archaeology has confirmed the credibility of the Bible.
>
> Therefore, archaeology has indirectly confirmed the inspiration of the Bible.

Certainly it is understood that archaeology has not confirmed all the facts of the Bible, since it has not checked all of them.[19] Nonetheless, it may be asserted that wherever archaeology has been able to check on the historicity of the Bible, it has supported the Bible. This fact increases the probability of the credibility and authority of the Bible in areas that have not been, and which cannot be, verified by archaeology.

THE ARGUMENT FROM ALTERNATE POSSIBILITY

One of the most interesting arguments for the inspiration of the Bible has been suggested by Charles Wesley.

> The Bible must be the invention either of good men or angels, bad men or devils, or of God.
>
> 1. It could not be the invention of good men or angels; for they neither would or could make a book, and tell lies all the time they were writing it, saying, "Thus saith the Lord," when it was their own invention.
>
> 2. It could not be the invention of bad men or devils; for they would not make a book which commands all duty, forbids all sin, and condemns their souls to hell to all eternity.
>
> 3. Therefore, I draw this conclusion, that the Bible must be given by divine inspiration.[20]

THE ARGUMENT FROM THE INDESTRUCTIBILITY OF THE BIBLE

One final point of consideration is the indomitable character of the Bible, or its ability to withstand attacks by its enemies. The

---

[19]Recently a leading Jewish archaeologist, Nelson Glueck, said, "It can be categorically stated that no archaeological discovery has ever controverted a biblical reference" (*Rivers in the Desert*, p. 31).

[20]Robert W. Burtner and Robert E. Chiles, *A Compend of Wesley's Theology*, p. 20.

enemies of the Bible have advanced from all quarters. From the political realm came the Diocletian Edict (c. A.D. 303), which commanded that the Scriptures be burned. Voltaire, the skeptic, predicted that the Bible and Christianity would be swept into obsolescence, but only fifty years after his death the Geneva Bible Society used his press and house to produce stacks of Bibles.[21] Modern attacks from science have battered against the Bible, but the Bible is again emerging the victor.[22] Jesus said, "Heaven and earth will pass away, but my words will not pass away" (Mark 13:31). As a result, it may be logically stated that

A book with proven indestructibility is best explained as God's Word.

The Bible is such a book.

Therefore, the Bible is best explained as God's Word.

SUMMARY AND CONCLUSION

The content of the present chapter is based upon the comprehensive claim, discussed in detail in chapters 4-8, that the Bible in its entirety is the Word of God. The thrust of the entire apologetic is that *the Bible claims to be and the Bible proves to be the Word of God*. Eleven of the traditional arguments have been surveyed, which, taken as a whole, present credentials for the claim of inspiration that is indisputable. Since the Bible does make such a strong claim for its inspiration, the possibility for explanations of its nature is very limited. This book could not be just the work of credible men and make the incredible claim that it is God-breathed. If the writers were lying at this point, then they certainly cannot be considered credible. On the other hand, if they were credible writers, and the Bible is God's Word, credentials for this claim may accordingly be expected. Such credentials are manifold, as they issue forth from the nature, unity, superiority, and universality of the Bible, as well as from archaeology, prophecy, Christian experience, and from Christ Himself.

[21]See Collett, p. 63.
[22]Cf. James H. Jauncey, *Science Returns to God.*

Part Two

———

CANONIZATION OF THE BIBLE

10

DETERMINATION OF CANONICITY

The first link in the chain of revelation "From God to Us" is inspiration, which is concerned with *what* God did, namely, that He breathed out (spirated) the Scriptures. The second link in the chain is canonization, which relates to the question of *which* books God inspired. Inspiration indicates how the Bible received its *authority*, whereas canonization tells how the Bible received its *acceptance*. It is one thing for God to give the Scriptures their authority, and quite another for men to recognize that authority. Canonization, then, concerns the recognition and collection of the God-inspired, authoritative books of the sacred Scriptures.

CANONICITY DEFINED

In the overall subject of canonicity, the first question to be considered is the determining principle: What is it that makes a book canonical? Various answers have been presented concerning the determining principle of canonicity; but, before they can be understood, it is necessary to trace briefly the development of the concept of the "canon."

LITERALLY

The original meaning of the term can be traced to the ancient Greeks, who used it in a literal sense: a *kanon* was a rod, ruler, staff, or measuring rod. The Greek word *kanon* is probably a derivative of the Hebrew *kaneh* (reed), an Old Testament term meaning measuring rod (Ezek. 40:3; 42:16).[1]

METAPHORICALLY

This literal concept provided the basis for a later metaphorical use of the word *kanon*, meaning standard, norm. Even in pre-Christian

[1]For the history of the word "canon" see Alexander Souter, *The Text and Canon of the New Testament*, rev. by C. S. C. Williams, pp. 154-56.

Greek, the word *kanon* bore the metaphorical meaning,[2] and the New Testament usage of the word bears the same metaphorical image. In II Corinthians 10:13-16 it bears the same sense of "sphere of action or influence."[3] Galatians 6:16 comes closest to the final theological significance of the word, as Paul says, "Peace and mercy be upon all who walk by this rule [*kanon*]."

THEOLOGICALLY

From the literal "ruler," the word was extended to mean a rule or standard for anything. In early Christian usage, it came to mean rule of faith, normative writings, or authoritative Scripture. The Fathers, from the time of Irenaeus, referred to the *kanon* of Christian teaching, which they called "The *Kanon* of the Church," "The *Kanon* of the Truth," and "The *Kanon* of Faith."[4] However, the first clear application of the word to the Scriptures came at about A.D. 350, with Athanasius.[5] The word *kanon* was applied to the Bible in both an active and a passive sense: one in which it was the canon or standard, and the other in which it was canonized or recognized to be canonical by the church. In this chapter canonicity is viewed in the active sense in which the Scriptures are the ultimate norm.

CANONICITY DESCRIBED

The Jews did not use the word canon (*kaneh*) in reference to their authoritative writings, although the theological concept of a canon or divine standard is certainly applicable to their sacred writings. Nevertheless, several other phrases or concepts used by the Jews are equivalent to the word canon.

SACRED WRITINGS

An inspired or canonical writing was considered sacred and was kept by the ark of the covenant (cf. Deut. 31:24-26). After the temple was built, the sacred writings were kept in the temple (cf. II Kings 22:8). This special attention and reverence paid to the Jewish Scriptures is tantamount to saying that they were considered canonical.

[2]For example, it was used to describe a standard in ethics, art, literature and even great epochs. See Brooke Foss Westcott, *A General Survey of the History of the Canon of the New Testament*, 7th ed., Appendix A, p. 512.
[3]Walter Bauer, *A Greek-English Lexicon of the New Testament and Other Early Christian Literature*, trans. by William F. Arndt and F. Wilbur Gingrich, p. 403.
[4]Westcott, p. 514.
[5]According to Westcott, p. 516, although certain derivatives of the Greek word were used by Origen.

Authoritative Writings

Another concept that is synonymous with canonicity is authority. The rulers of Israel were to be subject to the authority of the Scriptures. The Lord commanded that when a king "sits on the throne of his kingdom, he shall write for himself in a book a copy of this law, . . . and he shall read in it all the days of his life, that he may learn to fear the Lord his God" (Deut. 17:18-19). The Lord enjoined the same authoritative writings unto Joshua, saying, "This book of the law shall not depart out of your mouth, but you shall meditate on it day and night" (Joshua 1:8).

Books That Defile the Hands

Later, in the Talmudic tradition, the canonical or sacred books were considered those that "defiled the hands" of the users, because the books were so holy. For example, Tosefta Yadaim 3:5 of the Talmud says, "The Gospel and the books of the heretics do not make the hands unclean; the books of Ben Sira and whatever books have been written since his time are not canonical."[6] The books of the Old Testament, in contrast, do make the hands unclean, that is, they are canonical.

Books from the Prophetic Period

Josephus, in his *Contra Apion* 1:8, says,

> From Artaxerxes until our time everything has been recorded, but has not been deemed worthy of like credit with what preceded, because the exact succession of the prophets ceased. But what faith we have placed in our own writings is evident by our conduct; for though so long a time has now passed, no one has dared to add anything to them, or to take anything from them, or to alter anything in them.

That is, only the books written from Moses to Malachi, in the succession of Hebrew prophets, were considered to be canonical. With this the statement of the Talmud in Seder Olam Rabba 30 agrees when it says, "Up to this point [the time of Alexander the Great] the prophets prophesied through the Holy Spirit; from this time onward incline thine ear and listen to the sayings of the wise." So then, if a book was written after the prophetic period, it was not considered canonical. If it was written within the prophetic period, in the succession of Hebrew prophets, it was canonical.

[6]As quoted by R. H. Pfeiffer, *Introduction to the Old Testament*, p. 63, n. 10.

In brief, what were later called canonical writings were by the Jews considered to be those sacred and authoritative writings of the Hebrew prophets from Moses to Malachi. So sacred were these writings that they were preserved by the ark of the covenant in the temple. To touch them was to defile one's hands. To break them was to defile one's life. The Hebrew canon, then, was that collection of writings which conformed to the rule or standard of divine inspiration and authority.

CANONICITY DETERMINED

Once it is understood what canonicity means, the question of how these books received their canonicity must be considered. First, several inadequate views will be examined, views that fall short of explaining what it is that really determines the canonicity of a book.

SOME INADEQUATE VIEWS

Several insufficient suggestions have been offered as to the determining criteria of canonicity.

Age determines canonicity.[7] It has been suggested that canonicity is determined by antiquity. The general argument is that if the book was ancient it was venerated because of its age and placed among the prized collection of Hebrew literature. But, this view clearly does not measure up to the facts.

1. *Many ancient books are not in the canon.* That antiquity does not determine canonicity is apparent from the fact that numerous books, many of which are older than some canonical books, are not in the canon: "The Book of the Wars of the LORD" is mentioned in Numbers 21:14, and "The Book of Jasher" in Joshua 10:13 (AV),[8] neither of which is part of the Hebrew canon.

2. *Many young books were placed in the canon.* Most, if not all, of the canonical books were received into the canon soon after they were written. Moses' writings were placed by the ark while he was yet alive (Deut. 31:24-26). Daniel, a younger contemporary of Jeremiah, had accepted Jeremiah's book as canonical (cf. Dan. 9:2), and Ezekiel, another contemporary, made reference

[7]See W. H. Green, *General Introduction to the Old Testament: The Canon*, p. 34. He lists Wildeboer as holding this view and Hitzig as holding that Hebrew language is the test of canonicity (p. 29).

[8]For a more complete list of extrabiblical books contained in the Old Testament, see chap. 13.

to Daniel, although not to his writings (Ezek. 28:3). In the New Testament, Peter had a collection of Paul's books and considered them to be Scripture (II Peter 3:15-16). Since many old books were not accepted into the canon, and many young books were received, *age could not have been the determining factor of canonicity.*

Hebrew language determines canonicity. It has also been suggested that the Hebrew language is the key to canonicity. If a book was written in the "sacred" language of the Jews, it was placed with their sacred Scriptures, and if not, it was rejected. This view breaks down on two counts.

1. *Many books in the Hebrew language are not in the canon.* Most of the books written by the Hebrews were obviously in the Hebrew language, but they were not all accepted into the canon, as stated above. Even though some of these books were extant in the Hebrew language at the time of the recognition of the Old Testament Scriptures, for example, Ecclesiasticus and other Apocryphal books,[9] yet they have not been received into the Hebrew canon (see chap. 13).

2. *Some books not totally written in the Hebrew language are in the canon.* Parts of some of the books that were received into the Jewish canon were not in Hebrew at all, but in Aramaic. This fact is not only true of Daniel 2:4b–7:28, but of Ezra 4:8–6:18 and 7:12-26 as well. The thesis that the Hebrew language determines canonicity, then, breaks down for two reasons: some books in Hebrew were not accepted, whereas books which had some parts written in other languages were accepted as canonical.

Agreement with the Torah determines canonicity. To the Jews, ultimate criterion for all doctrine was the Torah, the law of Moses. This being the case, it has been suggested that all Hebrew religious literature that agreed with the teachings of the Torah was accepted into the canon, and all those books that disagreed with it were not. Of course, no book that contradicted the Torah would be accepted, since it was believed to be God's word, and no subsequent word from God could contradict a previous one. What this view does not account for are the numerous books that did agree with the Torah yet

---

[9]Some of the Apocryphal books found among the Dead Sea Scrolls were written in Hebrew, e.g., Tobit, Apocryphal Daniel, and Jubilees. Cf. Menahem Mansoor, *The Dead Sea Scrolls*, p. 203.

were not accepted into the canon. There are no doubt many non-canonical Old Testament books (see chap. 13) which agree with the Torah in their totality, but they were never considered to be canonical. For example, Elijah the prophet wrote a book that most certainly agreed with the Torah (II Chron. 21:12). Iddo the seer (II Chron. 12:15) also wrote one, as did others; yet, most of these were not accepted as a part of the canon. Likewise, in the New Testament there may have been books written by the Apostle Paul which were not extant, nor canonical, for example, "Epistle to the Laodiceans" (Col. 4:16)[10] and the so-called "Lost Letter to the Corinthians"[11] (referred to in I Cor. 5:9). Mere agreement with the Torah, or previous revelation, is not enough. The Jews no doubt thought that the Talmud and Midrash (see chap. 22) agreed with the Torah, but did not thereby consider them to be canonical. Furthermore, this view does not account for the manner by which the Torah itself became canonical.

Religious value determines canonicity. Still another view that merits consideration is that the religious value of a given book was the determining factor of its reception into the canon. It is almost redundant to say that a book would be rejected if it did not have any spiritual or religious value, for the canon was a *religious* canon, and only a book of religious value would be accepted as a part of it. The mistake in this view is similar to that of the preceding one, that is, there are many books of religious value that were not accepted into either the Old or New Testament collections. Any honest, objective reading of the Apocrypha will reveal much material of religious value (cf. Ecclesiasticus), as would reading some of the nonexistent books written by prophets or apostles. Furthermore, even if it be conceded that a book was accepted because of its religious value, this in no way explains *how it received its religious value.* The real question to be asked is: How (or from whom) did the books of spiritual import that agreed with the Torah (and God's previous revelations) receive their valued truth to begin with? Or, for that matter, where did the previous revelation in the Torah receive its truth and authority?

---

[10]Some scholars feel that "Laodiceans" is actually another name for "Ephesians," cf. chap. 15.

[11]Some have suggested that this so-called "Lost Letter to the Corinthians" is actually included in the canonical II Corinthians, and constitutes chaps. 10-13 of that epistle. Cf. Alfred Plummer, *II Corinthians* in *International Critical Commentary,* p. xxx.

A Mistake Common to the Inadequate Views of Canonicity

Underlying all the insufficient views of what determined canonicity is the failure to distinguish between the *determination* and the *recognition* of canonicity.

Canonicity is determined by God. Actually, a canonical book is valuable and true because God inspired it. That is, canonicity is determined or fixed conclusively by authority, and authority was given to the individual books by God through inspiration. The real question is not where a book received its divine authority, for this can only come from God alone, but how did men recognize that authority?

Authority is recognized by men of God. Inspiration determines canonicity. If a book was authoritative, it was so because God breathed it and made it so. How a book *received* authority, then, is determined by God. How men *recognize* that authority is another matter altogether (see discussion in chap. 11).

A More Sufficient View of Canonicity

Precisely speaking, canonicity is determined by God, in other words, the reason there are only sixty-six books in the canon is that God inspired only that many. That is, only sixty-six books were found to have the stamp of divine authority, because God only stamped that many, or invested that number with authority for faith and practice.

A book is valuable because it is canonical. A given book is not canonical because it was found to be valuable. Rather, it was found to be valuable because it was determined to be canonical by God. In other words, a book is not inspired because it is inspiring; it is inspiring because it is inspired.

A book is canonical because it is inspired. Edward J. Young presents the correct view, that *inspiration determines canonization,* as he writes,

> When the Word of God was written it became Scripture and, inasmuch as it had been spoken by God, possessed absolute authority. Since it was the Word of God, it was canonical. That which determines the canonicity of a book, therefore, is the fact that the book is inspired of God. Hence a distinction is properly made between the authority which the Old Testament possesses as

divinely inspired, and the recognition of that authority on the part of Israel.[12]

Although this discussion has primarily centered around the Old Testament, the principles are equally applicable to the New Testament.

CANONICITY DEFENDED

For the Christian the teaching of Christ is decisive. In this respect, Christ is not only the key to inspiration (chap. 6), but He is the key to canonicity as well.[13]

THE TESTIMONY OF CHRIST

Jesus taught definitely that God was the Originator of the Hebrew Old Testament. He quoted as authoritative or authentic most of the twenty-two books of the Hebrew canon.[14] He considered every section, "Law and Prophets" and "Law, Prophets, and Psalms" (Luke 24:27, 44), to be prophetic of Him. He believed that inspiration extended from Genesis through Chronicles (Matt. 23:35; tantamount to saying "Genesis to Malachi"). He asserted that the Old Testament as a whole was unbreakable Scripture (John 10:35); that it would never perish (Matt. 5:18); and that it must be fulfilled (Luke 24:44). He personally authenticated persons and events from Eden (Matt. 19:5) to Jonah in the "whale" (Matt. 12:40), including Daniel the prophet (Matt. 24:15), Noah and the flood (Luke 17:27), and the destruction of Sodom (Luke 17:29). Jesus not only defined the limits of the canon, that is, the twenty-two books of the Hebrew Old Testament, but He laid down the principle of canonicity, namely, the canon consists of that which is the "word of God." Illustrative of this point are Jesus' references to the Old Testament as the "word of God" (Mark 7:13), as that which "God said" (Matt. 19:5), or as that which was uttered "by the Spirit" (Matt. 22:43; Mark 12:36). As for the New Testament, Jesus promised that the Holy Spirit would guide the apostles into "all the truth" (John 16:13) and bring all things that He had taught them to their remembrance (John 14:26). Thus, the principle that "canonicity is determined by inspiration" was pronounced by Jesus concerning the Old Testament, and promised for the New Testament.

[12]Edward J. Young, "The Canon of the Old Testament," *Revelation and the Bible*, Carl F. H. Henry (ed.), p. 156.

[13]Everett F. Harrison, *Introduction to the New Testament*, p. 112.

[14]Henry (ed), *Revelation. . .* , pp. 121-34.

The Integrity of the Scriptures

At first, it may appear that a circular argument is used, when it is stated that "Christ is the key to canonicity," when all that is known about the teachings of Christ comes from that very canon, and the truth of that canon is being assumed in order to prove the underlying principle of the canon. However, such is not actually the case. What is presently being contended is that

Canonicity is determined by authority (inspiration).

Authority is known by Christ's testimony.

Christ's testimony is known by the authenticity of the record.

Since there is ample evidence to support the authenticity (and genuineness) of the New Testament (chap. 18), and since the New Testament reveals that Christ taught that divine authority is imparted to the Scriptures through the process of inspiration, the authority of Christ becomes the crux of the canonicity of the Bible.[15]

SUMMARY AND CONCLUSION

The history of the word "canon" indicates a development from a literal rod or ruler to the concept of a standard for something. Subsequently the word was applied to *the rule of faith,* that is, the normative writings or authoritative Scriptures, which was the standard of faith and practice. Just how this standard or canon was determined is the subject of some misunderstanding. With this in view, the present chapter has discussed that which determined canonicity. Several insufficient views have been suggested, for example, (1) age decided the issue; (2) Hebrew language determined it; (3) agreement with the Torah did; or (4) religious value determined whether or not a book was canonical. However, all these views share one common weakness: a failure to distinguish between the *determination* of canonicity (a work of God) and *recognition* of canonicity (a work of men). The biblical view is that inspiration determines canonicity; a book is valuable because it is inspired, and not inspired because men found it to be valuable. This view is clearly supported by Christ in the New Testament, and is therefore conclusive for the Christian, as "Christ is the key to canonicity."

[15]See Benjamin B. Warfield, *The Inspiration and Authority of the Bible.*

11

DISCOVERY OF CANONICITY

HOW CANONICITY WAS DISCOVERED

DEFINITION

Canonicity is determined by God. A book is not inspired because men made it canonical; it is canonical because God inspired it. It is not the antiquity, authenticity or even religious value that makes a book canonical or authoritative. On the contrary, a book is valuable because it is canonical, and not canonical because it is or was considered valuable. Inspiration determines canonization, and confusion at this point not only dulls the edge of authority but it mistakes the effect (a canonical book) with the cause (inspiration of God). Canonicity is *determined* or established authoritatively by God; it is merely *discovered* by man.

DISTINCTION

The distinction between God's determination and man's discovery is essential to the correct view of canonicity, and should be drawn carefully. This may be done by a careful comparison of the following two views. This comparison is shown in the accompanying chart. In the "Incorrect View"[1] the authority of the Scriptures is based

The Incorrect View	The Correct View
The Church Is Determiner of Canon	The Church Is Discoverer of Canon
The Church Is Mother of Canon	The Church Is Child of Canon
The Church Is Magistrate of Canon	The Church Is Minister of Canon
The Church Is Regulator of Canon	The Church Is Recognizer of Canon
The Church Is Judge of Canon	The Church Is Witness of Canon
The Church Is Master of Canon	The Church Is Servant of Canon

[1]It is not correct to identify this "Incorrect View" with that of the Roman Catholic Council of Trent or Vatican I or II. Vatican I pronounced that the books of the Bible are held by the church to be "sacred and canonical, not because, having been carefully composed by mere human industry, they were afterwards approved by her authority . . . but because, having been written by the inspiration of the Holy Ghost, they have God for their author, and have been delivered as such to the Church herself."

upon the authority of the church; the correct view is that the authority of the church is to be found *in* the authority of the Scriptures. The incorrect view places the church *over* the canon, while the proper position views the church *under* the canon. In fact, if in the column titled "Incorrect View," the word "church" be replaced by the word "God," then the proper view of the canon emerges clearly. It is God who *regulated* the canon; man merely *recognized* the divine authority God gave to it. God *determined* the canon, and man *discovered* it. Gaussen gave an excellent summary of this position when he wrote,

> In this affair, then, the Church is a servant and not a mistress; a depository and not a judge. She exercises the office of a minister, not of a magistrate. . . . She delivers a testimony, not a judicial sentence. She discerns the canon of the Scriptures, she does not make it; she has recognized their authenticity, she has not given it. . . . The authority of the Scriptures is not founded, then, on the authority of the Church: It is the Church that is founded on the authority of the Scriptures.[2]

HOW CANONICITY WAS DISCOVERED

THE PRINCIPLES INVOLVED

It is all very well to assume that God gave authority and hence canonicity to the Bible, but another question arises, namely, *How* did man discover or become aware of what God had done? How did the Church Fathers know when they had come upon a canonical book? The commonly accepted canonical books of the Bible themselves make reference to many other books that are no longer available, for example, "The Book of Jasher" (Joshua 10:13, AV); "The Book of the Wars of the LORD" (Num. 21:14). Then there are the Apocryphal books and the so-called "lost books" of the Bible, for example, a so-called "Lost Epistle of Paul to Corinth" (I Cor. 5:9); and possibly an "Epistle to the Laodiceans" (Col. 4:16). How did the Fathers know these were not inspired? Did not John (21:25) and Luke (1:1) indicate that there was a profusion of religious literature? Were there not false epistles (II Thess. 2:2)? What were the earmarks of inspiration that guided the Fathers in their recognition and collection of the inspired books? How did they sort out the true from the false, and the canonical from the Apocryphal?

From a study of the historical and biblical process of canonization,

[2]Louis Gaussen, *Theopneustia*, p. 137.

the use of five principles emerges. These principles guided the Fathers in the recognition of the canonical books over a period of two or three centuries. Stated in question form, they are as follows: (1) Is it *authoritative*—did it come with the authority of God? (2) Is it *prophetic*—was it written by a man of God? (3) Is it *authentic*[3]—did it tell the truth about God, man, etc.? (4) Is it *dynamic*—did it come with the life-transforming power of God? (5) Was it *received*, collected, read and used—was it accepted by the people of God? The characteristics sought by these questions were the earmarks of inspired books. If they were apparent, the book was accepted. If they were absent, the book was rejected. If they were not apparent, the book was doubted until it was fully tested. By these principles the Fathers *were guided* by the Holy Spirit to sort through the proliferation of religious literature in order to *discover* the books which God had *determined* to be canonical. It will be instructive to look at these principles individually in their actual historical operation.

Is it authoritative? This is perhaps the first and most important question that was asked by the Fathers. Does this or that book speak with authority? Can it be said of this book as it was of Jesus, "And they were astonished at his teaching, for he taught them as one that had authority" (Mark 1:22)? Does this book come with a divine "Thus saith the Lord"? Does it have a self-vindicating authority that commands attention as it communicates?

1. This is how the Prophets were *recognized*. The characteristic words "And the word of the Lord came unto the prophet," or "The Lord said unto," or "God spoke" so fill the prophetic pages of the Old Testament that they have become proverbial. This earmark of inspiration is so clear and resounding in the Prophets that it hardly became necessary to look for any other characteristic to mark them as divine in their origin.

2. Other books were *rejected* by the absence of authority, for example, the books of Pseudepigrapha.[4] These books did not have the "ring" of authority, or, if they claimed authority, the claim had a hollow sound. They provided no character to support their claim. In many cases the books were fanciful and magical, and hardly anyone mistook their "divine claims" as dogmatic commands

[3]Perhaps it would be better to use the word "Christocentric" at this point rather than "authentic," in accordance with the emphasis made by Christ in Luke 24:27, 44; however, the word "authentic" is used because it is more explicit: whereas all canonical books are "Christocentric," some are only implicitly so.
[4]See chap. 13.

from God. Their shallow pretentions were clearly not sovereign intentions, and so they were emphatically rejected.

3. This same principle of authority was the basis for some books being *doubted*. For a time the book of Esther, in which even the name of God is conspicuously absent, fell into this category. Finally, upon closer examination, Esther retained its place in the canon, but only because the Fathers were convinced that authority was present although some did not consider it observably present.[5] Perhaps the very fact that some canonical books were doubted at times, on the basis of one principle or another, argues both for the value of the principle and the caution of the Fathers in their recognition of canonicity. If so, it provides assurance that men really included no books that God wanted excluded from the canon.

Is it prophetic? The next question to be asked was: Was this book writen by a man of God? It seemed reasonable to assume that *the Word of God inspired by the Spirit of God for the people of God* would not be given through anyone other than a *man of God* (II Peter 1:20; Heb. 1:1). Thus, a book was judged as to whether or not it was genuinely written by the stated author who was a spokesman in the mainstream of redemptive revelation, either a prophet (whether in Old or New Testament times) or an apostle.

1. This was exactly the argument that Paul used in the support of his epistle to the Galatians (cf. 1:1-24). He argued that his message was authoritative because he was an authorized messenger of God, "an apostle—not from men nor through man, but through Jesus Christ and God the Father" (Gal. 1:1). He also turned the tables on his opponents who preached "a different gospel—not that there is another . . ." (Gal. 1:6-7), and which could not be true because they were "false brethren" (Gal. 2:4). It should be noted in this connection that occasionally the Bible *contains* true prophecies from individuals whose status as men of God is questionable, such as Balaam (Num. 24:17) and Caiaphas (John 11:49). However, granted that these prophecies were consciously given,[6] these prophets were not writers of Bible books, but were merely quoted by the actual writer. Therefore, these utterances are in the same category as the Greek poets quoted by the Apostle Paul (cf. Acts 17:28; I Cor. 15:33; Titus 1:12).

[5]See chap. 13 for support of Esther's canonicity.
[6]In the case of Caiaphas it would seem that the prophecy was given unwittingly.

2. As previously mentioned, Paul used the argument that a book from God must be written by a man of God against the false teachers opposing him at Galatia. It was also used as a reason for rejecting a letter that was forged, or written under false pretenses, as in II Thessalonians 2:2. A book cannot be canonical if it is not genuine.

   In this connection, however, it should be noted that a book might use the device of literary impersonation with no intent to deceive, in which the writer assumes the role of another for effect. Some scholars feel such is the case in the book of Ecclesiastes, where Koheleth wrote autobiographically as though he were Solomon.[7] Such a view is not incompatible with the principle herein presented, provided it can be shown to be a literary device and not a moral deception.

3. Because of this "prophetic" principle, II Peter was disputed in the early church.[8] On the basis of internal evidence (differences in the style of writing), it was felt by some that the author of II Peter could not be the same as the author of I Peter. But II Peter claimed to have been written by "Simon Peter, a servant and apostle of Jesus Christ" (1:1). Thus, the epistle was either a forgery or there was great difficulty in explaining its different style. Those who were disturbed by such evidence doubted the genuineness of II Peter and it was placed among the Antilegomena books for a time.[9] It was finally admitted to be canonical, but only on the grounds that it was also Petrine.

Is it authentic? This question of the Fathers asked, "Does the book tell the *truth* about God, man, etc., as it is already known by previous revelation?" And, is it a record of facts as they actually occurred? Obviously a book cannot contradict truth and still be truly God's.

1. This was no doubt the reason that the Bereans searched the Scriptures to see whether Paul's teaching was true (Acts 17:11). If the preaching of the apostle did not accord with the teaching of

---

[7]See Herbert Carl Leupold, *Exposition of Ecclesiastes*, pp. 8 ff. for a defense of this view by a Conservative scholar. Other orthodox scholars favor the Solomonic authorship. See Gleason L. Archer, Jr., *A Survey of Old Testament Introduction*, pp. 462-72.

[8]Even Eusebius, *Ecclesiastical History*, III, 3, in the fourth century said, "But the so-called second Epistle we have not received as canonical, but nevertheless it has appeared useful to many, and has been studied with other Scriptures." Loeb ed., I, 193.

[9]See chap. 15.

the Old Testament canon, then it could not be of God. Agreement with the rest of the known Word of God does not necessarily make a book canonical, but disagreement would certainly relegate a book to a noncanonical status.

2. Much of the Apocrypha was rejected because it was not authentic.[10] The Jewish Fathers and early Christian Fathers rejected, or considered second-rate, these books because they had historical inaccuracies and even moral incongruities. The Reformers rejected some because of what they considered heretical teaching.[11] The Apostle John strongly urged that "truth" be tested by the known standard before it be received (I John 4:1-6). Logically, a book from the God of truth *must* accord with the truth of God. If its claim is divine but its credentials are unauthentic, then the credentials must supersede the claim.

3. For this reason a few of the canonical books, such as James and Jude, have been doubted by some. It was thought that Jude could not have been authentic, since it quoted from unauthentic Pseudepigraphal books (Jude 9, 14).[12] Martin Luther questioned the full canonicity of James because he thought the book taught salvation by works, and this teaching was contrary to the doctrine of salvation by faith as it was clearly taught in other Scriptures.[13] Historically and uniformly, Jude and James have been vindicated and their canonicity recognized, but only when their teaching had been harmonized with the rest of the body of Scripture. What has compounded this problem has been the failure of men to see that further truth can be complementary and supplementary without being contradictory to existing truth. But, again, since the Fathers held a kind of "if in doubt throw it out" policy, the validity of their discernment of the canonical books is enhanced.

Is it dynamic? Another question was asked by the Fathers, although sometimes only implicitly: Does the book come with the

---

[10]See chap. 15.
[11]Such as praying for the dead, which II Maccabees 12:45 supports.
[12]See Jerome, *Lives of Illustrious Men,* chap. 4.
[13]Luther placed James at the end of the New Testament, saying, "I do not regard it as the writing of an apostle; and my reasons follow. In the first place it is flatly against St. Paul and all the rest of Scripture in ascribing justification to works . . . . Therefore, I cannot include him among the chief books, though I would not thereby prevent anyone from including or extolling him as he pleases, for there are otherwise many good sayings in him." See E. Theodore Bachmann (ed.), "Preface to Epistles of St. James and St. Jude," *Luther's Works,* XXXV, 396-97.

power of God? They believed the Word of God was "living and active" (Heb. 4:12),[14] and consequently ought to have a transforming force for edification (II Tim. 3:16) and evangelization (I Peter 1:23). If the obeyed message of a book did not effect its stated goal, if it did not have the power to change a life, then God was apparently not behind its message. A *message* of God would certainly be backed by the *might* of God.

1. The Apostle Paul applied this principle to the Old Testament when he wrote to Timothy, "And that from a child thou hast known the holy scriptures, which are able to make thee wise unto salvation" (II Tim. 3:15, AV). If it is of God, it will work—it will come to pass. This simple pragmatic test was given by Moses to try the truth of a prophet's prediction (Deut. 18:20 ff.). If his prophecy did not materialize, then it was not from God.

2. On this basis, much heretical literature and even some good non-canonical apostolical literature was rejected. Teachings that contained false prophecies (Matt. 24:11) or prophets that held to a false hope (I Kings 22:6-8 ff.) were, of course, to be rejected. But beyond this, even those books whose teaching was spiritual, but whose message was at best only devotional and not canonical, such as the vast amount of literature written in the apostolic and sub-apostolic period,[15] were to be refused a place in the canon. When transition is made from the canonical books of the New Testament to these other religious writings of the apostolic period, ". . . one is conscious of a tremendous change. There is not the same freshness and originality, depth and clearness. And this is no wonder, for it means the transition from truth given by infallible inspiration to truth produced by fallible pioneers."[16] The noncanonical books lacked power; they were devoid of the dynamic and dogmatic aspects found in inspired literature.

3. Because a book must come with edifying originality and power in order to be considered canonical, some books, such as the Song of Solomon and Ecclesiastes, were the subject of occasional doubts. Could a book that is sensual or another that is skeptical be of God? Obviously not. And as long as these books were thought of in that manner, they could not be acclaimed as can-

---

[14]Greek: "effectual, active, powerful," cf. Walter Bauer, *A Greek-English Lexicon of the New Testament and Other Early Christian Literature*, p. 265.
[15]See chap. 15.
[16]Louis Berkhof, *The History of Christian Doctrines*, p. 42.

onical. Eventually the messages of these books were seen as spiritual and hence the books were recognized as canonical. The principle, nevertheless, was applied to all the books impartially; some passed the test while others failed. Nonetheless, this much was certain: no book that lacked essential edificational or practical characteristics was considered canonical.

Was it received? The capstone of all the questions was: Has this book been *accepted* generally by the *people* of God? Compared to modern standards, transportation was slow and communication was poor during the first centuries of the Christian era. Thus, the full canonical lists were not universally agreed upon in any official way for a few centuries. This meant that when final decision was made and, in many cases even long before that, the collection and listing of books was being done by people to whom the book was not originally directed. So they necessarily had to depend upon testimony, circulation, usage, and the above mentioned four principles in order to make a final decision about the acceptance of the given books.

In a sense, then, the acceptance of a book by the church councils of later centuries is not a strong independent witness to the canonicity of that book. It is rather a confirmation, and does serve the obvious purpose of *making final* the decision and availability of the books. After all, if the latter Fathers had not collected and *disseminated* the books, what good would be accomplished by the fact that the earlier Fathers had *accepted* them? The continuation of the canonical books necessitated not only their *collection* and *recognition,* but also their *transmission* to subsequent generations.

Two important factors must be kept in view about the *acceptance* of the canonical books:

1. *Acceptance* actually includes both *initial* acceptance as well as subsequent and *final* acceptance by the church universal. It also means that the people of God to whom it was originally addressed actually received it as the word of God (cf. I Thess. 2:13).[17]

2. It is *acceptance by the people of God,* that is, by the true church (not by heretical sects or unbelievers) that is meant. Even the books of Moses were not accepted by all in his day, as R. Laird Harris states, "But how did the people of antiquity know these books were canonical? As a matter of fact, some didn't. Korah,

---

[17]Cf. chap. 14 for *where* and *when* the New Testament was finally canonized.

Dathan, and Abiram (Numbers 16) did not think much of Moses. But then the earth opened and swallowed them alive."[18] Nor, for that matter, did the scoffers accept Paul's writings (II Peter 3:15), nor Marcion the Gnostic the full canon of the New Testament.[19]

a. The principle of recognition by the people of God, although not always as sensationally vindicated as in the case of Korah, was nonetheless an active and operative one. Israel had accepted Moses' writings and so God enjoined them to Joshua for the people of his day (Joshua 1:8). Peter accepted the epistles of Paul in his second epistle, as he accorded them the same position as the "other scriptures" (II Peter 3:16). There is ample evidence within the New Testament to indicate that the canon was already beginning to be formed, as the people of God accepted the truth of God from the men of God (see chap. 14). This revelation was impressed on the hearts of God's people by the Holy Spirit as being the true message from on high.[20]

b. Ultimately all the noncanonical books met their fate by virtue of this principle. They did not bear the marks of authority and authenticity, so they did not reach the final historical level of canonicity. Thus, they were not accepted by the people of God either generally or officially. It is true that some noncanonical books found individual, local and temporary acceptance, but ultimately they too fell short of final and universal recognition.[21]

c. It is also true that some canonical books were temporarily and locally considered uncanonical, because they were not widely accepted by the earlier Fathers. Revelation is one such book, and III John another. According to Merrill C. Tenney, these two books were not clearly quoted or alluded to as definitely canonical until about A.D. 170.[22] The first unquestioned listing of II Peter as canonical did not occur until A.D. 367, although there is other evidence for its authenticity from a much earlier date.[23] Succeeding generations had only the writings of their forebears to which they could turn for information as to whether or not a book enjoyed an *initial acceptance.* If this evidence were scant or lacking, the book was doubted until, of its own intrinsic

---

[18]*Can I Trust My Bible?* a symposium, p. 69.
[19]He accepted a revised Luke and ten of Paul's epistles, but not the Pastorals.
[20]See Edward J. Young, "The Canon of the Old Testament" in Carl F. H. Henry (ed.), *Revelation and the Bible,* pp. 157, 168.
[21]See chap. 15.
[22]Merrill C. Tenney, *New Testament Survey,* p. 430.
[23]See chap. 15.

weight, and by virtue of other essential characteristics, it over-powered the objections and was given rightful recognition as a part of the canon of Holy Scripture.

THE PROCEDURE USED

Lest the impression be gained that these five principles were explicitly and mechanically put into operation by some specially appointed committee of Church Fathers commissioned to discover which books were inspired, a few words of explanation are needed. Just how did these principles operate in the history and consciousness of the early Christian church?

Some only implicitly present. It should be apparent that all of the earmarks of inspiration are necessary to demonstrate the canonicity of each book. At least none of them can be essentially lacking, even though they may not be conspicuously present. All of the five characteristics must be at least *implicitly* present, even though some of them are more dominant than others. For example, the dynamic ability is more obvious in the New Testament Epistles than in the Historical Books of the Old Testament, and the authoritative nature of the Prophets is more apparent than the Poetry. This is not to say that there is not an implicit "thus saith the Lord" in the Poetry, nor a dynamic in the redemptive history of the Old Testament. It does mean, however, that the Fathers did not always have in operation all of these principles in an explicit fashion.

Some are more important than others. Furthermore, it should be noted that some earmarks of inspiration are more important than others, in that the presence of one implies another or is a key to others. For example, if a book is authoritative (i.e., if it is from God), then it will be dynamic. That is, if it is from God, it will be accompanied with the transforming power of God. In fact, when authority was unmistakably present, the other characteristics of inspiration were automatically assumed to be present also. So it was that with regard to the New Testament books, the proof of Apostolicity (its prophetic nature) was often considered a virtual certainty of inspiration.[24] In addition, if the first three tests (is the book authoritative, prophetic and authentic?) could be verified explicitly, it was conceded that this was sufficient to establish that the book was canonical. Generally speaking, then, the Church Fathers were only explicitly concerned with authority, apostolicity and authenticity. The

[24]Benjamin B. Warfield, *The Inspiration and Authority of the Bible*, p. 415.

edificational earmark and the universal acceptance of a book were then implicitly assumed unless there was some doubt cast on the latter two which forced a reexamination of the former three tests for canonicity, as was the case with some of the Antilegomena (e.g., II Peter and II John). But even in these cases the positive evidence for the first three principles emerged victoriously over the supposed negative evidence on the latter two.

The witness of the Holy Spirit. The recognition of canonicity was not a mere mechanical matter settled by a synod or ecclesiastical council. It was a providential process directed by the Spirit of God as He witnessed to the church about the reality of the Word of God. Man of himself could not identify the Word of God, but the Holy Spirit opened the eyes of their understanding so that they could recognize God's Word. Jesus said, "My sheep hear my voice" (John 10:27). This is not to say that in some mystical way the testimony of the Holy Spirit in the hearts of believers settled the question of canonicity. The witness of the Spirit only established the reality of the canon, not its extent or limits.[25] The canon was established by a twofold method of faith and science. Objective principles were used, but the subjective testimony of the Holy Spirit was in operation, confirming the reality of God's Word to His people. In the providence of God, the principles were used to determine the extent of the canon, while the Holy Spirit gave assurance as to the reality of its essential message. The tests for canonicity were not mechanical means for measuring out the amount of inspired literature, nor did the Holy Spirit say, "This book or passage is inspired, that one is not." This would be a revelation, not an illumination. The Holy Spirit neither witnessed to the exact extent of the canon nor settled the matters of textual criticism. He did providentially guide the process which gave assent to the limits of the canon as well as give witness to the people of God as to the reality of God's Word wherever they read or heard it.

SUMMARY AND CONCLUSION

The most important distinction to be made at this point is between the *determination* and the *discovery* of canonicity. God is solely responsible for the first, and man is merely responsible for the last. *That* a book is canonical is due to *divine inspiration. How* this is known to be true is the process of *human recognition.* How men *dis-*

[25]Bernard Ramm, *The Witness of the Spirit,* pp. 93 ff.

covered what God had *determined* was by looking for the "earmarks of inspiration," which are the (1) authoritative, (2) prophetic, (3) authentic, (4) dynamic, and (5) accepted nature of the books. That is, it was asked whether the book (1) came with the *authority of God*, (2) *was written by a man of God*, (3) *told the truth* about God, man, etc., (4) came with the *power of God*, and (5) was *accepted by the people of God*. If a book clearly had the first earmark, the remainder were often assumed. The first three were used *explicitly* on most books, while the last two were usually applied *implicitly* only. It was by this procedure that the early Fathers sorted out the profusion of religious literature, discovered, and gave official recognition to the books that, by virtue of their divine inspiration, had been determined by God as canonical.

12

DEVELOPMENT AND HISTORY OF THE OLD TESTAMENT CANON

The fact *that* the canon developed is indisputable, but *how* it developed and *when* it was completed is a matter which must also be considered. Although inspiration determines canonicity, men are actively involved in the recognition of the canon. This process of recognition is a historical study; hence a review of the development of the Old Testament canon is presently in order.

PRELIMINARY CONSIDERATIONS

Much of the historical data necessary to provide a complete picture of the process of the canonization of the Old Testament is lost in the mists of antiquity. Enough information is available, however, to give a general overview of the development of the Hebrew canon.

THE THREE STEPS

The principles operative in the historical process of canonization are three: (1) inspiration by God; (2) recognition by men of God; and (3) collection and preservation of the books by the people of God.

Inspiration by God. As the previous discussion reveals (see chap. 10), God took the first step in canonization when He inspired the books. Thus, the simple answer to the question as to why there are only thirty-nine books in the Old Testament canon is that these are all that God inspired. Obviously, if God did not inspire and thus give divine authority to a book, no council of men could ever do it.

Recognition by men of God. Once God gave a book its authority, men of God gave assent to that authority by their recognition of it as a prophetic utterance. There is every reason to believe that this recognition followed immediately upon the publication of the message. As Edward J. Young states, "There is no evidence that these particular books existed among the ancient Jews for many years before

148

they were recognized as canonical. Indeed, if a book was actually revealed by God, is it conceivable that such a book would circulate for many years before anyone recognized its true nature?"[1] The evidence, in fact, is to the contrary. Moses' writings were received in his day (Exodus 24:3; Joshua 1:8), and Daniel, a contemporary of Jeremiah, had received the latter's book along with "*the* books" (Dan. 9:2).

Collection and preservation by the people of God. Moses' books were collected and preserved beside the ark (Deut. 31:26). "Samuel told the people the rights and duties of the kingship; and he wrote them in a book [literally, *the* book] and laid it up before the LORD" (I Sam. 10:25). Daniel had a collection of "the books" and there is every indication throughout the Old Testament that it was the rule to collect prophetic writings. During Josiah's day, the "law of Moses" was "found in the house of the LORD" (II Kings 23:24) where it had been stored. Proverbs 25:1 notes that "these . . . are the proverbs of Solomon which the men of Hezekiah king of Judah copied." Ezra the priest had preserved a copy of "the law of Moses" which he brought with him out of Babylon after the captivity (Ezra 7:6). Therefore, inspiration produced the canonical books, while subsequent recognition and collection preserved them for posterity.

TWO DISTINCTIONS

Two other factors are to be kept in mind in the history of the Old Testament canon.

Distinction between canon and other literature. A distinction must be made between the formal canon and Hebrew religious literature, such as the Book of Jasher (Joshua 10:13); the Book of the Wars of the Lord (Num. 21:14); the Visions of Iddo the Seer (II Chron. 9:29); the Book of the Acts of Solomon (I Kings 11:41) and many others.[2] Most of these books were part of Hebrew religious literature, but were never a part of their theological canon, the formal canon. There was evidently a profusion of religious lore in Hebrew, as is evident from the many noncanonical books (see chap. 13), but these were not a part of the "Law and Prophets," the "Sacred Scriptures," considered to be divine and authoritative.

Immediate recognition did not guarantee subsequent recognition.

[1]See Carl F. H. Henry (ed.), "The Canon of the Old Testament," *Revelation and the Bible,* p. 163.

[2]Willis J. Beecher lists twenty-five extracanonical books mentioned in Chronicles alone in his article on "Chronicles," *The International Standard Bible Encyclopaedia,* rev. ed., I, 630.

History Of The Old Testament Canon

	NATIONAL EVENTS	CANONICAL BOOKS	PROBABLE HISTORY OF THE MANUSCRIPTS & COPIES
1500 B.C.			
1400 B.C.		ORIGINAL PENTATEUCH JOB? JOSHUA ADDED	ORIGINAL PENTATEUCH SCROLLS STORED BESIDE ARK
1300 B.C.			
1200 B.C.			
1100 B.C.	SHILOH DESTROYED BY PHILISTINES AND TABERNACLE MOVED		ORIGINAL SCROLLS DISPERSED AND NEW COPIES MADE (?)
1000 B.C.		JUDGES & RUTH ADDED DAVIDIC PSALMS WRITTEN	SAMUEL, DAVID and LEVITES DISTRIBUTE COPIES THROUGHOUT ISRAEL
900 B.C.		PROVERBS, ECCLESIASTES, SONG OF SOLOMON SAMUEL ADDED	COPIES BROUGHT TO NORTHERN KINGDOM DURING ELIJAH'S REFORM?
800 B.C.		OBADIAH JOEL	
700 B.C.	ASSYRIANS CAPTURE SAMARIA	JONAH AMOS HOSEA MICAH ISAIAH	KINGS WRITTEN BY A SUCCESSION OF PROPHETS AND COLLECTED AND EDITED BY JEREMIAH (?) COPIES OBTAINED BY PRIEST AT ORDER OF SARGON II (II Kings 17:27-28)?
600 B.C.	EZEKIEL, ETC. TAKEN CAPTIVE JERUSALEM DESTROYED	NAHUM HABAKKUK ZEPHANIAH EZEKIEL JEREMIAH, LAM. KINGS	BOOK OF THE LAW RECOVERED IN THE TEMPLE COPIES BROUGHT TO THE PEOPLE FROM JERUSALEM DURING JOSIAH'S REFORM (II Chron 34:6–9, 21)?
500 B.C.	CYRUS CAPTURES BABYLON TEMPLE REBUILT	DANIEL HAGGAI, ZECHARIAH ADDED	
400 B.C.	EZRA RETURNS TO JERUSALEM	ESTHER, EZRA, CHRONICLES NEHEMIAH ADDED MALACHI ADDED	COPIES TAKEN TO SAMARIA AT TIME OF NEHEMIAH'S EXCLUSION (NEH. 13:28–30)?

Chart by JOHN REA

Another consideration is that immediate recognition of a book as inspired did not thereby guarantee subsequent recognition by all, as will become apparent from the debate over certain books among later Jews. In fact, there may have been an initial recognition and then, after a time lapse, subsequent doubts before a final confirmation. This is apparently what did happen with some books, for example, Ecclesiastes and the Song of Solomon. In reality, the problems of *transportation, transmission* (making copies) and sometimes even *translation* tended to slow down the final and universal confirmation of canonicity. As a case in point, parts of Daniel and Ezra were written in foreign languages, and this fact may account in part for their problem of retaining a place among the Prophets in the Hebrew canon.

PROGRESSIVE COLLECTION OF THE CANON

The standard critical theory has been that the books of the Hebrew Scriptures were canonized in three stages, according to their dates of composition, into the Law (*c.* 400 B.C.), Prophets (*c.* 200 B.C.), and Writings (*c.* A.D. 100).[3] However, this view is untenable in light of the fact that the complete canon, even with a threefold description, is known to have existed much earlier than A.D. 100, and possibly as early as 200 B.C. (see chap. 1). In fact, Jesus and Josephus both alluded to a threefold division of the Hebrew canon before A.D. 100. Furthermore, there is evidence that inspired books were added immediately to the canon as they were written.

The Law of Moses

Historically, Moses wrote first, so his books were the first to be recognized as canonical, and the constant reference to Moses' law by almost every canonical book after Moses' day demonstrates that Moses' law was immediately received as authoritative and continuously recognized as such.

Joshua. The Lord enjoined "the book of the law" to Joshua (Joshua 1:8), "which Moses . . . commanded" (Joshua 1:7) unto the people of his day (cf. also Joshua 8:31; 23:6).

David. David charged Solomon to keep the statutes, commandments, ordinances and testimonies that were "written in the law of Moses" (I Kings 2:3).

Solomon. Solomon, at the dedication of the temple, urged the peo-

[3]See Franz Buhl, *The Canon and Text of the Old Testament.*

ple, saying, "Let your heart therefore be wholly true to the Lord your God, walking in his statutes and keeping his commandments" (I Kings 8:61), which he had previously identified as the works of Moses (cf. vv. 53, 56).

Amaziah. It is written of King Amaziah that he acted not "according to what is written in the book of the law of Moses" (II Kings 14:6).

Manasseh. The wicked Manasseh did not live "according to all the law that . . . Moses commanded" (II Kings 21:8).

Josiah. Josiah turned to the Lord "with all his soul and with all his might, according to all the law of Moses" (II Kings 23:25).

Asa. In Asa's day Judah was commanded "to keep the law and the commandments" (II Chron. 14:4).

Jehoshaphat. During Jehoshaphat's reign the priests "taught in Judah, having the book of the law of the Lord with them" (II Chron. 17:9).

Jeremiah-Daniel. Around the time of the Babylonian exile, Jeremiah referred to "the law of the Lord" (Jer. 8:8). Daniel made reference to "the curse and the oath which are written in the law of Moses" (Dan. 9:11; cf. 9:13).

Ezra. In Ezra's time, the Levitical system was reinstituted "as it is written in the book of Moses" (Ezra 6:18).

Nehemiah. In Nehemiah's day, the priests "read from the book of Moses in the hearing of the people" (Neh. 13:1).

Malachi. Malachi, the last Old Testament prophet, admonished the people to "remember the law of my servant Moses, the statutes and ordinances that I commanded him at Horeb for all Israel" (Mal. 4:4).

From these passages, and others like them, it can readily be seen that the rest of the Old Testament after Moses considered his writings to be canonical.

The Prophets

The most common designation for the rest of the Old Testament is "the Prophets." This title, combined with "the Law," occurs about a dozen times in the New Testament (cf. Matt. 5:17; 7:12; Luke 24:27), whereas a threefold breakdown is suggested only once (Luke 24:44).

The character of a prophet. According to Ezekiel 13:9, it would seem that a true prophet was one who with his writings was "enrolled in the register of the house of Israel." It is specifically said that Joshua (Joshua 24:26) and Samuel (I Sam. 10:25) added writings to the official list.

In the general sense of the word, all of the books of the Old Testament were written by "prophets." Moses was a prophet according to Deuteronomy 18:15 and Hosea 12:13; Daniel and David are called prophets in the New Testament (Matt. 24:15; Acts 2:30). And, if the word "prophet" is broadly defined as one who receives and relates a revelation from God, King David is certainly to be regarded as a prophet, because he received a revelation "made clear by the writing from the hand of the LORD" (I Chron. 28:19). Even Solomon was a prophet, since God revealed the future to him (I Kings 3:13-14).

A priest could be a prophet (cf. Ezek. 2:2-5), as could a prince (cf. Dan. 1:3, 7). One did not have to belong to the "School of the Prophets" (I Sam. 19:20) or to be a "son of a prophet" (i.e., as student or apprentice of a prophet as Elisha was to Elijah, cf. II Kings 2:12) to be a prophet, as the testimony of Amos confirms (Amos 7:14). In this broad sense of the word "prophet," then, all of the Old Testament writers, including men from Moses the lawgiver to Amos the vinedresser, were prophets.

The continuity of the prophets. A prophet was one who spoke for God, and it was this characteristic which bound together the ministry of the prophets from Moses to Malachi. The succession of prophets produced both the substance and the structure of the Sacred Scriptures. The books of Chronicles, for instance, bear an unusual testimony to this fact, as the following survey indicates:

1. The history of David was written by Samuel, Nathan and Gad (I Chron. 29:29).

2. The history of Solomon was recorded by Nathan, Ahijah and Iddo (II Chron. 9:29).

3. The acts of Rehoboam were written by Shemaiah and Iddo (II Chron. 12:15).

4. The history of Abijah was added by Iddo (II Chron. 13:22).

5. Jehoshaphat's story was recorded by Jehu the prophet (II Chron. 20:34).

6. Hezekiah's story was told by Isaiah (II Chron. 32:32).

7. Manasseh's life story was recorded by unnamed seers (II Chron. 33:19).

8. The other kings had their histories recorded in other books (II Chron. 35:27).

To this list of writing prophets Jeremiah may be added, for his writings were added to theirs and the entire collection was designated "the books" by Daniel (Dan. 9:2).[4]

R. Laird Harris says:

> This continuity of writing prophets may be the solution to the problem of how Moses and Joshua could have written the accounts of their own death in historical narratives (cf. Deut. 34, Josh. 24). Each book completes the preceding and links the prophetic history together. Ruth was originally appended to Judges, and the genealogy of Ruth may have been added after David's rise to power in order to link it to Samuel and the Kings, which are a unit. Likewise, the last chapter of Kings parallels the material of Jeremiah 52, 39, 40, and 41. Similarly, the book of Chronicles ends with the same two verses that the Ezra-Nehemiah unit begins.[5]

In other words, the prophets undoubtedly recorded a continuous sacred history, tying their books together into a canonical unit as they were individually written. This practice of connecting books or documents by a footnote or statement is known as the "colophon principle" and also was used in nonbiblical writings.[6]

The completion of the Prophets. The continuity of the prophetic writings ended with Malachi. Several lines of evidence support this assertion:

1. There are intimations in some of the postexilic prophets that the next revelation from God would be just before the coming of Messiah (Mal. 4:5), and that there would be no true prophets in the intervening period (Zech. 13:2-5).

2. Furthermore, there is confirmation from the intertestamental period that there were indeed no more prophets after Malachi. In the Maccabean period, the people were waiting "until a prophet should arise" (I Mac. 4:45; 9:27; 14:41). *The Manual of Discipline* from the Qumran community (B.C.) also looked for the "coming of a prophet."[7]

---

[4]See R. Laird Harris, *Inspiration and Canonicity of the Bible*, p. 166.
[5]*Ibid.*, p. 168.
[6]See Alexander Heidel, *The Babylonian Genesis*, 2d ed., pp. 25 ff.
[7]1QS, *The Manual of Discipline*, trans. P. Wernberg-Moller, IX, 11.

3. Verification of this view also comes from Josephus;[8] the Talmud, which states, "After the latter prophets Haggai, Zechariah, and Malachi, the Holy Spirit departed from Israel";[9] and from the New Testament, which never quotes a post-Malachi book as canonical, and uses the expression "from . . . Abel to . . . Zechariah" (Matt. 23:35), which encompasses only the books from Genesis to II Chronicles, the last book in the Jewish arrangement of the Hebrew Old Testament (see chap. 6). Harris summarizes this view well when he says, "The chain of prophets evidently wrote a chain of histories from Genesis through Nehemiah, and the writings of these prophets were accepted, one by one, through the centuries, until, when the Spirit of Prophecy departed from Israel, the canon was complete."[10]

The Writings

Some books of the Prophets did not fit neatly into the continual sequence of the history of the prophets, such as the "four books of hymns and the precepts for human conduct" mentioned by Josephus.[11] This apparently led to a very early (at least by 200 B.C., and perhaps earlier) categorization of books into the later widely accepted threefold division of Law, Prophets and Writings. The earliest mention of a third group of books is in the "Prologue to Ecclesiasticus" (c. 132 B.C.), but it does not enumerate the books. Josephus (A.D. 37-100) is more explicit, saying that there were only four books in the third section.[12] No doubt he considered Esther to be with the other prophetic histories, whereas Ruth and Lamentations were counted with Judges and Jeremiah respectively, which accounts for his numbering twenty-two books in the Hebrew canon. This would also mean that Daniel was listed with the prophets.[13] Whatever the origin or status of the threefold division, the Septuagint (LXX) (c. 250 B.C.) felt no compunction whatever to follow it. Hence, it would seem best to agree with Robert Dick Wilson and R. Laird Harris that, so far as *canonization* is concerned, there were only two groups of books: the Law (five books) and the Prophets (seventeen books).[14]

[8]Josephus, *Against Apion*, I:8.
[9]Michael L. Rodkinson, Tractate "Sanhedrin," *Babylonian Talmud*, VII-VIII, 24.
[10]Harris, pp. 168-69.
[11]Josephus, *ibid*.
[12]These books were undoubtedly Job, Psalms, Proverbs and Ecclesiastes.
[13]See Harris, p. 140.
[14]Harris has modified his earlier view and now would permit an early threefold division, perhaps as a variant practice: "Was the Law and the Prophets Two-Thirds of the Old Testament Canon?" *Bulletin of Evangelical Theological Society*, Vol. IX, No. 4 (Fall, 1966), p. 170.

Having said this, it must also be admitted that there was an early (perhaps by 200 B.C.) *categorization* of books into three groups: the Law, the Prophets and the Writings. The reason for this is not altogether clear.

1. One possible explanation for this situation is that, because of the later distinction between men who held the prophetic office and those who had only the prophetic gift—and the resultant division of the canon into the Law, written by the lawgiver; the Prophets, written by prophets, and the Writings, written by nonprophets— there was a very early tendency to make this same distinction. Perhaps this would help explain why some of the books, for example, Ecclesiastes and Song of Solomon, were later disputed (see chap. 13).

2. It may have been felt by some, at a later date, that the books in the third category, that is, those not written by prophets, were not fully canonical, and thus not to be placed in the same section with the writings of the prophets.

3. Or, it may have been thought that the topical and festal significance of the books (e.g., the Five Rolls were read at the five annual feasts) served a more practical purpose when they were removed from the category of prophetic writings for liturgical reasons.

Whatever the reason for the later threefold *categorization*, it must be remembered that *canonization* was on a twofold basis: the Law and the Prophets. These divisions actually included all of the same books that were later given a threefold division in some circles, and which finally gained general acceptance among Jews by (or before) the fourth century A.D.

PRACTICAL CONFIRMATION

Historical data by which a complete picture of the development of the Old Testament canon may be traced is currently lacking. Nevertheless, important historical facts that serve as checkpoints in the overall process are available. To this material the present study now turns.

Confirmation of the Threefold Categorization

Even though the Old Testament Scriptures were apparently not

3. *Thus far all Old Testament books except Esther have been represented in the Dead Sea Scrolls. Here small Dead Sea Scroll fragments are under the scrutiny of scholars (Palestine Archaeological Museum)*

canonized in three groups and/or stages, there is early and continual evidence of this tendency to categorize the canonical books.

Prologue to Ecclesiasticus. Possibly the earliest reference is in the "Prologue to Ecclesiasticus" (*c.* 132 B.C.), which may refer to the use of a threefold division of the Old Testament by the writer's grandfather (*c.* 200 B.C.).

Jesus Christ. Jesus Himself on one occasion used a threefold division of the Old Testament (Luke 24:44), although He usually used the twofold classification (cf. Luke 24:27, where He speaks on the same subject, viz., Himself revealed in the Old Testament).

Philo. Just after the time of Christ (*c.* A.D. 40), Philo witnessed to a threefold division, making reference to the Law, the Prophets (or Prophecies), and "hymns and the others which foster and perfect knowledge and piety."[15]

[15]Philo, *De Vita Contemplativa*, III, 25. See F. H. Colson's translation of *The Contemplative Life* in *Philo*, p. 127: "In each house there is a consecrated room which is called a sanctuary or closet and closeted in this they are initiated into the mysteries of the sanctified life. They take nothing into it, either drink or food or any other of the things necessary for the needs of the body, but [1] laws and [2] oracles delivered through the mouth of prophets, [3] and psalms and anything else which fosters and perfects knowledge and piety."

Josephus. Josephus attested to the same divisions at about the same time (*c.* A.D. 37-100), and explicitly stated that the third section was made up of "hymns to God" and "precepts for the conduct of human life."[16]

Babylonian Talmud. By, or before, the fourth century A.D., the Babylonian Talmud gave the modern threefold division of Law (five books), Prophets (eight books), and Writings (eleven books). Thus, the tendency to categorize the canon into three divisions, which possibly began as early as 200 B.C., triumphed in its ultimate form before A.D. 400. This fact may be further confirmed at other checkpoints in the history of the Hebrew canon between these terminals.

Confirmation of the Twofold Canonization

The Talmudic tractate "Baba-Bathra" (14*b*-15*a*) refers to "the men of the Great Synagogue" (400 B.C. ff.). The tradition of the Great Synagogue is that of those Jewish scholars (fifth to third centuries B.C.) who followed Ezra in the exposition of the Law (cf. Neh. 9-10). It is believed that they formed an assembly which was responsible for the recognition and preservation of the Old Testament canon.[17] There are several lines of evidence that support the contention that they classified and recognized the Old Testament canon as a twofold division of Law and Prophets.

Old Testament links them together. First of all, as indicated above, the historical books of the Old Testament give evidence that they have been linked together as a prophetic unity from the time of Moses to Nehemiah.

Repeated use of "Law and Prophets." There is also the repeated use of the description "Law and Prophets" in the New Testament, a common Talmudic phrase, as well as the one used in the Maccabean period (cf. II Macc. 15:9) and by the Dead Sea community at Qumran.[18]

Acknowledgment in Daniel. Then too, there is the acknowledgment in the Old Testament book of Daniel of the "law of Moses" (Dan. 9:11, 13) as well as a group called "the books" (Dan. 9:2). The postexilic prophet, Zechariah, refers to the "former prophets" (Zech. 1:4; 7:7, 12), which also attests to a line of prophetic utterances.

---

[16]Josephus, I:8.
[17]See the Talmudic tractate "Pirke Aboth" ("Sayings of the Fathers") in *Living Talmud,* selected and translated by Judah Goldin, pp. 43 ff., which traces this tradition of the Great Synagogue.
[18]IQS, *The Manual of Discipline,* I, 3; VIII, 15; IX, 11.

Acknowledgment by succeeding prophets. The acid test, however, of this view of a gradually developing canon is the acknowledgment by succeeding prophets of the existence and/or authority of preceding prophetic utterances. For, if there were a gradually developing canon to which inspired books were added as they were written (presumably without a long delay), it is reasonable to expect not only continuity between the books but some recognition of the existence of the former books by the latter writers.

A survey of important Old Testament passages is sufficient to confirm this general thesis.

1. That the law of Moses was recognized and utilized by subsequent prophetic books is most evident from Joshua 1:7 to Malachi 4:4 (see above). There can be no doubt that all of the latter prophets stood in continuity with, and in dependence upon, the great prophet and lawgiver, Moses. There is a constant reechoing of his truth, and hearkening back to his precepts throughout the remaining pages of the Old Testament. Only the critical schools, which consider the Pentateuch to be a mosaic (a piece of literature from varied sources put together by redactors) rather than Mosaic, could possibly fail to see that a great prophet lived, taught and wrote a law that was reflected by other prophets of his nation for about a millennium after him.

2. The crucial question for consequent consideration is whether or not there is evidence of prophets since Moses' time who are in continuity with and/or have a recognition of the other biblical prophets that precede them. A mere glance at any good cross-reference Bible or concordance will reveal that such evidence is widely manifest in the historical books.

    a. Both Joshua and events in the book by his name are referred to by the book of Judges (1:1, 20, 21; 2:8).

    b. Ruth, originally appended to Judges, refers to "the days when the judges ruled" (1:1).

    c. The book of I Samuel continues the history of Israel after Judges, and II Samuel formed a unit with I Samuel in the Hebrew canon.

    d. Both I and II Kings (one book in the Hebrew canon) refer to the "law of Moses" (II Kings 14:6), and repeatedly speak of David as his life is told in I and II Samuel (I Kings 3:14; 5:7; 8:16; 9:5).

e. The books of I and II Chronicles, which give a parallel history to Samuel and Kings, likewise allude to former events. In fact, genealogies are traced all the way from the book of Genesis (I Chron. 1), including the one which is recorded only in Ruth (I Chron. 2:12-13).

f. Ezra-Nehemiah begin with the same two verses that close II Chronicles (36:22-23), refer to the "law of Moses" (Ezra 3:2; Neh. 13:1), and review Israel's entire history as it is recorded from Genesis through the captivity and restoration (Neh. 9).

3. The remainder of the Old Testament provides the final aspect of the "acid test" of the twofold canonical thesis. What is the evidence that these prophetical and poetical books were recognized and accepted into the canon soon after they were written?

a. The date of the writing of the book of Job is uncertain, but there is good evidence that the events in the book refer back to pre-Mosaic times, and there are striking similarities to the Pentateuch.[19] Ezekiel is the first to mention Job directly (14:14, 20), a fact which substantiates the existence of the book of Job by his day.

b. Parts of Psalms also occur in the historical books (cf. II Sam. 22; I Chron. 16). There is also the acknowledged fact that David spoke by the Holy Spirit (II Sam. 23:2).

c. The Solomonic writings (Song of Solomon, Proverbs, Ecclesiastes) are most likely included as part of the list in I Kings 4:32, namely, "He . . . uttered three thousand proverbs; and his songs were a thousand and five."

d. Many of the prophets also quote from or refer to the inspired writings of their predecessors. Daniel had a collection that he called "the books," which apparently included books from Moses (Dan. 9:13) to his contemporary, Jeremiah (Dan. 9:2), and "the prophets" in between, who had spoken to the kings, princes, fathers, and all the people of the land (Dan. 9:6). Jeremiah 26:18 quotes Micah 3:12, and Micah 4:1-3 quotes Isaiah 2:2-4 (or vice versa). There is also a dependence between Isaiah 2:4 and Joel 3:10; between Joel 3:16 and Amos 1:2; Obadiah 17*a* and Joel 2:32*b*, and many other instances. The prophets reflect a clear knowledge of Psalms; Jonah 2:2-9, for example, is filled with references from Psalms. Jonah 2:3, "All thy waves and thy billows passed over me," is from Psalm 42:7. Jonah 2:4 reflects a

[19]See "Introduction to the Book of Job," *Ellicott's Commentary*, IV, 4-5.

knowledge of Psalm 5:7, "I will worship toward thy holy temple" (cf. also Jonah 2:5 with Ps. 18:4-6).

It could not be expected that every book of the Old Testament would be referred to by succeeding prophets; the New Testament as a whole does not refer to every book in the Old Testament. However, there is substantial evidence to support the concept of *a growing canon:* books that were written by a man of God, came with the power of God, and told the truth about God, were *then and there* received by the people into the canon and preserved.

SUMMARY AND CONCLUSION

There are three steps to canonization: (1) inspiration by God; (2) recognition by men of God; and (3) collection and preservation by the people of God. This process of canonization is not to be confused with the collection of other religious writings. The history of the canon indicates a gradual development of the collection of prophetic books which were added continually to the Law as they were written.

The Old Testament canon was probably completed about 400 B.C., and perhaps by about 200 B.C., the twenty-two books that had undergone this process of canonization began to assume a threefold categorization: the Law, the Prophets and the Writings. One reason suggested is that they were eventually separated on the basis of whether the writer was *officially* a prophet, or whether he was a priest, prince or king through whom God had given a prophetic utterance. Another suggestion is that a third division may have been created for liturgical reasons (to fit their festal year).

Whatever the reason for a threefold categorization, there are several lines of evidence to support the view that the Old Testament was originally canonized into the twofold division of the Law (five books) and the Prophets (seventeen books): (1) the way in which the historical books are linked together into a unit; (2) the most common New Testament designation of the Old Testament, "Law and Prophets"; (3) the reference in Daniel to the Law and "the books" (9:2); and (4) the recognition of the "Former" prophetic books by the "Latter." Nevertheless, because of the early tendency to separate the Prophets into two groups, the final form of the Hebrew canon became threefold: the Law, the Prophets and the Writings.

13

THE OLD TESTAMENT APOCRYPHA AND PSEUDEPIGRAPHA

Once the "What?" (nature) and the "How?" (history) of the canon have been considered, the question "Which?" (extent of the canon) demands attention. Historically, the *number* of books in the canon has vied for polemic honors with the question of the *nature* of the canon. To borrow the terminology of the New Testament Fathers, the books of the Hebrew canon may be divided into four groups: (1) those accepted as canonical by virtually everyone, called Homologoumena (one word, agreement); (2) those which at one time or another have been disputed by some of the Fathers, called Antilegomena (spoken against); (3) those which were rejected by virtually everyone, called Pseudepigrapha (false writings, spurious); and (4) those which were accepted by some, called Apocrypha (hidden, secret). Each of these various classifications requires individual treatment.

THE BOOKS ACCEPTED BY ALL—HOMOLOGOUMENA

THE NATURE OF THE HOMOLOGOUMENA

The Homologoumena are books which once they were accepted into the canon were not subsequently questioned or disputed. They held a continual canonical status not only by early generations but by succeeding generations as well.

THE NUMBER OF THE HOMOLOGOUMENA

In all, the Homologoumena comprise thirty-four of the thirty-nine books in the English versions of the Protestant Old Testament. All of the Old Testament except the Antilegomena are in this body of books. That is, the Homologoumena include every book of the Protestant English Old Testament except Song of Solomon, Ecclesiastes, Esther, Ezekiel and Proverbs. Since the Homologoumena are not involved in the debate about the Old Testament, no space need be devoted to discussing them in this context. The question of the Antilegomena is important, however, and requires a more careful treatment.

THE BOOKS DISPUTED BY SOME—ANTILEGOMENA

The Nature of the Antilegomena

Several books which were generally, and ultimately, considered canonical were for one reason or another, at one time or another, disputed by some of the rabbis. Although this definition actually borrows the conclusion of the present section, these books classified as Antilegomena were originally accepted into the canon and were only subsequently disputed. To put it another way, these canonical books had their character and/or claims brought into question by later rabbis.

The Number of the Antilegomena

As has been stated, there are five books which fall into this category, and each one deserves individual treatment.

Song of Solomon. The basic reason that this book was challenged is that it seemed sensual to some. The school of Shammai expressed doubt about its canonicity, but eventually the view of Rabbi Akiba prevailed, when he said,

> God forbid!—No man in Israel ever disputed about the Song of Songs [that he should say] that it does not render the hands unclean [i.e., is not canonical], for all the ages are not worth the day on which the Song of Songs was given to Israel; for all the Writings are holy, but the Song of Songs is the Holy of Holies. And if aught was in dispute the dispute was about Ecclesiastes alone.[1]

However, as Rowley observes, the very fact that such a statement was necessary implies that there was some doubt concerning it.[2] If these doubts centered in the alleged sensual character, they were based upon a misunderstanding. Nevertheless, it is entirely possible "that God has placed this Song in the canon in order to teach us the purity and the sanctity of that estate of marriage which He Himself has established."[3] Whatever questions may arise about the interpre-

---

[1] Herbert Danby, *The Mishnah, Yadaim* 3:5, p. 782.
[2] H. H. Rowley, "The Interpretation of the Song of Songs," *Journal of Theological Studies*, XXXVIII (1937), pp. 337-63.
[3] Edward J. Young, *An Introduction to the Old Testament*, p. 355.

tation of the Song, there ought to be none about its inspiration and subsequent canonization.

Ecclesiastes. One of the main objections to this book was that it seemed skeptical. Some have called it the "Song of Skepticism."[4] Rabbi Akiba admitted that "if aught was in dispute [about Song of Solomon and Ecclesiastes] the dispute was about Ecclesiastes alone."[5] However, there is no necessity to come to this conclusion about the book. Ecclesiastes itself comes to a spiritual conclusion: "Fear God, and keep his commandments; for this is the whole duty of man" (12:13). There may be some doubt about man "under the sun," but there need be none about the ultimate teaching of the book, which goes "above and beyond the sun."

Esther. Because of the conspicuous absence of the name of God, this book encountered some difficulty in retaining its position in the Hebrew canon. The basis of challenge lay in the fact that the book seemed to be unspiritual. The basic question asked was: How can the book be God's Word when it does not even mention God's name? There are two possible explanations for this phenomenon which merit mention at this point. Some have suggested that since the Jews of the Persian exile "were no longer in the Theocratic line, so to speak, the *Name* of the covenant God is not associated with them."[6] Others have thought the omission of God's name to be an intentional one, to protect it from pagan plagiarization and the substitution for it of the name of a heathen god. In support of this contention is the observation of W. G. Scroggie, who indicated that the name of Jehovah (YHWH) may be seen four times in acrostic form in the book, in such a way and in such places that would place it beyond the realm of mere probability.[7] In any event, the absence of God's name is more than compensated for by the presence of His power and grace in the deliverance of His people, a fact which gives canonical worth to the book.

Ezekiel. This book was questioned by some because of its apparent anti-Mosaical teachings. The school of Shammai thought that the teaching of the book was not in harmony with the Mosaic law, and that the first ten chapters exhibited a tendency toward Gnosti-

[4] As cited in Herbert Carl Leupold, *Exposition of Ecclesiastes*, p. 19.
[5] Danby, p. 782; also see discussion in Young, p. 355.
[6] Young, p. 378.
[7] W. Graham Scroggie, *Know Your Bible*, Vol. I: *The Old Testament*, p. 96. The Jewish scholars did not doubt the canonicity of the Song of Solomon on the same grounds, for while no name or term for God appears in an English translation of the Song of Solomon, the Hebrew name for God, *Yah*, occurs at the end of 8:6.

cism.[8] However, no specific examples have been supplied which do in fact contradict the Torah. If there were actual contradictions, then of course the book could not be considered canonical. Hence, as in the case of the other disputed books, the arguments were centered about interpretation rather than inspiration.

Proverbs. The disputation over this book was based on the grounds that it is illogical (contradictory within itself). This charge is very clear in the Talmud, which states, "The book of Proverbs also they sought to hide, because its words contradicted one to another."[9] The supposed contradiction is found in Proverbs 26:4-5, where the exhortation is both to "answer a fool according to his folly" and not to do so. However, as the rabbis have observed, the obvious meaning intended is that there are occasions when a fool should be answered and others when he should not. Since the statements are in successive verses and in couplet form, it would appear that they carry an implicit impact similar to the current expression, "On the one hand— and on the other hand." In any event, the remainder of the verses give different reasons for the two kinds of advice, respectively; and, as a result, there is no contradiction to stand in the way of canonicity.

THE BOOKS REJECTED BY ALL—PSEUDEPIGRAPHA

There are a vast number of false and spurious writings which deserve mention at this point; not because anyone would seriously contend for their authority, but because they do represent the religious lore of the Hebrews in the intertestamental period. Strangely enough, the New Testament writers make use of a number of the books, for example, Jude 14-15 have a possible quotation from the Book of Enoch (1:9) and the Assumption of Moses (1:9); and an allusion from the Penitence of Jannes and Jambres is found in II Timothy 3:8. Of course, it should be remembered that the New Testament also quotes from the heathen poets Aratus (Acts 17:28); Menander (I Cor. 15:33); and Epimenides (Titus 1:12).[10] Truth is truth no matter where it is found, whether uttered by a heathen poet, a pagan prophet (Num. 24:17), or even a dumb animal (Num. 22:28). Nevertheless, it should be noted that no such formula as "it is written" or "the Scriptures say" is connected with these citations. It should also be noted that neither the New Testament writers nor the Fathers have considered these writings canonical.

[8]Young, p. 257.
[9]Tractate "Shabbath," 30b, Talmud, as cited in Young, p. 332.
[10]William H. Green, *General Introduction to the Old Testament: The Canon*, pp. 146 ff.

The Nature of the Pseudepigrapha

The Pseudepigrapha books are those books which are distinctly spurious and unauthentic in their overall content. While they claim to have been written by biblical authors, they actually express religious fancy and magic from the period between about 200 B.C. and A.D. 200. In Roman Catholic circles these books are known as the Apocrypha, a term not to be confused with an entirely different set of books known in Protestant circles by the same name (see below); although at times Protestants have referred to these same books as the "wider Apocrypha," or "Apocalyptic Literature." Most of these books are comprised of dreams, visions and revelations in the apocalyptic style of Ezekiel, Daniel and Zechariah. An outstanding characteristic of these books is that they depict the bright future of the Messianic kingdom, as well as the questions of creation, angels, sin, suffering and rewards for faithful living.

The Number of the Pseudepigrapha

The actual number of these books is not known certainly, and various writers have given different numbers of important ones. There are eighteen worthy of mention,[11] and they may be classified as follows:

Legendary	1. The Book of Jubilee
	2. The Letter of Aristeas
	3. The Book of Adam and Eve
	4. The Martyrdom of Isaiah
Apocalyptic	1. I Enoch
	2. The Testament of the Twelve Patriarchs
	3. The Sibylline Oracle
	4. The Assumption of Moses
	5. II Enoch, or the Book of the Secrets of Enoch
	6. II Baruch, or The Syriac Apocalypse of Baruch
	7. III Baruch, or The Greek Apocalypse of Baruch
Didactical	1. III Maccabees
	2. IV Maccabees
	3. Pirke Aboth
	4. The Story of Ahikar
Poetical	1. The Psalms of Solomon
	2. Psalm 151
Historical	1. The Fragment of a Zadokite Work

[11]Seventeen are in Robert Henry Charles, *The Apocrypha and Pseudepigrapha of the Old Testament in English.* Psalm 151 may be found in *The Septuagint Version of the Old Testament.* A Hebrew copy of Psalm 151 was found at Qumran.

THE BOOKS ACCEPTED BY SOME—APOCRYPHA

Hovering more closely to the borders of the canon are the Apocryphal books.

The Meaning of "Apocrypha"

Part of the mystery that surrounds the "extra" books is involved in the meaning of their very name, Apocrypha.

Classical and Hellenistic Greek. The word Apocrypha was used to describe something "hard to understand," or "hidden."

Patristic Greek. Later the word was used with the connotation of "esoteric," that is, something understood only by the initiated, or those within the inner circle of believers.

Early Fathers. Some of the early Fathers, for example, Irenaeus and Jerome, were among the first to apply the word Apocrypha to the list of noncanonical books, including the Pseudepigrapha.

Post-Reformation. Since the time of the Reformation, the word Apocrypha has come to mean "Old Testament Apocrypha." The basic etymology of the word is clear, meaning "hidden." The disputation about the Apocrypha centers in the reason for its being so labeled. Is "hidden" to be used in a good sense, indicating that these books were hidden in order to be preserved, or in the sense that their message was deep and spiritual? Or, is the word "hidden" used in the bad sense, indicating that the books were of doubtful authenticity, spurious? In order to answer these questions, the individual books must be examined carefully.

The Mix-up About the Apocrypha—The Two Canons

The confusion in the present issue appears to center about the two canons: The Palestinian Canon (containing twenty-two books in Hebrew, thirty-nine in English) and the Alexandrian Canon (with the additional fourteen or fifteen books). The former is the Hebrew canon, which arose in Palestine and was accepted by the Jews. The latter is the Greek canon, which allegedly arose in Alexandria, Egypt, where the Hebrew Scriptures were translated into the Greek Septuagint (LXX) at about 250 B.C. and following.

It has been thought by some that there were actually two canons: a broader canon containing the Apocrypha, and a narrower one without it. This two-canon hypothesis is based on the fact that the earliest extant copies of the Greek Septuagint (LXX) (*c.* fourth century

4. *Skyline of Alexandria, where the Septuagint was produced (Egyptian State Tourist Administration)*

A.D.) contain some fifteen additional books, while the Hebrew Bible has only the familiar thirty-nine Old Testament books.

Arguments in favor of accepting the Alexandrian Canon. The Alexandrian Canon, as it is known by extant Greek manuscripts, has the following fourteen or fifteen additional books, commonly called Apocrypha, interwoven among the other thirty-nine books of the Old Testament (see chart on p. 169). Only eleven of these fourteen or fifteen books are accepted as canonical by the Roman Catholic Church, which includes all but I and II Esdras (which are called III and IV Esdras) and the Prayer of Manasseh. However, according to the numbering of books in the Douay Old Testament, only seven additional books are indicated, making the total forty-six. The reason for this is that Baruch and the Letter of Jeremiah were combined into one book, having six chapters; the additions to Esther were added at the end of the book of Esther; the Prayer of Azariah was inserted between the Hebrew Daniel 3:23 and 24, making it Daniel 3:24-90 in the Douay Version; Susanna was placed at the end of the book of Daniel (chap. 13); and Bel and the Dragon was attached as chapter 14 of Daniel. Because three of the fifteen books were rejected, the remaining twelve books were incorporated into eleven, and since four of these books were added to the existing Old Testament books, only seven extra books appear in the Douay Old Testament table of contents. Nonetheless, the Roman Catholic Church has actually added eleven (twelve if Baruch and the Letter of Jeremiah are separated) pieces of Apocryphal literature to the Hebrew canon, in contrast to the Protestants who followed the Hebrew canon.

Type of Book	Revised Standard Version	Douay
Didactic	1. The Wisdom of Solomon (c. 30 B.C.)	Book of Wisdom
	2. Ecclesiasticus (Sirach) (132 B.C.)	Ecclesiastes
Religious Romance	3. Tobit (c. 200 B.C.)	Tobias
	4. Judith (c. 150 B.C.)	Judith
Historic	5. I Esdras (c. 150-100 B.C.)	III Esdras*
	6. I Maccabees (c. 110 B.C.)	I Machabees
	7. II Maccabees (c. 110-70 B.C.)	II Machabees
Prophetic	8. Baruch (c. 150-50 B.C.)	Baruch chaps. 1-5
	9. Letter of Jeremiah (c. 300-100 B.C.)	Baruch chap. 6
	10. II Esdras (c. A.D. 100)	IV Esdras*
Legendary	11. Additions to Esther (140-130 B.C.)	Esther 10:4—16:24
	12. Prayer of Azariah (second or first century B.C.) (Song of Three Young Men)	Daniel 3:24-90
	13. Susanna (second or first century B.C.)	Daniel 13
	14. Bel and the Dragon (c. 100 B.C.)	Daniel 14
	15. Prayer of Manasseh (second or first century B.C.)	Prayer of Manasseh*

*Books not accepted as canonical at the Council of Trent, 1546.

The reasons generally advanced in favor of this broader Alexandrian Canon are as follows:

1. The New Testament reflects the thought of the Apocrypha, and even refers to it (cf. Heb. 11:35 with II Macc. 7, 12).

2. The New Testament quotes mostly from the Greek Old Testament (LXX), which contained the Apocrypha.

3. Some of the early Church Fathers quoted and used the Apocrypha as Scripture in public worship.

4. Many of the Fathers accepted all of the books of the Apocrypha as canonical, for example, Irenaeus, Tertullian, and Clement of Alexandria.

5. Catacomb scenes depict episodes from the Apocrypha.

6. The great Greek manuscripts (Aleph, A, and B) interpose the Apocrypha among the Old Testament books.

7. The Syriac Church accepted them in the fourth century.

8. Augustine and the councils he presided over at Hippo (393) and Carthage (397) accepted them.

9. The Greek Church accepts them.

10. The Roman Catholic Church proclaimed them canonical at the Council of Trent (1546).

11. The Apocryphal books continued in the Protestant Bibles as late as the nineteenth century.

12. Some Apocryphal books written in Hebrew have been found among other Old Testament canonical books in the Dead Sea community at Qumran.

Arguments against accepting the Alexandrian Canon. In response to the alleged support for considering the Apocryphal books as canonical, the following reasons may be proffered, answering point by point the arguments given above.

1. There may be New Testament allusions to the Apocrypha, although few are indisputable, but there are no clear New Testament quotations from it. In any event, the New Testament never refers to any of the fourteen or fifteen Apocryphal books as authoritative or canonical.

2. It has not been proven that the Greek Old Testament (LXX) of the first century contained the Apocrypha. The earliest Greek manuscripts which include them date from the fourth century A.D. In addition to this, if they were in the LXX of apostolic

time, Jesus and the apostles implied their view of them by never once quoting them, although they are supposed to have been included in the very version of the Old Testament that they quoted.

3 and 4. While some individuals in the early church had a high esteem for the Apocrypha, no council of the entire church during the first four centuries favored them, and there were many individuals who vehemently opposed them, for example, Athanasius, Cyril of Jerusalem, Origen, Jerome.

5. Scenes from the catacombs do not prove the canonicity of the books whose events they depict. Such scenes at best could only prove the belief of those Christians in the historicity of the events portrayed.

6. The fact that the Apocryphal books were a part of the Greek manuscripts in the fourth century A.D. does not prove that they were a part of the first century canon, nor indeed that they were considered canonical by the apostolic church.

7. The Syrian Church did not accept these books until the fourth century A.D. In the second century A.D. the Syrian Bible (Peshitta) did *not* contain the Apocrypha.

8. Augustine is the single significant voice of antiquity that recognized the Apocrypha. But, even in his case several things should be noted: He omits Baruch and includes I Esdras, thus accepting one and rejecting the other in contrast to the Council of Trent; other writings of Augustine indicate that he held to a "secondary canonicity" for the Apocrypha, as compared to a "primary canonicity" for the Hebrew canon;[12] the councils at Hippo and Carthage were small, local councils dominated by Augustine and had no qualified persons present to judge the issue of canonicity. Augustine, not a trained Hebrew scholar, led early opposition to Jerome's use of the Hebrew Old Testament for his Latin Vulgate. Later, however, he recognized that the Septuagint was not inspired, and reverted to the authority of the Hebrew Scriptures.[13]

[12]Augustine, *The City of God*, XVIII, 36.
[13]Since the acceptance of the inspiration of the Septuagint was the basis upon which Augustine accepted the Apocrypha, his later acknowledgment of the superiority of Jerome's Hebrew text should also have led him to accept the authority of Jerome's Hebrew canon. Cf. chap. 24.

9. The Greek Church has not always accepted the Apocrypha, nor is its present position unequivocal. Not until the synods of Constantinople (1638), Jaffa (1642), and Jerusalem (1672) were these books declared canonical. And, even as late as 1839, their Larger Catechism expressly omitted the Apocrypha on the grounds that "they do not exist in the Hebrew."[14]

10. The Council of Trent was the first official proclamation of the Roman Catholic Church on the Apocrypha, and it came a millennium and a half after the books were written, in an obvious polemical action against Protestantism. Furthermore, the addition of books that support "salvation by works" and "prayers for the dead" at this time (1546), only twenty-nine years after Luther posted his Ninety-five Theses, is highly suspect.

11. Apocryphal books appeared in Protestant Bibles prior to the Council of Trent, and were generally placed in a separate section as they were not considered to be of equal authority. Even Roman Catholic scholars through the Reformation period made the distinction between the Apocrypha and the canon. Cardinal Ximenes made this distinction in his *Complutensian Polyglot* (1514-17) on the very eve of the Reformation. Cardinal Cajetan, who opposed Luther at Augsburg in 1518, published a *Commentary on all the Authentic Historical Books of the Old Testament* that did not include the Apocrypha in A.D. 1532. Luther spoke against the Apocrypha in his Bible published in 1543 by placing its books in the back.[15]

12. The discoveries at Qumran included not only the community's Bibles but their library with fragments of hundreds of books. Among these were some of the Old Testament Apocryphal books.[16] While the argument from silence is in itself generally a weak one, it may be said that as far as the present evidence goes, the fact that no commentaries on the noncanonical books have been discovered tends to support the contention that the Apocryphal books were not viewed as canonical by the Qumran community.

---

[14]H. S. Miller, *General Biblical Introduction*, 2d ed., rev., p. 114.
[15]Bruce M. Metzger, *An Introduction to the Apocrypha*, pp. 181 ff.
[16]Menahem Mansoor, *The Dead Sea Scrolls*, p. 203, lists the following fragments from the Apocrypha and Pseudepigrapha: Tobit, in Hebrew and Aramaic; Enoch in Aramaic; Jubilees, in Hebrew; Testaments of Levi and Naphtali, in Aramaic; Apocryphal Daniel literature, in Hebrew and Aramaic; Psalms of Joshua.

Therefore, all of the arguments urged in favor of the canonicity of the Apocryphal books merely prove that these books have been given varied degrees of esteem and recognition, usually falling short of full canonicity, until the Roman Catholic Church officially pronounced them canonical in 1546 at the Council of Trent. This recognition falls far short of the canonicity accorded the thirty-nine books of the Old Testament, and the overwhelming arguments in favor of rejecting the Apocrypha as part of the canon provide convincing evidence that the books are not God-breathed.

Arguments in favor of accepting the Palestinian Canon. The true canon is the Palestinian Canon. It was the canon of Jesus, Josephus and Jerome and, for that matter, the canon of virtually every qualified witness from before the time of Christ to the present. The arguments for accepting the Palestinian Canon (only the thirty-nine books of the Old Testament) as canonical are:

1. Some of the additional books have teaching which is unbiblical or heretical. Two of the main doctrines in dispute during the Reformation are supported by the Apocrypha: "prayers for the dead" (II Macc. 12:45-46) and "salvation by works" (Tobit 12:9). The canonical books of the Bible are against praying for the dead (Heb. 9:27; Luke 16:25-26; II Sam. 12:19). They are also strongly against salvation by works (Gen. 15:6; Rom. 4:5; Gal. 3:11).[17]

2. Some of the Apocryphal stories are extrabiblical and fanciful. The story of Bel and the Dragon is a good case in point. In it, the pagan priests of Bel try to deceive Daniel by using a trapdoor to go in and consume the food offered to Bel to prove that Bel is a "living God" who "eats and drinks every day" (v. 6). So, in order to assist the "living God," Bel, "in the night the priests came with their wives and children, as they were accustomed to do, and ate and drank everything" (v. 15). The same unauthentic ring may be heard in the other legendary books of Additions to Esther, Prayer of Azariah, and Susanna, as well as Tobit and Judith.

3. Much of the teaching of the Apocrypha is subbiblical and, at times, even immoral. Judith was assisted by God in a deed of falsehood (Judith 9:10, 13), while both Ecclesiasticus and Wisdom teach a morality based on expedience.

[17]Also see Wisdom 11:17, which teaches creation *ex hula* (out of preexisting matter) rather than *ex nihilo* (out of nothing), as in John 1:1-3 and Heb. 11:3.

Besides this low morality, the subbiblical nature of the Apocrypha can be seen in its historical and chronological errors. It is claimed that Tobit was alive when the Assyrians conquered Israel (722 B.C.) as well as when Jeroboam revolted against Judah (931 B.C.), yet his total life-span was only 158 years (14:11; cf. 1:3-5). Judith speaks of Nebuchadnezzar as reigning in Nineveh instead of Babylon (1:1). William H. Green concisely summarizes this evidence, as he writes, "The books of Tobit and Judith abound in geographical, chronological, and historical mistakes, so as not only to vitiate the truth of the narratives which they contain, but to make it doubtful whether they even rest upon a basis of fact."[18]

4. Most of the Old Testament Apocrypha was written in the postbiblical, intertestamental period. According to Josephus, the prophets wrote from Moses to Artaxerxes, and he adds, "It is true our history hath been written since Artaxerxes very particularly but hath not been esteemed of the like authority with the former by our forefathers, because there hath not been an exact succession of the prophets since that time."[19] The Talmud adds a similar thought, as it records, "After the latter prophets Haggai, Zechariah, . . . and Malachi, the Holy Spirit departed from Israel."[20] Since the Apocryphal books were written long after Artaxerxes' time (Malachi's day, 400 B.C.), namely, after about 200 B.C., then they could not be considered inspired. Not only does the Talmud testify to this end, but the canonical books of the Old Testament also imply this (see Zech. 1:5; Mal. 4:5), as do some of the statements in the Apocryphal books themselves (see chap. 12). In fact, there is no claim within the Apocrypha that it is the Word of God. It is sometimes asserted that Ecclesiasticus 50:27-29 lays claim to divine inspiration, but a closer examination of the passage indicates that it is *illumination* and not *inspiration* that the author claims to have.

Briefly then, with the possible exception of II Esdras, all of the Apocryphal books are postbiblical, since they were written after the time that the prophetic spirit had departed from Israel but before the prophet cried, "Prepare the way of the Lord" (Matt. 3:3), and "the time had fully come" (Gal. 4:4) when God spoke through His Son.

[18]Green, p. 195.
[19]Josephus, *Against Apion*, 1:8.
[20]Michael L. Rodkinson, Tractate "Sanhedrin," *Babylonian Talmud*, VII-VIII, 24.

5. Finally, all of the books of the Apocrypha are nonbiblical or uncanonical since none of them was ever accepted by the people of God as the canonical books were. In order for a book to be canonical, it must satisfy the tests of canonicity:

a. *Was it written by a "prophet" of God?* There is neither claim and/or proof that they were.

b. *Did it come with the authority of God?* No! There is a striking absence of the ring of authority in the Apocrypha. A step from the canon to the Apocrypha is like leaving the natural sunlight of God for the artificial candlelight of man, which at times becomes very dim indeed.

c. *Did it have the power of God?* There is nothing transforming about the Apocrypha. Its truth is not exhilarating, except as it is a repetition of canonical truth in other books.

d. *Did it tell the truth about God, man, etc.?* As was mentioned above, there are contradictions, errors, and even heresies in the Apocrypha. It does not stand the test of canonical truth.

e. *Was it accepted by the people of God?* It is this final question upon which the Apocrypha takes the final and fatal fall.

Testimony of antiquity against accepting Apocrypha. There is an almost unbroken testimony of antiquity *against* accepting the Apocrypha into the canon:

1. Philo, Alexandrian Jewish philosopher (20 B.C.-A.D. 40), quoted the Old Testament prolifically and even recognized the threefold division, but he never quoted from the Apocrypha as inspired.

2. Josephus (A.D. 30-100), Jewish historian, explicitly excludes the Apocrypha, numbering the books of the Old Testament as twenty-two. Neither does he quote these books as Scripture.

3. Jesus and the New Testament writers never once quote the Apocrypha although there are hundreds of quotes and references to almost all of the canonical books of the Old Testament.

4. The Jewish scholars of Jamnia (A.D. 90) did not recognize the Apocrypha.

5. No canon or council of the Christian church for the first four centuries recognized the Apocrypha as inspired.

6. Many of the great Fathers of the early church spoke out against the Apocrypha, for example, Origen, Cyril of Jerusalem, Athanasius.

7. Jerome (340-420), the great scholar and translator of the Vulgate, rejected the Apocrypha as part of the canon. He disputed across the Mediterranean with Augustine on this point. He at first refused even to translate the Apocryphal books into Latin, but later he made a hurried translation of a few of them. After his death, and literally "over his dead body," the Apocryphal books were brought into his Latin Vulgate directly from the Old Latin Version.

8. Many Roman Catholic scholars through the Reformation period rejected the Apocrypha.

9. Luther and the Reformers rejected the canonicity of the Apocrypha.

10. Not until A.D. 1546, in a polemical action at the Counter Reformation Council of Trent, did the Apocryphal books receive full canonical status by the Roman Catholic Church.

11. The acceptance of the Apocrypha at Trent is suspect because:

    a. It had been quoted against Luther in support of the Roman Catholic position (e.g., II Macc. 12:45-46, which favors prayers for the dead), and then added a few years later in a counter-Reformation attempt to refute Luther.

    b. Not all of the Apocrypha was accepted. Only twelve of the fifteen books were, and at least one of these omitted books (II Esdras)[21] is against prayers for the dead (cf. 7:105).

    c. In fact, the very history of this section of II Esdras is suspect. It was written by an unknown Jewish author in Aramaic (*c.* A.D. 100) and circulated in the Old Latin versions (*c.* A.D. 200). The Roman Catholic Vulgate printed it as an appendix to the New Testament (*c.* A.D. 400). Then it disappeared from Western Bibles until Protestants, beginning with Johann Haug (1726-42), began to print it in their Apocryphas based on Aramaic texts. In 1874 a long section (seventy verses from chap. 7) was found by Robert L. Bently in a library at Amiens. This was the first known Latin manuscript that contained 7:36-105 (as renumbered), and, as Metzger observes, "It is probable that the lost section was deliberately cut out of an ancestor of most extant Latin Manuscripts, because of dogmatic reasons, for the passage contains an emphatic denial of the value of prayers for

[21]Identified as IV Esdras in the Vulgate.

the dead."[22] From 1895 to the present this section has been printed in the Protestant Apocrypha.

Therefore, for some fifteen hundred years the Apocrypha had not been accepted as canonical by the people of God. Then, in 1546, just twenty-nine years after Luther posted his famous Ninety-Five Theses, the Council of Trent elevated the Apocrypha, or rather the part of it which supported their position, to the level of inspired Scripture, saying,

> The Synod . . . receives and venerates . . . all the books (including the *Apocrypha*) both of the Old and of the New Testament— seeing that one God is the Author of both . . . as having been dictated, either by Christ's own word of mouth or by the Holy Ghost . . . if anyone receive not as sacred and canonical the said books entire with all their parts, as they have been used to be read in the Catholic Church . . . let him be anathema.[23]

The Value of the Apocrypha

Even though the Apocrypha cannot be afforded a place in the canon of inspired books, it should not be dismissed as having no value. Some, as Jerome and Rufinus (A.D. 410), have held the Apocrypha to be a kind of "ecclesiastical" canon containing books to be preserved, read and used by the church. For many it has served as a sort of "homiletical" or "devotional" canon from which many of the Fathers have drawn illumination for life, art and preaching. Almost all agree that the Apocrypha has some historical value. It provides a most valuable source of information about the history and religion of the Jewish church in the intertestamental period. It is probably going too far to give the Apocrypha a semicanonical status, as did the Church of England, or a quasi-canonical status, as did the Eastern Church. Whatever place it may be accorded below this level, it clearly is not part of the theological canon of definitive and dogmatic books on doctrine.

SUMMARY AND CONCLUSION

Thirty-four of the thirty-nine books of the Old Testament are accepted by all Christians as part of the canon, called Homologoumena. The other five books, called Antilegomena, have been disputed by some but have retained their place in the canon. The

[22]Metzger, p. 23.
[23]Philip Schaff (ed.), *The Creeds of Christendom*, 6th ed., II, 81.

Psuedepigraphical books have been rejected as spurious by virtually everyone. A real battle has raged, however, over the fourteen or fifteen books of the Apocrypha written between 200 B.C. and A.D. 100. The Roman Catholic Church canonized them at Trent (1546); Protestants have rejected them; and the Church of England and the Eastern Orthodox Church have given them a status in between these positions. Whereas there is no doubt a devotional and even homiletical and historical value in them, yet they are not part of the theological canon to which the other thirty-nine books of the Old Testament belong because:

1. Some of their teaching is *unbiblical* or heretical.
2. Some of their stories are *extrabiblical* or fanciful.
3. Much of their teaching is *subbiblical*, at times even immoral.
4. Most of the Apocrypha was written in the *postbiblical* or intertestamental period.
5. Finally, all of the Apocrypha is *nonbiblical* or uncanonical, since it was not received by the people of God.

14

DEVELOPMENT AND HISTORY OF
THE NEW TESTAMENT CANON

PRELIMINARY CONSIDERATIONS

The history of the New Testament canon is similar to that of the Old Testament, although there is happily much more data available on the subject. Before this evidence is examined, a preliminary distinction must be made between the source and the stimuli for canonization.

THE SOURCE OF CANONIZATION

It has already been pointed out that God is the source of canonicity. A book is canonical because it is inspired, and it is inspired because God moved in and through the men who wrote it. In this sense, canonicity is passive; it is something received from God (see chap. 10). There is also an active sense of the word "canonization"; the sense in which the people of God were active in the recognition and collection of the books which God had inspired. The historical process of canonization is concerned with this latter sense.

THE STIMULI FOR CANONIZATION

From the human point of view there were several stimuli for the collection and final canonization of inspired books.

Books were prophetic. One of the initial reasons for collecting and preserving the inspired books was that they were prophetic. That is, since they were written by an apostle or prophet of God, they must be valuable, and if valuable, they should be preserved. This reasoning is apparent in apostolic times, by the collection and circulation of Paul's epistles (cf. II Peter 3:15-16; Col. 4:16). The postapostolic period continued to reflect this high regard for the apostolic writings of the New Testament by their voluminous and authoritative quotations from these inspired books.

Demands of early church. Closely connected with the foregoing reason for preserving the inspired books were the theological and ethical demands of the early church. That is, in order to know which books should be read in the churches (cf. I Thess. 5:27 and I Tim. 4:13) and which books could be definitely applied to the theological and practical problems of the Christian church (cf. II Tim. 3:16-17), it became necessary to have a complete collection of the books which could provide this authoritative norm for faith and practice.

Heretical stimulus. On the negative side of this there was the heretical stimulus. At least as early as A.D. 140, there was the heretical Marcion who accepted only limited sections of the full New Testament canon. Marcion's heretical canon, consisting of only Luke's gospel and ten of Paul's epistles, pointed up clearly the need to collect a complete canon of New Testament Scriptures.

Missionary stimulus. On the positive side, there was the missionary stimulus. Christianity had spread rapidly to other countries, and there was the need to translate the Bible into their native tongues. As early as the first half of the second century the Bible was translated into Syriac and Old Latin. But since the missionaries could not translate a Bible that did not exist, attention was necessarily drawn to the question of which books really belonged to the authoritative Christian canon.

Persecutions and politics. The final phase of full and general recognition of the whole canon of New Testament writings involved also a negative and political stimulus. The Diocletian persecutions of about 302/303-5 provided forceful motivation for the church to sort, sift, and settle on the New Testament Scriptures. For certainly the books they would risk their lives to preserve must have been considered sacred to them.

> . . . an imperial letter was everywhere promulgated, ordering the razing of the churches to the ground and the destruction by fire of the Scriptures, and proclaiming that those who held high positions would lose all civil rights, while those in households, if they persisted in their profession of Christianity, would be deprived of their liberty.[1]

Ironically enough, within twenty-five years of the edict to destroy the Scriptures, Constantine took positive action to preserve them. He commissioned Eusebius, the historian, to prepare fifty copies of the Scriptures at imperial expense in the following letter:

[1]Eusebius, *Ecclesiastical History*, VIII, 2. Loeb ed., II, 259.

Victor Constantinus, Maximus Augustus, to Eusebius

. . . I have thought it expedient to instruct your Prudence to order fifty copies of the sacred Scriptures, the provision and use of which you know to be most needful for the instruction of the Church, to be written on prepared parchment in a legible manner, and in a convenient, portable form, by professional transcribers thoroughly practiced in their art. The catholicus of the diocese has also received instructions from our Clemency to be careful to furnish all things necessary for the preparation of such copies; and it will be for you to take special care that they are completed with as little delay as possible.[2]

Both of these political actions prompted a careful examination and scrutiny of all religious writings in order to discover which were truly authoritative. And, in the same century as Diocletian's persecutions and Constantine's letter, the church began to give official recognition to the twenty-seven books of the New Testament, that is, in A.D. 363 (at Laodicea), and in A.D. 397 (at Carthage).

PROGRESSIVE COLLECTION

While the church did not give official recognition to the canon prior to the late fourth century, it is misleading to say there was no recognition before then. Like the Old Testament books, there is ample evidence available to confirm that the inspired books were received immediately as such, circulated, and even collected. The problem of the New Testament is somewhat different, however, in that the New Testament books were written during a half-century period by some eight or nine different writers, having destinations ranging from individuals (e.g., Philemon) to groups of churches (e.g., I Peter) located in centers extending from Jerusalem to Rome. The problems of transportation and translation would tend to obscure the authority and authenticity of books even though they had already gained recognition by the original recipients.

NEW TESTAMENT INDICATIONS

Within the New Testament itself, there is evidence of the concept of a developing canon of inspired books.

The principle of canonization. The determining factor in New Testament canonization was inspiration, and the primary test was apostolicity. If it could be determined that a book had apostolic authority, there would be no reason to question its authenticity or

[2] Philip Schaff (ed.), *The Nicene and Post-Nicene Fathers* (2d series), I, 549.

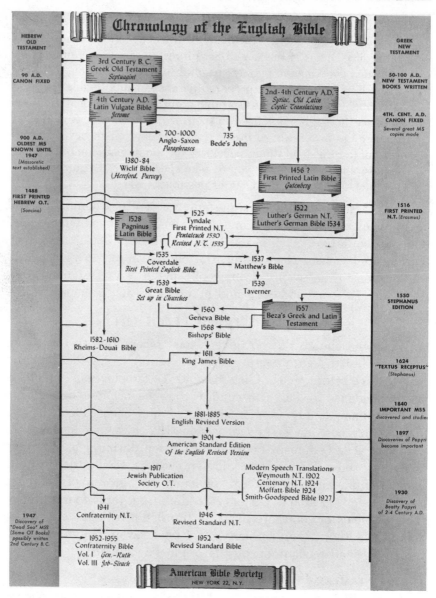

5. *The history of the English Bible (American Bible Society)*

veracity. In New Testament terminology, the church was "built upon the foundation of the apostles and prophets" (Eph. 2:20) whom Christ had promised to guide unto "all the truth" (John 16:13) by the Holy Spirit. The church at Jerusalem was said to have continued in the "apostles' teaching and fellowship" (Acts 2:42). The term "apostolic" as used for the test of canonicity does not necessarily mean "apostolic authorship," or "that which was prepared under the direction of the apostles,"[3] unless the word "apostle" be taken in its nontechnical sense, meaning someone *beyond* the twelve apostles or Paul. In this nontechnical sense, Barnabas is called an apostle (Acts 14:14; cf. v. 4), as is James (Gal. 1:19), and evidently others too (Rom. 16:7; II Cor. 8:23; Phil. 2:25). It appears rather unnecessary to think of Mark and Luke as being secretaries of apostles, or to argue that the writer of James was an apostle, to say nothing of Jude or the writer of Hebrews. In fact, the writer of Hebrews disclaims being an apostle, saying that the message of Christ "was attested to us [readers and writer] by those [the apostles] who heard him" (Heb. 2:3). It seems much better to agree with Gaussen,[4] Warfield,[5] Charles Hodge,[6] and most Protestants that it is apostolic authority, or apostolic approval, that was the primary test for canonicity, and not merely apostolic authorship. In the terminology of the New Testament, a book had to be written by an apostle or prophet (cf. Eph. 2:20). The real question, then, was "Is a book prophetic?" that is, "Was it written by a prophet of God?" The apostles were, of course, granted a prophetic ministry (John 14-16): John called himself "a fellow servant with . . . the prophets" (Rev. 22:9), and Paul considered his books prophetic writings (cf. Rom. 16:25-26; Eph. 3:3-5). Individuals in the New Testament besides those called apostles were granted a prophetic ministry, in accordance with the promise on the day of Pentecost (Acts 2:17-18), as was manifest in Agabus and the other prophets from Jerusalem (Acts 11:27-28), not to mention the "gift of prophecy" evident in the New Testament church (cf. I Cor. 12:29).

The progress of canonization. A close look at the New Testament reveals that these prophetic writings were being sorted from among

---

[3]R. Laird Harris attempts to defend this view, however, making Mark and Luke to be secretaries to Peter and Paul, respectively, etc.; cf. *Inspiration and Canonicity of the Bible*, p. 270.
[4]Louis Gaussen, *Theopneustia*, p. 319.
[5]Benjamin B. Warfield, *The Inspiration and Authority of the Bible*, p. 455.
[6]Charles Hodge, *Systematic Theology*, I, 153.

the nonprophetic writings, even from oral traditions, and a canon was being formed during apostolic times.

1. *Selecting procedure.* John implies that there was a selecting process going on among the apostles themselves, dealing with the problem of which particular truths should be preserved in written form. He writes that "Jesus did many other signs . . . which are not written in this book" (John 20:30), and "were every one of them to be written," he adds, "I suppose that the world itself could not contain the books that would be written" (John 21:25). Luke speaks of other written sources on the life of Christ, from which he compiled "an orderly account" based on "eyewitnesses" in order that "the truth" might be known (Luke 1:1-4). This evidence seems to imply that there were other written records of Christ's life which were not entirely true. There are several references to the authority of apostolic oral tradition or teaching (cf. I Thess. 2:13; I Cor. 11:2). These "traditions" meant that there was authoritative teaching by original eyewitnesses to Christ's life. Some have suggested that this was in fact the *kerygma* (authoritative apostolic pronouncement about Christ), or a sort of "canon within the canon."[7] Whether or not this *kerygma* was used as the test for canonicity is uncertain, but it is clear that there were apostolic criteria for sorting out oral traditions of an Apocryphal nature. John speaks of a false belief regarding his own death, which was "spread abroad among the brethren" as a distortion by Jesus' own disciples of something spoken from the lips of Jesus (John 21:23-24). No doubt there were other incidents of this nature also. However, though these may have been believed among the early disciples, they were nowhere taught as apostolic truth, at least not in the canonical writings. They were not part of the authoritative oral message of the eyewitnesses and therefore never became part of the teaching of the written record.

2. *Reading procedure.* Another indication within the New Testament itself that a canon was being formed is the repeated injunction that certain books should be read to the churches. Paul commanded that I Thessalonians be "read to all the brethren" (5:27). Revelation 1:3 promised a blessing to all who read "the words of the prophecy" and kept it; in fact, it gave a warning to

[7]See Herman Ridderbos, "The Canon of the New Testament," *Revelation and the Bible,* Carl F. H. Henry (ed.), pp. 191 ff.

those who "hear the words of the prophecy of this book" and do not keep them. The key to canonicity implicit in these injunctions appears to be authority, or prophecy. If a writing was prophetic, it was to be read with authority to the churches.

3. *Circulating procedure.* Those writings which were read as authoritative to the churches were circulated and collected by the churches. The book of Revelation was circulated among the churches of Asia Minor, as John was told to "write what you see in a book and send it to the seven churches" (Rev. 1:11). Paul commanded the Colossians, saying, "When this letter has been read among you, have it read also in the church of the Laodiceans; and see that you read also the letter from Laodicea" (Col. 4:16).[8] This is a crucial passage, since it indicates that the authority of one epistle included a larger audience than just the one to which it was written. Thus, as the book of Revelation was circulated throughout the churches, so other epistles were to be exchanged, and prophetic messages were to be read with all authority.

4. *Collecting procedure.* This circulating procedure no doubt led to the habit of collecting prophetic and apostolic writings, such as those alluded to in II Peter 3:15-16, where the author speaks of "all his [Paul's] letters" as being on a level with "the other scriptures." As has already been noted (see chap. 6), the apostles considered the collection of Old Testament writings to be divine Scripture; therefore, as the New Testament prophets wrote inspired books, these were added to the collection of "the other scriptures." Thus, by the time of II Peter (c. A.D. 66),[9] Paul's epistles were in the canon.[10] Since most of the General Epistles were written after Paul's, it cannot be expected that they would be mentioned. Nevertheless, Jude probably is referring to Peter's book, and he seems to regard it as Scripture (cf. Jude 17-18 and II Peter 3:2-3).

---

[8]Some scholars believe that this letter from Laodicea is the epistle called Ephesians in modern English Bibles. Cf. discussion of this matter in F. F. Bruce, and E. K. Simpson, *Commentary on the Epistles to the Ephesians and Colossians*, pp. 310-11. Others, however, have suggested that it is Philemon instead of Ephesians. See discussion in Everett F. Harrison, *Introduction to the New Testament*, pp. 308-9.

[9]Harrison, p. 401.

[10]Lewis Foster argues that Luke made the earliest collection of Paul's epistles as a kind of third volume following his gospel and Acts sequence. See his article, "The Earliest Collection of Paul's Epistles," *Bulletin of the Evangelical Theological Society*, Vol. X, No. 1 (Winter, 1967), pp. 44-53.

5. *Quotation procedure.* If Jude quoted from Peter's writing when he said, "You must remember, beloved, the predictions of the apostles of our Lord Jesus Christ" (v. 17), then he not only verified that Peter's writing was accepted into the canon by that time, but that the books received were immediately and authoritatively quoted as Scripture. Paul (I Tim. 5:18) quoted from the gospel of Luke (10:7) with the same formula he used to quote the Old Testament. It would be too much to expect that every book of the New Testament would be verified in this way, but enough of them are referred to (at least some of Paul's, one of Luke's and perhaps one of Peter's—a substantial part of the New Testament) in order to demonstrate that there was a canon of New Testament books even during New Testament times. The absence of any quotation from some of the smaller and more personal epistles may be explained by their size and nature.

In summary, the primary test of canonicity in New Testament times was apostolic or prophetic authority. Those writings which came to local churches (or individuals) were read, circulated, collected and even quoted as a part of the canon of the Scriptures. These writings supplemented, and formed an integral part of the inspired Word of God along with the previously recognized Old Testament Scriptures.

Apostolic Fathers

What has been said of the development of the New Testament canon, as seen in the inspired writings of the New Testament itself, is even more apparent in the writings of the younger contemporaries, the Apostolic Fathers. A sample survey will suffice to show that by the middle of the second century every book of the New Testament was referred to, presumably as canonical, by at least one of these Fathers.

The Gospels

1. Matthew was quoted by the *Epistle of Pseudo-Barnabas* (*c.* 70-79) on several occasions, for example, 4:14 (Matt. 20:16; 22:14); 5:12 (26:31); 6:13 (19:30; 20:16); 7:3 (27:34) and 12:11 (22:45); in addition to several allusions. The *Didache* (*c.* 70-130) quotes Matthew rather extensively (cf. Matt. 6:9-13).

2. Mark was cited by the *Epistle of Pseudo-Barnabas* in only one

clear example, 5:9 (Mark 2:17), but 12:11 quotes the parallel passage in Matthew 22:45 and/or Luke 20:44. Papias (c. 70-163) wrote five treatises entitled *Interpretation of the Oracles of the Lord* (c. 120), which included the four Gospels.[11]

3. Luke was revised by the Gnostic Marcion (c. A.D. 140) and appeared in his sharply abridged canon of Scriptures. *The Muratorian Fragment* (c. 170-80) began with Mark, and refers to Luke as the third gospel and follows with John, Acts, etc.[12]

4. John was cited by Papias, and listed in the Muratorian Canon. It was also cited and alluded to in the epistles of Ignatius (c. 110-17), for example, *Ephesians* 5:2 (John 6:33), *Ephesians* 17:1 (John 12:3). Clement of Rome cited John 17:3 in his *Epistle to the Corinthians* 43:5 (c. 95).

Acts

Acts appeared in the *Muratorian Fragment*, and was quoted by Polycarp (69-155), the disciple of John, in his *Philippians* 1:2 (Acts 2:24). The *Shepherd of Hermas* quotes Acts in several instances, for example, Vision II: 2.7 (Acts 10:35); Vision III: 7.3 (Acts 2:38; 10:48; 19:5); Similitude IX: 28.2 (Acts 15:26); X: 2.3; 4.1 (Acts 2:11; 2:1).

The Epistles

1. Romans is frequently cited by Clement of Rome in his *Epistle to the Corinthians*, for example, 33:1 (Rom. 6:1); 35:6 (Rom. 1:29-32); 50:6 (Rom. 4:7-9). Polycarp quotes Romans on several occasions in his *Epistle to the Philippians*, for example, 5:2 (Rom. 8:17); 6:1 (Rom. 12:17); 6:3 (Rom. 14:10, 12); 10:1 (Rom. 13:8). The *Didache* (5:1-2) cites Romans 1:29-30 and 12:9, respectively.

2. First Corinthians was cited in the *Didache* 10:6 (I Cor. 16:22); 13:1-2 (I Cor. 9:13-14); and 16:6 (I Cor. 15:22; cf. Matt. 24:30-31). The *Shepherd of Hermas*, Mandate 3:6 (I Cor. 7:11; cf. Matt. 5:32; 19:9; and Mark 10:11); and Mandate 4:4.1 (I Cor. 7:38-40) also cites I Corinthians.

3. Second Corinthians was cited by Polycarp, *Philippians* 2:2 (II Cor. 4:14); 4:1 (II Cor. 6:7), as it was by the *Shepherd*,

[11]See Eusebius, III, 39. Loeb ed., I, 291.
[12]See C. R. Gregory, *Canon and Text of the New Testament*, pp. 129-33.

Similitude 9:13. 7-8 (II Cor. 13:11); and the *Epistle to Diognetus* (*c.* 150), 5:7 (II Cor. 10:3); 5:12 (II Cor. 6:9-10); 5:15-16 (II Cor. 4:12; 6:10).

4. Galatians was frequently quoted by many writers such as Polycarp, *Philippians* 3:3 (Gal. 4:26); 5:1 (Gal. 6:7); 5:3 (Gal. 5:17); *Epistle to Diognetus* 6:5 (Gal. 5:17); and 10:5 (Gal. 6:2).

5. Ephesians, one of Paul's prison epistles, was cited by Clement of Rome in his *Corinthians* 46:6 (Eph. 4:4-6); 59:3 (Eph. 1:18); by Ignatius in his *Smyrnaeans* 1:2 (Eph. 2:16); *Polycarp* 1:3 (Eph. 4:2); 5:1 (Eph. 5:25, 29); alluded to in *Pseudo-Barnabas* 6:10 (Eph. 2:10; 4:22-24).

6. Philippians was often quoted by Polycarp in his *Philippians* 9:2 (Phil. 2:16); 11:3 (Phil. 4:15); 12:3 (Phil. 3:18); and *Shepherd*, Similitude 5:3.8 (Phil. 4:18); 9:13. 7-8 (Phil. 2:2; 3:16; 4:2); and by Ignatius, *Smyrnaeans* 4:2 (Phil. 4:13); 11:3 (Phil. 3:15).

7. Colossians was cited by Polycarp, *Philippians* 10:1 (Col. 1:23); 11:2 (Col. 3:5); Ignatius, *Ephesians* 10:2 (Col.1:23); *Trallians* 5:2 (Col. 1:16); and *Epistle to Diognetus* 10:7 (Col. 4:1).

8. First Thessalonians 5:13 was cited several times in the *Shepherd* (Vision 3:6.3; 3:9.2, 10; Similitude 8:7.2); the *Didache* 16:7 also quotes this epistle (I Thess. 4:16); it is used by Ignatius, *Ephesians* 10:1 (I Thess. 5:17); and *Romans* 2:1 (I Thess. 2:4).

9. Second Thessalonians is less frequently cited, but Ignatius uses it as the basis of his statement in his *Philadelphians* 4:3 (II Thess. 3:5). Polycarp also uses this epistle in his *Philippians* 11:3 (II Thess. 1:4) and 11:4 (II Thess. 3:15). *Dionysius of Corinth* (*c.* A.D. 170) also quotes this epistle.

10. First Timothy was repeatedly used by Clement of Rome in his *I Corinthians*, as it was in Polycarp's *Philippians*. The *Shepherd*, Similitude 8:2.9, cites I Timothy 2:4, and the *Didache*, 13:1-2, quotes I Timothy 5:17-18.

11. Second Timothy is used in *Pseudo-Barnabas* 5:6 (II Tim. 1:10), as it is in the *Shepherd*, Mandate 3:2 (II Tim. 1:14).

12. Titus is frequently quoted by Clement of Rome in his *I Corinthians; Pseudo-Barnabas* 1:4-6 and 14:5 cite Titus 1:1-3, 7 and 2:14, respectively, as does the *Epistle to Diognetus* 9:1-2 (Titus 3:3-5).

13. Philemon was a personal letter, and its nature is reflected in its use: *Ignatius* makes allusions to it, and the *Muratorian Fragment* lists thirteen of Paul's epistles.

14. Hebrews was frequently cited by Clement of Rome in his *I Corinthians;* it was also quoted in the *Ancient Homily* (often called *II Corinthians* of Clement of Rome) 11:6 (Heb. 10:23); the *Shepherd* frequently used this epistle, for example, Vision 2:2.7 (Heb. 11:33); Vision 2:3.2 (Heb. 3:12).

15. James is repeatedly used in the *I Corinthians* of Clement of Rome, as it is in the *Shepherd,* Vision 3:9.6 (James 5:4); Mandate 2:2.7 (James 4:11; 1:27); 11:5 (James 3:15).

16. First Peter is used in *Pseudo-Barnabas* 4:12 (I Peter 1:17); 6:2 (I Peter 2:6) 7:2 (I Peter 4:5); the *Shepherd* quotes I Peter 5:7, 4:13, 15-16; 4:14 in Vision 3:11.3, Similitude 9:28.5, and 9:28.6, respectively.

17. Second Peter (2:6-9) is quoted in *I Corinthians* 11:1 by Clement of Rome. It is also used in *Pseudo-Barnabas* 15:4 (II Peter 3:8).

18. First John is cited in the *Shepherd,* Mandate 3:1 (I John 2:27); Similitude 6:5-6 (I John 3:22).

19. Second John is listed in the *Muratorian Fragment,* and cited in Polycarp, *Philippians* 7:1 (II John 7).

20. Third John is listed in the *Muratorian Fragment.*

21. Jude is listed in the *Muratorian Fragment* and is cited in *The Martyrdom of St. Polycarp, Bishop of Smyrna.* Preface (Jude 2).

Revelation

The book of Revelation was cited in the *Didache* 10:3 (Rev. 4:11); 16:4 (Rev. 13:2, 13), as well as in the *Shepherd,* Vision 4:2.1 (Rev. 21:2). Papias accepted the authority of Revelation, and it was cited in the *Ancient Homily* 17:7 (Rev. 11:13), and by Justin Martyr and Dionysius of Corinth.

While many of these citations may be disputed if modern critical approaches are used, it should be noted that by the standards of classical civilization these would be considered legitimate quotations. Therefore, works are regarded as quoted when they would possibly be misquoted or alluded to in modern parlance.

In summary, the first hundred years of the existence of the twenty-seven books of the New Testament reveal that virtually every one of them was quoted as authoritative and recognized as canonical by men who were themselves the younger contemporaries of the Apostolic Age.

PRACTICAL COMPLETION AND VERIFICATION

Of course there was not universal agreement by all the early Fathers, in either the second or even the third century, on all of the canonical books. However, some Fathers and canons recognized almost all of the books before the end of the second century, and the church universal was in agreement by the end of the fourth century.

Recognition by Individuals

Some outstanding Fathers of the second century show their acceptance of most of New Testament canon, and there is no reason to believe they did not also accept the rest of it.

Polycarp (*c.* A.D. 150). The younger contemporary and disciple of the Apostle John, Polycarp quotes from Matthew, John, the first ten of Paul's epistles, I Peter, and I and II John. Since most of the rest of the books were small, it could not be expected that he would refer to them. As a result, the argument from silence that Polycarp did not know or accept them is a weak one at best.

Justin Martyr (A.D. 140). Justin Martyr considered all the Gospels as Scripture, plus most of Paul's epistles, as well as I Peter and Revelation. It is noteworthy that Justin had occasion to refer to Mark, Luke, John and Revelation, not cited by Polycarp, and not to refer to Philippians or I Timothy, which would tend to confirm the thesis that both men accepted more books than those from which they quoted.

Irenaeus (*c.* A.D. 170). The first early Father who himself quoted almost every book of the New Testament was Irenaeus, the disciple of Polycarp. He quoted or considered as authentic twenty-three of the twenty-seven books, omitting only Philemon, James, II Peter and III John. Clement of Alexandria (c. A.D. 200) has almost an identical list, with the exception of his omission of II Timothy and II John. Philemon and III John may not have been quoted because of their brevity, leaving only II Peter and James in question. In this connection it is interesting to note that the *Shepherd* of Hermas (c. A.D. 140) referred to James, and the book of II Peter had already been quoted as Scripture in Jude. Thus, before the end of the second century some individuals had recognized almost all of the twenty-seven books, and the remainder were recognized by others even before that time.

RECOGNIZED BY CANONS (AND TRANSLATIONS)

Another confirmation that the New Testament canon was formed as early as the second century comes from canonical lists and translations; and, it goes without saying, a translation assumes a canon by those individuals doing the translation.

The Old Syriac. This translation of the New Testament was in circulation in Syria about A.D. 400, but represented a text dating from the end of the second century.[13] It included all of the twenty-seven New Testament books except II Peter, II and III John, Jude and Revelation. Westcott notes: "Its general agreement with our own [canon] is striking and important; and its omissions admit of easy explanation."[14]

The Old Latin. This was translated prior to A.D. 200 and served as the Bible of the Western church as the Syriac did in the East. This Latin version contained all the New Testament books except Hebrews, James and I and II Peter.[15]

The Muratorian Canon (A.D. 170). Aside from Marcion's heretical canon (A.D. 140), the earliest canonical list is in the *Muratorian Fragment.* This list coincides exactly with the Old Latin, omitting only Hebrews, James and I and II Peter. Westcott argues for the probability of a break in this manuscript that may once have included these books.[16] It does seem strange that Hebrews and I Peter should be omitted, while Philemon and III John were included. This feature is just the opposite of the lists of Irenaeus and Clement of Alexandria.

---

[13]Bruce M. Metzger, *The Text of the New Testament*, p. 69.
[14]Brooke Foss Westcott, *A General Survey of the History of the Canon of the New Testament*, 7th ed., pp. 249-50.
[15]*Ibid.*, p. 263.
[16]*Ibid.*, p. 223.

Codex Barococcio (A.D. 206).[17] Another interesting testimony to the late second century status of the New Testament canon comes from a codex titled "The Sixty Books." When examined, this list proves to include sixty-four of the familiar sixty-six books of the English Bible; only Esther and Revelation are omitted. This codex not only tends to confirm what the other individuals and translations said about canonicity, but it gives further support for some of the books they omitted. While Revelation is omitted from this list, it had formerly been supported by Justin Martyr, Irenaeus, Clement of Alexandria, Tertullian, and the Muratorian Canon.

RECOGNITION BY COUNCILS

As can be readily seen from the examination of quotations (by individuals) and canonical lists, there were a few books that were rather persistently unrecognized. Eusebius summed up the situation in his day by acknowledging all twenty-seven books, but stating that James, II Peter, II and III John and Jude were "spoken against" (Greek: *Antilegomena*).[18] However, whatever doubts existed in his day gradually faded during the next fifty years, when Athanasius (*c.* 367), the "Father of Orthodoxy," clearly and emphatically listed all twenty-seven books as canonical, saying,

> Again it is not tedious to speak of the books of the New Testament. These are, the four gospels, according to Matthew, Mark, Luke, and John. Afterwards, the Acts of the Apostles and Epistles (called Catholic), seven, viz. of James, one; of Peter, two; of John, three; after these, one of Jude. In addition, there are fourteen Epistles of Paul, written in this order. The first, to the Romans; then two to the Corinthians; after these, to the Galatians; next, to the Ephesians; then to the Philippians; then to the Colossians; after these, two to the Thessalonians, and that to the Hebrews; and again, two to Timothy; one to Titus; and lastly, that to Philemon. And besides, the Revelation of John.[19]

The councils of Hippo (A.D. 393) and Carthage (A.D. 397) were under the influence of Augustine. At these councils the New Testament canon which was ratified agreed with the present-day canon of twenty-seven books;[20] however, they accepted a variation of the Alex-

[17]Westcott, Appendix D, p. 567.
[18]Eusebius, III, 25. Loeb ed., I, 257-59.
[19]Athanasius, *Letters*, No. 39 (Easter, 367) paragraph 5, *The Nicene and Post-Nicene Fathers* (2d series), IV, 552.
[20]This also agreed with Augustine's list in his treatise *On Christian Doctrine*, II, 8, 13, as translated in Philip Schaff (ed.), *The Nicene and Post-Nicene Fathers* (1st series), II, 538-39.

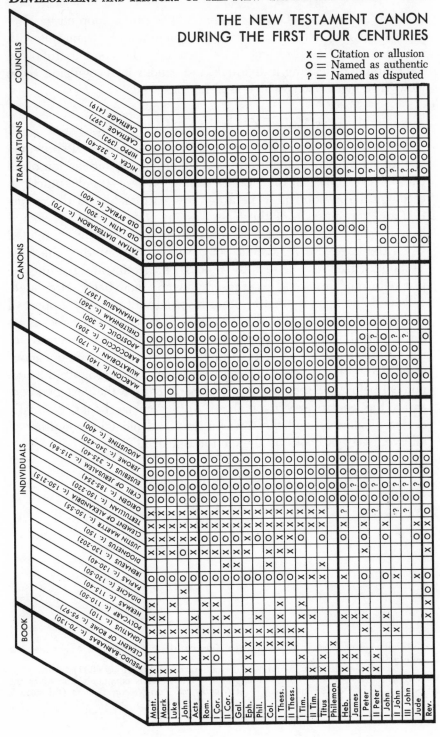

THE NEW TESTAMENT CANON DURING THE FIRST FOUR CENTURIES

x = Citation or allusion
o = Named as authentic
? = Named as disputed

andrian Canon of the Old Testament.[21] The canon adopted by Hippo and Carthage is verification of the contention of Athanasius with regard to the New Testament.[22] Therefore, the councils followed the example of leading individuals and canons in recognizing those New Testament books which God had inspired.

SUMMARY AND CONCLUSION

God is the source of canonicity and, in His providence, He provided several stimuli which finalized the recognition and ratification of all twenty-seven books of the New Testament. These stimuli—practical, theological and political in nature—were instrumental in the collection and transmission of the New Testament Scriptures. It should be remembered, however, that the canon was actually completed when the last New Testament book was written. Within the New Testament itself may be seen the process of selecting and reading the prophetic and apostolic writings that were then being circulated, collected and even quoted in other inspired writings. In support of this view of canonization, the Apostolic Fathers may be cited as referring to all of the New Testament books within about a century of the time they were written. Individuals, translations and canons show that all but a very few books were generally recognized as canonical before the second century closed. During the next two centuries the controversy over these Antilegomena books gradually erased all doubts, and there was a final and official recognition of all twenty-seven books by the church universal.

[21]Philip Schaff, *History of the Christian Church*, III, 608-9; also see Augustine, *The City of God*, XVIII, 36.

[22]The complete list of Old and New Testament books for Hippo (393) is also given in Canon XXIV of the Council of Carthage (419), and is commonly known as the "African Code"; cf. Philip Schaff, *The Nicene and Post-Nicene Fathers* (2d series), XIV, 453-54.

15

THE NEW TESTAMENT APOCRYPHA
AND PSEUDEPIGRAPHA

The books involved in the canonicity of the New Testament may be divided into four classes: (1) Homologoumena, books accepted by virtually everyone as canonical; (2) Antilegomena, books disputed by some; (3) Pseudepigrapha, books rejected by everyone as unauthentic; and (4) Apocrypha, books accepted by some as canonical or semicanonical. These classifications are comparable with those of Eusebius, who categorized them into: (1) acknowledged books; (2) disputed books; (3) spurious books; and (4) heretical books, which are "absurd and impious."

BOOKS ACCEPTED BY ALL—HOMOLOGOUMENA

NATURE OF THE HOMOLOGOUMENA

The Homologoumena are those books which have been universally acclaimed as canonical from their beginning. They have appeared in virtually every ancient version and orthodox canonical list, as well as having been widely quoted as Scripture. None of these books was deliberately deleted from the circulating canon in orthodox circles or brought into question by any prominent Father. Of course, the exact number of these books will vary depending on one's definition of "orthodox" and "prominent"; but, for the most part, there is little disagreement on this point.

THE NUMBER OF THE HOMOLOGOUMENA

Generally speaking, twenty of the twenty-seven books of the New Testament are considered to be undisputed. This includes all of the books from Matthew through Philemon, plus I Peter and I John. It is true that some have also included the latter three books (Philemon, I Peter, I John) among the disputed books; however, it is probably better to refer to these as omitted rather than disputed books. A disputed book is characterized as one that is retained and yet questioned, not merely one that is not quoted nor included in a given list. Unless there is clear evidence that a book was absent from a canonical list or from a Father's quotation (or enumeration) because it was considered of doubtful authenticity or authority, it would be better not to classify it as Antilegomena. In either event, if the seven disputed books were extended to ten, they, interestingly enough, would still be among the last books in the order of the New Testament.

THE DISPUTED BOOKS—ANTILEGOMENA

THE NATURE OF THE ANTILEGOMENA

It has already been implied that the reason for certain books having been classed as Antilegomena consists in the fact that these books possessed neither uniform nor universal recognition in the early church. They were books which became the subject of canonical controversy and had, as it were, their canonical "ins" and "outs." It should be said, however, that these books were seldom considered anticanonical, or even uncanonical; but they were given a sort of semicanonical status, as has sometimes been accorded to the Old Testament Apocrypha (see chap. 13).

THE NUMBER OF THE ANTILEGOMENA

There are seven significant books in the Antilegomena, that is, seven books that may be properly called "disputed books." Of a possible ten such books there is good early evidence for the canonicity of I Peter, I John, and even the brief epistle to Philemon (see chap. 14). Certainly there is almost no evidence that those who possessed these three books did not consider them authentic and apostolic. The seven books which came in question for various reasons are Hebrews, James, II Peter, II and III John, Jude and Revelation. In order to clearly understand the issue at stake, the books "spoken against" (Antilegomena) must be carefully and individually considered.

Hebrews. This book was questioned because of its anonymity. In the East, where it was considered Pauline, it was readily received. The West was slower, however, since they were not certain of its apostolic authorship, and possibly because the heretical Montanist sect appealed to Hebrews for one of their erroneous doctrines.[1] In the fourth century, through the influence of Jerome and Augustine, the

[1]Everett F. Harrison, *Introduction to the New Testament,* p. 345.

West finally recognized the epistle as canonical. One other reason that the West was slow in its deliberation was its stress upon apostolic authorship rather than apostolic authority as the correct test of canonicity (see chap. 13).

James. This was questioned as to its veracity, although some questioned its authorship as well. The supposed conflict with Paul on justification by faith held back full acceptance as late as the time of Eusebius.[2] Even during the Reformation period, Luther had doubts about James, calling it "a right strawy epistle," and placing it at the end of his New Testament, with Hebrews, Jude and Revelation, in a lesser position. As a result of the work of Origen, Eusebius (who personally favored James), Jerome and Augustine, the West finally recognized its complementary nature to Paul's epistles and hence, its canonicity.

II Peter. Its genuineness was questioned. In fact, no other book in the New Testament has been questioned as persistently as II Peter. Even Calvin seemed to be unsure of it. Jerome stated that the hesitancy to accept II Peter was due to dissimilarity of style with I Peter.[3] Whether, as Jerome thought, this characteristic is due to a different amanuensis may never be fully settled. It is clear, however, that ample evidence is now available to attest that this epistle is rightly attributed to the Apostle Peter.[4]

1. Another reason for rejecting II Peter has been the claim that it is a second century work, but W. F. Albright has pointed out the reminiscences of Qumran literature in II Peter, and dates it before A.D. 80.[5]

2. The recently discovered Bodmer manuscript, (P 72), which contains the earliest known copy of II Peter (late third century), reveals that it was in use and highly respected by Coptic Christians in Egypt during the third century.[6]

3. Besides the possible allusions to II Peter in *Pseudo-Barnabas* 15:4 (cf. II Peter 3:8), there is the testimony of Origen, Eusebius, Jerome and Augustine which finally triumphed. Warfield keenly

[2]Eusebius, *Ecclesiastical History*, II, 23. Loeb ed., I, 179.
[3]Jerome, *Catalogus Scriptorum Ecclesiasticorum* as cited by Harrison, p. 389.
[4]Harrison, pp. 386 ff.
[5]William Foxwell Albright, *From the Stone Age to Christianity*, 2d ed., pp. 22-23.
[6]Marchant A. King, "Notes on the Bodmer Manuscript of Jude and 1 and 2 Peter," *Bibliotheca Sacra*, Vol. CXXI, No. 481 (Jan.-Mar., 1964), pp. 54-57; or see "The Text of I Peter in Papyrus 72," *Journal of Biblical Literature*, LXXXX (Sept., 1961), 253.

observes that there is more evidence for II Peter than there is for Herodotus and Thucydides.[7]

4. Furthermore, there is positive internal evidence for the authenticity of II Peter. For although there are some marked differences, there are some close similarities to I Peter both linguistically and doctrinally.[8]

II and III John. These were also questioned as to their genuineness. Because of their private nature and limited circulation, they enjoyed neither a widespread nor an early acceptance. The author identified himself not as an apostle but as an elder, a fact which also hindered its acceptance. All their liabilities notwithstanding, these two epistles were more widely recognized than II Peter, being recognized in the Muratorian Canon as well as by some of the Fathers in the second century. Furthermore, the similarity of style and thought to I John, and the use of "elder" by apostles on other occasions (I Peter 5:1), argues strongly for the Johannine authorship.

Jude. This was disputed on the question of authenticity. The majority of those who questioned Jude did so on the basis of its reference to the Pseudepigraphal Book of Enoch (vv. 14-15; cf. Enoch 1:9), and possibly also to the Assumption of Moses (v. 9). Origen hints at this in his day[9] and Jerome specifically says this is the reason it was challenged.[10] It is interesting to note that Tertullian defended Jude as authoritative because it *did* refer to Enoch.[11] However, "the explanation that has most commended it is that Jude's citation of Enoch does not demand approval of the work as a whole, but extends only to those portions that he utilizes for his purpose. This situation is not materially different from Paul's references to pagan poets (Acts 17:28; I Cor. 15:33; Titus 1:12)."[12] The external evidence for Jude is widespread from the time of Irenaeus (*c.* A.D. 170). Like II Peter, the recently published Bodmer papyrus Codex P 72 from Egypt confirms the use of Jude during the third century. In fact, traces of Jude's influence may be found in the *Didache* (2:7).

Revelation. This was included in the Antilegomena because its authenticity was challenged. The doctrine of *chiliasm* (millennialism) was the focal point of the controversy which lasted longer than

[7]Benjamin B. Warfield, *Syllabus on the Special Introduction to the Catholic Epistles,* pp. 116-17.
[8]J. D. Douglas (ed.), *The New Bible Dictionary,* p. 978.
[9]Origen, *Commentary on Matthew,* 18:30.
[10]Jerome, *Lives of Illustrious Men,* chap. 4.
[11]Tertullian, *On the Apparel of Women,* I:3, *Ante-Nicene Fathers,* IV, 16-17.
[12]Harrison, p. 404.

that over any other New Testament book. It is a curious thing that Revelation was one of the first books to be recognized in existing writings of the Apostolic Fathers, and one of the last to be questioned. Evidence for its immediate reception in the first century is probable, since the "seven churches" to which it was addressed would naturally want to preserve a work that related to them so directly. There is external evidence for its recognition from the time of the *Shepherd* of Hermas, continuing on into the second century until the Montanists began to attach their unique form of millennialism to it. Around the middle of the third century, Dionysius, the Bishop of Alexandria, raised his influential voice against the Apocalypse. His views prevailed through the time of Eusebius of Caesarea to the time of Athanasius and the Council of Carthage (A.D. 397) when this trend was reversed. It seems clear that the question was not one of inspiration, but interpretation and association with particular doctrinal emphases that occasioned the dispute. Once the air was cleared of these, the authentic apostolic authority of Revelation was vindicated.

As with Revelation, so with all of the disputed books: once the question of authenticity or genuineness was settled, there was no problem about the canonicity. If it was clear that a book was written by a "prophet of God," and it told the "truth about God, man, etc.," then it was recognized to be the "word of God."

THE BOOKS REJECTED BY ALL—PSEUDEPIGRAPHA

THE NATURE OF THE PSEUDEPIGRAPHA

During the first few centuries, numerous books of a fanciful and heretical nature arose that are neither genuine nor valuable as a whole. Eusebius called these "totally absurd and impious." Virtually no orthodox Father, canon or council considered these books to be canonical and, so far as the church is concerned, they have historical value only, indicating the heretical teachings of Gnostic, Docetic and ascetic groups, as well as the exaggerated fancy of religious lore in the early church. At best, these books were revered by some of the cults and referred to by some of the orthodox Fathers, but they were never considered canonical by the mainstream of Christianity.

THE NUMBER OF THE PSEUDEPIGRAPHA

There was apparently a large number of these books even in the first century (cf. Luke 1:1-2). By the ninth century, Photius listed some 280 of them, and more have subsequently been discovered. The following list includes some of the more important Pseudepigraphal books of the New Testament:

GOSPELS

1. *The Gospel of Thomas* (first century), a Gnostic view of Jesus' childhood miracles.

2. *The Gospel of the Ebionites* (second century), Gnostic Christians maintained Old Testament practices in this work.

3. *The Gospel of Peter* (second century), a Docetic and Gnostic forgery.

4. *Protevangelium of James* (second century), a story from Mary to the massacre of babies.

5. *The Gospel of the Egyptians* (second century), ascetic teaching against marriage, meat and wine.

6. *Arabic Gospel of Childhood* (?), childhood miracles in Egypt. Zoroastrian magi.

7. *The Gospel of Nicodemus* (second or fifth century), contains *Acts of Pilate* and *Descent of Jesus*.

8. *The Gospel of Joseph the Carpenter* (fourth century), the writing of the Monophysite cult that glorified Joseph.

9. *The History of Joseph the Carpenter* (fifth century), Monophysite version of life of Joseph.

10. *The Passing of Mary* (fourth century), bodily assumption and advance stage of Mary worship.

11. *The Gospel of Nativity of Mary* (sixth century), promotes Mary worship and is the basis of the *Golden Legend*, a thirteenth century best seller on the lives of the saints by James of Orogeny.

12. *The Gospel of Pseudo-Matthew* (fifth century), visit to Egypt and later boyhood miracles.

13-21. *The Gospel of the Twelve; The Gospel of Barnabas; The Gospel of Bartholomew; The Gospel According to the Hebrews; The Gospel of Marcion; The Gospel of Andrew; The Gospel of Matthias; The Gospel of Peter; The Gospel of Philip;* etc.

ACTS

1. *The Acts of Peter* (second century), contains legend that Peter was crucified upside down.

2. *The Acts of John* (second century), ascetic, Docetic and Gnostic influences.

3. *The Acts of Andrew* (?), story of imprisonment and death of Andrew, Gnostic and ascetic.

4. *The Acts of Thomas* (?), deeds and martyrdom of Thomas who went to India.

5-8. *The Acts of Paul; The Acts of Matthias; The Acts of Philip; The Acts of Thaddaeus;* etc.

EPISTLES

1. *The Letter Attributed to Our Lord*, response to request for healing by king of Mesopotamia. Jesus said He would send someone after His resurrection.

2. *The Lost Epistle to Corinthians* (second-third century), forgery based on I Corinthians 5:9, found in the fifth century Armenian Scriptures.

3. *The (6) Letters of Paul to Seneca* (fourth century), forgery, recommending Christianity to Seneca's students.

4. *The Epistle of Paul to the Laodiceans,* forgery of an epistle mentioned in Colossians 4:16 (listed also under Apocrypha).

APOCALYPSES

1. *The Apocalypse of Peter.*
2. *The Apocalypse of Paul.*
3. *The Apocalypse of Thomas.*
4. *The Apocalypse of Stephen.*[13]

Although the canons, councils and orthodox Fathers never considered the Pseudepigrapha to be inspired, because of their exaggerated fancy and heretical tendencies, they no doubt reflect fragments of truths behind their excesses, and they do reveal the consciousness (and corruption) of sections of the church even in the early centuries.

[13]For critical introduction to these extracanonical books and others see Edgar Hennecke's *New Testament Apocrypha,* Wilhelm Schneemelcher (ed.), Vol. I.

BOOKS ACCEPTED BY SOME—APOCRYPHA

THE NATURE OF THE APOCRYPHA

The distinction between the Pseudepigrapha and the Apocrypha in most cases is a valid one, but it becomes rather tenuous in other instances.

For the most part, these books were not received as canonical and, like the Pseudepigrapha, they were used heretically by the sects and even homiletically by the orthodox. Nonetheless, on the whole they have one further characteristic, namely, they were not only part of the informal homiletical canon but sometimes appeared in local ecclesiastical canons and Bible translations. The first seven in the list below are what Souter called "Books of Temporal and Local Canonicity," or books that "had canonicity, or something very like it, in a particular church for a particular period, but were afterward dropped."[14] There can be little doubt that some of the Fathers and churches considered some of these books to be canonical. Nevertheless the testimony of the church in general, as well as the final canonical decisions, reveals that their judgment was faulty. Still, local acceptance and wide circulation of some of these books manifest their value as well as their esteem.

THE NUMBER OF THE APOCRYPHA

Here again, the number is somewhat arbitrary, because it is based on two distinctions that are difficult to determine precisely, that is, the difference between the "homiletical" and "ecclesiastical" canons, and between the "orthodox" and "heretical" Fathers. In a general way, the latter may be determined by the canons and creeds of the church councils of the first five centuries, while the former by whether or not the book was used only homiletically, or theologically and authoritatively. The following list, and perhaps more, fits into the category of books used at least ecclesiastically, and possibly canonically.

Epistle of Pseudo-Barnabas (c. A.D. 70-79). This widely circulated epistle is found in the Sinaitic manuscript (Aleph), and mentioned in the table of contents of *Bezae* (D) (c. 550). It was quoted as Scripture by Clement of Alexandria and Origen. It parallels the canonical epistle to the Hebrews in style although it is more allegorical and mystical than Hebrews, and there is some debate as to whether it is a first or second century document. Nonetheless, it may

[14]Alexander Souter, *The Text and Canon of the New Testament,* pp. 178-81.

be concluded with Westcott that "while the antiquity of the Epistle is firmly established, its Apostolicity is more than questionable."[15]

Epistle to the Corinthians (c. A.D. 96). Dionysius of Corinth (160-80) says that this epistle by Clement of Rome was read publicly at Corinth and elsewhere,[16] and it is found in the Alexandrian manuscript (A) of the New Testament (c. 450). Andrews sums up the situation on this epistle, saying,

> Today no one would put in a plea for its recognition as Scripture, yet from a historical point of view the Epistle has no little interest for us. . . . It gives us a very good conception of the Christian belief at the time. . . . It contains explicit references to Paul's first Epistle to the Corinthians, and gives several quotations from the Epistle to the Hebrews, and so proves that these books were widely circulated and recognized before the close of the first century.[17]

Ancient Homily, or the so-called Second Epistle of Clement (c. A.D. 120-40). This was known and used in the second century. In the Alexandrian manuscript (A) it is placed after the book of Revelation, with *I Clement* and the *Psalms of Solomon* as a sort of appendix. There is no clear evidence, however, that it was considered fully canonical, at least not on any broad scale.

Shepherd of Hermas (c. A.D. 115-40). This is the most popular of all the noncanonical books of the New Testament. It is found in Sinaiticus (Aleph), in the table of contents of *Bezae* (D), in some Latin Bibles, quoted as inspired Scripture by Irenaeus and Origen, and Eusebius recognized that "it was publicly read in the churches" and "deemed most necessary for those who have need of elementary instruction." The *Shepherd* has been aptly called the "Pilgrim's Progress" of the early church. Like Bunyan's great allegory, it ranks second only to the canonical books in its circulation, as well as in its dramatization of spiritual truths. In other words, it is like Ecclesiasticus of the Old Testament Apocrypha—ethical and devotional, but not canonical.

Didache, Teaching of the Twelve (c. A.D. 100-20). This was held in high regard by the early church. Clement of Alexandria quoted it as Scripture, and Athanasius listed it among the sacred writings

---

[15]Brooke Foss Westcott, *A General Survey of the History of the Canon of the New Testament*, p. 41.
[16]Cf. Eusebius, IV, 23. Loeb ed., I, 383.
[17]Herbert T. Andrews, *An Introduction to the Apocryphal Books of the Old and New Testaments*, C. F. Pfeiffer (rev. and ed.), p. 102.

along with Judith and Tobit. This book is of great importance from the historical point of view, giving the opinion of the church of the early second century on the essential truths of Christianity, and it forms a bridge between the New Testament and the patristic literature;[18] nevertheless, the verdict of history is at one with Eusebius who placed it among the "rejected books."

Apocalypse of Peter (*c.* 150). This is perhaps the oldest of the noncanonical New Testament apocalypses, and it enjoyed great popularity in the early church. It is mentioned in the *Muratorian Fragment,* in the table of contents of *Bezae* (D), and is quoted by Clement of Alexandria. Its description of heaven is picturesque, and its pictures of hell are grotesque, depicting it as a lake of "flaming mire" or "a lake of pitch and blood and boiling mire." Its imagery had a wide influence on medieval theology, and was a source from which Dante's *Inferno* was derived. As to its authenticity, even the *Muratorian Fragment* had questions, saying that some would not permit it to be read in the churches. The church in general has agreed with that feeling.

The Acts of Paul and Thecla (170). This was quoted often by Origen and is in the table of contents of *Bezae* (D). Stripped of its mythical elements, it is the story of the conversion and testimony of an Iconian lady, Thecla, based on Acts 14:1-7. It no doubt embodies a genuine tradition, as such noted scholars as W. M. Ramsay and A. Deissmann have argued, but most scholars are inclined to agree with A. Harnack, who said it contains "a great deal of fiction and very little truth."

Epistle to the Laodiceans (fourth century?). This was known to Jerome, and was included in many Latin Bibles from the sixth to the fifteenth centuries. It is a forgery based on the reference of Paul in Colossians 4:16. A book by this name is mentioned in the *Muratorian Fragment,* although it may be another name for Ephesians,[19] which does not have "to the Ephesians" (in 1:1) in the leading manuscripts (Aleph, B, P 46). To quote J. B. Lightfoot, "The Epistle is a centro of Pauline phrases strung together without any definite connection or any clear object."[20] As late as A.D. 787, the Council of Nicea (II) warned against it, terming it "a forged epistle." It reappeared as late as the Reformation era in German and even in English Bibles. "Un-

---

[18]An interesting illustration of this transition may be seen in the case of baptism. The change from immersion to affusion may have been alluded to in *Didache* 7:1-4.
[19]Harrison, pp. 310-11.
[20]J. B. Lightfoot, *Saint Paul's Epistles to the Colossians and to Philemon,* p. 285.

like most forgeries it had no ulterior aim. . . . It has no doctrinal peculiarities. Thus it is quite harmless, so far as falsity and stupidity combined can ever be regarded as harmless."[21]

The Gospel According to the Hebrews (A.D. 65-100). Probably the earliest noncanonical gospel, it has survived only in a few fragmentary quotes culled from various Fathers of the church.[22] According to Jerome, some called it "the true Matthew," although this seems unlikely from its quotations, which bear little relation to the canonical Matthew. In fact, it is questionable whether it deserves to be called Apocryphal rather than Pseudepigraphal, since there is no evidence that it had any more than a homiletical usage. And, even if evidence be educed that it had a limited ecclesiastical use, it certainly was not canonical; as a matter of fact, it is not even extant.

Epistle of Polycarp to the Philippians (c. A.D. 108). In one sense, Polycarp is the most important of the Apostolic Fathers. He was a disciple of the Apostle John, and the teacher of Irenaeus. He lays no claim to inspiration for himself, but says that he "always taught the things he had learned from the apostles, and which the Church has handed down, and which alone are true."[23] There is very little originality in this epistle, as it borrows both matter and style from the New Testament, and particularly from Paul's epistle to the Philippians. Even though it was not considered canonical, it is a valuable testimony to the existence of most of the New Testament canon which he interweaves into his writing.[24]

The Seven Epistles of Ignatius (c. A.D. 110). These letters indicate a definite familiarity with the teachings of the New Testament, but have a marked peculiarity of style. Their teaching shows a strong belief in the unity of the visible church, with a bishop-centered government. Bishop J. B. Lightfoot has ably defended the genuineness of these epistles, but virtually no one contends for their canonicity.

EVALUATION OF THE NEW TESTAMENT APOCRYPHA AND PSEUDEPIGRAPHA

A brief evaluation of this vast body of early Christian literature will serve to focus on their significance in the early church as well as for the church today.

[21]*Ibid.*
[22]Andrews, p. 109.
[23]Irenaeus, *Against Heresies,* III, 3:4.
[24]Westcott, p. 37.

The Value of the New Testament Pseudepigrapha. In general, these books have no positive theological value, and almost no historical value, except as they reflect the religious consciousness of the church during early centuries. Their value may be thus summarized:

1. They contain, no doubt, the kernel of some correct traditions that, by careful "demythologizing," may furnish some supplementary historical facts about the early church.

2. They reflect the ascetic, Docetic and Gnostic tendencies and heresies of early Christianity.

3. They show a popular desire for information not given in the canonical Gospels, such as information about the childhood of Jesus, and the lives of the apostles.

4. They manifest an illegitimate tendency to glorify Christianity by means of pious frauds.

5. They display an unhealthy desire to find support for doctrinal interests and heretical teachings under the guise of apostolic authority.

6. They reveal an unwholesome attempt to fill up supposed lacks in the canonical writings.

7. They demonstrate the incurable tendency of depraved curiosity to arrive at heretical and fanciful embellishments of Christian truth (e.g., Mary worship).

The Value of the New Testament Apocrypha. There is no doubt that the theological and historical value of most of these books is much higher than that of the Pseudepigrapha. In brief, they are valuable, but not canonical.

1. They provide the earliest documentation of some of the canonical books of the New Testament.

2. They reveal the general teaching of the subapostolic church.

3. They form a bridge between the apostolic writings of the New Testament and the patristic literature of the third and fourth centuries, thus providing some clues to that transition.

4. They possess hints as to the rise of later false teachings and heresies (e.g., allegorical interpretation in *Pseudo-Barnabas,* or baptismal regeneration in the *Shepherd*).

5. They contain much of historical value about the practices and policies of the early church.

With the above values in mind, it should be emphasized that none of these books are to be considered canonical or inspired. Several reasons may be proffered in support of this contention. (1) None of them enjoyed any more than a *temporary* or *local* recognition. (2) Most of them never did have anything more than a semicanonical status, being appended to various manuscripts or mentioned in tables of contents. (3) No major canon or church council included them as inspired books of the New Testament. (4) The limited acceptance enjoyed by most of these books is attributable to the fact that they attached themselves to references in canonical books (e.g., Laodiceans to Col. 4:16), because of their alleged apostolic authorship (e.g., Acts of Paul), or because apostolicity was misunderstood to mean "from the Apostolic Age" rather than "from an apostle" or "with apostolic authority." Once these issues were clarified, there remained little doubt that they were not canonical.

SUMMARY AND CONCLUSION

On the question of New Testament canonicity, twenty of the twenty-seven books were never seriously questioned in orthodox circles, namely, the Homologoumena. The other seven books, called Antilegomena, were questioned by some Fathers for a time, but were finally and fully recognized by the church generally. There are numerous books that were never accepted by anyone as authentic or canonical which are called Pseudepigrapha. The final class of books is called Apocrypha. These were books of good quality and integrity which had a local and temporary acceptance, although they were never widely nor finally considered to be canonical.

Part Three

TRANSMISSION OF THE BIBLE

16

LANGUAGES OF THE BIBLE

There are three links in the chain "from God to us": inspiration, canonization and transmission. In the first, God gave the message to the prophets who received and recorded it. Canonization, the second link, dealt with the recognition and collection of the prophetic writings. In effect, the objective disclosure was complete when the sixty-six books of the Bible were written, and then recognized by their original readers. However, in order for succeeding generations to share in this revelation the Scriptures had to be copied, translated, recopied and retranslated. This process not only provided the Scriptures for other nations, but for other generations as well. This third link is known as transmission of the Bible.

Since the Scriptures have undergone some two thousand years of transmission, it is only natural to ask: How much has the Bible suffered in the process? Or, to put it more precisely: Is the twentieth century English Bible an accurate reproduction of the first century Greek Testament and the Hebrew Old Testament? The answer to this question comes from the science of textual criticism, which will now be traced in terms of the transmission of the biblical text.

WHY GOD CHOSE WRITTEN LANGUAGES

Several alternatives were open to God in His choice of a means for communication of His truth to men. As a matter of fact, a wide variety of the media of communication were actually utilized by God "in time past," as He "spake unto the fathers by the prophets" (Heb. 1:1, AV).

WHAT GOD COULD HAVE USED

God could have chosen to continue to communicate with men as He did initially in biblical times.

Sometimes God spoke through angels. (Cf. Gen. 18-19, 22; Exodus 3.) In fact, their very name means "messenger." Their ministry

211

began in Genesis (chaps. 18-19), and continued through the very last chapter of the Bible (Rev. 22:8 f.). However, the very nature of this celestial intrusion into the terrestrial made it a special revelation which did not lend itself to permanence. There were certain distinct limitations in having to call upon angels to convey everything that God wished to say to every man under every circumstance in every age. One could imagine quite an endless invasion from outer space in order to care for all the details of truth transmitted to billions of people, many of which have short memories.

Visions and dreams. This was another means of communication which God occasionally chose to utilize (cf. Dan. 7:1; Gen. 41). This means of revelation had more potential for universality and individuality than did angels, since it did not involve the mass of heavenly traffic, and since it could even be worked into one's personal experience more readily. However, this method also has serious handicaps. For one thing, visions and dreams tend to be subjective and personal rather than objective and universal. For another, even their ecstatic impact could wear off and be forgotten.

The Urim and Thummim and the Lot. These methods were sometimes used to determine God's will (see Exodus 28:30; Prov. 16:33). However, they were limited in the scope of the content of truth they could convey. Apparently, all they could indicate was a yes or no answer to questions that men happened to direct toward God. Thus, their scope was quite limited when compared with a detailed description of God's declarations to men found in other media of transmission.

The voice of conscience, and creation. One's conscience (Rom. 2:15) as well as creation (Ps. 19:1 ff.) no doubt revealed God's truth; but, here again the amount of truth was limited, subjective (particularly with reference to conscience), and subject to corruption. Romans 1:18-19 admits to the revelation of creation; but, while it is "clearly seen," men "suppress the truth in unrighteousness" (NASB). Conscience, of course, is subject not only to culture and conditioning, but to corruption (I Cor. 8:7) as well, and it can even be "seared" (I Tim. 4:2).

The audible voice and the direct miracle. These were also media of divine communication (see I Sam. 3 and Judges 6:40), but they suffered from the same intrinsic difficulties that the other means had, namely, they were good ways for God to speak to one man on one occasion and for one specific purpose. Nevertheless, it would be a strain on the divine economy to expect a repeat performance of these feats in speaking to all men everywhere. This is not to say that all of these methods were not good; they were in fact the ways by which God did speak to the prophets. There was, however, "a more excellent way" to communicate; it was a more precise, more permanent, and more easily disseminated revelation which was just as personal.

WHAT GOD CHOSE TO USE

It was no doubt desirable to speak *to* the prophets "in divers manners," but the best way to speak to the men of all ages through the prophets was to *record* the communication. While no one can doubt that language, whether written or spoken, is not a "perfect" means of communication, it cannot be denied that it was the "best" means available, nor that the best means was "adequate." In other words, what means could one devise to convince anyone that language is not adequate to communicate something other than a language itself? It is incongruous to observe that the scholars who raise a voice against the adequacy of language have found language adequate enough to convey their view that language is not adequate! The time-tested superiority of a written record of truth was the one God chose to use in order to make permanent and immortalize His message to men. There were several decided advantages to this medium of revelation.

Precision. One of the advantages of language over the other media of communication mentioned is the matter of precision. It is a common experience that thoughts become more precise as they are expressed. In this connection it may be said that a student can understand better with a pencil than with any other instrument; because, if a thought can be apprehended and expressed in writing, it must have been clearly understood. Another illustration of the precision of language is the difference between one's active and his passive vocabularies. It is possible to read and understand, in a general way, more words than one can use or write in a specific way. This is true because the accurate usage of words requires a more precise understanding of them, and precision is attained by expression. The proof of this point is the fact that mankind's most treasured knowledge to date is in the form of written records and books. It is understandable, then, that God should choose to have His truth conveyed by books as precisely as is possible.

Propagation. There is another advantage to written revelation, namely, the matter of propagation. It is possible to make more precise copies of a written medium than a spoken one. No one will disagree that a written copy can be, and usually is, a much more accurate reproduction than an oral tradition. No matter how careful the communication is made orally, there is always a greater chance for change and corruption of the original than with a written record. A simple experiment will suffice to convince the skeptic. The word-of-mouth story passed around a circle of friends returns with amazing emendations in a few short minutes. In fact, it is astounding to note that Jesus' disciples misinterpreted and mistransmitted a simple oral tradition which they thought they had heard Jesus say (cf. John 21:23). Thus, in order to accurately transmit revealed truth, written records were made and copied by hand, until the invention of movable type in the printing process. Once the movable type had been invented (in the fifteenth century), the advantage of the printed page, and ability to reproduce it on a mass scale, became most apparent.

Preservation. A final advantage of writing is the matter of preservation. Failing memories are sometimes a blessing, but they are a decided disadvantage in the retention of the repertoire of revelation. It is always better to "make a note of it," or to "put it on record." As a matter of fact, it is difficult to imagine the adjudication of justice in a court without a record of testimony, to say nothing of the vacillation of memory in other realms. A written record has one additional advantage as well, namely, it can stimulate memory and conjure up within the individual's imagination a host of personal implications that are latent within the given symbols or words of that record. Words, then, are not so wooden as to prevent a "personal blessing" for the individual reader, particularly in light of the fact that biblical words are only the objective vehicle through which the Holy Spirit applies truth personally and subjectively to each reader individually (cf. John 16:13; I Peter 1:11).

WHICH LANGUAGES GOD CHOSE

Having discussed why God chose to commit His truth to men by way of writing, it is only natural to examine which languages He chose. Ostensibly, it could be expected that He who "accomplishes all things according to the counsel of his will" (Eph. 1:11), and who brought forth Christ "when the time had fully come" (Gal. 4:4), would have chosen languages that were particularly suited to the purpose of His revelation. Happily, such is the case with the biblical languages as the following examination will reveal.

OLD TESTAMENT LANGUAGES: THE SEMITIC FAMILY

The migrations of the descendants of Noah as recorded in Genesis 10 and 11 make mention of the sons of Shem, after whom the Semitic languages receive their name. These genealogical tables explicitly denote the geographical relationships of the children of Noah as they were known to one living in the Near East during the second millennium B.C. Although these tables present political relationships implicitly, they have little or no bearing on their linguistic relationships. Nevertheless, the Semitic family of languages forms the basis of the Old Testament, and a survey of its various divisions should provide needed clarification.

The Eastern Division. This division of the Semitic family boasts of having Akkadian as its spokesman. This language was the common language of all Southwest Asia during the height of the Old Babylonian and Assyrian empires, a fact evidenced by the Amarna Letters which were sent by petty kings in Syria and Palestine to the Pharaohs in Egypt around 1400-1360 B.C. This language was not used in the Old Testament.

The Southern Division. This division has two chief groups: the Arabic and the Ethiopic. Neither of these languages was used in the Old Testament. Ethiopic was the language of Ethiopia (Cush), a country referred to in each section of the Old Testament (cf. Gen. 10:7 f.; Isa. 45:14; Ps. 68:31). Arabic, the most widely spoken Semitic language today, swept over the Semitic-speaking peoples with the rise of Islam in the seventh century A.D.

The Northern Division. This division of Semitic is represented by Amorite and Aramaic (Syriac).[1] The Amorites inhabited Palestine before and during Israel's occupation (cf. Gen. 10:16; 15:16; Deut. 7:1; Joshua 10:6; II Chron. 8:7), but their language was not used in the writing of the Old Testament. Aramaic was the language of the

---

[1]Most scholars oversimplify the divisions of the Semitic branch to the point of error, which is ill-advised and unnecessary; e.g., Mario A. Pei, *The World's Chief Languages* (4th ed.), pp. 29-30; *Encyclopaedia Britannica* (1954 ed.), XX, 314-18; and even *Webster's Third International Dictionary*, p. 38.

Syrians, and was used in all three sections of the Old Testament, either in writing or in place names (cf. Gen. 10:22; 31:47; II Kings 18:26; Isa. 36:11; Jer. 10:11; Ezra 4:7–6:18; 7:12-26; Dan. 2:4–7:28).

The Northwest Division. This division of the Semitic family includes the Canaanite subdivision as well as Aramaic elements, and is represented by four dialects: Ugaritic, Phoenician, Moabite and Hebrew.

Ugaritic is not used in the Old Testament, but it has been instrumental in further study of the cognate Hebrew language of the Old Testament. This was the language of the Ras Shamra Tablets, being discovered in Northern Syria since 1929, which provides another key to the Canaanite dialects.

Phoenician is another important language which was not used in the Old Testament, although these people are mentioned in all three sections (cf. Gen. 10:8-12; I Kings 5:6; Neh. 13:16; Ezek. 27:9; Zeph. 1:11). The contribution of the Phoenicians is a major one, since it was they who introduced the alphabet to other languages,[2] thus making writing much less cumbersome than it was for the Akkadians.

Lot's descendants developed two dialects of Hebrew: Moabite by way of his oldest daughter, and Ammonite by way of the younger. Neither of these languages were used in the Old Testament; however, their nations are referred to repeatedly in all three sections of the Old Testament. The Moabite Stone (*c.* 850 B.C.) is the first really long inscription in any Canaanite language that has been discovered (found in 1868 at Dibon), and is the account of the Moabite king, Mesha, concerning the revolt mentioned in II Kings 1:1; 3:4-27.

Hebrew is by far the most important language of the Old Testament.[3] Most of the Old Testament is written in it, and it is called "the language of Judah" (II Kings 18:26, 28), as well as "the language of Canaan" (Isa. 19:18). Except for the portions mentioned above (cf. Aramaic in particular), the Old Testament was written in this language. During its long history, Hebrew has developed into the Biblical, Mishnaic, Rabbinic, Medieval, and Modern dialects.

---

[2] See F. F. Bruce, *The Books and the Parchments,* rev. ed., pp. 15-32, for an excellent discussion on "The Bible and the Alphabet."
[3] *Ibid.,* pp. 33-47 discusses "The Hebrew Language."

NEW TESTAMENT LANGUAGES: SEMITIC FAMILY AND INDO-
    EUROPEAN FAMILY

There is no need to retrace the various divisions of the Semitic
family, and the Indo-European family is traced in more detail at
a later point;[4] hence, the present discussion deals with the individual
languages involved in the New Testament.

The Semitic Family. This is represented by both Hebrew and
Aramaic (Syriac). Most of the Hebrew influence is seen in the
Greek translation of the former's idiom. This may be seen in the
use of the expression "and it came to pass"; the use of two nouns
rather than an adjective and a noun (cf. I Thess. 1:3, Eph. 1:13),
and calling someone a child or son of a given quality if he has that
quality (cf. Luke 10:6; Eph. 2:3).[5] Aramaic was no doubt the
spoken language of the Lord and His disciples. It was the source
of such words as Cephas, Matthew, Abba (Mark 14:36), and Mara-
natha (I Cor. 16:22, AV). It is also noteworthy that in the very hour
of His agony on the cross, Jesus cried out in His native Aramaic
tongue, " 'Eli, Eli, lama sabachthani?' that is to say, 'My God, my
God, why hast thou forsaken me?' " (Matt. 27:46).

The Indo-European Family. Even more prominent are Latin and
Greek. While Latin was used in the Eastern Roman Empire mostly
by the legions, it made its influence felt in the Rabbinical Hebrew,
spoken Aramaic, and Greek writings.[6] Its influence in the New
Testament is found mainly in loanwords, for example, centurion
(Mark 15:39, 44-45); tribute (Matt. 17:25; Mark 12:14, AV); legion
(Matt. 26:53). In addition to this, the inscription on the cross was
written in Latin, Hebrew and Greek.[7] The Greek of the New Testament has been quite problematic through the centuries. The basic
language of the New Testament, it has gone through a series of
changes similar to Latin, Hebrew and English. There are five basic
periods of Greek: Homeric, Attic, Koine, Byzantine, and Modern.
Until the late nineteenth century, the language of the New Testament (Koine) was considered a sort of special "Holy Ghost" language, since it was not specifically identifiable with any of the other
four periods, and the vocabulary was somewhat different. However,
with the discovery in the late nineteenth century of first century
letters and other documents in Egypt, this view began to give way

[4]See chap. 28.
[5]See Joseph Angus, *The Bible Handbook,* Samuel G. Green, rev., pp. 181-84.
[6]Bruce, pp. 48-57.
[7]For a comprehensive list of New Testament Latinisms, see *Ibid.,* pp. 72-73.

to the current view, that the New Testament was written in the language of the common people. It should be pointed out that Koine, or Hellenistic Greek, "is not confined to the vernacular speech. There was a flourishing *koine* literature in the centuries before and after the time of Christ."[8] It was this language that was most widely known throughout the world: its alphabet was derived from the Phoenicians, its language and culture were not limited to a given geographical area, it became the official language of the empires into which Alexander's conquests were divided, and even the Romans used Greek in their literature as fluently as they did Latin. This language was not a special "Holy Ghost" language, but its appearance was certainly providentially directed, as Paul implied in his statement "When the time had fully come, God sent forth his Son" (Gal. 4:4).

WHY GOD CHOSE THESE LANGUAGES

Now that the background and development of the biblical languages have been traced, it remains to examine how they fit God's purpose of revelation. What was it that made these languages, above others, particularly appropriate channels for God's truth? In theorizing about this point, it would be imprudent to overlook a very practical purpose for God's choice of both major and minor languages, namely, they were the primary languages of the times and the people to whom God was speaking.

MINOR LANGUAGES

Aramaic. This language, which shows influence in both vocabulary and form in the New Testament, was the local language of the land of Palestine and much of Syria when Jesus and the apostles lived and ministered. It was no doubt the language that Jesus used in day-to-day conversation.[9] Furthermore, Aramaic had been the

---

[8]*Ibid.*, p. 65, but also see this entire chapter, entitled "The Greek Language," pp. 58-73.

[9]Some have argued that the Gospels were originally written in Aramaic (cf. C. C. Torrey, *The Four Gospels*). Although certain others have shared this view, there are serious objections against it. W. F. Albright has pointed out that "there is absolutely no trace so far of a continuous Aramaic literary tradition spanning the interval between the Achaemenian and earliest Hellenistic period on the one hand, and the second century A.D. on the other" (*The Background of the New Testament and Its Eschatology*, Davies and Daube [eds.], p. 155). Besides the fact that there has been no objective evidence for the existence of Aramaic originals of the Gospels, the view is rendered improbable by the broad Greek constituency of the early church, as well as by the commission of Christ that His followers take the gospel into all the world. Greek, and not Aramaic, was the only language spoken throughout the Mediterranean world.

lingua franca of the Near East in the sixth through fourth centuries B.C., until the conquests of Alexander the Great. This was the language of the documents, mostly papyri, left by the Jewish colony at Elephantine (near modern Aswan, Egypt) during the fifth century B.C.

Latin. On the other hand, Latin, which made its influence felt in the New Testament, was the military and political language of the Roman Empire. This Empire included Herod's Palestine; and, it was only natural that the New Testament would include the use of Latin and Latinisms to some degree.

MAJOR LANGUAGES

It would be too much to suppose, however, that Hebrew and Greek, the major biblical languages, were chosen by God because they just happened to be the ones available when He decided to speak to man. The Christian theist who believes in special as well as general Providence will expect that God planned the very languages to fit the message and the age to which the message was addressed. On this assumption, an inquiry into these purposes may be briefly pursued.

Hebrew: its biographical suitability. The Old Testament is primarily the biography of a people and God's dealings with them. Hebrew was the primary language in which the Old Testament was written, and it was particularly suited for this kind of biographical expression for at least two reasons.

1. It is a *pictorial* language, speaking with vivid, bold metaphors which challenge and dramatize the story. The Hebrew language possesses a facility to present "pictures" of the events narrated. "The Hebrew thought in pictures, and consequently his nouns are concrete and vivid. There is no such thing as neuter gender, for the Semite everything is alive. Compound words are lacking. . . . There is no wealth of adjectives. . . ."[10] The language shows "vast powers of association and, therefore, of imagination."[11] Some of this is lost in the English translation, but even so, "much of the vivid, concrete, and forthright character of our English Old Testament is really a carrying over into English of something of the genius of the Hebrew tongue."[12] As a pictorial lan-

[10]Elmer W. K. Mould, *Essentials of Bible History,* rev. ed., p. 307.
[11]Mary Ellen Chase, *Life and Language in the Old Testament,* p. 87.
[12]Bruce, p. 45.

guage, Hebrew presents a vivid picture of the acts of God among a people who became examples or illustrations for future generations (cf. I Cor. 10:11). Since the Old Testament was intended as a biographical book for believers, it was fitting for these truths to be presented graphically in a "picture-language."

2. Further, Hebrew is a *personal* language. It addresses itself to the heart and emotions rather than merely to the mind or reason. Sometimes even nations are given personalities (cf. Mal. 1:2-3). Always the appeal is to the person in the concrete realities of life and not to the abstract or theoretical. Hebrew is a language through which the message is felt rather than thought. As such, the language was highly qualified to convey to the individual believer as well as to the worshiping community the personal revelation of the living God in the events of the Jewish nation. It was much more qualified to record the realization of revelation in the life of a nation than to propositionalize that revelation for the propagation among all nations. F. F. Bruce summed up these characteristics well, when he wrote,

> Biblical Hebrew does not deal with abstractions but with the facts of experience. It is the right sort of language for the record of the self-revelation of a God who does not make Himself known by philosophical propositions but by controlling and intervening in the course of human history. Hebrew is not afraid to use daring anthropomorphisms when speaking of God. If God imparts to men the knowledge of Himself, He chooses to do so most effectively in terms of human life and human language.[13]

Greek: its evangelistic suitability. The foundation of God's revelation of Christ was laid in the biography of the Old Testament. The interpretation of the revelation of Christ was made in the theological language of the New Testament. New Testament Greek was appropriately adapted to this end of propositionalizing and propagating the truth about Christ for two basic reasons.

1. Greek was an *intellectual* language. It was more a language of the mind than of the heart, a fact to which the great Greek philosophers gave abundant evidence. Greek was more suited to codifying a communication or reflecting on a revelation of God in order to put it into simple communicable form. It was a language that could more easily render the credible into the intelligible than could Hebrew. It was for this reason that New Testa-

[13]*Ibid.*

ment Greek was a most useful medium for expressing the propositional truth of the New Testament, as Hebrew was for expressing the biographical truth of the Old Testament. Since Greek possessed a technical precision not found in Hebrew, the theological truths which were more generally expressed in the Hebrew of the Old Testament were more precisely formulated in the Greek of the New Testament.

2. Furthermore, Greek was a nearly *universal* language. The truth of God in the Old Testament, which was initially revealed to one nation (Israel), was appropriately recorded in the language of that nation (Hebrew). But the fuller revelation given by God in the New Testament was not restricted in that way. In the words of Luke's gospel, the message of Christ was to "be preached in his name to all nations" (Luke 24:47). The language most appropriate for the propagation of this message was naturally the one that was most widely spoken throughout the world. Such was the common (Koine) Greek, a thoroughly international language of the first century Mediterranean world.

It may be concluded, then, that God chose the very languages to communicate His truth which had, in His providence, been prepared to express most effectively the kind of truth He desired at that particular time, in the unfolding of His overall plan. Hebrew, with its pictorial and personal vividness, expressed well the biographical truth of the Old Testament. Greek, with its intellectual and universal potentialities, served well for the doctrinal and evangelistic demands of the New Testament.

SUMMARY AND CONCLUSION

The written word, with all of its limitations, was by far the most adequate means of conveying the truth of God because it could be more precisely presented, more easily preserved from corruption, and more effectively propagated. Therefore, when God—who spoke to the prophets by visions, dreams or angels—desired to speak through the prophets to succeeding generations, He chose to have them *write* their revelation. In the providence of God the Hebrew and Greek languages were prepared to express most appropriately the kind of revelation God desired for their particular days. Hebrew was a language well fitted to depict God's deeds in the biography of the Old Testament, and Greek was particularly suited to the expression and propagation of the doctrines of the New Testament.

17

WRITING MATERIALS

Before proceeding to the mechanics of transmission, it is needful to consider the materials used by the men of God in their communication of the message of God. This study involves the development of writing, the description of materials, and the divisions of the text, in order to make it more usable.

THE DEVELOPMENT OF WRITING

The Old Testament has nothing to say about the origin of writing, which seems to have been invented early in the fourth millennium B.C.,[1] but it does assume writing on the part of Moses,[2] who wrote not earlier than about 1450 B.C.[3] Many earlier records of writing have been discovered in various places. But, what was the character of these records? Were they drawings? Symbols? If so, what did they symbolize?

ADVANCES IN THE DEVELOPMENT OF WRITING

Three stages in the development of writing may be discerned: pictograms, ideograms and phonograms.

Pictograms. These were representations which long antedated the origin of writing, and played a role in the development of it. They were actually crude pictures which represented objects such as the sun, an old man, an eagle, an ox, a lion. As long as these pictograms represented nothing other than the object itself, there would be no difficulty in using them. However, as time passed the use of pictures to depict ideas appeared and the pictograms lost their dominant position in recorded communication.

Ideograms. These were the new items which superseded the pictogram. They were pictures which actually represented ideas rather than objects. Here the picture of the sun might represent heat; an

---

[1]See Samuel Noah Kramer, *History Begins at Sumer,* or any basic up-to-date work on the subject of writing in Sumer and/or Egypt.
[2]F. F. Bruce, *The Books and the Parchments,* rev. ed., p. 15.
[3]If the late date for Exodus is accepted, *c.* 1270 B.C.

old man might represent old age; an eagle, power; an ox, strength; a lion, regality. Thus, a long stride toward writing was taken; although writing in the modern sense was still a long way off. But ideograms, actually a particular use of pictograms, were not the only extension of pictograms.

Phonograms. These were another extension of pictograms. They were really representations of sounds rather than objects or ideas. Thus, a representation of the sun might speak of a son rather than the sun; a picture of a bear might be used to express "the verb 'to bear'; the picture of a bee to express the verb 'to be.' "[4] As a result, another step was taken in the direction of written languages, but there was still a long succession of events necessary before writing in the modern sense was achieved.

Ideographic and phonographic writings were later intermingled with simple syllabic writing, and this with a more sophisticated system of cuneiform, wedge-shaped signs was used by the Sumerians. Merrill F. Unger adequately summarizes the situation as he writes,

> Those who first attempted to reduce human speech to writing did not at once perceive the chasm that separates the spoken words from the characters in which they are symbolized. They wrote as they spoke in unbroken succession, inscribing the letters in closest proximity to each other, without separating them into words, much less into sentences, paragraphs and chapters.[5]

Although letters were used in writing by the time of Moses, they were consonants only, as vowels were added much later. Hence, an unbroken succession of consonants covering an entire tablet, later a scroll, and still later a codex (sheets of papyrus bound into a book form), would appear before the reader of a given text. Needless to say, even this was still far from the modern concept of writing.

AGE OF WRITING

Although the witnesses to writing in antiquity are far from abundant, there is sufficient evidence available to indicate that it was the hallmark of cultural achievement. During the second millennium B.C. there were several experiments which led to the development of the alphabet and written documents. In Palestine itself there have been very few documents which have survived from the preexilic period, but the evidence from surrounding territories makes it reasonable to

[4]Bruce, p. 23.
[5]Merrill F. Unger, *Introductory Guide to the Old Testament,* 2d ed., p. 115.

assume that the Israelites shared in the act of writing even earlier than the beginning of the Davidic kingdom. Several lines of evidence may be called upon to witness to the fact that writing was most certainly practiced by the Israelites prior to the time of the Moabite Stone of Mesha, king of Moab, which dates from about 850 B.C. It was this item that was used by the late-nineteenth century higher critical writers, for example, Graf and Wellhausen, as the earliest example of writing in Palestine. As a matter of fact, the higher critical view was formulated prior to the discovery of the material discussed below. The testimony of these discoveries overwhelmingly disproves that position.

6. *Cuneiform (Assyrian) inscription in stone from the palace of King Sargon II, Eighth century* B.C. *(The Louvre)*

Evidence from Mesopotamia. This dates from about 3500 B.C. and includes cuneiform tablets of the Sumerians. The successors to the Sumerians used the latter's cuneiform script in developing their own individual languages.[6] Leonard Woolley discovered many temple tablets in the ruins of ancient Ur of the Chaldees which date from about 2100 B.C.; however, they are antedated by many other tablets, including some dating to about 3500 B.C. found in Uruk (the Erech

[6]See Bruce, pp. 9-21, for an excellent discussion on the whole problem of alphabets, languages, etc. Also see Sir Frederic G. Kenyon, *Our Bible and the Ancient Manuscripts*, 4th ed., rev. and enlarged, pp. 3-15.

of Gen. 10:10) and Kish. The Sumerian flood narrative found at Nippur dates from about 2100 B.C.

Egyptian discoveries. These confirm those found in Mesopotamia, and they are dated about 3100 B.C. The hieroglyphic script first appeared in Egypt just prior to the founding of Dynasty I (c. 3100 B.C.), while its successors, the hieratic and demotic scripts, both appeared prior to the exilic period in Israel's history. Among the early Egyptian writings are *The Teachings for Kagemni* and *The Teaching of Ptah-Hetep* which date from about 2700 B.C. There are, in addition to these witnesses, other testimonies which illustrate the use of writing in Egypt prior to the time of Moses, Joseph, and even Abraham, regardless of the dates ascribed to each of these individuals. Furthermore, the Israelites must have been aware of writing techniques prior to their exodus from Egypt, for Moses was raised as a child with great position in the household of the pharaoh during the New Kingdom period. The New Testament record indicates the Hebrew traditional position, as Stephen bears witness in his famous sermon when he relates that "Moses was instructed in all the wisdom of the Egyptians, and he was mighty in his words and deeds" (Acts 7:22). This learning most likely included writing on papyrus, as papyrus was used in writing earlier than Dynasty V (c. 2500 B.C.).

East-Mediterranean testimony. This dates from about 2500 B.C., where pictographic signs were used in Byblos (Gebal) and Syria. As early as about 3100 B.C. there was writing used on cylinder seal impressions in Byblos. Leonard Woolley's discoveries at Atchana (in northern Syria) appear to have been contemporaneous to the records found by Sir Arthur Evans at Knossos, Crete. These records date into the mid-second millennium B.C., and they indicate that written records were used in these great commercial centers in pre-Mosaic and Mosaic times. In addition, they also indicate the connection between the mainland of Asia and the island bridge of Europe, namely, Crete.

Early Palestinian and Syrian contributions. These also date from the middle of the second millennium B.C. Alphabetic inscriptions from the turquoise mines in southern Sinai date from about 1500 B.C. A pottery fragment from Gezer is dated from about 1800 to 1500 B.C.; the Lachish dagger inscription is contemporary, as are inscriptions from Shechem, Beth-Shemesh, Hazor, and Tell el-Hesi. The Ras Shamra tablets, from the coastal site in northwest Syria identified as Ugarit, date from about 1500 to 1300 B.C. There they employed the

7. *The Moabite Stone
(The Oriental Insti-
tute)*

same diplomatic language as the Tel el-Amarna tablets (*c.* 1380 B.C.)
from the ancient Egyptian capital of Amenhotep IV (Akhenaton).
At Ras Shamra were also found specimens of the Canaanite language
written in alphabetic form. These writings were made by inscribing
unique cuneiform signs on clay tablets, known as the Ugaritic tablets
(see chap. 16).

All of the above evidence is extant from the period prior to the
Moabite Stone of Mesha, king of Moab. The event recorded on the
Moabite Stone is that revolt against Israel recorded in II Kings 1:1
and 3:4-27. Although the preceding evidence is not direct, it is overwhelming in its denunciation of the higher critical position. It is also
overwhelming in its demarcation of the history of writing before the

time of Moses. As a result, the over 450 biblical references to writing may be seen as reflective of the cultural diffusion between Israel and her neighbors.

ACTIVITY OF BIBLICAL WRITERS WITHIN LITERATE HISTORY

The foregoing discussion makes the assertion that "Moses and the other Biblical writers wrote during the literate age of man" almost redundant. Nevertheless, the biblical record itself asserts that its writers wrote. Several of the more than 450 biblical references may be called upon to indicate this fact.

The Law. This makes reference to several kinds of writing done by Moses and his predecessors (cf. Gen. 5:1[7]; Exodus 17:14; 24:4; 34:27-28; Num. 17:2-3; Deut. 31:9, 19, 22, 24).

The Prophets. These indicate that writing was employed by several individuals even prior to the time of the Moabite Stone (cf. Joshua 8:30-34; 18:4-9; 24:26; Judges 8:14; I Sam. 10:25), which further militates against the higher critical view.

The Writings. These also relate that individuals were writing before the time of the Moabite insurrection recorded in II Kings 1:1 and 3:4-27 (cf. Prov. 1:1 with 22:20; II Chron. 35:4).

THE DESCRIPTION OF MATERIALS AND INSTRUMENTS

WRITING MATERIALS

The materials upon which the ancients wrote were also used by the writers of Scripture. Several of these items may be indicated.

Clay. This was not only used in ancient Sumer as early as about 3500 B.C., but it was used by Jeremiah (17:13) and Ezekiel (4:1). This material would be inscribed while it was still damp or soft. It would then be either dried in the sun or baked in a kiln to make a permanent record.

Stone. This was used in Mesopotamia, Egypt and Palestine, as is evidenced by the Code of Hammurabi, the Rosetta Stone, and the Moabite Stone. The biblical writers also made use of stone as a writing material (cf. Exodus 24:12; 31:18; 32:15-16; 34:1, 28; Deut. 5:22; 27:2-3; Joshua 8:31-32). Also at the Dog River in Lebanon and at Behistun in Iran royal inscriptions were carved on cliff faces.

Papyrus. This was used in ancient Gebal (Byblos) and Egypt

[7]The clause, "this is the generation of" or "the book of the generations of," occurs twelve times in Genesis and probably indicates the divisions of early family records of the patriarchs; cf. Gen. 2:4; 5:1; 6:9; 10:1, 31; 11:10, 27; 25:12-13, 19; 36:1, 9; 37:2.

from about 3100 B.C. It was made by pressing and gluing two layers of split papyrus reeds together in order to form a sheet. A series of papyrus sheets were joined together to form a scroll. It is this type of papyrus "scroll" that is mentioned in Revelation 5:1, though it is translated "book" in the Authorized Version. The Apostle John used papyrus for his epistles (cf. II John 12).

Vellum, parchment, leather. These are various quality grades of writing material made from animal skins of calf or antelope, sheep or goat, and cow or bull, respectively. While these substances are not mentioned directly as writing materials in the Bible, some type of animal skin may have been in mind in Jeremiah 36:23. It could hardly have been vellum, as Frederic Kenyon has indicated that vellum was not known prior to about 200 B.C.[8] Most likely it was leather, for the king used a knife on it. Parchments are, on the other hand, clearly mentioned in Paul's request to Timothy (II Tim. 4:13). The chief difference in the use of these materials seems to be that leather was prepared for writing on *one* side only (as a scroll), while parchment or vellum was prepared on *both* sides (as in a codex).

Miscellaneous items. Writing also was done in the biblical narrative upon such things as metal (Exodus 28:36; Job 19:24; Matt. 22:19-20); a wooden writing board recessed to hold a wax writing surface (cf. Isa. 8:1; 30:8; Hab. 2:2; Luke 1:63); precious stones (Exodus 28:9, 11, 21; 39:6-14); and potsherds (Job 2:8), better known as ostraca, as found in such locations as Samaria and Lachish in Palestine. Still another item used in ancient writing in Egypt, Greece, Etruscan and Roman Italy, but not mentioned in the Bible, was linen.

WRITING INSTRUMENTS

Several different instruments were necessary in the production of written records on the various materials mentioned above:

Stylus. A three-sided instrument with a beveled head, the stylus was used to make incursions into clay and wax tablets. It was sometimes called a "pen," as in Jeremiah 17:1.

Chisel. A chisel was used in making inscriptions in stone, as in Joshua 8:31-32. Job wished that his words might be engraved with an iron "pen" in the rock forever (Job 19:24).

Pen. This was employed in writing on papyrus, vellum, leather and parchment, as indicated in III John 13.

[8]Kenyon, pp. 43 f.

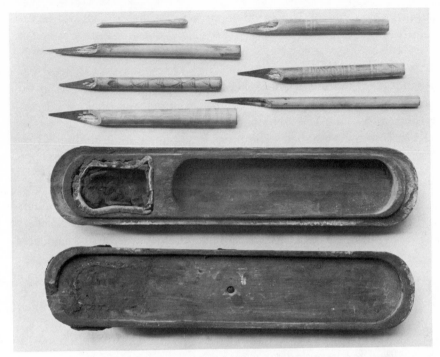

8. *Ancient writing equipment from Egypt. Biblical writers may have used something similar (British Museum)*

Penknife. This was used in Jeremiah 36:23 to destroy a scroll, the material of which was probably tougher than papyrus. It was also used to sharpen the writer's pen after it had begun to wear down.

Inkhorn and ink. These were necessary concomitants of the pen, and they served as the container and fluid used for writing on papyrus, vellum, leather and parchment. Thus, just as writing and its materials were available for the biblical writers, so were the instruments necessary for their vital task.

THE DIVISIONS OF THE TEXT

Writing material and instruments were the means by which revelation could be expressed in the media of language. However, the ancients for the most part felt no need for dividing the text into such smaller and meaningful units as chapters, paragraphs or verses. These divisions came into being much later than the time when the Scriptures began to be preserved in written form. Since the procedure of textual division did not take place in both Testaments simultaneously, each is treated separately before they are observed jointly.

THE OLD TESTAMENT

Chapters (sections). There were apparently some divisions in the autographs of the Old Testament: for example, the book of Lamentations, and Psalm 119,[9] which are indicated by the use of the letters of the Hebrew alphabet. These cases are not numerous but do reflect at least some natural divisions in the Hebrew text.

1. *Palestinian Sections* were begun prior to the Babylonian captivity (586 B.C.), and consisted of 154 sections for the Pentateuch. These sections were called *sedarim* (*seder*, singular), and were designed to provide lessons sufficient to cover a three-year cycle of reading.[10]

2. *Babylonian Sections* appeared during the captivity (prior to 536 B.C.), when the Torah was divided into fifty-four sections called *parashiyyoth* (*parashah*, singular). These were later subdivided into 669 sections for reference purposes. These sections were utilized for a single-year cycle.

3. *Maccabean Sections* appeared during the period at about 165 B.C. These fifty-four sections, corresponding with the *sedarim* of the Law, covered the Prophets, and were called *haphtarahs*.

4. *Reformation Sections.* After the Protestant Reformation, the Hebrew Bible for the most part followed the same chapter divisions as the Protestant Old Testament. These divisions were first placed in the margins in 1330. They were printed into the text of the *Complutensian Polyglot* (1517), and the text was divided in the edition of Arias Montanus (1571).

Verses

1. *Ancient verse* indications were merely spaces between words, as the words were run together continuously through a given book. Each book was separate and there were no vowel points until the Masoretes added them (fifth to tenth century A.D.).

---

[9]W. Graham Scroggie, *Know Your Bible*, I, 122-23.
[10]H. S. Miller, *A General Biblical Introduction*, p. 165, seems to imply that this sectioning was not the earliest; he favors making the *parashiyyoth* (*parashah*) antedate it instead. However, Bruce, p. 121, indicates the view followed in the text.

After the Babylonian captivity, for the purpose of public reading and interpretation, space stops were employed, and still later additional markings were added. These "verse" markings were not regulated, and differed from place to place. It was not until about A.D. 900 that the markings were standardized.

2. *Reformation verse indications* appeared in the sixteenth century. In the Bomberg edition (1547), every fifth verse was indicated; in 1571 Montanus indicated each verse in the margin for the first time.

THE NEW TESTAMENT

Ancient Sections

The autographs of the New Testament were undoubtedly written in an unbroken manner, similar to the Old, especially since they consisted mostly of shorter books than the Gospels and Acts. However, there was an early sectioning that took place, and it is commonly referred to as the old Greek division into paragraphs (*kephalaia*). These divisions appeared prior to the Council at Nicea (325), and differed from modern chapter divisions; for example, Matthew 2:1–2:15 (1); 2:16-23 (2); 3:1–4:16 (3); 4:17-22 (4).[11] During the fourth century, the Codex Vaticanus (B) utilized another system of marking sections, for example, Matthew 1:1-5 (1); 1:6-11 (2); 12-16 (3); 17 (4); 18-23 (5); 24-25 (6). This system is not completely known today, as the Vaticanus manuscript is broken at Hebrews 9:14. As a result, only the *kephalaia* markings are known from that point. Eusebius of Caesarea attempted another means of sectioning the New Testament. He devised a system of short paragraphs, which he cross-referenced on a series of tables, for the Gospels. These paragraphs were longer than modern verses, but shorter than current chapters. Matthew had 335 sections, Mark had 233 (later changed to 241), Luke had 342, and John 232.[12]

Modern Sections

1. *The English New Testament.* It was not until the thirteenth century that these sections were changed, and then only gradually.

[11]Eberhard Nestle, *Novum Testamentum Graece* (*Editio vicesima tertia*), p. 82*, explains its markings of these old Greek paragraphs (*kephalaia*) and the old Greek descriptive headings (*titloi*) in its apparatus.
[12]Miller, p. 165, is apparently incorrect in his tabulations at this point. For the correct totals see Nestle, pp. 82*-83*.

Stephen Langton, a professor at the University of Paris, and afterward Archbishop of Canterbury, divided the Bible into the modern chapter divisions (*c.* 1227).[13] This was prior to the introduction of movable type in printing. Since the Wycliffe Bible (1382) followed this pattern, these basic divisions have been the virtual base upon which the Bible has been printed to this very day, as the Wycliffe Bible has been basic to subsequent versions and translations.

2. *The Latin New Testament (Vulgate).* This was printed by Gutenberg in 1456, and is known as the Mazarin Bible. This edition followed the thirteenth century chapter divisions, and paved the way for such sectioning in the Rheims-Douay Version (1581-1609), which became the authoritative English edition by decree of Pope Sixtus V in 1585. The only major revision it experienced was by Bishop Challoner (1691-1781).

3. *The Greek New Testament.* This was first printed in 1516, by Desiderius Erasmus. It was done in an effort to beat Cardinal Ximenes to the market, as the latter's work was already printed but bogged down in ecclesiastical machinery in the matter of publication. Erasmus followed the chapter divisions of the Mazarin Bible (1456) and therefore gave the same chapter divisions to the Protestant world that Mazarin gave to the Catholics. This provided a valuable common ground for cross-references of biblical texts between Catholics and Protestants.

Modern Verses. These were actually developed later than the chapters. This was apparently an effort to further facilitate cross-references, and make public reading easier. These markings first occur in the fourth edition of the Greek New Testament published by Robert Stephanus, a Parisian printer, in 1551. These verses were introduced into the English New Testament by William Whittingham of Oxford in 1557.[14] In 1555, Stephanus introduced his verse

[13]The traditional view has been stated in the text, but others have held that Cardinal Hugo of St. Cher (d. 1263) was the pioneer in this effort, in the preparation of a concordance (*c.* 1244). Cf. Kenyon, p. 190, for the former view; Bruce, p. 121, for the latter. Miller, pp. 10-11, presents both views. M. H. Black, "The Printed Bible," in S. L. Greenslade (ed.), *The Cambridge History of the Bible,* II, 419, avoids the problem altogether by saying, "The chapters had always been divided in printed Bibles; the division itself, Berger says, dates from the thirteenth century."

[14]F. F. Bruce, *The English Bible: A History of Translations,* pp. 85-86, indicates that Whittingham was married to John Calvin's sister (or sister-in-law), and succeeded John Knox as the pastor of the English church in Geneva; hence, his influential position in the preparation of the Geneva Bible (1560).

divisions into a Latin Vulgate edition, from which they have continued to the present day.

THE WHOLE BIBLE

Latin Vulgate. The first Bible to use both the modern chapter and verse divisions was the Latin Vulgate edition of Robert Stephanus (1555). He had previously used these divisions in his Greek New Testament (1551).

Geneva Bible. The first English Bible to incorporate both the modern chapter and verse divisions was the Geneva Bible (1560). It was actually done in two parts: in 1557, the New Testament was done by Whittingham, as a stopgap measure, and, in 1560, the entire Bible was completed in the same tradition. It employed modern chapter and verse divisions, and even introduced italicized words into the text where English idiom required fuller treatment than a simple Greek translation. More of this is considered later. It is sufficient to note here that the Bible had attained its "modern" character before the translation work of either the Rheims-Douay or the so-called authorized versions of the Bible.

SUMMARY AND CONCLUSION

A brief history of the development of writing indicates a progressive development from pictograms, through ideograms, to phonograms, before the time of the biblical writers. Hence, the Bible is correct in assuming the development of writing; and the late nineteenth century view that Moses and others lived in preliterate history is totally unfounded in the light of modern archaeological discoveries; namely, from Mesopotamia, Egypt, Western Asia, Crete, and even Palestine. With the development of writing, there must have been a development of writing materials and instruments. These too appeared in ample time to be utilized in the recording of divine revelation.

The divisions of the autographs were quite different from those of modern Bibles; a survey of the divisions of the record reveals that the process began over a half millennium before the earthly ministry of Christ, and took almost two millennia to come to its current form. These divisions, it has been shown, are *not of divine origin,* but are rather the efforts of man to "find his way" more adequately through that revelation which *is* of divine origin.[15] It was also indicated that

[15]Archibald T. Robertson, *Introduction to the Textual Criticism of the New Testament,* p. 100, states accordingly, "The first step in interpretation is to ignore the modern chapters and verses."

the period which evidenced a rise in opposition to papal authority had, as a concomitant, the rise in making the Bible a more practically workable source of authority. Most of these innovations were well established before the translation of either the Rheims-Douay or the so-called authorized versions of the Bible.

18

MANUSCRIPT TRANSMISSION, PREPARATION AND PRESERVATION

In order to fully appreciate the total process by which the Bible was transmitted from the first to the twentieth century, certain mechanical items must be discussed (e.g., preparation, age and preservation of manuscripts). Along with these technical matters of transmission, certain definitions are basic to the understanding of this central "link" in the chain "from God to us." The following discussion is an overview of the next several chapters (19-30) and is intended as an introduction to the whole subject of transmission.

THE PROCESS OF TRANSMISSION

GENUINENESS AND AUTHENTICITY DISTINGUISHED

As the terms "authority" and "canonicity" were basic to Sections I and II, the words "genuineness" and "authenticity" are fundamental to this third section. Unfortunately, there is some confusion about the meaning of these terms, as their usage is somewhat interchangeable in theological circles.

Genuineness. As used here, genuineness refers to the truth of the origin of a document, that is, its authorship. It answers the question: Is this document really from its alleged source or author? Is it genuinely the work of the stated writer? As such, genuineness is primarily the subject of Special Introduction, which on the whole deals with such things as the authorship, date and destiny of the biblical books. General Introduction, on the other hand, is concerned with the topics of authority, canonicity and authenticity.

Authenticity. This refers to the truth of the facts and *content* of the documents of the Bible. Authenticity deals with the integrity (trustworthiness) and credibility (truthfulness) of the record. A book may be genuine without being authentic, if the professed writer is the real one, even if the content is untrue. Then, again, a book may be authentic without being genuine, if the content is true but the professed writer is not the actual one. In such a case, the book would be called forged or spurious, regardless of the truthfulness or falsity of its content. Biblical books of course must be both genuine and authentic or they cannot be inspired, since in either case there would be a falsehood. However, General Introduction does not deal explicitly with genuineness (authorship); it deals with the integrity of the text based on its credibility and authority. It is assumed that a biblical book, which has divine authority, and hence credibility, and has been transmitted with integrity, will automatically have genuineness. If there be a lie in the book regarding its origin and/or authorship, how can its content be believed?

GUARANTEE OF AUTHENTICITY (AND GENUINENESS)

The whole chain of revelation must be examined in order to demonstrate with certainty that the fact and route of revelation are found in the history of the Bible known to Christians today. A complete chain "from God to us" will consist of the following necessary "links."

Deity. This is the first link in the chain of revelation. The existence of a God who desires to communicate Himself to man is the one irreducible axiom of this entire study. Evidence that there is such a God is the subject of theology and philosophy,[1] but this fact is assumed at this juncture.

Apostolicity. The next link is apostolicity. That God accredited and directed a group of men known as prophets and apostles to speak authoritatively for Him is the repeated claim of the biblical writers (see chaps. 4-5, 7), and the evidence that what they wrote was God's word is examined in chapter 9.

Canonicity. A somewhat parenthetic but necessary link is canonicity. It answers the historical question: Which are the inspired prophetic and apostolic books, and how are they known? They are those books which were written by men of God, that came with the authority and power of God, told the truth about God, man, etc., and were accepted and collected by the people of God (see chaps. 10-15).

Authority. The direct result of apostolicity is authority, as circumscribed by the limits of canonicity. The teaching of men who were divinely accredited for that purpose is divinely authoritative teaching. In this sense, authority is just a logical link, consequent upon

[1]For a thorough defense of the standard arguments for the existence of God, see Stuart Cornelius Hackett, *The Resurrection of Theism.*

apostolicity as apostolicity is, in turn, dependent upon deity, or, rather, upon God's desire to communicate to men.

Authenticity. Likewise, authenticity is the necessary result of authority which is derived from apostolicity, deity, etc. Whatever is spoken by God must be true, since God is the very standard of truth itself (cf. Heb. 6:18). The Scriptures are authentic (true in content) if they are the prophetic voice of God.

Integrity. This is the historic evidence that links authenticity and credibility. Anything authentic or true is of course credible. The question is: Does the twentieth century Bible possess integrity? To put it another way: Does it adequately and accurately reproduce the original apostolic writings known as the autographs?

1. *Autographs.* Sometimes these were inaccurately called "originals" and sometimes incorrectly defined as the original writing from the hand of an apostle or prophet. In reality the authentic apostolic writings produced under the direction and/or authorization of a prophet or apostle are the autographs.

   a. An autograph would not necessarily have to be written by an apostle's own hand. Paul often used a secretary (cf. Rom. 16:22), as did Jeremiah (cf. Jer. 36:27).

   b. Nor does an autograph necessarily have to be the "first edition" of a book. Jeremiah, for example, wrote two editions of his scroll to Jehoiakim (cf. Jer. 36:28). Similarly, some students of the Gospels have suggested that Mark may have had two editions.[2] In such cases both editions are inspired, but the latter supersedes the former in a supplementary and complementary sense, in somewhat the same way that the New Testament does the Old Testament.

2. *Ancient Versions.* The autographs are not extant,[3] so they must be reconstructed from early manuscripts and versions. The earliest versions, or translations of the New Testament into other languages, for example, the Syriac and Latin, extend back to the threshold of the second century. They began to appear just over a generation from the time the New Testament was completed (see chaps. 22-23).

3. *Citations of the Fathers.* The corroborative quotations of the

[2]Merrill C. Tenney, *New Testament Survey*, p. 157.
[3]For a suggested reason as to why God permitted the autographs to perish, see p. 32.

Church Fathers from the first few centuries, totaling over 36,000, include almost every verse of the New Testament. Some of these citations begin in the first century, and they continue in an unbroken succession from that time (cf. chap. 25).

4. *Manuscript Copies.* These were in Greek and extended practically to the first century in fragmentary form, and to the third and fourth centuries in completed copies. The earliest manuscripts, known as uncials, were written in capital letters throughout. Later manuscripts, known as minuscules, were written in lower case letters or in flowing letters, cursives. Some manuscripts were written on scrolls, and others as books, codex form, from which they are known as codices (chaps. 19-20).

5. *Modern Versions.* The ancient manuscripts are the most important witnesses to the autographs and, by the method of textual criticism (chaps. 26-27), they form the basis for the modern versions of the Bible (chaps. 29-30). Some early modern versions were based on medieval versions (cf. chap. 24); however, since the discoveries of the great manuscripts of the New Testament and other miscellaneous items, most recent versions and translations are based on the latter. These discoveries form the basis of the critical Greek text rather than the so-called Received Text used as the authority of the earlier modern versions. In the minds of most modern textual scholars, this so-called "critical" text represents an objective attempt to reconstruct the autographs. It is a scientific approach to the question of integrity, and it concludes that the present Greek text (after Nestle) is probably over 99 percent accurate in reproducing the exact words of the autographs.

Credibility.. The right to be believed—credibility—is based on the authenticity of the text. This, in turn, is founded upon divine authority, which is guaranteed by the ministry of the Holy Spirit and the integrity of the text.

1. *Objective credibility.* This is based on (1) the integrity of the text via the science of textual criticism, which yields a Bible that is probably over 99 percent trustworthy or credible. (2) Second, there is the objective evidence supplied by apologetics which likewise confirms the Bible to be the Word of God (cf. chap. 9). (3) The critic will, of course, stress the weakness of the link of

9. *An orthodox Jewish scribe in Jerusalem transcribing the Torah on parchment (Matson Photo Service)*

integrity which is only "probably" some "99 percent" sure, and not "actually" a full "100 percent" certain. There are two "welds" for these "cracks" in the chain. For the providence of God and the witness of the Holy Spirit provide assurance to the believer that the chain is unbroken.

2. *Subjective assurance.* Before discussing the subjective assurance which welds together any potential cracks in the chain of the Bible's transmission, it should be emphasized that a 99 percent probability is as good as can be obtained by the historical method. Similar textual methods applied to other ancient documents yield a much lower percent of certitude (see chap. 26).

   a. In fact, human beings do not require any more assurance for credibility. The game of life is played, and must be, quite often on much lower odds.

   b. Second, the providence of God, a characteristic which is consonant with a self-revealing God, is the force that welds together the entire chain of communication. Any alleged "cracks" are welded by God, who providentially planned the process of communication and, therefore, is the One who perfects its product. The chain, then, has no "real cracks," because it is God who welds it together.

c. Finally, there is, transcending the entire chain, the direct witness to the hearts of the children of God by the Spirit of God that the Bible is the Word of God. However, this subjective witness should not be used to "short circuit" the objective evidence; rather it is used to complete the circuit which brings the power and truth of God to man. History is replete with illustrations of the danger of mysticism as well as rationalism. Any attempt to bypass God's truth in its objective form, whether in its original oral form or its final written form, is doomed to the dismal dungeon of defeat. The Spirit of God speaks through the Word of God, and the Word of God has been transmitted by a historical process superintended by the providence of God. This truth is based upon the best objective and subjective certainty.

THE PREPARATION, AGE AND PRESERVATION OF MANUSCRIPT COPIES

Another factor which enhances confidence in the fidelity of the transmitted text is derived from a consideration of the copying and subsequent care of manuscripts.

THE PREPARATION OF MANUSCRIPT COPIES

The Old Testament. It is impossible to fix with certainty the beginning of Hebrew writing, although it was pre-Mosaic. Thus, from an early date the Scriptures were copied. These copies were made according to different criteria, depending on the purpose of the manuscript being copied. There are no manuscripts in existence dating from before the Babylonian captivity (586 B.C.), but there was a great flood of copies of the Scriptures dating from the Talmudic period (c. 300 B.C.-A.D. 500). During this period there were two general classes of manuscript copies.

1. *The synagogue rolls* were regarded as "sacred copies" of the Old Testament text, and were used in public meeting places. Separate rolls contained the Torah (Law) on one roll, portions of the Nebhiim (Prophets) on another, the Kethubhim (Writings)

on two others,[4] and the Megilloth ("five rolls") on five separate rolls. The Megilloth were no doubt produced on separate rolls to facilitate their being read at the annual feasts.[5] Strict rules were employed, so that these rolls would be copied scrupulously. Samuel Davidson related these rules rather meticulously when he wrote,

[1] A synagogue roll must be written on the skins of clean animals, [2] prepared for the particular use of the synagogue by a Jew. [3] These must be fastened together with strings taken from clean animals. [4] Every skin must contain a certain number of columns, equal throughout the entire codex. [5] The length of each column must not extend over less than 48 or more than 60 lines; and the breadth must consist of thirty letters. [6] The whole copy must be first-lined; and if three words be written without a line, it is worthless. [7] The ink should be black, neither red, green, nor any other colour, and be prepared according to a definite recipe. [8] An authentic copy must be the exemplar, from which the transcriber ought not in the least deviate. [9] No word or letter, not even a *yod*, must be written from memory, the scribe not having looked at the codex before him . . . . [10] Between every consonant the space of a hair or thread must intervene; [11] between every new *parashah*, or section, the breadth of nine consonants; [12] between every book, three lines. [13] The fifth book of Moses must terminate exactly with a line; but the rest need not do so. [14] Besides this, the copyist must sit in full Jewish dress, [15] wash his whole body, [16] not begin to write the name of God with a pen newly dipped in ink, [17] and should a king address him while writing that name he must take no notice of him.[6]

2. *The private copies* were regarded as "common copies" of the Old Testament text and were not used in public meetings. These rolls, although not governed by such strict rules as the synagogue rolls, were prepared with great care. They were frequently ornamented, often took a codex form, sometimes included marginal notes and commentaries. Since they were private copies, the desires of the purchaser were paramount in choosing such things

[4]Three of these books were on one roll of poetry: Job, Psalms and Proverbs; and three other books were on the other: Daniel, Ezra-Nehemiah and Chronicles.

[5]At the Passover, the Song of Songs was read; at Pentecost, it was Ruth; Tabernacles featured Ecclesiastes; Purim used Esther; and on the Anniversary of the Destruction of Jerusalem, Lamentations was read.

[6]Samuel Davidson, *The Hebrew Text of the Old Testament*, 2d ed., p. 89, as cited in James Hastings (ed.), *A Dictionary of the Bible*, IV, 949.

as the size, material, form, and ink color, and seldom did an individual have a collection of scrolls which contained the entire Old Testament.

The New Testament. While the autographs of the New Testament have long since disappeared, there is enough evidence to warrant the statement that these documents were written in rolls and books made of papyrus. The Old Testament had been copied into the "books and the parchments," but the New Testament was probably written on papyrus[7] between about A.D. 50 and 100.[8] During this period, papyrus rolls were used, and papyrus survived long periods of time only when placed in rather unusual circumstances. By the early second century, codices were introduced but they too were still generally made of papyrus.[9] As a by-product of the persecutions, culminating with the Edict of Diocletian,[10] the Scriptures were jeopardized and not systematically copied. It was with the Letter of Constantine to Eusebius[11] that systematic copying of the New Testament began in the West. From this time, vellum and parchment were used along with the papyrus. It was not until the Reformation era that printed copies of the Bible became available.

THE AGE OF MANUSCRIPTS

Since there was no printing process available at the time of manuscript copying of the Scriptures, the age of manuscripts must be determined by other means than a publisher's date. This process of dating is not nearly so accurate as finding the publication date printed on the title page of a modern book, but it is relatively accurate.

Materials. The materials of a given manuscript copy may provide the basis for discovering its date. Chapter 17 mentioned such materials as stone (not used for manuscripts), papyrus, vellum, parchment and leather. For present purposes, only those materials which could be utilized in making rolls and/or books will be considered.

1. Skins were possibly the earliest materials used, and they were at first of coarse texture and made rather heavy, bulky rolls. These materials were used early in Hebrew history, and led to refinements in the postcaptivity period.

[7]F. F. Bruce, *The Books and the Parchments,* rev. ed., pp. 176-77.
[8]Sir Frederic G. Kenyon, *Our Bible and the Ancient Manuscripts,* pp. 98-102.
[9]Papyrus was much less expensive to obtain than was vellum or parchment.
[10]See chap. 14.
[11]See chap. 14.

2. Papyrus rolls were used in the New Testament period, largely because of their inexpensive character when compared with vellum and parchment.

3. Papyrus codices were introduced when attempts at collecting the individual rolls revealed that there was a need to make them less cumbersome to handle. Formerly each book or group of books was written on a single roll, but this multiplicity of rolls was replaced by codices in the early second century.

4. Vellum was prepared from animal skins, chiefly from lambs and young goats, and was rather costly. It was used for more expensive copies of manuscripts.

5. Parchment was used as early as the days of the New Testament composition (cf. II Tim. 4:13). Since there are various qualities of parchment and vellum writing material made from animal skins, they were often used during the same period of time. Codices of these two materials did not appear generally until after the Edict of Diocletian, and were the primary materials used in manuscript copying in the Middle Ages.

6. Redressed parchment was used for copying manuscripts after the original writing had become faded. Sometimes parchments were "erased" and "rewritten," as in the case of the Codex Ephraemi Rescriptus (C), also known as a palimpsest (Greek, "rubbed out again") *rescriptus* (Latin, "rewritten"). Needless to say, these manuscripts would be of a later date than the earlier text on the parchment.

7. Paper was invented in China in the second century A.D.; it was introduced into Eastern Turkestan as early as the fourth century, manufactured in Arabia in the eighth century,[12] introduced into Europe in the tenth century, manufactured in Europe in the twelfth century, and became common by the thirteenth century. There were, of course, developments in the manufacture of paper, for example, with hemp, flax, linen, and rag content. Thus, the materials used in the manufacture of writing material on which manuscripts were copied, assist in determining their age.

Letter size and form. Evidence is also provided by letter size and form for the date of a given manuscript. The earliest form of

[12]After the Arabs captured Samarkand (704); see *The Catholic Encyclopedia*, IX, 615.

Hebrew writing was in the prong-type letters of the old Phoenician alphabet. This style prevailed until the return from the Babylonian captivity in Nehemiah's time (c. 444 B.C.).[13] After Nehemiah, the Jews apparently adopted the Aramaic script, as it became the vernacular language during the fifth century B.C. At this time the Hebrew Old Testament was translated into Aramaic and then, after about 200 B.C., it was copied in the square letters of Aramaic script. The square characters of extant manuscripts are not identical to those of this early period, but they are direct descendants.[14] The discovery of the Dead Sea Scrolls of Qumran in 1947 brought even more precision to the study of Hebrew paleography, as it has brought a large quantity of early biblical and nonbiblical manuscripts to light. For the first time these manuscripts have provided examples of Hebrew texts from prechristian times, a thousand years earlier than the oldest Hebrew Old Testament manuscripts previously available. The Qumran manuscripts reveal three main types of text among them, and indicate differences in matters of spelling, grammatical forms and, to some extent, wording from the Masoretic text.[15] By the time of the Masoretes (c. A.D. 500-1000), the principles of the late Talmudic period (c. A.D. 300-500) became rather stereotyped.[16]

Greek manuscripts were written in two general styles during the New Testament period: literary and nonliterary. The New Testament was probably written in nonliterary style. In fact, for the first three centuries, the New Testament was undoubtedly circulated outside the channels of ordinary book trade. While the literary hand was well-rounded, graceful and handsome, the nonliterary hand was smaller, square lettered, sprinkled with variants, and exhibited a lack of literary exactness generally. The written repositories of Christian tradition were not plentiful during the first three centuries, and the records which were preserved included various oral and written traditions according to the individual interpreters involved in the given historical situation. Coupled with the tenuous position of the church prior to the time of Constantine's letter to Eusebius in the fourth century, the period of the establishment of the canon witnessed attempts at textual emendation and alteration according

---

[13]Bruce, p. 22; also see Merrill F. Unger, *Introductory Guide to the Old Testament*, pp. 123-25.

[14]Hastings, IV, 949.

[15]For further study of this matter see Millar Burrows, *More Light on the Dead Sea Scrolls*, and Frank Moore Cross, Jr., *The Ancient Library of Qumran and Modern Biblical Studies*.

[16]Hastings, IV, 949.

to the prevailing fashions or whims among scribes. Not until the late third or early fourth century were serious attempts at recension of the manuscripts actually tried with success, and these have left little direct historical evidence. These matters belong to the discipline of textual criticism and restoration, however, and require no further elaboration at this juncture. The style of writing was slow and laborious during the early centuries of the church, as the letters were capital (uncial),[17] written separately, and without breaks between words or sentences. Uncial manuscripts were copied through the tenth century; but, before they became less prominent, a new form of writing was introduced into the field, which is called minuscule or cursive writing. By the time of the tenth century, the demand for manuscript copies caused the faster cursive style to outstrip the cumbersome uncial style. Thus, by the golden age of manuscript copying, the eleventh through fifteenth centuries, this new running hand, employing small and connected letters, was the dominant form of manuscript copying. It was superseded in the fifteenth century by printed manuscripts, after the introduction of movable type by Johann Gutenberg.

Punctuation. Further light is added to the age of a given manuscript by its punctuation. At first, words were run together, and very little punctuation was used. "During the sixth and seventh centuries, scribes began to use punctuation marks more liberally."[18] The actual process of change proceeded from spaceless writing, to spaced writing, addition of end punctuation (periods), commas, colons, breath and accent marks (seventh-eighth centuries), interrogation marks, etc. This was a long, slow process which was rather complete by the tenth century, in time again for the minuscules and the golden age of manuscript copying.

Text Divisions. The text divisions into sections, chapters and verses have been treated in chapter 17 and need only be mentioned at this point. It was not until the thirteenth century that modern chapter divisions appeared, and not until the sixteenth century that modern verses were introduced. But this development occurred prior to the mass distribution of the printed Bible, and augmented the influence of the Authorized and Rheims-Douay versions of the English Bible.

[17]"Uncial letters were an adaptation of the lapidary capitals used for inscriptions in stone, tablets, and the like; minuscule letters, as the name implies, were smaller and more akin to ordinary cursive hands." Bruce, p. 182. Also see Kenyon, p. 15, n. 1.

[18]Bruce M. Metzger, *The Text of the New Testament,* p. 26; also see his book *en passim* for a fuller treatment of the subject of punctuation in manuscripts.

Miscellaneous factors. Also involved in the dating of a given manuscript were such miscellaneous factors as the size and shape of letters within the uncial and minuscule groupings of manuscripts.[19] Ornamentation is another factor in dating of manuscripts; from the fourth to the late ninth centuries the ornamentation of manuscripts became more elaborate in the uncial manuscripts. After that time, they became less ornate and less carefully copied. These factors helped to increase the popularity of the minuscules, which went through a similar development. Spelling was modified during the centuries, just as it is in living languages, and this point helps date manuscripts. The color of the ink used is another important factor. At first, only black ink was used, but green, red and other colors were added later. Finally, the texture and color of parchment help date a manuscript. The means of parchment production changed, quality and texture were modified, and the aging process added another cause for color change in the material.

THE PRESERVATION OF MANUSCRIPTS

Although manuscripts give information as to their date, and their quality is governed by their preparation, the preservation of given manuscripts adds vital support to their relative value for the textual critic and student of the Bible. This may be illustrated by a cursory treatment of manuscript preservation in general.

The Old Testament manuscripts. These manuscripts generally fall into two general periods.

1. *The Talmudic period* (*c.* 300 B.C.-A.D. 500) produced a great flood of manuscripts which were used in the synagogues and for private study. In comparison to the later Masoretic period, for the temple and synagogues there were very few, but they were careful "official" copies. By the time of the Maccabean revolt (168 B.C.), the Syrians had destroyed most of the existing manuscripts of the Old Testament. The Dead Sea Scrolls (*c.* 167 B.C.-A.D. 133) have begun to make an immense contribution to Old Testament critical study. There were many manuscript copies, confirming for the most part the textual tradition of the Masoretes.[20]

---

[19]For a brief, thorough description of the changing character of writing in manuscripts, see Hastings, IV, 953.
[20]See chap. 19 for a full treatment of the manuscripts of the Old Testament text.

2. *The Masoretic period* (fl. *c.* A.D. 500-1000) of Old Testament manuscript copying indicates a complete review of established rules, a deep reverence for the Scriptures, and a systematic renovation of transmission techniques.

The New Testament manuscripts. These manuscripts fall into four general periods.

1. *The first three centuries* witnessed a composite testimony as to the integrity of the New Testament Scriptures. Because of the illegal position of Christianity, it cannot be expected that many, if any, complete manuscripts from that period are to be found. Therefore, textual critics must be content to examine whatever evidence has survived, that is, nonbiblical papyri, biblical papyri, ostraca, inscriptions and lectionaries which bore witness to the manuscripts of the New Testament.[21]

2. *The fourth and fifth centuries* brought a legalization of Christianity and a multiplication of manuscripts of the New Testament. These manuscripts, on vellum and parchment generally, were copies of earlier papyri, and bear witness to this dependence.[22]

3. *From the sixth century onward,* monks collected, copied and cared for New Testament manuscripts in the monasteries. This was a period of rather uncritical production, and it brought about an increase in manuscript quantity, but with a corresponding decrease in quality.

4. *After the tenth century,* uncials gave way to minuscules, and copies of manuscripts multiplied rapidly.

The Classical Writings of Greece and Rome. These writings illustrate the character of biblical manuscript preservation in a candid fashion.[23] In contrast to the total number of the over 5,000 New Testament manuscripts known today, the *Iliad* of Homer has only 643, *The Peloponnesian War* of Thucydides only eight, while Tacitus' works rely on but two manuscripts. The abundance of biblical evidence would lead one to conclude that "the Christian can take the whole Bible in his hand and say without fear or hesitation that he holds in it the true word of God, handed down without essential

---

[21]See chap. 21 for a discussion of these miscellaneous items.
[22]See chap. 20 for an examination of New Testament manuscripts.
[23]Fuller treatment of this material may be found in chap. 26.

loss from generation to generation throughout the centuries."[24] Or, in other words,

> The number of manuscripts of the New Testament, of early translations from it, and of quotations from it in the oldest writers of the Church, is so large that it is practically certain that the true reading of every doubtful passage is preserved in some one or other of these ancient authorities. This can be said of no other ancient book in the world.[25]

SUMMARY AND CONCLUSION

Between the autograph and the modern Bible extends an important link in the overall chain "from God to us" known as *transmission*. It provides a positive answer to the question: Do Bible scholars today possess an accurate copy of the autographs? Obviously, the authenticity and authority of the Bible cannot be established unless it be known that the present copies have *integrity*. In support of the integrity of the text, an overwhelming number of ancient documents may be presented. For the New Testament, beginning with the second century ancient versions and manuscript fragments and continuing with abundant quotations of the Fathers and thousands of manuscript copies from that time to the modern versions of the Bible, there is virtually an unbroken line of testimony. Furthermore, there are not only countless manuscripts to support the integrity of the Bible (including the Old Testament since the discovery of the Dead Sea Scrolls), but a study of the procedures of preparation and preservation of the biblical manuscript copies reveals the fidelity of the transmission process itself. In fact, it may be concluded that no major document from antiquity comes into the modern world with such evidence of its integrity as does the Bible.

[24]Kenyon, p. 55.
[25]*Ibid.*

19

OLD TESTAMENT MANUSCRIPTS

THE MASORETIC TEXT

What are the nature and amount of the documentary evidence for the original text of the Old Testament? Sir Frederic Kenyon posed this "great, indeed all important question" when he wrote, "Does this Hebrew text which we call Masoretic faithfully represent the Hebrew text as originally written by the authors of the Old Testament books?"[1] The answer to this question arises from a careful examination of the number and nature of Hebrew manuscripts of the Old Testament.

THE NUMBER OF MASORETIC PERIOD MANUSCRIPTS: FEW[2]

Just how many Old Testament manuscripts are extant in the Hebrew language? Until recently, very few of them were known. The current edition of the Hebrew Bible, Kittel's *Biblia Hebraica*, is based on only four of the following Hebrew manuscripts and primarily on only one of them (Leningrad Codex).

Copies of Hebrew Manuscripts.

1. The Cairo Codex (A.D. 895) is perhaps the oldest known Masoretic manuscript of the Prophets, and it includes both the Former and the Latter Prophets. It was written by Moses ben Asher in Tiberias, Palestine.

2. The Leningrad Codex of the Prophets (A.D. 916) contains only the Latter Prophets (Isaiah, Jeremiah, Ezekiel, and the Twelve), and was written with a Babylonian punctuation.

[1]Sir Frederic G. Kenyon, *Our Bible and the Ancient Manuscripts*, rev. by A. W. Adams, p. 88.
[2]Compared to over 5,000 manuscripts of the New Testament, there were relatively few manuscripts of the Old Testament, especially before the discovery of those in the Cairo Geneza (1890) and the DSS (1947 ff.). The first collection of manuscripts made by Benjamin Kennicott (1776-80), published at Oxford, lists readings from 615 manuscripts and 52 printed editions. Giovanni de Rossi (1784-88) published 731 manuscripts and 300 printed editions. See Kenyon, pp. 70-71.

3. The Aleppo Codex (A.D. 930) of the whole Old Testament is no longer complete. It was rescued from a burning synagogue in Aleppo in 1948 and smuggled out of Syria to Israel. The codex is to become the main authority for a new edition of the Hebrew Bible to be published in Jerusalem. It was corrected and punctuated by Aaron ben Asher in A.D. 930.

4. The British Museum Codex (Oriental 4445) (A.D. 950) is an incomplete manuscript of the Pentateuch which dates from around the middle of the tenth century and has proved to be an important witness to the text. It now contains only Genesis 39:20 through Deuteronomy 1:33.

5. The Leningrad Codex (A.D. 1008) is the largest and only complete manuscript of the entire Old Testament. It is part of the Firkowitsch Collection brought from the Crimea to the Royal Library at Leningrad. It was completed in A.D. 1008, copied from a corrected codex prepared by Rabbi Aaron ben Moses ben Asher before A.D. 1000.[3] The manuscript is on vellum, in three columns of twenty-one lines each to the page. It has vowel points and accents above the line, in accordance with the custom of the Babylonian scribes.

6. The Reuchlin Codex of the Prophets (A.D. 1105), now at Karlsruhe, contains a text in the recension of ben Naphtali, another Tiberian Masorete whose work like ben Asher helps to verify the fidelity of the Leningrad Codex of the Old Testament.

7. Cairo Geniza fragments (sixth-ninth centuries A.D.), discovered during the rebuilding of the synagogue at Cairo, Egypt, in 1890 and now in scattered collections throughout libraries of the world including the British Museum, Bodleian Library, Oxford and Cambridge. Over one hundred twenty biblical manuscripts have been identified by Paul Kahle from these fragments, plus other Targums and rabbinical writings.[4]

Causes for the Scarcity of Hebrew Manuscripts. Several reasons have been suggested for the paucity of early Hebrew manuscripts.

The first and most obvious reason is a combination of antiquity and destructibility. Two or three thousand years is a long time to

[3]Dates here are taken from Kenyon, pp. 84 ff.
[4]Kenyon, p. 77. See B. J. Roberts, *The Old Testament Text and Versions.* His index has numerous references to these manuscripts, especially p. 56.

expect the elements and the destructiveness of man to leave these ancient documents unmolested. However, the discovery of various collections of ancient records such as some 20,000 cuneiform tablets of the Mari Letters, dating back to about 1700 B.C., do show that preservation is possible. Nonetheless, no such biblical finds are known.

Second, perhaps it should be noted that the Jews were beset with two difficulties that the Babylonians did not experience in this respect. From Moses' time on, writing was primarily done on animal skins, which do not last as long as clay tablets. Furthermore, the Jews over the centuries were forced to "live out of a suitcase" because of their many persecutions and exiles. They have not been able to transport multitudes of manuscripts from country to country. When consideration is given to the possibility for preservation within their homeland, it must be remembered that the city of Jerusalem was conquered forty-seven times between 1800 B.C. and A.D. 1948. The chances for survival of manuscripts from the biblical period in such a place are virtually nil. Perhaps this accounts for the fact that the few Masoretic manuscripts now available are those which have been preserved outside the land of Palestine.

Another reason for the scarcity of Hebrew manuscripts centered around the sacred scribal laws demanding ceremonial burial of worn or flawed manuscripts. According to Talmudic tradition,[5] any manuscript that contained a mistake or error, and all those that were aged beyond use, were systematically and religiously destroyed. Such a practice undoubtedly decreased the number of discoverable manuscripts appreciably.

A final reason to be suggested dates back to the fifth and sixth centuries of our era, when the Masoretes (Jewish scribes) standardized the Hebrew text. It is believed that when their great work of vocalizing (putting in the vowel letters) and standardizing the Scriptures was completed, they systematically and completely disposed of all the deviating manuscripts.[6] Archaeological discoveries, or the lack of them, tend to support this judgment. Thus it is certain that the printed Masoretic text as it appears today is based on relatively few manuscripts, none of which antedates the tenth century of the Christian era.

[5]Cf. Kenyon, p. 79; see also *The Massorah* (4 vols.), C. D. Ginsburg (compiler); and F. F. Bruce, *The Books and the Parchments*, rev. ed., pp. 117 ff.
[6]Cf. Samuel Davidson, *Introduction to the Old Testament*, p. 89; also see Kenyon, pp. 78 ff.

THE NATURE OF THE MASORETIC MANUSCRIPTS: GOOD

The next and very logical question to be asked then is: How good are the few Hebrew manuscripts which remain? There are several lines of evidence which suggest that although the number of Masoretic manuscripts is small, their quality is very good.

Very few variants. There are very few variants in the texts available, since they are all descendants of one text type[7] which was established about A.D. 100. This cannot be said of the New Testament manuscripts, where over 200,000 variants appear in some 5,000 manuscripts. Kenyon illustrates the paucity of variations in the Masoretic text by contrasting the Leningrad Codex of the Prophets, which is Babylonian (Eastern), with the standard Palestinian text (Western) of Ezekiel, where the Masoretic text is sometimes corrupt. A critical comparison reveals that there are only sixteen real conflicts between the two texts.[8] The fidelity of the New Testament text depends upon the multiplicity of manuscripts; whereas, in the Old Testament, the accuracy of the text results from the ability and reliability of the scribes who transmitted it.

Reverence for the Bible. With respect to the Jewish Scriptures, however, it was not scribal accuracy alone that guaranteed their product, but rather their almost superstitious reverence for the Bible. According to the Talmud, there were specifications not only for the kind of skins to be used and the size of the columns, but there was even a religious ritual necessary for the scribe to perform before writing the name of God. Rules governed the kind of ink they were to use, the spacing of words, and also forbade their writing anything from memory. The lines, and even the letters, were counted methodically. If a manuscript was found to contain even one mistake, it was discarded and destroyed (cf. chap. 18). This scribal formalism was responsible, at least in part, for the extreme care exercised in copying the Scriptures. It was also the reason why there were only a few manuscripts (as the rules demanded the destruction of defective items), as well as why those which are extant are of good quality.

Comparison of duplicate passages. Another line of evidence is found in the comparison of the duplicate passages of the Old Testament Masoretic text itself. Several psalms occur twice (e.g., Ps. 14 and 53), much of Isaiah 36-39 is also found in II Kings 18-20,

---

[7]Kenyon, pp. 70-72, which shows that the work of Paul Kahle on the Geniza manuscripts has modified this view of only one Masoretic text type.
[8]Kenyon, p. 45.

Isaiah 2:2-4 is almost exactly parallel to Micah 4:1-3, Jeremiah 52 is a repeat of II Kings 25, and large portions of Chronicles are found in Samuel and Kings. An examination of these passages shows not only a substantial textual agreement but, in some cases, almost a word-for-word identity. Therefore it may be concluded that the Old Testament texts have not undergone radical revisions, even if it were assumed that these parallel passages had identical sources.

Proof from archaeology. A substantial proof for the accuracy of the Old Testament text has come from archaeology. Numerous discoveries have confirmed the historical accuracy of the biblical documents, even down to the obsolete names of foreign kings on occasion. Reference should be made at this point to Robert Dick Wilson's classic work, *A Scientific Investigation of the Old Testament,* or the more recent work of William F. Albright, *From the Stone Age to Christianity,* in support of this view. One interesting example may be cited from even more recent findings than these. Until recently the reference to "So, king of Egypt" (II Kings 17:4) has often been used to illustrate the total ignorance of the writer of the book. No such king of Egypt was known to history. Now it is known, from the Egyptian spelling of the city of Sais—the capital of an Egyptian province in the western delta of that time (*c.* 725 B.C.)— that the text should read "To So [Sais], to the king of Egypt."[9] Tefnakhte was the king of this Egyptian province at the time, and Hoshea, king of Israel, was appealing to him for help to withstand the Assyrians. Rather than a manifestation of complete ignorance of the facts of its day, the biblical record thus reflects a great knowledge by the writer of his day, as well as precision in textual transmission.

Evidence from the Septuagint. Perhaps the best line of evidence comes from the Greek translation (third and second centuries B.C.) of the Old Testament known as the Septuagint (LXX). For the most part this Alexandrian translation reflects an almost literal book-for-book, chapter-by-chapter translation of the Hebrew Scriptures as they are found in the Masoretic text, with the common stylistic and idiomatic differences.

> The fact is that if we discard our Hebrew Bibles, the Septuagint, though sounding strange in places, would be a very satisfactory

---

[9]This problem has been brilliantly handled in two articles: Hans Goedicke, "The End of 'So,' King of Egypt," pp. 64-66, and William F. Albright, "The Elimination of King 'So,'" p. 66, both in *The Bulletin of the American Schools of Oriental Research,* No. 171 (Oct., 1963).

copy of the Old Testament. Indeed, for the first three centuries of the Christian Church, when most Christians spoke Greek fluently, the Septuagint was used almost exclusively.[10]

Furthermore, the Septuagint was the Bible of Jesus and the apostles. Most New Testament quotations are taken from it directly, even when it differs from the Masoretic text. These differences will be discussed subsequently, but on the whole the Septuagint closely parallels the Masoretic text, and is a confirmation of the fidelity of the tenth century A.D. Hebrew text.[11]

Close parallel between the Septuagint and Masoretic text. If no other evidence were available, the case for the fidelity of the Masoretic text could be brought to rest with confidence upon the foregoing lines of evidence alone. It appeared to be a careful and correct reproduction of the autographs. But, with the discovery of the Dead Sea Scrolls in 1947 and following, there is now another and almost overwhelming substantiation of the received Hebrew text of the Masoretes. Critics of the Masoretic text charged that the manuscripts were few and late; now, however, there is available, through the Dead Sea Scrolls, many and early manuscript fragments that provide a check on the whole Old Testament. These checks date about a thousand years before the great Masoretic manuscripts of the tenth century A.D. Before the discoveries in the Cairo Geniza and the Dead Sea caves, the Nash Papyrus (a fragment of the Ten Commandments and Shema, Deut. 6:4-9), dated between 150 B.C. and A.D. 100, was the only known scrap of the Hebrew text dating from before the Christian era.

THE DEAD SEA SCROLLS

Before showing how the amazing new evidence from Qumran bears on the state of the Hebrew text, a word should be said about the discovery of the scrolls, which are viewed by W. F. Albright as "the greatest manuscript discovery of modern times."[12]

DISCOVERIES

Ironically, and perhaps providentially, this great manuscript discovery was hit upon by chance when an Arab shepherd boy (Mu-

---

[10]R. Laird Harris, "How Reliable Is the Old Testament Text?" in *Can I Trust My Bible?* a symposium, p. 128.

[11]The best manuscript representative of the LXX is Vaticanus (Codex B), dated *c.* A.D. 325.

[12]J. C. Trever, "The Discovery of the Scrolls," *Biblical Archaeologist*, XI (Sept., 1948), 55.

10. *Qumran caves where the Dead Sea Scrolls were found (Giovanni Trimboli)*

hammad adh-Dhib) was pursuing a lost goat seven and one-half miles south of Jericho and a mile west of the Dead Sea. Here in a cave he found some jars containing several leather scrolls. Later explorations in this and nearby caves produced thousands of manuscript fragments which had once constituted about four hundred books thought to belong to the library of the Essenes. The Essenes were a Jewish religious sect dating from about the time of Christ. They had broken away from the temple-centered worship at Jerusalem, and had established their own monastic and Messianic community in the Judean desert near Qumran.

The first discovery was made in March, 1947, and subsequent explorations produced amazing finds through 1956. In all there were eleven caves containing scrolls and/or fragments excavated near Qumran between February 15, 1949, and February, 1956. Much material of interest to the archaeologist was discovered, but the discussion here is limited to the manuscripts that bear on the text of the Old Testament.

DESCRIPTION OF THE DISCOVERIES

Cave I. This cave was discovered first by the Arab shepherd boy. From it he took seven more or less complete scrolls and some fragments including the following:

1. St. Mark's Monastery Isaiah Scroll (Isaiah A, or IQIs[a]). It is a popular copy with numerous corrections above the line or in the margin and is the earliest known copy of any complete book of the Bible.

2. Manual of Discipline, a scroll containing rules and regulations of the Qumran sect.

3. Commentary on the book of Habakkuk, containing the text of

11. *The Qumran Community, where the Dead Sea Scrolls were produced (Giovanni Trimboli)*

the first two chapters of the Prophet Habakkuk with a running interpretation.

4. Genesis Apocryphon, first known as the Lamech Scroll, containing Apocryphal accounts in Aramaic of some of the patriarchs of Genesis.

5. Hebrew University Isaiah (Isaiah B, or IQIs^b) is incomplete but its text agrees more closely with the Masoretic text than does Isaiah A.

6. War Scroll, whose full title is War of the Sons of Light Against the Sons of Darkness, gives an account of preparation for the end-time war between the Qumran sect and their enemies.

7. Thanksgiving Hymns contain about thirty hymns which resemble Old Testament psalms.[13]

Cave I was officially excavated between February 15 and March 9, 1949. It yielded fragments of Genesis, Leviticus, Deuteronomy, Judges, Samuel, Isaiah, Ezekiel, Psalms, and some nonbiblical works including Enoch, Sayings of Moses (previously unknown), Book of Jubilee, Book of Noah, Testament of Levi, Tobit, and the Wisdom of Solomon. An interesting fragment of Daniel, containing 2:4 (where the language changes from Hebrew to Aramaic) also comes from this cave. Fragmentary commentaries on Psalms, Micah and Zephaniah were also found in Cave I.[14]

Cave II. This cave, first discovered and pilferred by the Bedouins, was excavated between March 10 and 29, 1952. Fragments of about a hundred manuscripts, including two of Exodus, one of Leviticus, four of Numbers, two or three of Deuteronomy, one of Jeremiah, Job, Psalms, and two of Ruth, were found. However, nothing so spectacular as the manuscripts found in some of the other caves was uncovered.

Cave III. This was found by the archaeologists and searched on March 14, 1952. It disclosed two halves of a copper scroll with directions to sixty or sixty-four sites containing hidden treasures. These sites were mostly in and around the Jerusalem area, ranging from north of Jericho to the Vale of Achor. Thus far, search for the treasures has been unfruitful. Various views have emerged to explain this scroll. It has been suggested that it is the work of a crank, or

---

[13]Taken from Menahem Mansoor, *The Dead Sea Scrolls*, pp. 2-3.
[14]For a more detailed list of the manuscript fragments from the various caves see *Biblical Archaeologist* (Sept., 1965), pp. 87-100.

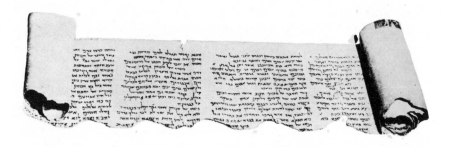

12. *The Habakkuk Commentary (Y. Yadin and The Shrine of the Book)*

part of the people's folklore, or possibly a record of the deposits of the tithe money and sacred vessels dedicated to the temple service.[15]

Cave IV. This cave (Partridge Cave), after being ransacked by the Bedouins, was searched in September, 1952, and it proved to be the most productive cave of all. Literally thousands of fragments were recovered either by purchase from the Bedouins or by the archaeologists' sifting the dust on the floor of the cave. These scraps represent hundreds of manuscripts (nearly four hundred of which have already been identified), including about one hundred copies of Bible books (all except Esther). The fragment of Samuel (4QSam^b) is thought to be the oldest known piece of biblical Hebrew, dating from the fourth century B.C. Also found were a few fragments of commentaries of the Psalms Isaiah and Nahum. The entire collection of Cave IV is believed to represent the scope of the Qumran library, and judging from the relative number of books found, their favorite books seemed to be Deuteronomy, Isaiah, Psalms, and the Minor Prophets, in that order. An interesting fragment containing some of Daniel 7:28; 8:1 (where the language changes back from Aramaic to Hebrew) was found.

Cave V. This cave was excavated in September, 1952. Fragments of Tobit and some biblical books, all in an advanced stage of deterioration, were found.

Cave VI. This cave was investigated on September 27, 1952, and produced, strangely enough, mostly papyrus instead of leather fragments. Papyrus pieces of Daniel, I Kings and II Kings were among the finds.

[15]See John M. Allegro, *The Treasure of the Copper Scroll*, 2d rev. ed.

Caves VII—X. These caves were examined between February 2 and April 6, 1955. The contents are interesting to the expert archaeologist, but not relevant to the present study of textual criticism.

Cave XI. This cave was excavated in January or February, 1956. It produced a well-preserved copy of some of the Psalms, including the Apocryphal Psalm 151, which was hitherto known only in Greek texts. Altogether, this manuscript contains the whole or part of thirty-six canonical psalms, ranging from Psalm 93 through 150. In addition to these, a very fine scroll of part of Leviticus, some large pieces of an Apocalypse of the New Jerusalem, and an Aramaic Targum (paraphrase) of Job were discovered.

Murabba'at Discoveries. Prompted by the original finds, the Bedouins have pursued their search and found caves to the southeast of Bethlehem which have produced self-dated manuscripts and documents from the Second Jewish Revolt (A.D. 132-35). Systematic exploration and excavation of these caves began on January 21, 1952. The dated manuscripts proved to be later and helped to establish the antiquity of the Dead Sea Scrolls. From these caves came another scroll of the Minor Prophets (the last half of Joel through Haggai), which closely supports the Masoretic text. The oldest known Semitic papyrus (a palimpsest), inscribed the second time in the ancient Hebrew script (dating from the seventh-eighth centuries B.C.), was found here.[16] As can readily be seen, there is now a mass of material of the Old Testament text, more than scholars will be able to absorb in some decades. Much of this material has already been published,[17] but much more from Caves IV and XI still remains to be published.

DATING THE DISCOVERIES

The question of dating these manuscripts from the Dead Sea has been settled by several lines of evidence.

Carbon 14. This was applied to half of a two-ounce piece of linen wrapping from one of the scrolls in Cave I by Dr. W. F. Libby of the University of Chicago in 1950. Results indicated an age of 1,917 years with a two-hundred-year (10 percent) variant, which left the date somewhere between 168 B.C. and A.D. 233.

---

[16]See D. Barthelemy and J. T. Milik, *Ten Years of Discovery in the Judean Wilderness.* Another site known as Khirbet Mird has produced manuscript materials. On April 3, 1960, a parchment fragment (first century A.D.) of Psalm 15 and part of Psalm 16 was discovered at Wadi Murabba'at. See T. L. Cass, *Secrets from the Caves,* p. 164.

[17]See Geza Vermes, trans., *The Dead Sea Scrolls in English.*

Paleography and Orthography. Another means of dating was found in paleography (ancient writing forms) and orthography (spelling), which indicated a date for some of the manuscripts before 100 B.C. Photographs of the complete Isaiah scroll mailed to him by John Trever were examined by W. F. Albright, who wrote,

> There is no doubt in my mind that the script is more archaic than the Nash papyrus . . . I should prefer a date around 100 B.C. . . . What an absolutely incredible find! And there can happily not be the slightest doubt in the world about the genuineness of the manuscript. [18]

Archaeology. Collaborative evidence for an early date came from archaeology. The accompanying pottery was analyzed as Late Hellenistic (*c.* 150-63 B.C.), and Early Roman (*c.* 63 B.C. to A.D. 100). The coins found in the monastery ruins proved by their inscriptions to extend from 135 B.C. to A.D. 135. The cloth was analyzed as to type and pattern, and it, too, supported the early date.

Final evidence came from the Murabba'at Discoveries south of Bethlehem, where self-dated manuscripts were discovered in 1952. Bearing dates from A.D. 132-35, these proved to be paleographically younger than the Dead Sea Scrolls. Practically the only source of evidence urged against the great antiquity of the scrolls was internal evidence, but that proved to be a double-edged argument.[19] There can be no reasonable doubt that the Qumran manuscripts came from the century before Christ and the first century A.D. Thus, they are one thousand years older than the Masoretic manuscripts of the tenth century. Before 1947, the Hebrew text was based on three partial and one complete manuscript dating from about A.D. 1000. Now, thousands of fragments are available, as well as complete books, containing large sections of the Old Testament from one millennium before the time of the Masoretic manuscripts.

The recent discovery of fourth century B.C. papyri in Aramaic cursive in caves southeast of Samaria shows by paleography that datings proposed for 40 Ex^r (*c.* 250 B.C.) and 4Q Sam^b (*c.* 225 B.C.) now appear to be minimal.[20]

DETAILS OF THE TEXT

The nature and number of these finds are of critical value for

[18]Trever, p. 55.
[19]See Solomon Zeitlin, *The Dead Sea Scrolls and Modern Scholarship.*
[20]*Biblical Archaeologist* (Dec., 1963), pp. 119 ff.

establishing the true text. With innumerable fragments of the entire Old Testament, there are abundant samples from which to draw comparisons with the Masoretic text. What does such a comparison reveal? All of the evidence has not been critically analyzed to date, but a decade and a half of scholarship has produced the following general conclusions.

Similarity to Masoretic Text. The scrolls give an overwhelming confirmation of the fidelity of the Masoretic text. Millar Burrows, in his valuable work entitled *The Dead Sea Scrolls*, writes, "It is a matter of wonder that through something like a thousand years the text underwent so little alteration. As I said in my first article on the scroll, 'Herein lies its chief importance, supporting the fidelity of the Masoretic tradition.' "[21] R. Laird Harris points out that "evidently the difference between the standard text of A.D. 900 and the text of 100 B.C. is not nearly so great as that between the Neutral and Western text in the New Testament study."[22] Gleason Archer observes that the two copies of Isaiah discovered in Qumran Cave I "proved to be word for word identical with our standard Hebrew Bible in more than 95% of the text. The 5% of variation consisted chiefly of obvious slips of the pen and variations in spelling."[23] To return to the original and "all important question" which Kenyon stated a generation ago, as to whether "this Hebrew text which we call Masoretic faithfully represents the Hebrew text as originally written by the authors of the Old Testament," it may now be more confidently asserted than ever before that the Dead Sea discoveries have enabled us to answer this question in the affirmative with much greater assurance than was possible before 1948.[24]

Difference from Masoretic Text. Next to the substantial agreement between the scrolls and the Masoretic text, the most important contribution these Dead Sea manuscripts make to textual criticism of the Old Testament is in the area of variant readings which they provide. Millar Burrows states, "I still feel that the amount of agreement with the Masoretic text is the manuscript's most significant feature, but having said that, I agree that the variants constitute its second point of importance."[25] This raises the question of what some of the variants are, and what constitutes their significance.

[21]Millar Burrows, *The Dead Sea Scrolls*, p. 304.
[22]R. Laird Harris, *Inspiration and Canonicity of the Bible*, p. 99.
[23]Gleason L. Archer, Jr., *A Survey of Old Testament Introduction*, p. 19.
[24]See F. F. Bruce, *Second Thoughts on the Dead Sea Scrolls*, pp. 61-69.
[25]Burrows, p. 304.

Some of the important variants show a close parallel to the Greek text (Septuagint).

1. A fragment from Cave IV containing Deuteronomy 32:8 reads, "according to the number of the sons of God," which is translated "angels of God" by the Septuagint (LXX), as in Genesis 6:4 (margin); Job 1:6; 2:1; and 38:7. The Masoretic text reads, "according to the number of the children of Israel."

2. The Masoretic text of Exodus 1:5 reads "seventy souls," while the LXX, and the New Testament quote taken from it (cf. Acts 7:14), read "seventy-five souls." A fragment of Exodus 1:5 from the Qumran Scrolls reads "seventy-five souls," in agreement with the Septuagint.

3. Hebrews 1:6 (AV), "Let all the angels of God worship him," is a quote from the LXX of Deuteronomy 32:43. This quotation is not in agreement with the Masoretic text, but one of the scroll fragments containing this section tends to confirm the Greek text (LXX).

4. The famous Isaiah 7:14 passage reads, "she shall call his name" in the Masoretic text, but the LXX and now the great Isaiah scroll read, "His name shall be called," a matter of one less consonant of the Hebrew alphabet.

5. The Greek version of Jeremiah is sixty verses (one-eighth) shorter than the Hebrew text of Jeremiah. The fragment of Jeremiah (4Q Jer^b) supports some of these omissions.

6. In Cave XI a copy of Psalm 151 was found which was previously unknown in the Hebrew text although it appeared in the Septuagint. There were also some Apocryphal books found in the Hebrew manuscripts of the Qumran caves, which had previously been known only in the LXX.[26]

This should by no means be construed as a uniform picture, since there are not many deviants in the Dead Sea Scrolls from the Masoretic text to begin with, and in some cases the variants do not consistently agree with the LXX, while in a few cases they do not agree at all. However, even Orlinsky, who is one of the foremost defenders of the Masoretic text against proposed emendations based on the Dead Sea Scrolls, admits, "But this much may be said: The *LXX* translation, no less than the Masoretic Text itself, will have gained

[26]Vermes, *The Essene Writings of Qumran*, p. 296.

considerable respect as a result of the Qumran discoveries in those circles where it has long—overlong—been necessary."[27]

In summary of the evidence thus far presented, it may be said that there are three basic textual traditions of the Old Testament: the Masoretic, the Samaritan (see chap. 22), and the Greek (LXX). On the whole, the Masoretic text is the best, but in several passages the Septuagint (LXX) is better.

The general fidelity of the Hebrew text. The basic problem is to determine how great the difference between the Hebrew text and the Greek traditions is in general, and between the Dead Sea Scrolls and the Masoretic text in particular. One answer has been given in the decision of the translators of the Revised Standard Version of Isaiah. Only thirteen readings were adopted in preference for the complete Isaiah scroll (IQ Is[a]) over the Masoretic text. Eight of these were previously known from ancient versions, and few of them were significant changes.[28]

Another way to approach this problem is by a simple comparison of the variants in a given chapter. Of the 166 words in Isaiah 53, there are only seventeen letters in question. Ten of these letters are simply a matter of spelling, which does not affect the sense. Four more letters are minor stylistic changes, such as conjunctions. The remaining three letters comprise the word "light," which is added in verse 11, and does not affect the meaning greatly. Furthermore, this word is supported by the LXX and IQ Is[b]. Thus, in one chapter of 166 words, there is only one word (three letters) in question after a thousand years of transmission—and this word does not significantly change the meaning of the passage. This sample is typical of the whole Isaiah A manuscript.[29] Thus, the Dead Sea Scrolls lend assurance to the reader of the dependability of the Old Testament text, or, as Millar Burrows affirms, "The general reader and student of the Bible may be satisfied to note that nothing in all this changes our understanding of the religious teaching of the Bible."[30]

Attempts to establish a family tree of textual traditions. The discovery of the Dead Sea Scrolls, with their various variant readings, has reopened the whole question of the Old Testament textual traditions. Some tentative attempts to reconstruct a family tree of these

[27]Harry M. Orlinsky, "The Textual Criticism of the Old Testament" in G. E. Wright (ed.), *The Bible and the Ancient Near East*, p. 121.
[28]Burrows, pp. 305 ff.
[29]Harris, p. 124.
[30]Burrows, p. 320.

manuscript traditions have been made.[31] Since the Masoretic text (fourth century A.D.) stemmed from a single source which was standardized by Hebrew scholars at about A.D. 100, the discovery of manuscripts antedating this period casts new light on the history of the Old Testament text before this recension. From among the Dead Sea Scrolls several textual traditions can be observed.

1. The Proto-Masoretic Text Type. This textual type, which was the predecessor of the later Masoretic text, is clearly represented at Qumran, chiefly in Isaiah, Ezekiel and the Twelve (Minor Prophets), although fragments from among the Law and Historical books also preserve this text type. Most of the manuscripts of the Law from Cave IV are aligned with the Proto-Masoretic type. With the exception of the Writings (whose textual type has not been clearly determined as yet), the remaining books of the Old Testament are represented among the scrolls and fragments in a Proto-Masoretic text type.

2. The Proto-Septuagint Text Type. This is represented at Qumran by manuscripts of Joshua, Samuel (e.g., 4QSam[a, b]), and Jeremiah (e.g., 4QJer[a]). The text of 4QSam[b] agrees systematically with the LXX against the Masoretic type by a ratio of thirteen to four. In 4QSam[a] the ratio of agreement with the LXX type text is even higher. The other historical books (Joshua and Kings), insofar as they are preserved by the fragments, also support the Proto-Septuagint text type. A few manuscripts of the Pentateuch from Cave IV also support this tradition, for example, the Exodus manuscript (4QEx[a]) and the manuscript containing Deuteronomy 32:43. From the Prophets there is a Jeremiah fragment (4QJer[b]) that follows the LXX very closely. In the LXX, Jeremiah is one-eighth shorter than the Masoretic text, and in Jeremiah 10 of this manuscript there are four verses omitted and one shifted, exactly as it is in the Qumran literature. Hitherto there were no Hebrew manuscripts supporting the shorter LXX version of Jeremiah.

3. The Proto-Samaritan Text Type. This is also known among the Dead Sea Scrolls. From Cave IV came a Paleo-Hebrew manuscript of Exodus[32] and one of Numbers (4QNum[b]) in "square"

---

[31]The discussion here is taken from Frank Moore Cross, Jr., *The Ancient Library of Qumran and Modern Biblical Studies*, pp. 121-45. See also Barthelemy and Milik, chap. 2.

[32]Published by Patrick W. Skehan, "Exodus in the Samaritan Recension from Qumran," *Journal of Biblical Literature* (1955), pp. 182-87.

History Of The Old Testament Text

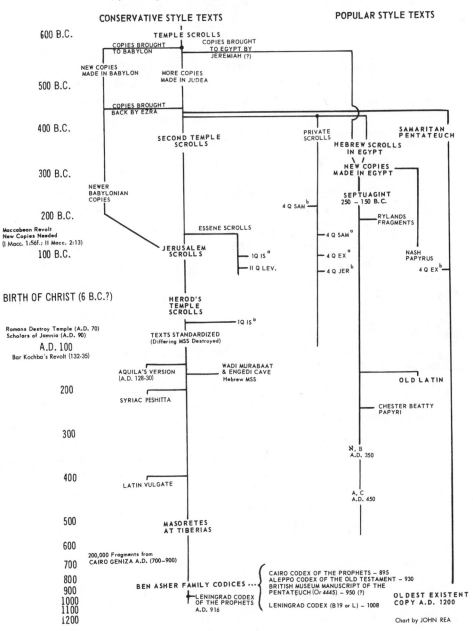

CONSERVATIVE STYLE TEXTS   POPULAR STYLE TEXTS

600 B.C.   TEMPLE SCROLLS
          COPIES BROUGHT   COPIES BROUGHT
          TO BABYLON   TO EGYPT BY
                                JEREMIAH (?)

          NEW COPIES
          MADE IN BABYLON   MORE COPIES
500 B.C.   MADE IN JUDEA

          COPIES BROUGHT
          BACK BY EZRA

400 B.C.   SECOND TEMPLE   PRIVATE   SAMARITAN
                  SCROLLS   SCROLLS   PENTATEUCH
                                      HEBREW SCROLLS
                                      IN EGYPT
                                      NEW COPIES
300 B.C.   MADE IN EGYPT

          NEWER
          BABYLONIAN   SEPTUAGINT
          COPIES   250 – 150 B.C.
                              4 Q SAM^b RYLANDS
200 B.C.   ESSENE SCROLLS   FRAGMENTS
Maccabean Revolt
New Copies Needed   4 Q SAM^a
(I Macc. 1:56f.; II Macc. 2:13)   NASH
100 B.C.   JERUSALEM   4 Q EX^a PAPYRUS
                  SCROLLS
                        1Q IS^a 4 Q JER^b 4Q EX^b
                        II Q LEV.

BIRTH OF CHRIST (6 B.C.?)
                  HEROD'S
                  TEMPLE
                  SCROLLS
Romans Destroy Temple (A.D. 70)   1Q IS^b
Scholars of Jamnia (A.D. 90)
A.D. 100   TEXTS STANDARDIZED
Bar Kochba's Revolt (132-35)   (Differing MSS Destroyed)

                  AQUILA'S VERSION   WADI MURABAAT
                  (A.D. 128-30)   & ENGEDI CAVE   OLD LATIN
200   Hebrew MSS
                  SYRIAC PESHITTA
                                                      CHESTER BEATTY
300   PAPYRI

                                      ℵ, B
400   A.D. 350
                  LATIN VULGATE

                                      A, C
500   MASORETES   A.D. 450
                  AT TIBERIAS
600
          200,000 Fragments from
700   CAIRO GENIZA A.D. (700–900)
                                      CAIRO CODEX OF THE PROPHETS – 895
800   ALEPPO CODEX OF THE OLD TESTAMENT – 930
900   BEN ASHER FAMILY CODICES ··· BRITISH MUSEUM MANUSCRIPT OF THE
1000   PENTATEUCH (Or 4445) – 950 (?)   OLDEST EXISTENT
1100   LENINGRAD CODEX   LENINGRAD CODEX (B19 or L) – 1008 COPY A.D. 1200
1200   OF THE PROPHETS
                  A.D. 916
                                      Chart by JOHN REA

script which give collateral witness to a Samaritan kind of text. The Numbers manuscript is not a consistent witness to the Samaritan text or even to a Proto-Samaritan type, since it shows striking contact with the LXX tradition.

Attempts to draw the lines of relationship between these textual families are in the embryonic stage, and the situation calls for dedicated scholarship in the days to come. The accompanying chart by Dr. John Rea, former instructor in Old Testament at Moody Bible Institute, is helpful in summarizing and visualizing the relationship on this family tree of the Old Testament textual traditions.

SUMMARY AND CONCLUSION

Several lines of evidence supported the faithfulness of the Masoretic text even before the discovery of the Dead Sea Scrolls in 1947: (1) the fact that there were so few variants in the Masoretic text, (2) the substantial, at times literal, agreement of the LXX translation, (3) the scrupulous rules of the scribes, (4) the similarity of duplicate passages within the Hebrew Old Testament, and (5) the archaeological confirmation of the historical accuracy of the text. Consequently, although there were relatively few Masoretic manuscripts, they were known to be of good quality even prior to 1947.

The discovery of the Dead Sea Scrolls did, however, dismiss any remaining doubts about the fidelity of the Masoretic text by providing scholars with hundreds of manuscripts including almost every book of the Old Testament, which antedate the extant Masoretic manuscripts by a thousand years. The results of scholarly comparison reveal that the Masoretic text and the various text types of the Dead Sea manuscripts are substantially identical. The variants that do occur are probably not so great as those which separate the New Testament textual traditions. The significance of the variants is that they reopen the whole field of Old Testament textual families, which is only beginning to take shape.

20

NEW TESTAMENT MANUSCRIPTS

INTRODUCTORY CONSIDERATIONS

The integrity of the Old Testament text was established primarily by the fidelity of the transmission process which was later confirmed by the Dead Sea Scrolls. The fidelity of the New Testament text, however, rests in the multiplicity of the extant manuscripts. Whereas the Old Testament had only a few complete manuscripts, all of which were good, as the result of ancient rabbinical textual work the New Testament has more copies—although of poorer quality (more variants)—which enable the present-day textual critic to establish the true text.

DEFINITION OF MANUSCRIPT

A manuscript is a handwritten literary composition in contrast to a printed copy. An original manuscript is the first one produced, usually called an autograph. There are no known original manuscripts of the Bible; in fact, none are needed because of the abundance of manuscript copies.

DIFFERENT KINDS OF MANUSCRIPTS

New Testament manuscripts written in a formal printed style somewhat similar to capital letters are known as uncials (or majuscules).[1] Uncial manuscripts of Greek and biblical literature flourished from the third to the sixth centuries A.D. Gradually, during the next two centuries, the style degenerated until a reform in handwriting was initiated, consisting of smaller letters in a running hand, called "minuscules."[2] Minuscule manuscripts in Greek are dated from the ninth to the fifteenth centuries; nevertheless, this "running hand," known also as "cursive," was employed by the Greeks for nonliterary, everyday documents from antiquity. The cursive hand proved to

[1] The word "uncial" is derived from *uncia* (Latin), meaning "a twelfth part," implying that the letter was one-twelfth the size of a normal line. Cf. *Classical Philology*, XXX (1935), 247-54.
[2] "Minuscule" is derived from *minusculus* (Latin), meaning "rather small."

be more practical than the more formal "book hand" (uncial), and became popular almost immediately throughout Western Europe, with the exception of some liturgical writers who employed uncials as late as the tenth and eleventh centuries.

Testimony to the fidelity of the New Testament text comes primarily from three sources: Greek manuscripts, ancient translations, and patristic citations. The first source is the most important and can be subdivided into three classes commonly termed the papyri, the uncials and the minuscules. The most distinguishing feature of each has been chosen for these designations, for the papyrus manuscripts were also written in uncial letters. The second and third classes are differentiated by the style of writing, since both used vellum or parchment as the writing substance.

MANUSCRIPTS ON PAPYRUS (SECOND-THIRD CENTURIES)[3]

P52 John Rylands Fragment (a.d. 117-38)

This papyrus fragment (2½ by 3½ inches) from a codex is the earliest known copy of any portion of the New Testament. It dates from the first half of the second century, and probably between a.d. 117-38. Adolf Deissmann argued that it may even be earlier.[4] The papyrus piece, written on both sides, contains portions of five verses from the gospel of John (18:31-33, 37-38). Although this is a short fragment, it has proven to be the closest and most valuable link in the chain of transmission. Because of its early date and location (Egypt), some distance from the traditional place of composition (Asia Minor), this portion of the gospel of John tends to confirm the traditional date of the composition of the gospel about the end of the first century. This fragment belongs to the John Rylands Library at Manchester, England.

P45, 46, 47 Chester Beatty Papyri (a.d. 250)

This important collection of New Testament papyri now resides in the Beatty Museum near Dublin. It consists of three codices, and contains most of the New Testament. P45 is comprised of pieces of thirty leaves of a papyrus codex: two from Matthew, two from John, six from Mark, seven from Luke, and thirteen from Acts. The orig-

[3]Unless otherwise noted, the following discussion and dating system are after Bruce M. Metzger, *The Text of the New Testament.*
[4]*Ibid.,* p. 39, n. 2.

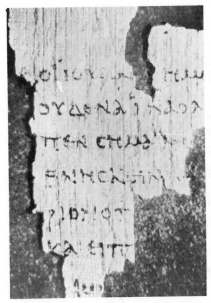

13. The John Rylands Fragment of John 18:31-33 (John Rylands Library)

14. A page of Romans from a Beatty-Michigan papyrus dating about A.D. 250 (University of Michigan Library)

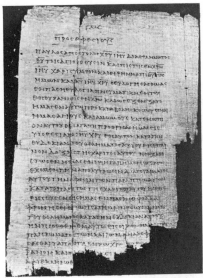

15. The first page of Ephesians from a Beatty-Michigan papyrus dating about A.D. 250 (University of Michigan Library)

16. The Bodmer Papyrus (P 66) dates from about A.D. 250. John 1:1-14 is pictured (Bodmer Library)

inal codex consisted of some 220 leaves, measuring ten by eight inches each. Several other small fragments of Matthew from these papyri have appeared in a collection at Vienna.[5] The type of text represented in Mark is nearer to the Caesarean family.[6] The other Gospels stand between the Alexandrian and Western type text. Acts is clearly nearer to the Alexandrian family of manuscripts. P46 consists of eighty-six slightly mutilated leaves (11 by 6½ inches), stemming from an original that contained 104 pages of Paul's epistles. These epistles include Romans, Hebrews, I Corinthians, II Corinthians, Ephesians, Galatians, Philippians, Colossians, I Thessalonians, and II Thessalonians. Portions of Romans and I Thessalonians, and all of II Thessalonians, are missing from the present manuscripts, which were arranged in descending order according to size. Like P45, P46 dates from about A.D. 250. In general, the text is closer to the Alexandrian type. P47 is made up of ten slightly mutilated leaves of the book of Revelation, measuring 9½ by 5½ inches. Of the original thirty-two leaves, only the middle portion, 9:10–17:2, remains. In general, it agrees with the Alexandrian text of Codex Sinaiticus (Aleph), but shows frequent independence. This papyrus dates from about A.D. 250 or later. Thirty of the leaves are owned by the University of Michigan, Ann Arbor.

P66, 72, 75 BODMER PAPYRI

The most important discovery of New Testament papyri since the Chester Beatty manuscripts was the acquisition of the Bodmer Collection by the Library of World Literature at Culagny, near Geneva. P66, dating from about A.D. 200 or earlier, contains 104 leaves of John 1:1–6:11; 6:35b–14:15; and fragments of forty other pages, John 14-21. The text is a mixture of the Alexandrian and Western types, and there are some twenty alterations between the lines which invariably belong to the Western family.[7] P72 is the earliest known copy of Jude, I Peter and II Peter. It dates from the third century and contains several Apocryphal and canonical books, in the following order: Nativity of Mary, Apocryphal Correspondence of Paul to the Corinthians, the Eleventh Ode of Solomon, the Epistle of Jude, Melito's Homily on the Passover, a Fragment of a Hymn, the Apology of Phileas, Psalm 33, Psalm 34, I Peter, and II Peter. This papyrus was apparently a private codex measuring 6 by 5¾ inches, pre-

[5]*Ibid.*, p. 37, n. 2.
[6]For a discussion of the meaning of "textual families," see chap. 27.
[7]Metzger, p. 40.

pared by some four scribes and having definite affinities to the Alexandrian textual tradition, and particularly the Sahidic version.[8] P75
is a codex of 102 pages (originally 144) measuring 10¼ by 5⅓ inches,
containing Luke and John in clear and carefully printed uncials, and
dated between A.D. 175 and 225. It consequently is the earliest
known copy of Luke. Its text is very similar to Codex Vaticanus (B),
although it occasionally agrees with the Sahidic version.[9]

Actually, there are some seventy-six[10] papyri manuscripts of the
New Testament, of which the foregoing are merely the more important representatives. The papyri witness to the text is invaluable,
ranging chronologically from the very threshold of the second century, within a generation of the autographs, and including the content of most of the New Testament. All this is still extant from within
the first two hundred years after the New Testament itself was
written.

UNCIAL MANUSCRIPTS ON VELLUM AND PARCHMENT
(FOURTH-NINTH CENTURIES)

As a whole, the most important manuscripts of the New Testament
are generally considered to be the great uncials, which date from the
fourth and following centuries.

CODEX VATICANUS (B)

The Codex Vaticanus is perhaps the oldest uncial on parchment
or vellum (c. 325-50), and one of the most important witnesses to
the text of the New Testament. This manuscript was probably written by the middle of the fourth century; however, it was not known
to textual scholars until after 1475 when it was cataloged in the
Vatican Library. For the next four hundred years scholars were prohibited from studying it.[11] After that time, a complete photographic
facsimile was made of it, 1889-90, and another of the New Testament
in 1904. It includes most of the Old Testament (LXX), the New
Testament in Greek, and the Apocrypha, with the exception of I
Maccabees, II Maccabees, and the Prayer of Manasses. Also missing
is Genesis 1:1—46:28; II Kings 2:5-7, 10-13; Psalms 106:27—138:6;

---

[8]*Ibid.*, pp. 40-41.
[9]A more detailed analysis appears in *ibid.*, p. 42.
[10]See "Check-list of the Greek Papyri of the New Testament," *ibid.*, pp. 247-56.
[11]Constantin Tischendorf (in 1843-66) and S. P. Tregelles (in 1845) were permitted to look at it for a few hours. They were not permitted to copy the manuscript, but
Tregelles secretly memorized much of it. For a more complete story of Codex Vaticanus (B), see G. L. Robinson, *Where Did We Get Our Bible?* p. 111.

17. *Codex Sinaiticus opened to John 21:1-25 (British Museum)*

18. *The Monastery of St. Catherine of Mount Sinai is a repository of ancient manuscripts (Biblical Archaeologist)*

19. *Codex Alexandrinus opened to II Peter 3 (British Museum)*

20. *Papyrus 1532. This third century fragment shows Hebrews 12:1-11 (British Museum)*

and Hebrews 9:14 to the end of the New Testament. Mark 16:9-20 and John 7:53–8:11 were purposely omitted from the text. This codex was written in small and delicate uncials on fine vellum. It has three columns of forty-two lines per page, except for the Old Testament poetical books which have only two columns. It contains 759 leaves measuring 10 by 10½ inches: 617 in the Old Testament, and 142 in the New. The manuscripts are divided into sections: Matthew has 170 sections, Mark has 61, Luke 152, John 80, etc. The Codex Vaticanus is a possession of the Roman Catholic Church, and is housed in the Vatican Library, Vatican City, Italy. This manuscript is generally regarded as an excellent example of the Alexandrian type text.

CODEX SINAITICUS ℵ (ALEPH) (c. 340)

This fourth century Greek manuscript is generally considered to be the most important witness to the text because of its antiquity, accuracy, and lack of omissions. The story of the discovery of Aleph is one of the most fascinating and romantic in textual history.[12] It was found in the monastery of St. Catherine at Mount Sinai by the German Count Tischendorf, who was living in Prussia by permission of the czar. On his first visit (1844), he discovered forty-three leaves of vellum, containing portions of the LXX (I Chronicles, Jeremiah, Nehemiah and Esther), in a basket of scraps which the monks were using to light their fires. He secured it and took it to the University Library at Leipsig, Germany. It remains there, known as the Codex Frederico-Augustanus. Tischendorf's second visit, in 1853, proved unfruitful; but in 1859, under the authority of Czar Alexander II, he returned again. Just before he was to return home empty-handed, the monastery steward showed him an almost complete copy of the Scriptures and some other books. These were subsequently acquired as a "conditional gift"[13] to the czar. This manuscript is now known as the famous Codex Sinaiticus (Aleph). It contains over half the Old Testament (LXX), and all of the New, with the exception of Mark 16:9-20 and John 7:53–8:11. All of the Old Testament Apocrypha, with the addition of the *Epistle of Barnabas*, and a large por-

---

[12]For the details of this story see Metzger, pp. 42-45.

[13]Actually, Tischendorf pulled a bit of "ecclesiastical diplomacy" in convincing the monastery that it would be to their advantage for them to give the manuscript to the czar, whose influence as protectorate of the Greek Church could be to their advantage. In return for the manuscript, the czar gave them a silver shrine, 7,000 rubles for the library at Sinai, 2,000 rubles for the monks in Cairo, and conferred several Russian decorations on the authorities of the monastery.

tion of the *Shepherd* of Hermas are also included. This codex was written in large clear Greek uncials on 364½ pages (plus the forty-three at Leipsig), measuring 13½ by 14 inches. Each page has four columns about 2½ inches wide, except the Old Testament poetical books where there are only two wider columns per page. The material is good vellum, made from antelope skins. Originally the manuscript underwent several scribal "corrections," known by the seglum א (Aleph), and then, at Caesarea (in the sixth or seventh century) a group of scribes introduced a large number of alterations, known as א*ᶜᵃ* or א*ᶜᵇ*. In 1933 the British government purchased Aleph for the British Museum for £100,000, about $500,000 at that time. It was published in a volume entitled *Scribes and Correctors of Codex Sinaiticus* (London, 1938). The text type is Alexandrian in general, but has definite strains of Western readings.

CODEX ALEXANDRINUS (A) (*c.* 450)

This well-preserved manuscript from the fifth century ranks second only to B and Aleph as representative of the New Testament text. Though some have dated this manuscript in the late fourth century,[14] it is probably the result of fifth century scribes of Alexandria, Egypt. In 1078 this codex was presented to the Patriarch of Alexandria, after whom it was named. In 1621 it was taken to Constantinople by Cyril Lucar, who was transferred to patriarchal duties there. Lucar gave it to Sir Thomas Roe, English ambassador to Turkey in 1624, to present to King James I. James died before it reached England, and the manuscript was given to Charles I in 1627, too late for use in the King James Version of 1611. In 1757, George II presented it to the National Library of the British Museum. It contains the whole Old Testament, except for several mutilations (Gen. 14:14-17; 15:1-5, 16-19; 16:6-9; I Kingdoms [I Sam.] 12:18–14:9; Psalms 49:19–79:10), and most of the New Testament (only Matt. 1:1–25:6; John 6:50–8:52 and II Cor. 4:13–12:6 are missing). However, the manuscript also contains I and II Clement and the Psalms of Solomon, with some parts missing. The manuscript contains 773 leaves, 639 of the Old Testament and 134 of the New. The page size is 10¼ by 12 inches, and is written in two columns of fifty or fifty-one lines per page. The large square uncials are written on very thin vellum, and are divided into sections marked by large letters. Codex

---

[14]Sir Frederic G. Kenyon, *Our Bible and the Ancient Manuscripts*, rev. ed., p. 129.

Alexandrinus is in the possession of the National Library of the British Museum. The text is of varied quality. The Gospels are the oldest example of the Byzantine text, which is generally regarded as inferior.[15] The remainder of the New Testament, which was probably copied from a different source, ranks with Aleph and B as a representative of the Alexandrian type of text.[16]

Codex Ephraemi Rescriptus (C) (c. 345)

The Ephraemi Rescriptus Codex probably originated in Alexandria, Egypt. It was brought to Italy by John Lascaris at about 1500, and was later purchased by Pietro Strozzi. Catherine de Medici, an Italian who was the wife and mother of French kings, acquired it about 1533. At her death, the manuscript was placed in the National Library at Paris, where it remains today. Most of the Old Testament is missing from this codex, except parts of Job, Proverbs, Ecclesiastes, Song of Solomon, and two Apocryphal books: The Wisdom of Solomon, and Ecclesiasticus. The New Testament lacks II Thessalonians, II John, and parts of other books.[17] The manuscript is a palimpsest (rubbed out, erased) *rescriptus* (rewritten) which originally contained the Old and New Testaments, but they were erased by Ephraem, who wrote his sermons on the leaves. By chemical reactivation, Tischendorf was able to decipher the almost invisible writing.[18] Only 209 leaves survive: 64 from the Old and 145 (out of an original 238) from the New Testament. The pages are 9½ by 12¼ inches, with one wide column of forty to forty-six lines (usually forty-one). Located in the National Library, Paris, C is a compound of all the major textual types, agreeing frequently with the inferior Byzantine family. The manuscript has been corrected by two scribes, in texts referred to as C² or C^b (sixth century Palestine) and C³ or C^c (ninth century Constantinople).

Codex Bezae (D) (Codex Cantabrigiensis) (c. 450 or c. 550)

This is the oldest known bilingual manuscript of the New Testament. It was written in Greek and Latin and may have originated in southern Gaul (France) or northern Italy. It was found in 1562 by Theodore deBèze (Beza), the French theologian, at St. Irenaeus Mon-

[15]Cf. Metzger, p. 49.
[16]*Ibid.*, p. 47.
[17]F. H. A. Scrivener, *A Plain Introduction to the Criticism of the New Testament*, 4th ed., Edward Miller (ed.), I, 121, lists these in detail.
[18]For an up-to-date correction of Tischendorf's edition (Leipzig, 1843), see Robert W. Lyon's article in *New Testament Studies*, V (1959), 266-72.

astery, Lyons, France. In 1581 Beza gave it to Cambridge University. This manuscript contains the four Gospels, Acts, and III John 11-15, with variations from other manuscripts indicated. Present omissions in Greek include Matthew 1:1-20; 6:20–9:2; 27:2-12; John 1:16–3:26; Acts 8:29–10:14; 21:2-10, 15-18; 22:10-20; and 22:29–28:31. In Latin, Matthew 1:1-11; 6:8–8:27; 26:65–27:1; I John 1:1–3:16; Acts 8:20–10:4; 20:31–21:2; 21:7-10; 22:2-10; and 22:20–28:31 are omitted. There are 406 leaves (8 by 10 inches), with one column of thirty-three lines to the page. The Greek text is on the left page, and the Latin on the right. The order of the books is Matthew, John, Luke, Mark, etc. Third John 11-15 is found in Latin only. In each book the first three lines are in red ink. The manuscript is located in the Cambridge University Library. The Gospels are Western in type but, as Metzger points out, "no manuscript has so many and such remarkable variations from what is usually taken to be the normal New Testament Text."[19]

CODEX CLAROMONTANUS (D^2 or D^{p2})[20] (c. 550)

This codex is a sixth century complement of D, containing much of the New Testament missing in Codex Bezae. D^2 seems to have originated in Italy or Sardinia.[21] It was named after a monastery at Clermont, France, where it was found by Beza. After Beza's death, the codex was owned by several private individuals. Finally, King Louis XIV purchased it for the National Library at Paris in 1656. Tischendorf fully edited it in 1852. It contains all of Paul's epistles and Hebrews, although Romans 1:1-7, 27-30 and I Corinthians 14:13-22 are missing in Greek, while I Corinthians 14:8-18 and Hebrews 13:21-23 are missing in the Latin. Like D, D^2 is a bilingual manuscript, containing 533 pages, seven by nine inches. It was written in a single column of twenty-one lines. It was artistically written on thin, high quality vellum. The Greek is good, but the Latin is grammatically inferior in some places. The manuscript is now located in the National Library, Paris. D^2 is distinctly Western, although the readings in the Epistles are not so striking as those in the Gospels and Acts.

CODEX BASILIENSIS (E)

This is an eighth century manuscript of the four Gospels on 318

---

[19]Metzger, p. 50.
[20]D^{p2} stands for D^{Paul}, since it supplements D with the Pauline epistles.
[21]Kenyon, pp. 207-8. Also see Alexander Souter, *The Text and Canon of the New Testament*, p. 28.

leaves. It is presently in the library of the University of Basel, Switzerland, and has a Byzantine type text.

CODEX LAUDIANUS 35 (E² or Eᵃ)

This dates from the late sixth or early seventh century. It contains Acts in both Greek and Latin, arranged in very short lines of one to three words. The text type is mixed, sometimes agreeing with D, but more often with the Byzantine family.[22] It is the earliest known manuscript containing Acts 8:37.

CODEX SANGERMANENSIS (E³ or Eᵖ)

This is a ninth century copy of D² in Greek and Latin and therefore has no independent value for the textual critic.

CODEX BOREELIANUS (F)

This contains the four Gospels, dates from the ninth century, and is a typically Byzantine type text.

CODEX AUGIENSIS (F² or Fᵖ)

This is a ninth century manuscript of Paul's epistles in Greek and Latin (with large omissions) but Hebrews is in Latin only. It is now at Trinity College, Cambridge. The text is Western and was published by F. H. A. Scrivener in 1859.

CODEX WOLFII A (G)

Also called Codex Harleianus, this codex dates to the tenth century. It contains the four Gospels with many lacunae (omissions).

CODEX BOERNERIANUS (G³ or Gᵖ)

Dating from the ninth century, this codex contains Paul's epistles in Greek with a literal Latin translation between the lines (interlinear). It has the name but not the narration of the Apocryphal Epistle to the Laodiceans. The text is closely akin to F². It is possibly of Irish origin, and apparently was part of the same codex as Δ (see Codex Sangallensis).

CODEX WOLFII B (H)

This codex contains the four Gospels with many lacunae. It dates from the ninth or tenth century, and now resides in the Public Library, Hamburg. The text is Byzantine.

[22]Constantin Tischendorf edited it in 1870.

CODEX MUTINENSIS (H² or Hª)

This is a ninth century copy of Acts (seven chapters missing), now in the Grand Ducal Library at Modena. The text is Byzantine.

CODEX COISLINIANUS (H³ or Hᵖ)

This is an important codex of Paul's epistles, dating from the sixth century. The forty-three leaves known to exist today are divided among the libraries at Paris, Leningrad, Moscow, Kiev, Turin and Mount Athos. The text is Alexandrian.

CODEX WASHINGTONIANUS II (I)

This is a manuscript of the Pauline Epistles in the Freer Collection at the Smithsonian Institute. There are 84 surviving leaves of the original 210. It dates from the fifth or sixth century and has portions of all of Paul's letters and Hebrews, except Romans. The text is a good representative of the Alexandrian family, agreeing more closely with Aleph and A than B.

CODEX CYPRIUS (K)

This is a ninth or tenth century complete copy of the four Gospels with a typically Byzantine text.

CODEX MOSQUENSIS (K² or Kᵃᵖ)

This is a ninth or tenth century codex of Acts, the General Epistles, and Pauline Epistles with Hebrews. The text is a form of Von Soden's I-text (see chap. 26).

CODEX REGIUS (L)

This is an eighth century codex of the Gospels. It is badly written but represents a good text type, often agreeing with B. Its unique feature is the presence of two endings to the gospel of Mark. The first is the shorter ending, reading as follows:

> But they [the women] reported briefly to Peter and those with him all that they had been told. And after this, Jesus himself sent out by means of them, from east to west, the sacred and imperishable proclamation of eternal salvation.[23]

The second ending is the traditional verses 9-20 found in the King James Version.

---

[23]As translated by Revised Standard Version in note on Mark 16:8.

CODEX ANGELICUS (L² or Lᵃᵖ)

This codex is a ninth century copy of Acts, the General Epistles, and the Pauline Epistles. It is a Byzantine type text.

CODEX PAMPIANUS (M)

This codex contains the four Gospels. It is a Byzantine text, with admixtures of Caesarean. It dates from the ninth century.

CODEX PURPUREUS PETROPOLITANUS (N)

This codex, written in the sixth century in silver letters on purple vellum, is a deluxe parchment. Of the 462 original leaves, some 230 known leaves are scattered around the world. The text is dominantly Byzantine, although B. H. Streeter regarded it as a weak member of the Caesarean family.[24]

CODEX SINOPENSIS (O)

This codex is another sixth century deluxe edition, written with gold ink on purple vellum. It is now in Bibliotheque Nationale, Paris. It contains forty-three leaves of Matthew 13-24, and five smaller leaves in Caesarean type text.

CODEX PORPHYRIANUS (P² or Pᵃᵖʳ)

This is one of the few uncial manuscripts containing the book of Revelation. It also contains Acts, the General, and the Pauline Epistles; however there are omissions. The text is Koine (Byzantine) with sporadic I (Western) readings in Acts and Alexandrian in the other books. It is now in Leningrad.

CODEX NITRIENSIS (R)

Now in the British Museum, this codex is a palimpsest of Luke from the sixth century, over which an eighth or ninth century treatise of Severus of Antioch was written. It also contains 4,000 lines of Homer's *Iliad*. The text is Western.

CODEX VATICANUS 354 (S)

This is one of the earliest self-dated manuscripts of the Gospels, A.D. 949. It resides in the Vatican Library (No. 354), and the text is Byzantine.

---

[24]B. H. Streeter, "Codices 157, 1071 and the Caesarean Text," *Quantulacumque, Studies Presented to Kirsopp Lake* (1937), pp. 149-50.

CODEX BORGIANUS (T)

This is a valuable fifth century fragment of Luke 22-23 and John 6-8. The text closely resembles B.

CODEX MOSQUENSIS (V)

Now in Moscow, this codex is a nearly complete copy of the four Gospels from the eighth or ninth century. The manuscript is in uncials to John 8:39, where it shifts to thirteenth century minuscules. The type of text is Byzantine.

CODEX WASHINGTONIANUS I (W)

This dates from the fourth or early fifth century. It was purchased by Charles F. Freer of Detroit in 1906, from a dealer in Cairo, Egypt. Professor H. A. Sanders, of the University of Michigan, edited it between 1910 and 1918. The manuscript contains the four Gospels, portions of all the Pauline Epistles except Romans, Hebrews, Deuteronomy, Joshua and Psalms. The portions missing from the codex are Mark 15:13-38; John 14:25—16:7; some from Paul's epistles; Deuteronomy 5:16—6:18; Joshua 3:3—4:10; and some of the psalms. The Gospels manuscript has 187 leaves, 374 pages of good vellum. Each page (5⅝ by 8¼ inches) has one column of thirty lines, consisting of small, slanting uncials clearly written. The Gospels include Matthew, John, Luke and Mark, in that order. Mark has the long ending (16:9-20) attached; however, a most noteworthy insertion follows Mark 16:14:

> And they excused themselves, saying, "This age of lawlessness and unbelief is under Satan, who does not allow the truth and power of God to prevail over the unclean things of the spirits. Therefore reveal thy righteousness now"—thus they spoke of Christ. And Christ replied to them, "The term of years for Satan's power has been fulfilled, but other terrible things draw near. And for those who have sinned I was delivered over to death, that they may return to the incorruptible glory of righteousness which is in heaven."[25]

The manuscript of Deuteronomy and Joshua has 102 leaves (10½ by 12½ inches), with two columns per page, and is written on thick vellum. The mutilated manuscript of Psalms has portions of 107 leaves that originally measured eleven by fourteen inches, written in single columns. This codex is located in the Smithsonian Institute, Wash-

[25]As cited by Metzger, p. 54.

ington, D. C. As to text type, it is mysteriously mixed, as though it were compiled from various manuscripts of different families. Matthew and Luke 8:13—24:25 are Byzantine, but Mark 1:1—5:30 is Western, resembling the Old Latin. Mark 5:31—16:20 is Caesarean, like P45, whereas Luke 1:1—8:12 and John 5:12—21:25 are Alexandrian. John 1:1—5:11, which was added in the seventh century, is a mixture of Alexandrian and Western readings.

CODEX DUBLIENSIS (Z [Zeta])

This is a palimpsest of 299 verses from Matthew. It dates from the fifth or sixth century, and agrees chiefly with Aleph.

CODEX SANGALLENSIS (Δ [Delta])

This is a ninth century Greek-Latin interlinear manuscript of the four Gospels (John 19:17-35 missing). It agrees with the Alexandrian text in Mark, and the Byzantine elsewhere.

CODEX KORIDETHI (Θ [Theta])

This is a ninth century copy of the Gospels. It is very much like the Byzantine text in Matthew, Luke and John. Mark, however, is akin to the third or fourth century text used by Origen and Eusebius of Caesarea.

CODEX TISCHENDORFIANUS III (Λ [Lambda])

This codex contains the text of Luke and John, and is of the Byzantine type.

CODEX ZACYNTHIUS (Ξ [Xi])

This is a twelfth or thirteenth century palimpsest preserving most of Luke 1:1—11:33. It is an Alexandrian type text akin to B, and is the earliest known New Testament manuscript with a marginal commentary.

CODEX PETROPOLITANUS (Π [Pi])

This is an almost complete ninth century copy of the four Gospels. With a Byzantine type text, it heads a subfamily akin to A.

CODEX ROSSANENSIS (Σ [Sigma])

This is a sixth century copy of Matthew and Mark. It is the earliest known Bible adorned with watercolored pictures. The text often agrees with the Byzantine, but has certain Caesarean readings.

CODEX BERATINUS (Φ [*Phi*])

This is another sixth century deluxe edition, containing Matthew and Mark (with large lacunae), with a mixed textual type (Koine, Western and Caesarean).

CODEX ATHOUS LAURAE (Ψ [*Psi*])

This is an eighth or ninth century manuscript containing the Gospels from Mark 9 onward, Acts, the General Epistles, Pauline Epistles, and Hebrews. The ending of Mark is the same as L. The text is primarily Byzantine, with some portions of Alexandrian.

CODEX ATHOUS DIONYSIOU (Ω [*Omega*])

This dates from the eighth or ninth century and is a virtually complete copy of the four Gospels. It is one of the oldest examples of the Byzantine type text.

There is a total of about 297 uncial manuscripts of the New Testament, of which only the more important ones have been listed. The most important of these are ℵ (Aleph), B, A, and C, none of which were available to the King James translators. The only great Greek uncial available in 1611 was D, and it was used only slightly in the preparation of the Authorized Version. This fact alone indicated the need of a revised version based on better manuscripts long before it was actually accomplished.

MINUSCULE MANUSCRIPTS (NINTH-FIFTEENTH CENTURIES)

As the dates would indicate, most minuscule manuscripts do not possess the high quality of the earlier uncials. However, this is not always the case, since some minuscules are late copies of good and early texts. Their main importance, then, will rest in the accent they place on the textual families and not in their multitude, there being some 2,646 of them, plus 1,997 lectionaries, making a total of 4,643. Some of the more important minuscules are listed below.

THE ALEXANDRIAN FAMILY

This is represented by manuscript 33, the "Queen of the Cursives," dating from the ninth or possibly the tenth century. It contains the entire New Testament except Revelation, and is now in the possession of the Bibliotheque Nationale, Paris. Although it is predominantly Alexandrian type, it shows traces of Byzantine in Acts and the Pauline Epistles.

THE CAESAREAN TEXT TYPE

This has survived in family 1, in which are included manuscripts 1, 118, 131, and 209, all of which date from the twelfth to the fourteenth centuries. Analysis of Mark reveals a textual type similar to Θ (Theta). Hence, it harks back to the Caesarean text of the third and fourth centuries.

AN ITALIAN SUBFAMILY OF CAESAREAN

This is represented by about a dozen manuscripts known as family 13 (including 13, 69, 124, 346, 543, 230, 788, 826, 828, 983, 1689, and 1709).[26] These manuscripts were copied between the eleventh and fifteenth centuries. One of their interesting characteristics is that they contain the section about the adulterous woman (John 7:53—8:11) following Luke 21:38 instead of after John 7:52.

Manuscript 28. This is an eleventh century copy of the Gospels having many noteworthy readings, especially in Mark where the text follows the Caesarean type.

Manuscript 61. This consists of the entire New Testament, dating from the late fifteenth or early sixteenth century. It was the first manuscript found containing I John 5:7, the single basis by which Erasmus was compelled to insert this doubtful passage into his Greek New Testament in 1516.

Manuscript 69. This contains the entire New Testament and dates from the fifteenth century. It is an important member of family 13.

Manuscript 81. This was written in A.D. 1044 and is one of the most important of all minuscules. Its text in Acts agrees frequently with the Alexandrian text type.

Manuscript 157.[27] This is a twelfth century codex of the Gospels following the Caesarean type.

Manuscript 383. This is a thirteenth century codex of Acts and the Epistles having the Western type text in Acts.

Manuscript 565. This is one of the most beautiful of all known

---

[26]The first four manuscripts in this list were formerly thought to be of the "Syrian" type text. Cf. Kenyon, *Our Bible* . . . , p. 153.

[27]A colophon, found in Λ (Lambda), 20, 164, 215, 262, 300, 376, 428, 565, 686, 718, and 1071, states that they were copied and corrected "from ancient manuscripts at Jerusalem." This item is known as the "Jerusalem colophon"; see *Journal of Theological Studies*, XIV (1913), 78 ff., 242 ff., 359 ff.

manuscripts. It has all the Gospels on purple vellum in gold letters. Mark is closely akin to Θ (Theta), in support of the Caesarean text.

Manuscript 579. This is a thirteenth century copy of the Gospels. Matthew belongs to the late Byzantine group, whereas the other Gospels belong to a good Alexandrian text, often agreeing with B, Aleph, and L.

Manuscript 614. This is a thirteenth century copy of Acts and the Epistles, with a great number of pre-Byzantine readings. Many of these readings agree with the Western type text.

Manuscript 700. This is an eleventh or twelfth century codex which is remarkable for its divergent readings. It has some 2,724 deviations from the Received Text, and some 270 not found in any other manuscript.[28]

Manuscript 892. This is a ninth or tenth century codex of the Gospels, with remarkable readings of an early (Alexandrian) type.

Manuscript 1241. This contains the whole New Testament except Revelation. It dates from the thirteenth century, and the text often agrees with C, L, Δ, Ψ, and 33.

Manuscript 1224. This includes the whole New Testament, dates from the ninth or tenth century, and heads a host of members into family 1224, which witnesses to the Caesarean text.

Manuscript 1739. This is a very important codex from the tenth century, based directly on a fourth century Alexandrian type manuscript. It has marginal notes taken from the writings of Irenaeus, Clement, Origen, Eusebius and Basil.

Manuscript 2053. This is a thirteenth century copy of Revelation. Together with codices A, C, and 2344, it is one of the best sources for the text of the Apocalypse.

Manuscript 2344. This is an eleventh century codex of the New Testament, minus the Gospels and parts of the Old Testament. It agrees frequently with Manuscript 2053.

SUMMARY AND CONCLUSION

Whereas there are many variant readings in New Testament manuscripts,[29] there are a multitude of manuscripts available for comparison and correlation of these readings in order to arrive at the correct one. Just how this is done is discussed in detail in chapter 26. It is sufficient to remember that while there are only 643 manu-

[28]Metzger, p. 64.
[29]See chap. 26.

scripts by which the *Iliad* is reconstructed, nine or ten good ones for Caesar's *Gallic Wars*, twenty manuscripts of note for Livy's *History of Rome,* and only two by which Tacitus is known, yet there are about 5,000 Greek manuscripts to attest the New Testament.[30]

Furthermore, the time lapse between the original composition and the earliest manuscript copy is very significant. The oldest manuscript for the *Gallic Wars* is some nine hundred years later than Caesar's day. The two manuscripts of Tacitus are eight and ten centuries later, respectively, than the original. In the case of Thucydides and Herodotus, the earliest manuscript is some thirteen hundred years after their autographs. But with the New Testament it is very different.[31] In addition to the complete manuscripts only three hundred years later (B, ℵ), most of the New Testament is preserved in manuscripts less than two hundred years from the original (P 45, 46, 47), some books of the New Testament from little over one hundred years after their composition (P 66), and one fragment (P 52) comes within a generation of the first century. So definite is the evidence for the New Testament that no less a scholar than the late Sir Frederic Kenyon could write,

> The interval then between the dates of original composition and the earliest extant evidence becomes so small as to be in fact negligible, and the last foundation for any doubt that the Scriptures have come down to us substantially as they were written has now been removed. Both the *authenticity* and the *general integrity* of the books of the New Testament may be regarded as finally established.[32]

Add to their proximity to the autographs not only the multiplicity of the New Testament manuscripts, but the prolific quotation by the early Church Fathers (chap. 25) and the plurality of early versions (chap. 23), and without entering into the mechanics by which the character of the New Testament text is established, it can be readily understood why no book from the ancient world comes to us with more abundant evidence for its integrity than does the New Testament.

---

[30]Metzger, pp. 31-33, lists the number of manuscripts of the Greek New Testament as follows: 76 papyri, 250 uncials, 2,646 minuscules, and 1,997 lectionary manuscripts. This would total 4,969. J. Harold Greenlee adds that about 95 percent of these date from the eighth century onward, *Introduction to New Testament Textual Criticism,* p. 62. This would leave a chain of some 250 manuscripts stretching back to the early second century.

[31]On this point compare the excellent little book by F. F. Bruce, *The New Testament Documents, Are They Reliable?* pp. 16-20.

[32]Sir Frederic G. Kenyon, *The Bible and Archaeology,* pp. 288 f.

21

PAPYRI, OSTRACA, INSCRIPTIONS AND LECTIONARIES

The transmission of the New Testament text can be traced rather clearly and completely from the late second and early third centuries to modern times by means of the great biblical manuscripts (see chap. 20). Although the textual evidence linking these manuscripts with the first century is scant, consisting of a few fragments like P52 and some quotations from the Apostolic Fathers, there is evidence that the type of Greek (i.e., vocabulary, grammar, style, etc.) represented by the New Testament is that of the first century. Support for this thesis has come from the nonbiblical papyri and ostraca discovered at Oxyrhynchus and elsewhere in Egypt since 1896.

THE NONBIBLICAL PAPYRI

The epoch-making discovery of the papyri, ostraca and inscriptions was destined to transform the world's understanding of the New Testament background. It also led to the classification of the New Testament as a book of the common man of the first century, instead of some especially mysterious writing which was given to man in a "Holy Ghost" language.

Several scholars stand out in the epochal task of reclassification: Moulton in England (see Moulton and Milligan's *Vocabulary of the Greek New Testament, Illustrated from the Papyri and Other Non-Literary Sources*, 1914-29), A. T. Robertson in the United States (see his *A Grammar of the Greek New Testament in the Light of Historical Research*), and Adolf Deissmann in Germany who wrote the results of his work in *Light from the Ancient East*.[1] The works of these men and others point indisputably to the conclusion that the New Testament was not written as classical literature, nor was it

[1]Unless otherwise noted, the factual content of this chapter is dependent upon the monumental work of Adolf Deissmann, *Light from the Ancient East*.

written in a special "Holy Ghost" language, but it is a lucid example of first century colloquial speech—Koine Greek.

DISCOVERIES BEARING ON THE LANGUAGE OF THE NEW TESTAMENT

There is a wealth of evidence that the New Testament was not written in a "perfect language," as some of the Latin Fathers contended. Examples may be cited from the nonliterary papyri in several areas to demonstrate that the New Testament is really a record in late colloquial Greek.

Phonology. Without engaging in the phonological trifles of the papyri, it will be sufficient to mention here that the same accent and inflections found in the New Testament (which differ from classical Greek), which were once thought to be a special "New Testament" or "biblical Greek" phenomenon, are known in abundance from the papyri.[2] So extensive is the evidence, says Deissmann, "as to make it impossible any longer to ignore the morphological identity of the 'New Testament idiom' with the Hellenistic colloquial language."[3]

Vocabulary. The field of linguistics abounds with evidence which confirms the contention that the New Testament, known from second and third century manuscripts, was the work of first century writers. Formerly there were some 550 words thought to be "biblical," that is, unique to the LXX and the New Testament. The list has been narrowed to about fifty (1 percent of the New Testament) since the discovery of the papyri. As a result of this evidence, Deissmann concludes that "unless a word is recognized as Christian or Jewish at sight, we must consider it ordinary Greek until the contrary is proved."[4] Two examples will suffice to illustrate this point: *agapē* (love) and *apokalupsis* (unveiling). The former is a typical "biblical word" and the latter was mistakenly limited to the Bible by Jerome, although Plutarch (A.D. 46-125) used it.[5] Now, as a result of the papyri, they are known to be common words in secular literature as well. As a matter of fact, *agapē* is found in the prayer of a devotee to the god Isis. It is no doubt true that the New Testament adopted and modified the meaning of these words, but the words were not

---

[2]According to Deissmann, two of the classical works on this aspect of the Koine Greek are Winer's *A Grammar of the Idiom of the New Testament Greek*, and Karl Dieterich's *Researches on the History of the Greek Language from the Hellenistic Period to the Tenth Century A.D.*
[3]Deissmann, p. 73.
[4]*Ibid.*, p. 78.
[5]*Ibid.*

created by the New Testament writers. They were common, current words in the culture of the first century.[6]

Syntax. Several phrases formerly thought to be "Hebraisms" have been found in the papyri, for example, *blepein apo* (beware of) and *duo duo* (two by two). *Pleres* (full), which was once held to be a nominative of the Holy Spirit from John 1:14,[7] has its parallel in the papyri along with many others.[8]

Style. The paratactic style of John may be singled out as a test case on style, since it is so often considered Semitic. The "I am's" and even the "and . . . and" construction have their parallel in the Fayum papyrus number 108,[9] the inscription of Asclepius in Rome, and many others. Hence, even the style of John may not be as Semitic as it once seemed.

The verdict, then, of historical philology based on the contemporary nonliterary texts is that the "sacred books are so many records of popular Greek, in its various grades" and "taken as a whole the New Testament is a book of the people."[10]

DISCOVERIES BEARING ON THE NEW TESTAMENT AS LITERATURE

Was the New Testament "something written for the public cast in artistic form" or was it the "product of life and not art," being literature only in a secondary sense? To answer this question the papyri and letters written on other materials provide numerous samples of the "everyday" correspondence and other nonliterary writings of the first century or before.

Leaden Tablet from Chaidari, near Athens. This is the oldest known Greek letter, coming from the third or fourth century B.C. The notable feature of this letter is its epistolary form. It illustrates that the praescript is not part of the address; the address was printed on the outside after the thin lead tablet was folded. According to Deissmann this was doubtless the case with Paul's letters as well.

Letter to Appolonius from Zoilus. From the third century B.C. comes a piece of religious correspondence that provides a remarkable parallel to the form of religious experiences reflected in Paul's

---

[6]*Ibid.,* p. 707.
[7]The adjective *pleres* in John 1:14 "full of grace and truth" seems to be in the nominative case whereas it should be genitive to agree with *autou,* "his glory." It was once claimed that the Holy Spirit led the apostle to write the nominative because Jesus is always our Nominative. But the inscriptions show the word had become indeclinable by the first century.
[8]Deissmann, pp. 122-24.
[9]*Ibid.,* p. 134.
[10]*Ibid.,* p. 143.

letters. The writer, a religious devotee of the god Serapis, expressed a very similar attitude toward his god as Paul did toward Christ.[11]

Ostracon Letter to Portis. This is a private receipt from an Egyptian landowner to his tenant; it employed the apparently common custom of using an amanuensis. Deissmann suggests that this letter may parallel Galatians 6:11, in that a secretary could write a better letter than could the slow, large, working hand of Paul or another author.[12]

From Apion to Epimachus. This is an interesting letter having a typical "Pauline" beginning. Like Paul's letters, it begins, "I thank God. . . ."

Numerous other letters. There is a letter, written by a farmer, having an uncial body and a cursive signature,[13] just the reverse of Galatians. Very similar to Luke 15, is the letter containing a prodigal's confession to his mother.[14]

From these and many other examples it has been concluded that the New Testament Epistles were really letters written in the form, style and vocabulary current at the time of the first century.[15] The New Testament is a book "of the people, by the people, and for the people." It was written in the lingo of the *laos* (laity).

DISCOVERIES BEARING ON CULTURAL AND RELIGIOUS BACKGROUND OF THE NEW TESTAMENT

Another area illuminated by the papyri is the cultural and religious backdrop of the first century. Indications of this context are found in Jesus' handling of the Roman denarius (Matt. 22:19), Paul's preaching on the Athenian inscription (Acts 17:23), and the burning of the magical books at Ephesus (Acts 19:19).

Cultural similarity. Basically the same Hellenistic culture prevailed throughout the Mediterranean world as is illustrated by the common census tax (Luke 2:3), the procedure of delivering a criminal to the people (cf. Barabbas, Matt. 27:15), and even the price of a sparrow (Luke 12:6). These very same customs and practices

[11]*Ibid.*, pp. 154-61.
[12]*Ibid.*, p. 166. It is also possible that Paul said, "See how large letters I have written with my own hand," for effect, and not because he could not write well.
[13]*Ibid.*, pp. 172 ff.
[14]*Ibid.*, pp. 187 ff.
[15]Deissmann overdraws his conclusion when he says that these letters were only raised to the level of epistles when the church later canonized them, and promulgated their contents as the sacred text (p. 240). Although these letters were not artistic literature, they were intended for the church public and for circulation (see chap. 14), and there is no reason why a "letter" cannot communicate God's truth as well as an "epistle."

are known from the papyri to have existed in Egypt as well as Palestine and throughout the Mediterranean world.

Competing Cults. Judaism, imperial religion, and the mystery religions were all missionary religions. The dispersed Jews left ample evidence of their religious escapades; the *Letter to Zoilus* illustrates the religious zeal of the heathen religions, and the monuments have yielded enough information to reconstruct the beliefs of Mithraism.[16] It was into this whirlpool of religious missionary zeal that Christianity inserted its claim to be a world religion.

Private devotions. One of the most significant areas of illumination from the papyri is the private devotions of unnumbered individual personalities which have become an open book for the world. In these nonliterary texts there arise, as it were, the living voices of a soldier, a wife, a religious propagandist, and others. This evidence is so clear that Deissmann concludes, "Anyone coming from the soul life of the New Testament to the papyri finds himself in no strange world."[17]

Language of moral expressions. To the biblical student, familiar with the phraseology of the New Testament, it will be no surprise to find among the inscriptions the well-known "I have fought a good fight," "Love your husbands," "Rebuke not an elder."[18] The list of sins (excepting idolatry and covetousness) are also similar. It seems that both Christian and pagan writers shared a common core of culture and terminology which was imbued with the content of their own unique experience and meaning.

Language of popular religion. One of the marks of the popular style of Paul is his employment of technical phraseology common to the technical language of magic.[19] A Leyden papyrus has a parallel to the Galatians 6:17 expression, "the marks of Jesus." First Corinthians 5:5 is exemplar to the formula of the ancient custom of execration, or the devoting of a person to the gods of the lower world.[20] Likewise, technical expressions were adapted from the ritual of cursing, for example, "delivered to Satan" (I Tim. 1:20), which has been found in the London Magical papyrus.[21]

Language of popular law. The inscriptions and papyri provide

---

[16]See Franz Cumont's monumental work, *Textes et Monuments figurés relatifs aux Mystères de Mithra.*
[17]Deissmann, p. 299.
[18]*Ibid.*, pp. 309 ff.
[19]*Ibid.*, p. 301.
[20]*Ibid.*, p. 302.
[21]*Ibid.*

outstanding illustrations of Paul's famous analogies from slavery. Manumission (release from slavery) is described by Paul in such terms as "you were bought with a price" (I Cor. 6:20; 7:23) and "for freedom Christ has set us free" (Gal. 5:1). This legal language, which provided Paul with some of his most illustrative metaphors, is abundantly evident in the temple inscriptions and the nonliterary papyri.

Language of emperor worship. One of the closest parallels, and the one that caused the greatest difficulty to Christianity, was the similarity of phraseology applied to Christ by Christians with that applied to Caesar by the Romans. The Christian antipathy toward emperor worship was strongly rooted in its monotheistic heritage (cf. Deut. 6:4). The following phrases, applied by the New Testament to Christ, were also appellations used in reference to Caesar:

1. "Lord" was used of Nero.[22]

2. "Lord's Day" was a direct contrast to "Imperial Day," or "Augustus' Day."[23]

3. "Parousia" and "epiphany" were used to refer to the presence or appearance of Caesar.[24]

4. Many of the Caesars (e.g., Domitian, Nero) claimed deity for themselves and received worship.[25]

It was this identity of terms which occasioned the tremendous persecution and martyrdom of so many of the early Christians.

CONCLUSIONS

Avoidable conclusion. Lest the conclusion be drawn that common language necessitates common meaning and experience, it should be indicated at this point that the New Testament used modes of expression of its day but did not necessarily use the same meanings. The meaning of a word must be determined by the usage of that word in its context, as representative of the experience of the author. Christian content is obviously different from pagan content and usage. The same words used by the different religions could, at best, only be expected to have a parallel, not an identical meaning, in Christianity. In other words, the Christian's experience was different from the heathen's, even though the form of expression may have

[22]*Ibid.*, p. 354.
[23]*Ibid.*, p. 359.
[24]*Ibid.*, p. 370.
[25]*Ibid.*, p. 347.

been similar. Certainly Paul used the language of the *heathen*, but he invested it with the meaning of *heaven* (cf. Acts 17:22-32).

Unavoidable conclusions. Although it need not be concluded that the New Testament reflects the same meaning as the contemporary profane usage of first century words, there are some conclusions which do seem unavoidable in light of the papyri.

1. The New Testament was not written in any so-called "Holy Ghost" Greek. Instead, it was written in the common (Koine) trade language of the Roman world. The language of the masses, the merchants, and the marketplace was the instrument used in transmitting the Greek New Testament.

2. The "Pauline" and other styles of Greek syntax, and even the New Testament vocabulary, were all commonly used in the first century. In fact, so decisive were the papyri discoveries for New Testament studies that new standard Greek lexicons (dictionaries) have come into existence.[26] This in turn has led to the publishing of new commentaries.

3. The conclusion sometimes overlooked, yet implicit in the foregoing conclusions, is the fact that if the Greek of the New Testament was the common language of the first century, then *the New Testament must have been written in the first century.*[27] Obviously the New Testament was written in the language of its day and that day was the first century. A book that reflects first century vocabulary and literary forms, and that resembles first century religious modes of expression, can scarcely be a second or third century fraud. In fact, the papyri have provided the biblical scholar with the "missing link" in his chain of transmission from the autographs to the modern Bible. Manuscript evidence is very good, dating back into the second century. From that point, thousands of papyri[28] take the stylistic evidence to the very hands of the apostles in the first century.

[26]The work of Joseph Henry Thayer, *A Greek-English Lexicon of the New Testament*, has been superseded by the translation of Walter Bauer's *Griechisch-Deutsches Wörterbuch zu den Schriften des Neuen Testaments und der übrigen urchristlichen Literatur* (4th rev. and augmented ed., 1952), by William F. Arndt and F. Wilbur Gingrich, *A Greek-English Lexicon of the New Testament and Other Early Christian Literature.*

[27]Millar Burrows has seen this point. See his book, *What Mean These Stones?* pp. 53-54.

[28]According to Allen P. Wikgren, there are some 25,000 papyri (biblical and nonbiblical) that shed light on the biblical text and early Christianity; about half of these have been published. See his article, "Papyri, Biblical and Early Christian," *The Twentieth Century Encyclopedia of Religious Knowledge*, ed. Lefferts A. Loetscher, Vol. K-Z, p. 839.

BIBLICAL AND RELATED PAPYRI, OSTRACA, AND INSCRIPTIONS

To complete the picture, brief mention should be made of some of the other papyri and ostraca that relate to the understanding of the Bible text. Since the most important papyri manuscripts were previously treated (see chap. 20), only a few supplementary and related finds need be mentioned here.

New Testament Ostraca Fragments

Ostraca are broken pieces of pottery which were frequently used as a writing material by the poorer classes in antiquity, as they could not afford papyrus. There is an interesting find of twenty pieces of a seventh century copy of the Gospels on ostraca, which probably represents a poor man's Bible. Ostraca were long overlooked by scholars, who apparently desired not to condescend in their academic pursuits to the rubbish lest they be called a "potsherd among the potsherds" (Isa. 45:9, RV). But from these rubbish heaps has come additional light on the biblical text. In Wilkens' work, *Greek Ostraca*, some 1,624 specimens of these humble records of history are listed.[29]

New Testament Inscriptions

The wide distribution and variety of ancient inscriptions testifies to the existence and importance of the biblical texts. There is an abundance of engravings on walls, pillars, coins, monuments, and other things which have preserved a witness to the New Testament. For the most part, however, these are not of importance in establishing the text of the New Testament; their role is merely that of a supplementary witness to the already abundant evidence of other New Testament manuscripts.

The Sayings of Jesus

A group of noncanonical sayings of Jesus have been discovered among the papyri. These writings are known as the "Logia of Jesus" (Grenfell and Hunt), a few samples of which follow:

> Jesus saith: Unless you fast to the world, you will not find the Kingdom of God; and unless you "sabbatize" the Sabbath, you will not see the Father.

---

[29]Deissmann, p. 50, n. 5, also lists several other sources of Egyptian, Coptic, and Greek Ostraca.

Jesus saith: Lift the stone and there you will find me, split the wood and I am there.

Jesus saith: I stood in the midst of the world, and I appeared in the flesh, and I found all drunken, and I found none thirsty among them, and my soul grieves over the sons of men for they are blind in their hearts and do not see. . . .[30]

A comparison of these "sayings" with familiar canonical quotes manifests their Apocryphal tone. Even in New Testament times there was an abundance of oral "sayings" of Christ (cf. John 21:23, 25); many of them are recorded in the four Gospels, and at least one more is found in Acts 20:35. There can be little doubt that many more "sayings" took on a local and even heretical flavor as time passed, and they in turn gave rise to collections of "sayings."

LECTIONARIES

A final testimony to the text of the New Testament, which has hitherto been generally undervalued, are the numerous lectionaries, church service books, containing selected readings from the New Tes-

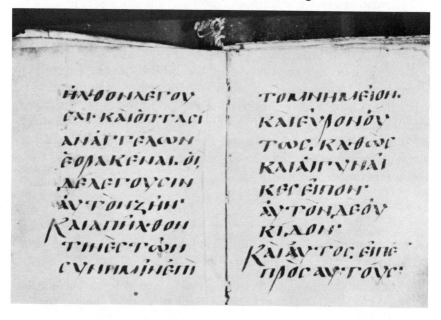

21. A seventh century lectionary, now in the library of St. Catherine's Monastery, showing Luke 24:23-25 (Biblical Archaeologist)

[30]See Robert M. Grant, The Secret Sayings of Jesus, pp. 47 ff.

tament. These lectionaries served as manuals, and they were read throughout the church year.

Nature

The great majority of the lectionary readings consisted of passages taken from the Gospels.[31] The rest of them contained portions of Acts, either with or without the Epistles. They were often elaborately adorned, and sometimes even included musical notations. It may be admitted with Wikgren that:

> The origin of the lectionary still remains obscure. We are ignorant of the exact circumstances and date of the transition from early usage of nonlectionary manuscripts . . . to lectionary proper. . . . However, various converging lines of evidence historical, liturgical and textual, point to Syria, possibly Antioch, in the mid-fourth century as a likely place and date for this event:[32]

Date

Since there was a continued ecclesiastical use of uncial manuscripts long after the minuscule type had superseded them, the lectionaries are difficult to date on the basis of paleography alone. Most lectionaries probably originated at a date ranging from the seventh to the twelfth centuries, with a dozen leaves and fragments dating from the fourth to the sixth centuries, five or six of which are papyri.[33]

Number

Although Gregory listed about 1,545 known in his day,[34] there are about 2,000 Greek lectionaries.[35] In view of this multitudinous witness to the New Testament text, it is difficult to understand why they have not hitherto enjoyed a more significant role in textual criticism.[36]

Value

It must be admitted, however, that lectionaries are only of a sec-

---

[31]Morton Enslin, *Christian Beginnings,* pp. 496 ff., suggests that lectionaries originate from the first century, and that this idea was borrowed from the practice of the Jewish synagogue.

[32]Wikgren, p. 650.

[33]*Ibid.*

[34]Caspar René Gregory, *Canon and Text of the New Testament,* pp. 384-93.

[35]Bruce M. Metzger lists the number of Greek lectionaries at 1,997, *The Text of the New Testament,* p. 33.

[36]Lectionaries are now coming into their own in textual study. The new critical apparatus of the United Bible Societies' *Greek New Testament* has extensive references to the lectionaries.

ondary value in establishing the New Testament text. (1) They contain all of the New Testament many times over, with the exception of Revelation and parts of Acts. (2) As a result of recent scholarship on the lectionaries, they are assuming a more significant role in establishing the true text. Lectionary text types are predominantly Byzantine, but there are certain groups which are characterized by Alexandrian and Caesarean readings. (3) Lectionaries have also influenced the understanding of specific passages, for example, John 7:53—8:11 and Mark 16:9-20.[37]

SUMMARY AND CONCLUSION

It is generally recognized that the discovery of the nonbiblical papyri has cast a flood of light on the understanding of the New Testament. This light shows that the New Testament was written in the language and style of first century colloquial Greek. In the past it has been overlooked sometimes that this fact, at the same time, indicates that the Greek New Testament, as it is known to scholars from third and fourth century manuscripts, was *written in the first century*. The nonliterary papyri provide another link between the apostles and the early manuscript copies. This link has hitherto been made up of small fragments and quotations, but it is now supported by thousands of papyri manuscripts. Further support for the text of the New Testament may be found in the ostraca, inscriptions, and hundreds of lectionaries.

[37]See John W. Burgon, *The Last Twelve Verses of the Gospel According to St. Mark*, chap. 10.

22

TRANSLATIONS CONTAINING
THE OLD TESTAMENT TEXT

In addition to the multitude of manuscript copies of the biblical text and the miscellaneous materials, the great ancient versions provide a very important witness to the text of the Scriptures. This chapter is primarily concerned with the great ancient translations of the Old Testament: the Samaritan Pentateuch, the Aramaic Targums, and the Septuagint (LXX). Before these works are viewed, however, several basic definitions and distinctions must be considered.

DEFINITIONS

There are more precise definitions of some of the basic words than are generally followed in popular usage. The careful scholar will avoid confusing these terms.

TRANSLATION, LITERAL TRANSLATION, AND TRANSLITERATION

Translation. A translation is simply the rendering of a given composition from one language into another. As an example, if the New Testament were translated into Spanish, it would be a translation. If, in turn, this Spanish translation were translated into French, or even back into Greek, it would result in another translation. To be specific about translations, Erasmus published the first printed Greek New Testament in 1516; however, the whole Apocalypse was not found in the original Greek, so he translated the Latin text into Greek. Hence, he published a translation of the Apocalypse.

Literal Translation. This is a specific kind of translation. It is one that expresses, as far as is possible, the exact meaning of the original words. It is a word-for-word translation and therefore is more rigid in its renderings than a mere translation. Consequently, a literal translation reveals the influence of Hebraisms and Greek idioms because it translates the precise word order rather than the idea contained in the original text.[1]

Transliteration. This is the rendering of the letters of one language into the corresponding letters of another. This results in many foreign words being introduced into a given language. To illustrate, the Greek words *angelos* and *evangelion* may be cited. *Angelos* is translated into English as "messenger," but it is transliterated as "angel." Likewise, *evangelion* is translated "gospel" and transliterated "evangel." It was the process of transliteration that rendered the Greek word *biblos,* through Latin and French, into English as "Bible" (chap. 1).

Version

A version is a translation from the original language of a literary text into any other language. In this sense, the Authorized Version and the Rheims-Douay Version are actually not even versions; the former being the fifth revision of Tyndale's Version, while the latter is a translation of the Latin Vulgate.[2] Both Tyndale's Version and Jerome's Vulgate, on the other hand, are versions of the original languages, and qualify according to this definition of a version because they were translated from the original languages.

Revision, or Revised Version

This title is given to those works which are actually translated from another language, usually the original, and have been carefully and systematically reviewed and examined for the purpose of correcting errors or making other necessary emendations. The Authorized Version (King James Version) is an example of such a revision. Using the caption "Revised Version," but actually meaning revision, is the Rheims-Douay-Challoner edition of the Rheims-Douay Bible (1582, 1609). Another example of a revision is the Confraternity edition of the New Testament (1941).

Recension

A recension is the product of critically and systematically revising a text, although such works may not be called recensions. Some outstanding examples of recension are the Revised Version (1881, 1885), American Standard Version (1901), the Revised Standard Version

---

[1]An excellent example of a literal translation is the work of Robert Young, *Young's Literal Translation of the Holy Bible,* 3d ed.
[2]These two versions are treated at length in chap. 29.

(1945, 1952), the Challoner revisions of the Rheims-Douay (between 1749 and 1763), and the Confraternity of Christian Doctrine revision of the New Testament. This same description has been applied to the New English Bible.

Paraphrase

Paraphrases are free translations or restatements of sentences, passages or works in an attempt to keep the original sense while expressing the meaning more fully or clearly. Such treatments appear early and frequently in English translation work. One of the most popular examples of paraphrase today is J. B. Phillips' New Testament.

Commentary

A commentary is simply the comment on, or explanation of, Scripture. These occur early in the history of Bible transmission, for example, the Midrash.[3] There are a great multitude of Bible commentaries available in many languages, and they add valuable insight into the problem of gathering materials to verify and vindicate the texts of the Old and New Testaments as they appear in the manuscripts, inscriptions, etc. It is important to note, however, that the major role in making use of the manuscript evidence of Scripture is played by the versions of the Bible.

DISTINCTIONS

Ancient, Medieval and Modern Works Distinguished

In dealing with the works bearing witness to the Bible, it is important to distinguish between their three general categories: the ancient, medieval and modern.

Ancient works. Ancient works containing parts of the Old and/or New Testaments appeared before the period of the church councils began (*c.* A.D. 350). These items include such works as the Samaritan Pentateuch, The Aramaic Targums, the Talmud, the Midrash, and the Septuagint (LXX). After the apostolic period, there were such works as Aquila's version, Symmachus' revision, Origen's Hexapla, and the Syriac versions.[4]

---

[3]In recent years, some Bible translations, known as "expanded" or "amplified" translations, have contained a sort of implicit (sometimes explicit) commentary within the text, e.g., Kenneth S. Wuest, *The New Testament: An Expanded Translation; The Amplified Bible.*

[4]For the material beginning with Aquila's version see discussion below. Latin versions, including Jerome's Vulgate, will be treated in chap. 24.

Medieval contributions. These cover those works containing parts of the Old and/or New Testaments from about 350 to about 1400. Of primary concern in this group is the Vulgate of Jerome (*c.* 340-420). It was this work that dominated Bible translation and commentary production up to the Reformation period. It was the basis for such works as Caedmon's paraphrases, Bede's *Ecclesiastical History of the English Nation,* and Wycliffe's translation of the Bible. This latter work was the first complete Bible in English, and rounds out the medieval period.[5]

Modern counterparts. Modern counterparts containing parts of the Old and/or New Testaments actually begin with the work of William Tyndale (*c.* 1492-1536), who translated his version directly from the original languages. In fact, it is this version, completed by Myles Coverdale, that begins what may be properly called Protestant Bible translation, for it is at this point that the Latin Vulgate is set aside in favor of the original languages for all except Roman Catholics.[6] Since Tyndale's day, multitudes of renderings have been produced containing all or parts of the Old and/or New Testaments.[7]

ANCIENT RENDERINGS DISCUSSED

Two important facts about ancient versions merit treatment in the consideration of God's communication to man.

The purpose of the materials indicates their importance. These works were used to help disseminate the message of the autographs to those who were followers of the Lord. They were also used to assist God's people in keeping their religion pure. Therefore, such items as the Samaritan Pentateuch and the Targums were in use before the time of Christ. After the introduction of Christianity into the world, this new proselyting religion used such things as versions and commentaries to meet the needs of the church in its evangelization, expansion and establishment.

Proximity of the ancient renderings to the autographs. This proximity also indicates their importance. These works take the Bible scholar back to the very threshold of the autographs, for example, the Samaritan Pentateuch may be from the period of Nehemiah's rebuilding of Jerusalem; and, while it is not really a version, it does

[5]For a fuller treatment of the English translations of the Bible prior to the Authorized Version see chap. 28 and William E. Nix, "Theological Presuppositions and Sixteenth Century English Bible Translation," *Bibliotheca Sacra,* CXXIV, Nos. 493 and 494 (Jan.-Mar., Apr.-June, 1967), pp. 42-50, 117-24.

[6]This in turn helped lead to the decree enunciating the Vulgate as authoritative at the Council of Trent (1546-63).

[7]For expanded treatment of this point, see chaps. 29-30.

indicate the need for careful study in tracing the true text. The Septuagint (LXX) was translated in Alexandria, Egypt (beginning c. 280-250 B.C.). It is sufficient evidence to weaken the higher critical view of the evolutionary canon, even if no other material is considered. Some of the New Testament versions date from the middle of the second century A.D., quite close to the date of John's writings. As a result, these versions, translations, paraphrases and commentaries warrant consideration by the careful student of Scripture if he desires to rest his text upon the foundation of that material which may be scientifically verified and affirmed.

DELINEATION OF MAJOR ANCIENT WORKS

THE SAMARITAN PENTATEUCH

This work is not a version in the strict sense of the word. It is rather a manuscript portion of the text itself. It contains the five books of Moses, and is written in a palaeo-Hebrew script, quite similar to that found on the Moabite Stone, Siloam Inscription, Lachish Letters, and some of the older biblical manuscripts from Qumran.[8] It was in 1616 that Pietro della Valle first discovered a form of the Samaritan text; however, it was known to such Fathers of the church as Eusebius of Caesarea and Jerome. The textual tradition is independent of the Masoretic text, the reasons for which a review of the history of the Samaritans will adequately illustrate.

The roots of the Samaritan race actually can be traced back to the time of David. It was during these years that the northern portion of the kingdom engineered an abortive revolt. After Solomon's death, the two kingdoms were divided, as Jeroboam wrested control of the ten northern tribes from the hands of Solomon's son, Rehoboam. During the reign of Omri (c. 880-874 B.C.), a northern king, Samaria was made the capital (I Kings 16:24), and the term Samaritans became applied to the entire kingdom rather than merely to the inhabitants of the city. In 732 B.C. the Assyrian Empire, under Tiglath-pileser III (745-727), conquered the northeast portion of Israel and followed its established policy of deportation of inhabitants and importation of other captive peoples into the area. Under Sargon II, in 721 B.C., the same procedure was followed after the Assyrians had captured the rest of Israel. Not all of the Israelites were deported, and intermarriage was imposed upon those who were not deported. This method was used as an attempt to guarantee that no revolt would ensue, as

8F. F. Bruce, *The Books and the Parchments*, rev. ed., p. 129.

there would be an automatic denationalization and commingling of cultures (II Kings 17:24–18:1). At first these colonists worshiped their own gods; but, by or after the time of Judah's return from the Babylonian captivity, they appeared to want to follow Israel's God. However, they were rebuffed by the Jews and, as a result, opposed Israel's restoration (cf. Ezra 4:2-6; Neh. 5:11–6:19). Nevertheless, in about 432 B.C. the daughter of Sanballat was married to the grandson of the high priest Eliashib. This resulted in the expulsion of the couple, and provided the historical incident for the break between the Jews and the Samaritans (cf. Neh. 13:23-31). During the conflict the Jews overstressed the foreign element in the ancestry of the Samaritans, and called them Cutheans after the name of the Middle-Babylonia city, Cuthah, from whence the Assyrians imported the foreign element into Samaria (cf. II Kings 17:24, 30). The Samaritans were still looked upon with scorn during New Testament times

22. *Samaritan high priest and Samaritan Pentateuch (Howard F. Vos)*

(John 4:3-45). They are still a separated group in Palestine; some 250 live in the original area in Nablus and about 50 reside in Tel Aviv.

The Samaritan religion as a separate system of worship actually dates from the expulsion of the high priest's grandson, whose name was probably Manasseh, in about 432 B.C.[9] At this time a copy of the Torah may have been taken to Samaria, and placed in the temple built on Mount Gerizim at Shechem (Nablus), where the rival worship and priesthood were established. The fifth century date may account for the palaeo-Hebrew script,[10] as well as categorization of books into only two groups: The Law, and what the Samaritans regarded as the noncanonic books.[11] Their adherence to the Torah, as well as their isolation from the Jews, has resulted in another textual tradition for the Law. In addition, the Samaritan Pentateuch has illustrated the Jewish-Samaritan hostility quite effectively, as it emphasizes the importance of Mount Gerizim instead of Jerusalem, and inserts additional material into the text, for example, after Exodus 20:2-17 and Deuteronomy 5:6-21.

The Samaritan Pentateuch was first published in the Paris Polyglot (1645), and then in the London Polyglot (1657). It was quickly regarded as superior to the Masoretic text, then, after careful study, it was relegated to an inferior status, and has just recently been raised to a higher level of appreciation, though still secondary to the Masoretic text.[12] The earliest manuscript of the Samaritan Pentateuch dates from the mid-eleventh century, and this is only a fragmentary part of a fourteenth century parchment, the Abisha scroll.[13] The oldest codex of the Samaritan Pentateuch bears a note regarding its sale in A.D. 1149-50, but it is actually a much older manuscript. Another copy is owned by the New York Public Library dating from about 1232. The merits of this textual tradition may be seen in the fact that its approximately 6,000 variants from the Masoretic text are

[9]Josephus, *Antiquities of the Jews*, IX, 7; also see XIII, 9. It should be noted that Josephus misplaces this incident, putting it in the period of Alexander the Great, a century later than Nehemiah's record. He does, however, name the priest, Manasseh, and relates that the temple at Shechem was built for him; he also refers to the Samaritans as Cutheans, as mentioned above.

[10]However, its script may be the result of a deliberate attempt to give it an archaistic character, as in the case of that manuscript attributed to Abishua, the great-grandson of Aaron. Cf. J. D. Douglas (ed.), *The New Bible Dictionary*, p. 1257.

[11]See chap. 12; also see R. Laird Harris, *Inspiration and Canonicity of the Bible*, p. 143.

[12]It was highly esteemed by Morinus, who first published the text in 1632; Wilhelm Gesenius condemned it as worthless in 1815; Sir Frederic Kenyon, following Geiger and Kahle, renders it as valuable to the study of textual criticism.

[13]See Bruce, pp. 127-29.

relatively few, mainly orthographic, and rather insignificant (see chap. 26). It also illustrates the purity of the Masoretic text, as the latter was governed by much stricter rules. Kenyon rightly states that when the LXX and the Samaritan Pentateuch agree against the Masoretic text, "they represent the original reading,"

> but when the *LXX* and the Masoretic Text are opposed, it is possible that, sometimes the one may be right and sometimes the other; but in any case the difference is one of *interpretation*, not of *text*. Then, again, there can be no doubt that the authors of the Septuagint made many actual mistakes of translation.[14]

Since this text tradition covers the best documented portion of the Old Testament, its contributions indicate cultural trends in the Hebrew social setting: the sectarian insertions of the Samaritans, the repetition of commands given by God, trends toward popularizing the Old Testament text, tendencies to modernize antique word forms, and the simplifying of difficult Hebrew sentence constructions.[15]

THE ARAMAIC TARGUMS

Origin of Targums. There is evidence that the scribes were making oral paraphrases of the Hebrew Scriptures into the Aramaic vernacular as early as the time of Ezra (Neh. 8:1-8). These paraphrases were not strictly translations, but were actually aids in understanding the archaic language forms of the Torah. The translator or interpreter involved in this work was called a *methurgeman*. The necessity for such helps arose from the fact that Hebrew was becoming less and less familiar to the ordinary people as a spoken language. By the close of the last centuries B.C., this gradual process had continued until almost every book in the Old Testament had its oral paraphrase or interpretation (Targum). During the early centuries A.D., these Targums were committed to writing, and an official text came to the fore, since the Hebrew canon, text and interpretation had become well solidified before the rabbinical scholars of Jamnia (c. A.D. 90), and the expulsion of the Jews from Palestine in A.D. 135. The earliest Targums were apparently written in Palestinian Aramaic during the second century A.D.; however, there is evidence of Ara-

---

[14]Sir Frederic G. Kenyon, *Our Bible and the Ancient Manuscripts,* 4th ed., pp. 91-92.
[15]Cf. Gleason F. Archer, Jr., *A Survey of Old Testament Introduction,* p. 37.

maic Targums from the pre-Christian period.[16] These early official Targums contained the Law and the Prophets, but the Writings were included in unofficial Targums in later times. It is interesting to note that a pre-Christian Targum of Job was written in Palestinian Aramaic and discovered in Cave XI at Qumran. Cave IV contained a Targum of the Pentateuch. These unofficial Aramaic Targums were superseded by official texts in the second century A.D. The official Palestinian Targums of the Law and Prophets were practically swallowed up by the Babylonian Aramaic Targums of the Law and Prophets during the third century. Targums on the Writings were apparently done on an unofficial basis, and have already been mentioned.

Outstanding Targums. During the third century A.D., there appeared in Babylonia an Aramaic Targum on the Torah. This Targum was possibly a recension of an earlier Palestinian tradition, but may have originated in Babylonia. It has been traditionally ascribed to Onkelos (Ongelos), a name probably confused with Aquila.[17] Another Babylonian Aramaic Targum accompanies the Prophets (Former and Latter), and is known as the Targum of Jonathan ben Uzziel. It dates from the fourth century A.D., and is freer and more paraphrastic in its rendering of the text. Both of these Targums were read in the synagogues: Onkelos along with the Torah, which was read in its entirety, and Jonathan along with selections from the Prophets (*haphtaroth*, pl.). Since the Writings were not read in the synagogues, there was no reason to have official Targums for them, although unofficial copies were used by individuals. During the middle of the seventh century, there appeared a Targum of the Pentateuch called the Pseudo-Jonathan Targum. It is a mixture of the Onkelos Targum and Midrash materials. The Jerusalem Targum, still another Targum, appeared at about 700, but it has survived in fragments only. None of these Targums is important to the textual critic, but they are all rather significant to the study of hermeneutics, as they indicate the manner in which Scripture was interpreted by rabbinical scholars.

[16]Bruce, pp. 133-45, where these materials are discussed and several quotations of the Targums are presented. Also cf. Harris, pp. 154-59.

[17]Aquila is the name of the scholar who made a slavishly literal Greek translation of the Hebrew Old Testament as a substitute for the LXX (discussion below); the confusion of the names was undoubtedly enhanced by the rigid rendering of the text of this Targum, which is itself regarded as a recension by many scholars.

The Talmud

Following the first period of Old Testament scribal tradition, the period of the Sopherim (c. 400 B.C.–c. A.D. 100), there appeared a second, the Talmudic period (c. A.D. 200-c. 500), which was followed by the better known Masoretic tradition (c. 500-c. 1000). Ezra worked with the first of these groups, and they were regarded as the Bible custodians until after the time of Christ.[18] Between A.D. 100 and 500, the Talmud (instruction, teaching) grew up as a body of Hebrew civil and canonical law based on the Torah. The Talmud basically represents the opinions and decisions of Jewish teachers from about 300 B.C. to A.D. 500, and it consisted of two main divisions: the Mishnah and the Gemara.

Mishnah. The Mishnah (repetition, explanation, teaching) was completed at about A.D. 200, and was a digest of all the oral laws from the time of Moses. It was regarded as the Second Law, the Torah being the First Law. This work was written in Hebrew, and it covered traditions as well as explanations of the oral law.

Gemara. The Gemara (to complete, accomplish, learn) was written in Aramaic rather than Hebrew, and was basically an expanded commentary on the Mishnah. It was transmitted in two traditions, the Palestinian Gemara (c. A.D. 200), and the larger and more authoritative Babylonian Gemara (c. A.D. 500).

The Midrash

The Midrash (textual study, textual interpretation) was actually a formal doctrinal and homiletical exposition of the Hebrew Scriptures written in Hebrew and Aramaic. They were collected into a body of material between 100 B.C. and A.D. 300. Within the Midrash were two major parts: the Halakah (procedure), a further expansion of the Torah only, and the Haggada (declaration, explanation), being commentaries on the entire Old Testament. These Midrashim differed from the Targums in that the former were actually commentaries, while the latter were paraphrases. The Midrashim contain some of the earliest extant synagogue homilies on the Old Testament, including such things as proverbs and parables.

The Septuagint (LXX), or Alexandrian Version

Just as the Jews had abandoned their native Hebrew tongue for Aramaic in the Near East, so they abandoned the Aramaic in favor

---

[18]See Archer, pp. 54-58, for a discussion of the contributions of each of these scribal traditions to Old Testament textual criticism.

of Greek in such Hellenistic centers as Alexandria, Egypt. During the campaigns of Alexander the Great, the Jews were shown considerable favor. In fact, Alexander was sympathetic toward the Jews as a result of their policies toward him in the siege of Tyre (332 B.C.). He is even reported to have traveled to Jerusalem to do homage to their God. As he conquered new lands, he built new cities which frequently had Jewish inhabitants, and frequently named them Alexandria.

After his great conquests and sudden death, Alexander's empire was divided into several dynasties: Ptolemaic Egypt, the Seleucid dynasty in Asia Minor, and Antigonid Macedonia, as well as several minor kingdoms. It was in Ptolemaic Egypt, named after Ptolemy I Soter, son of Lagus, that many Jews resided, in the city of Alexandria. Ptolemy I was governor of Egypt from 323 to 305, when he became king and reigned until his death in 285. He was succeeded by his son Ptolemy II Philadelphus (285-246 B.C.), who followed the Pharaonic practice of marrying his sister, Arsinoë II.

It was during the reign of Ptolemy Philadelphus that full political and religious rights were granted to the Jews. Egypt also underwent a tremendous cultural and educational program under the patronage of Arsinoë II, spearheaded by the founding of the Museum at Alexandria and the translation of great works into Greek. It was in this period that the Hebrew Old Testament was being translated into Greek, the first time it had ever been extensively translated. The leaders of Alexandrian Jewry had a standard Greek version produced which is known as the Septuagint (LXX),[19] the Greek word for "seventy"; it was undoubtedly translated during the third and/or second centuries B.C.; it is purported to have been written as early as the time of Ptolemy Philadelphus in a Letter of Aristeas to Philocartes (c. 130-100 B.C.).[20]

This Letter of Aristeas relates that the librarian at Alexandria persuaded Ptolemy Philadelphus to translate the Torah into Greek for use by Alexandrian Jews. As a result, six translators were selected

[19]It should be noted that the term Septuagint applies strictly to the Pentateuch, which was probably the only portion of the Old Testament translated during the time of Ptolemy II Philadelphus. "The Jews might have gone on at a later time to authorize a standard text of the rest of the Septuagint, but . . . they lost interest in the Septuagint altogether. With but few exceptions, every manuscript of the Septuagint which has come down to our day was copied and preserved in Christian, not Jewish, circles." Bruce, p. 150.

[20]No one seems to date the LXX precisely, and the dates given range from before c. 150 B.C. Bruce, pp. 69-73, 146-62, states the general consensus of opinion as it appears in the text.

from each of the twelve tribes, and the translation was completed in just seventy-two days. The details of this story are undoubtedly fictitious, but the letter does relate the authentic fact that the LXX was translated for the use of Greek-speaking Jews of Alexandria.

The quality of translation in the Septuagint is not consistent throughout. There are four observations which may be made on the quality of the work at this point. (1) The LXX varies in excellence in that it ranges from slavishly literal renderings of the Torah to free translations in the Writings. (2) The LXX was not designed to have the same purpose as the Hebrew text, as it would be primarily used publicly in the synagogues while the latter would be used for more scholarly purposes. (3) The LXX was the product of a pioneer venture in the transmission of the Old Testament Scriptures, and an excellent example of such a work. (4) The LXX was generally loyal to the readings of the original Hebrew text, as has been observed in chapter 19. As a result of this quality, the importance of the LXX is easily ascertainable: It bridged the religious gap between the Hebrew- and Greek-speaking peoples, as it met the needs of the Alexandrian Jews; it bridged the historical gap between the Hebrew Old Testament of the Jews and the Greek-speaking Christians who would use it with their New Testament, and it provided a precedent for missionaries to make translations of the Scriptures into various languages and dialects; it bridges the textual criticism gap by its substantial agreement with the Hebrew Old Testament text (Aleph, A, B, C, et al.). While the LXX does not measure up to the excellence of the Hebrew text, it does indicate the latter's purity.

It was as a result of Jewish criticism during the early centuries of Christianity that a reaction set in among the Jews against the Septuagint. This reaction has proved to be helpful to the textual critic, as it produced a new wave of translations and versions of the Old Testament. Some of the new works included the Greek translations known as Aquila's version and Symmachus' revision, and even led to the great work of textual criticism in the mid-third century, the *Hexapla* of Origen. Before proceeding on to these items, it seems advisable to recall that the foregoing ancient translations provide a valuable witness to the text of the Old Testament. For example, the LXX preserves a textual tradition from the third or second century B.C., while the Samaritan Pentateuchal tradition may date from the fifth century B.C. Although the Septuagint and the Samaritan Pentateuch, together with the Masoretic text, form three separate textual traditions, nevertheless, when critically evaluated, they provide overwhelming support for the integrity of the Old Testament text. In fact, the two former texts provide some of the closest links to the autographs available to textual scholars, even closer than many Hebrew manuscript copies.

Greek Versions of the Old Testament in the Christian Era. F. F. Bruce has advanced two basic reasons for the rejection of the Septuagint by Jewish Bible scholars in the first centuries of the church. In the first place, it had been adopted by the Christians as their own version of the Old Testament, and was freely used in the propagation and defense of their faith. Second, about the year A.D. 100 a revised edition of the standard Hebrew text of the Old Testament was established, first the Pentateuch and later the remainder of the Old Testament. It was the end of this process of revision that resulted in the Masoretic text.[21]

Opposition to the Septuagint found expression in the writings of such a man as Justin Martyr, in his *Dialogue with Trypho the Jew* (chap. 73) and his *First Apology* (chap. 41). These works, written at about 140, followed the pattern of the New Testament writers in quoting from the LXX rather than the Hebrew text, and gave a basis of accusation by Trypho for not following the Hebrew text, which he regarded as authoritative. Thus, since there was no authority acceptable to both camps, and since Christianity was rapidly emerging from its Judaistic antecedents, the Jewish scholars decided to counteract the trend. As a result, several translations were attempted which would help preserve the Old Testament for future generations.

1. *Aquila's version* (*c.* 130-50) was a new translation of the Old Testament into Greek. It was done for Greek-speaking Jews, but not before some interesting events had taken place. Aquila is reported to have been a relative of the Emperor Hadrian. He is said to have moved to Jerusalem from Sinope as a civil servant, and there he was converted to Christianity. He was not able to completely extricate himself from some of his prechristian ideas and habits, and he was publicly rebuked by the elders of the church. As a result, he took offense, forsook Christianity, and turned to Judaism. Having become a Jewish proselyte, he stud-

[21]*Ibid.*, pp. 150-52.

ied under the famed Rabbi Aqiba and translated the Old Testament into Greek.

While much of this story is probably fictitious, he was undoubtedly a Jewish proselyte from the coast of the Black Sea. He appears to have flourished during the first half of the second century, and he did make a new translation of the Hebrew Old Testament into Greek; he is the Aquila wrongly associated with the Targum Onkelos as mentioned earlier in this chapter. This translation (version) was a rigidly slavish one; for although the words were Greek, the thought patterns and sentence structures followed the Hebrew rules of composition. His translation became the official Greek translation of the Scriptures used among the nonchristian Jews, and it has survived only in fragments and quotations.

2. *Theodotion's revision* (*c.* 150-85) occupies the next place of interest in Greek translations of the Old Testament. The exact place of this work is disputed, but it appears to have been a revision of an earlier Greek version: either of the LXX, possibly of Aquila's, or of another Greek version.[22] Theodotion is reported to have been a native of Ephesus, and either a Jewish proselyte or an Ebionite Christian.[23] His revision was much freer than Aquila's version, and in a few instances his work even replaced some of the older Septuagint renderings among Christians. Daniel, as translated by Theodotion, soon replaced the older

[22]Authorities are quite divided over this issue, as well as the date of Theodotion's revision. Merrill F. Unger, *Introductory Guide to the Old Testament*, 2d ed., p. 159, says it is a revision of the LXX, and dates it "early in the second century, possibly before Aquila." Archer, p. 42. dates it *c.* 180 or 190, but offers no solution to the problem of its source, as he writes that Theodotion's work is "a revision of an earlier Greek version, whether *LXX* or of some other is much disputed." He, incidentally, dates Aquila's work earlier. Kenyon, p. 104, says: "But of recent years the view has been gaining ground that what Theodotion revised was not the Septuagint but another independent version. The reasons for this are that 'Theodotionic' readings are found in the New Testament. . . ." Bruce, p. 153, suggests that Theodotion "seems to have . . . taken an older Greek translation belonging to the pre-Christian era—one, indeed, which appears to lie behind some of the Old Testament quotations in the New Testament, particularly in Revelation—and revised it in accordance with the standard Hebrew text." He further states that the date for this revision is the late second century A.D. H. G. G. Herklots, *How Our Bible Came to Us*, pp. 117-19, 156, tends to agree with Bruce, and even adds that it was Theodotion, not Aquila, who was an Ephesian Jewish convert, and that his translation was "a free revision of the *LXX* rather than an independent translation (after H. B. Swete)." Bruce's position appears to be the most feasible, in that it is comprehensive enough to absorb the essential characteristics of the other views into a common and tenable position.

[23]The Ebionites were a Jewish-oriented faction in the early church. They appeared very early as a legalistic group within the church, and may have been the element involved in the disputation with Paul and Barnabas which led to the Jerusalem Council in Acts 15.

LXX version, and even superseded it in Christian catalogs. It is possible that his rendering of Ezra-Nehemiah superseded the older LXX version, as may be seen by comparing it with the Apocryphal I Esdras, which is a much looser and expanded version.[24]

3. *Symmachus' revision* (*c*. 185-200) seems to have followed Theodotion's in time, as well as theological commitment.[25] Symmachus was either an Ebionite, as Jerome thought, or a Samaritan convert to Judaism, as Epiphanius held. The purpose of Symmachus was to make an idiomatic Greek version and, as a result, he was at the opposite pole to Aquila. He was concerned with the sense of his rendering rather than the letter of the Hebrew; nevertheless, he exhibited high standards of accuracy, and influenced later Bible translators, as was seen by Frederic Kenyon who wrote,

> The special feature of this translation is the literary skill and taste with which the Hebrew phrases of the original are rendered into good and idiomatic Greek. In this respect Symmachus approaches nearer than any of his rivals to the modern conception of a translator's duty; but he had less influence than any of them on the history of the Greek Bible. Curiously enough, he had more influence upon the Latin Bible: for Jerome made considerable use of him in the preparation of the Vulgate.[26]

4. *Origen's Hexapla* (*c*. 240-50). The work of Old Testament translation led to four Greek textual traditions by the third century A.D.: the Septuagint, and versions by Aquila, Theodotion and Symmachus. This muddled state of affairs set the stage for the first really outstanding attempt at textual criticism, the *Hexapla* of Origen of Alexandria (A.D. 185-254). Because of the many divergencies between the existing manuscripts of the LXX, the discrepancies between the Hebrew text and the LXX, and the attempts at revising the Old Testament Greek translations, Origen appears to have settled upon a course which would give the Christian world a satisfactory Greek text of the Old Testament. His work was essentially a recension rather than a version, as he corrected textual corruptions and attempted to unify the Greek text with the Hebrew.

---

[24]Cf. Kenyon, p. 57, and Bruce, p. 153.
[25]Archer, p. 41, dates Symmachus' revision prior to Theodotion's, but this view tends to counter the mainstream of opinion.
[26]Kenyon, p. 57.

Thus, his twofold aim was to show the superiority of the various revisions of the Old Testament over the corrupted LXX, and to give a comparative view of the correct Hebrew and the divergent LXX, as he followed the view that the Hebrew Old Testament was a sort of "inerrant transcript" of God's revealed truth to man.

The arrangement of the *Hexapla* (sixfold) was in six parallel columns. Each column contained the Old Testament in a particular version or the original Hebrew, and it was far too bulky to be marketable in ancient times.[27] The six columns were arranged as follows: column one, the Hebrew original; column two, the Hebrew original transliterated into Greek letters; column three, the literal translation of Aquila; column four, the idiomatic revision of Symmachus; column five, Origen's own revision of the LXX; and column six, the Greek revision of Theodotion. In his *Hexapla* of Psalms, Origen added three additional columns, but actually only two of these are different translations. He also made a separate work called the *Tetrapla*, that is, the *Hexapla* with columns one and two omitted.[28] This tremendous work has not survived the ravages of time, but Eusebius and Pamphilus did publish the fifth column, Origen's translation of the LXX with additions, which is extant in the fourth or fifth century Codex Sarravianus (G). This codex contains portions of Genesis through Judges, and is the only Greek edition of any significance preserved; there is a Syriac translation of the *Hexapla* dating from the seventh century, and some manuscripts of it have been preserved.[29]

The accomplishment of the *Hexapla* is observable in what it has discovered and disclosed in matters of textual criticism. Origen had discovered many corruptions, omissions, additions and transpositions in the copies of the Septuagint of his day. Often these discoveries were observed in comparing the various revisions of the Old Testament into Greek, but Origen was primarily concerned with bringing the texts of the LXX and the Hebrew Old Testament into greater conformity. Thus, his attention was primarily focused on the Hebrew text of column one and his personal translation of the LXX in column five. In disclosing the problems uncovered in his work, Origen used an

[27]Cf. Herklots, pp. 119-20.
[28]Eusebius, *Ecclesiastical History*, VI, 16. Loeb ed., II, 51-53.
[29]See Archer, p. 39; Kenyon, p. 59; Bruce, p. 156; Herklots, pp. 119-23.

elaborate system of critical markings. Thus, the reader would be able to see the corruptions which were corrected, omissions and additions as indicated, and where transpositions of words were made in order to agree with the Hebrew text as then settled. When passages occurred in the Septuagint but not in the Hebrew, Origen would indicate it with an obelus ($-$), a horizontal diacritical stroke. When a passage occurred in the Hebrew but not the Septuagint, Origen would insert that passage from Theodotion's version and mark its beginning with an asterisk ($\times$ or ÷). To mark the close of either of these corrections, he would insert a metobelus ($\times$).[30] When transposed passages of short length differing from the Hebrew and other versions were observed, he would permit them to remain in their setting, but would mark them with an asterisk and obelus combined (÷ $-$ or $\times$ $-$) and use the metobelus at the close. If the transposed passage were long, the Hebrew order would be restored in order to gain better conformity with the latter. While this task was of monumental significance, it is well for the modern textual critic to observe the difference between his own and Origen's objectives, as has been so succinctly stated by Kenyon:

> For Origen's purpose, which was the production of a Greek version corresponding as closely as possible with the Hebrew text as then settled, this procedure was well enough; but for ours, which is the recovery of the original Septuagint text as evidence for what the Hebrew was before the Masoretic text, it was most unfortunate, since there was a natural tendency for his edition to be copied without the critical symbols, and thus for the additions made by him from Theodotion to appear as part of the genuine and original Septuagint.[31]

This unfortunate situation did in fact take place, and the transcribed Septuagint text without the diacritical markings led to the dissemination of a corrupted Greek Old Testament text, rather than the achievement of a Septuagint version in conformity with the Hebrew text of the day.

Bruce has written, "If Origen's *Hexapla* had survived entire,

---

[30]Kenyon, pp. 58-59; however, Archer, p. 39, indicates that the insertion into the LXX would be from any of the other versions, not just Theodotion's. The various signs are given differently in Herklots, p. 120. There, they are the obelus ($-$ or $--$ or ÷), the asterisk (*), and the metobelus (: or /. or /.).

[31]Kenyon, p. 59.

it would be a treasure beyond price."[32] This is certainly true, as it would have given the standard Hebrew text of the third century A.D., have aided in the disputation over Hebrew pronunciation, and have given information about the Greek versions of the Old Testament in Origen's day. Nevertheless, the text has not survived (as indicated above). It was housed in the library at Caesarea until the Saracens conquered and burned the city in 638. The *Hexapla* manuscript was probably destroyed at this time, but the fifth column has survived, largely through the Syriac translation of Bishop Paul of Tella (*c.* 616), known as the Syro-Hexaplar text, and its subsequent faithful reproduction in an eighth century copy which is housed in the museum at Milan.

5. *Other recensions of the Septuagint.* Early in the fourth century, Eusebius of Caesarea and his friend Pamphilus published their own editions of Origen's fifth column. Hence, they advanced the version of the LXX which became the standard in many places. In addition to their efforts, two other scholars attempted to revise the Greek text of the Old Testament. The first of these was Hesychius, an Egyptian bishop martyred in 311. This recension is preserved only in the quotations from the text made by church writers in Egypt. As a result, the recovery of the recension of Hesychius is dependent upon quotations of such Egyptians as Cyril of Alexandria (d. 444). The works of Chrysostom (d. 407) and Theodoret (d. *c.* 457) may be used to recover still another recension of the Old Testament text: the Lucian Recension. Lucian, a resident of Samosata and Antioch, was also martyred in A.D. 311. Thus, by the time of Jerome, as Swete observes, Christians could read the "Old Testament in the recension of Lucian, if they lived in North Syria, Asia Minor, or Greece; in that of Hesychius, if they belonged to the Delta or the valley of the Nile; in Origen's Hexaplaric edition, if they were residents at Jerusalem or Caesarea."[33]

SUMMARY AND CONCLUSION

The various ancient translations of the Old Testament provide the textual scholar with valuable witnesses to the text. The Septuagint,

---

[32]Bruce, p. 155.
[33]Henry Barclay Swete, *An Introduction to the Old Testament in Greek,* p. 85.

for example, preserves a textual tradition from the third century B.C., and the Samaritan Pentateuchal tradition may date from the fifth century B.C. These and the Masoretic text provide three Old Testament textual traditions, which, when critically evaluated, supply an overwhelming support for the integrity of the Old Testament text. The witness of the Samaritan Pentateuch, and especially that of the LXX with its revisions and recensions, is by no means a minor one in the confirmation of this textual integrity.

23

TRANSLATIONS CONTAINING BOTH OLD AND NEW TESTAMENT TEXTS

SYRIAC VERSIONS OF THE OLD AND NEW TESTAMENTS

Among the multitudes in Jerusalem on the day of Pentecost were "Parthians and Medes and Elamites and residents of Mesopotamia, Judea and Cappadocia, Pontus and Asia, Phrygia and Pamphylia, Egypt and the parts of Libya belonging to Cyrene, and visitors from Rome, both Jews and proselytes, Cretans and Arabians" (Acts 2:9-11). These individuals would undoubtedly need the Scriptures in their own tongues if they were to be able to study them. It is for this reason that some believe that the Syriac version of the Old Testament dates from the centuries before Christ, while others hold that the version was translated during the early Christian centuries. It is probable that the Old and New Testaments stemmed from separate traditions at first, and were later brought together. Therefore, it is best to treat these traditions separately.

THE LANGUAGE AND THE EARLY CHURCH

The Syriac (Aramaic) language of the Old Testament, and indeed of the Gospels, was comparable to the Koine in Greek and the Vulgar in Latin. It was the common language of the market. Since the Palestinian Jews of our Lord's time undoubtedly spoke Aramaic, the language common to this entire region, it is reasonable to assume that the Jews in nearby Syria also spoke it. In fact, Josephus relates the proselyting work of Jews in the first century in the areas east of ancient Nineveh, near Arbela.[1] This movement of Judaism in the middle of the first century paved the way for the spread of Christianity into Syria, from where it spread into Central Asia, India, and even as far as China. The basic language of this branch of Chris-

[1] Josephus, *Antiquities of the Jews*, Vol. XX, No. 2, pp. 1 ff., tells of the conversion of Helena, queen of Adiabene, and her son Izates to Judaism.

tianity was Syriac, or what F. F. Bruce has called "Christian Aramaic." It was actually a dialect of Aramaic which differed from the Aramaic of the Palestinian Jews who wrote in the Western dialect of that language.

The Syriac Peshitta

Once the church began to move out from Syria in a missionary effort, the need for a version of the Bible in the language of those parts made itself urgently manifest.[2] Thus, contemporary to the formation of the Jewish Targum in Aramaic, the Christians were translating the Bible into a more usable dialect of the same language, although they used a distinctive variation of the Aramaic alphabet.[3] The Syriac Bible corresponding to the Latin Vulgate is known as the Peshitta, meaning "simple." While this name dates from the ninth century, and is of uncertain origin,[4] the text of the Old Testament Peshitta undoubtedly stems from the period between the mid-second and early third centuries. It appears to have been the work of many hands, and possibly was done in the area at or near Edessa.

The translation of the Old Testament was probably from the Hebrew language, but was later revised in conformity with the LXX. The Syriac Pentateuch resembles the Targum of Onkelos,[5] following the Masoretic text, but subsequent books demonstrate a rather unsystematic and not too thorough influence from the LXX. Where the Syriac Peshitta follows the Masoretic text, it gives valuable aid to securing that text, but it is not too reliable as an independent witness to the text of the Old Testament. One important contribution of the Peshitta comes in the study of canonicity, as it omits the Apocryphal books of the Alexandrian Canon.

The standard Syriac edition of the New Testament is generally believed to stem from a fifth century revision by Rabbula, the bishop of Edessa (411-35). His revision was actually a recension of earlier Syriac versions which were brought into an approximation of the Greek manuscripts then in use in Constantinople (Byzantium). It, plus the Christian recension of the Syriac Old Testament, has come

---

[2]The role of Antioch, Syria, is readily seen in such passages as Acts 6:5; 11:26; 13:1; etc.

[3]Cf. F. F. Bruce, *The Books and the Parchments*, p. 193; also see Gleason L. Archer, Jr., *A Survey of Old Testament Introduction*, p. 44.

[4]Merrill F. Unger, *Introductory Guide to the Old Testament*, p. 168, suggests that the name Peshitta (simple) was presumably used to denote its character in contrast to the complex symbols used in Syro-Hexaplaric version.

[5]P. E. Kahle, *The Cairo Geniza*, 2d ed., p. 273, states that "there can be no doubt that the closest contact exists between the Syriac Pentateuch and the Old Palestinian Targum."

to be known as the Peshitta. Rabbula ordered that a copy of his recension be placed in every church in his diocese, which led to its widespread circulation during the middle and late fifth century. Hence, while there are many witnesses for the Peshitta, they are not nearly so authoritative in reclaiming the Bible text as are some earlier Old Syriac witnesses. This fact is largely because of their being brought into conformity with the Byzantine text type.[6] It is important to note at this point that the Peshitta was "the 'authorized version' of the two main opposed branches of Syriac Christianity, the Nestorians and the Jacobites, indicating that it must have been firmly established by the time of their final cleavage, well before the fifth century."[7]

THE SYRO-HEXAPLARIC VERSION

As has been mentioned above, the Syro-Hexaplar text was a Syriac translation of the fifth column of Origen's *Hexapla*. This work was done under the sponsorship of Bishop Paul Tella in about 616. This work has never actually taken root in the Syrian churches, partly due to its excessively literal rendering of the Greek, in violation of Syriac idiom. The manuscript portions which have been preserved are in the Codex Mediolanensis, and consist of II Kings, Isaiah, the Twelve, Lamentations, and the Poetical books (except Psalms). It is their literal character that makes the Syro-Hexaplar manuscripts valuable aids in ascertaining the correct text of the *Hexapla*, especially in light of the fact that Origen's text was never published in its entirety, and since it was probably destroyed in the burning of Caesarea by the Muslims in 638. The Pentateuch and the historical books were in existence as late as 1574, but have subsequently disappeared. The text is basically Byzantine, with marked Western influences.

THE DIATESSARON OF TATIAN (*c.* 170)

Tatian was an Assyrian Christian and follower of Justin Martyr in Rome. Upon returning to his native country, he made a "scissors and paste" harmony of the Gospels. This work was done at about A.D. 170, and is known as the *Diatessaron* (from the Greek word

---

[6]See chaps. 25-26 for detailed presentation of textual families and their relative merit in terms of textual criticism. At this point, however, it is noted that of the 250 or more manuscripts of the Syriac Peshitta, the earliest date from the fifth century.
[7]Bruce, pp. 194-95.

having a musical meaning, "through the four"). Tatian's work is known mainly through indirect references,[8] and may have been originally written in Syriac, a language similar to the Aramaic of the New Testament, or more likely it was written in Greek and subsequently translated into Syriac.[9] It was the widespread popularity of the *Diatessaron* which probably caused Rabbula and Theodoret, bishop of Cyrrhus in 423, to abolish its use in the early fifth century. This attitude was undoubtedly based upon the fact that Tatian belonged to the heretical sect of the Encratites, as identified by Eusebius.

> He established his own type of doctrine, telling stories of invisible Aeons, like the followers of Valentinus, and rejecting marriage as corruption and fornication similarly to Marcion and Saturninus. And as his own contribution, denied the salvation of Adam. But a little later a certain man named Severus strengthened the above mentioned heresy, and is the reason why those who have sprung from it obtained the name Severiani from him. . . . Their former leader Tatian composed in some way a combination and collection of the gospels, and gave this the name of *The Diatessaron*, and this is still extant in some places. . . .[10]

Tatian's work was so popular that Ephraem, a Syrian Father, wrote a commentary on it. Nevertheless, Theodoret had all the copies (about two hundred) of the *Diatessaron* destroyed because he felt the potential danger of their corrupting influence on the Christians who would use Tatian's text. In its place, Theodoret presented another translation of the Gospels of the Four Evangelists. Ephraem's commentary and the *Diatessaron* in Syriac are both lost, but an Armenian translation of the former has survived,[11] as have two Arabic translations of the latter. Hence, while the original *Diatessaron* would bear heavily on New Testament textual criticism, its secondary and tertiary witness merely supports primary materials, as influence is evident from both Eastern and Western texts.

---

[8]A fragment of Tatian's *Diatessaron* was found at Dura-Europos. Cf. Bruce, pp. 195-200.

[9]Cf. J. Harold Greenlee, *An Introduction to New Testament Textual Criticism*, pp. 48-49; Alexander Souter, *The Text and Canon of the New Testament*, C. S. C. Williams (rev.), pp. 50-52; also see Bruce, pp. 196-98; and Sir Frederic G. Kenyon, *Handbook to the Textual Criticism of the New Testament*, pp. 221-26.

[10]Eusebius, *Ecclesiastical History*, IV, 29. Loeb ed., I, 397.

[11]See Bruce M. Metzger, *The Text of the New Testament*, pp. 91-92, and his "Tatian's *Diatessaron* and a Persian Harmony of the Gospels," *Chapters in the History of New Testament Textual Criticism*, pp. 97-120, for an up-to-date extensive treatment of this subject matter.

THE OLD SYRIAC MANUSCRIPTS

The *Diatessaron* was not the only form of the Gospels used among the Syrian churches; among the scholars, at least, there was a tendency to read the Gospels in separate forms. Even before the time of Tatian, there were quotations of the Bible from the Syriac by such writers as Hegesippus, a Jewish scholar turned Christian, during the second century. This Old Syriac text of the Gospels, representative of the Western type text, has survived in two manuscripts: a parchment known as the Curetonian Syriac and a palimpsest manuscript known as the Sinaitic Syriac. These Gospels were called "The Gospel of the Separated Ones," indicating that they were separated, not interwoven, and also suggesting that other "harmonies" were in existence. The Curetonian is a fifth century manuscript named after William Cureton, the man who discovered it in 1858. The Sinaitic is an earlier manuscript, fourth century, although it is sometimes corrupted where the Curetonian manuscript is not. This manuscript was found in 1892 by Mrs. Agnes Smith Lewis and her twin sister, Mrs. Margaret Dunlop Gibson, in the monastery of St. Catherine, where Tischendorf had earlier discovered Codex א (Aleph). While there are differences in these manuscripts, they are representatives of the same version of a text which "dates from the close of the second or beginning of the third century."[12] No Old Syriac texts of the remainder of the New Testament have survived, though they have been reconstructed.[13] With this information, it would appear that the Old Syriac is much more valuable in terms of textual reconstruction than any other Syriac versions.

OTHER SYRIAC VERSIONS

There are three other Syriac versions that require comment, but they are all later versions than those already discussed, and not nearly so significant to the textual critic. In 508 a new Syriac New Testament was completed, which included the books omitted by the Peshitta (II Peter, II John, III John, Jude and Revelation). This version was actually a Syriac revision of the whole Bible by the rural Bishop Polycarp (*chorepiskopos*), under the direction of Zenaia (Philoxenus), Jacobite bishop of Mabbug (Hierapolis), in eastern Syria. Sir Frederic Kenyon states:

---

[12]Metzger, *The Text* . . . , p. 69.
[13]*Ibid.*, these reconstructions are based upon citations of the text as it is found in the writings of the Fathers of the Eastern Church.

... [this] version was written in free and idiomatic Syriac, being the most literary in form of all the translations of the New Testament into this language. The Greek text underlying it was that of the great mass of later manuscripts, which (as is abundantly clear from other evidence also) was firmly established as the standard type of text in the Greek-speaking Church at the time when Polycarp prepared this version of the Scriptures for Philoxenus.[14]

This version is known as the Philoxenian Syriac, and reveals that it was the sixth century before the Syrian church accepted all the books of the New Testament as canonical.

In 616, Thomas of Harkel (Heraclea), also bishop of Mabbug, reissued the Philoxenian version. He either merely added some marginal notes, or thoroughly revised the earlier edition, making it much more literal, a problem much too complex to be handled at this point.[15] This version is known as the Harklean version, and its "apparatus of Acts is the second most important witness to the Western text, being surpassed in this respect only by Codex Bezae."[16] The Old Testament portion of this work was done by Paul of Tella, as related above.

The third Syriac version is known as the Palestinian Syriac. This translation is known mainly from a lectionary of the Gospels, as no book of the New Testament exists complete in this version. The text of this version probably dates from the fifth century, and it is in fragmentary form only. The present witness to this text is seen in three eleventh and twelfth century lectionaries, and these follow the pattern of the earlier Greek lectionaries.

COPTIC VERSIONS

Coptic is the latest form of ancient Egyptian writing. Prior to Christian times, Egyptian writing was done in hieroglyphic, hieratic, and demotic scripts. The Greek language, with seven demotic characters added, became the written mode with the beginning of the Christian era. This system of writing came to be called Coptic, and the Bible was translated into its several dialects.[17]

---

[14]Kenyon, pp. 165-66. However, experts disagree on this point; e.g., Vaganay, Souter and Vööbus, cf. Greenlee, p. 49, n. 4.

[15]See sources mentioned in footnotes 27 and 28 of this chapter for materials pertaining to this matter.

[16]Metzger, *The Text* . . . , p. 71.

[17]The best treatment of the following materials may be found in Metzger, *The Text* . . . , pp. 79-81; and H. G. G. Herklots, *How Our Bible Came to Us*, pp. 72-74.

Sahidic (Thebaic)

The Coptic dialect of Upper (southern) Egypt was Sahidic. In the region of Thebes, virtually all of the New Testament was translated into Sahidic by the beginning of the fourth century. As early as the third century, portions of the New Testament were translated into this dialect. Manuscripts in this dialect represent the earliest Coptic versions of the New Testament, as may be seen by the fact that Pachomius (c. 292-c. 346), the great organizer of Egyptian monasticism, required his followers to be diligent in the study of the Scripture. Since the Sahidic was so early in Egypt, its evidence to text type carries considerable weight. Basically, the underlying text is Alexandrian, although the Gospels and Acts follow the Western type.

Bohairic (Memphic)

In Lower (northern) Egypt, around the Delta, another dialect of Coptic was used along with the Greek. This was in the area of Alexandria, and its centrality in Christian history is reflected by the fact that Bohairic became the basic dialect of the Egyptian church. The Bohairic versions appear somewhat later than the Sahidic, probably due to the continuing widespread use of Greek in the Delta area, and have survived only in late manuscripts. The only early manuscript is the Bodmer papyrus codex of the gospel of John (Papyrus Bodmer III). Although badly mutilated at the beginning, it is in much better condition following John 4; and it casts added light on two textual problems: John 5:3b-4 and John 7:53—8:11.[18] "The Greek prototype of the Bohairic version appears to be closely related to the Alexandrian text-type."[19]

Middle Egyptian Dialects

In the region between Thebes and Alexandria is the third area of a Coptic dialect. Fragments of these "Middle Egyptian" dialects, which Greenlee classifies as Fayumic, Achmimic, and sub-Achmimic,[20] have been discovered. No New Testament book is extant in these dialects, but John is almost complete. One fourth century papyrus codex in the Fayumic dialect contains John 6:11—15:11, and is closer to the Sahidic than the Bohairic text.[21] Thus, these

[18]See chap. 26 for a discussion of John 7:53—8:11.
[19]Metzger, The Text . . . , p. 80.
[20]Greenlee, p. 51.
[21]This codex is housed at the University of Michigan, Ann Arbor, and its affinities to the Sahidic are two for every one to the Bohairic. Cf. Elinor M. Husselman, The Gospel of John in Fayumic Coptic.

manuscripts appear to follow the Alexandrian type of text. The Old Testament in both dialects follows the LXX.

OTHER VERSIONS

Ethiopic Version

As Christianity moved through Egypt into Ethiopia, a need arose for another translation of the Bible. While there is no authoritative statement on the subject, the Old Testament appears to have been translated from the Greek into Ethiopic beginning in the fourth century A.D., with revisions made in light of the Hebrew text. This translation seems to have been completed by the seventh century, at which time the New Testament was translated. The complete translation was probably done by Syrian monks, who moved into Ethiopia during the Monophysite Controversy, in the fifth and sixth centuries, and the rise of Islam, in the seventh and eighth centuries. That their influence was great is seen in the fact that this church is Monophysite in the present day.[22] There have been two recensions of the Ethiopic New Testament, "one in the fifth, the other in the twelfth century."[23] The text of the Ethiopic version was later influenced by Coptic and Arabic versions, and may itself have been based on Syriac rather than Greek manuscripts. These manuscripts were undoubtedly of fourth or fifth century heritage, and thus reduce the Ethiopic to a minor position in textual study, as they bear the marks of their admixture, but are of basic Byzantine origin. The Old Testament includes the noncanonical I Enoch (I Enoch 1:9 is quoted in Jude 14-15)[24] and the Book of Jubilees. These books indicate the breadth of the accepted books included in the Ethiopic version, and their secondary character as translations, even though they were revised in accordance with Hebrew manuscripts. There are over one hundred manuscript copies extant, but none are earlier than the thirteenth century, and these are from late sources. While these little-known manuscripts may deserve more thorough study, it is probable that they will remain neglected because of their late date.

Gothic Version

It is not clear exactly when Christianity penetrated into the Ger-

[22]As is the Coptic church, which has exerted a profound influence on its Ethiopic counterpart, as may be seen in the Coptic influence in later Ethiopic manuscripts.
[23]A. T. Robertson, *An Introduction to the Textual Criticism of the New Testament*, p. 129; but Greenlee, p. 52, says it was the fourteenth century.
[24]This book is to be distinguished from II and III Enoch. See Bruce, p. 171.

manic tribes in the regions of the Rhine and Danube rivers. It is certain that this area was evangelized prior to the Council at Nicea (325), as Theophilus, bishop of the Goths, was in attendance. The Goths were among the chief Germanic tribes, as their role in the events of the fifth century clearly indicates. In the area of the lower Danube, the Ostrogoths were the first of these tribes to be evangelized. Their second bishop, Ulfilas (311-81), the "Apostle of the Goths," led his converts into the land now known as Bulgaria. There he translated the Greek Bible into Gothic. This enterprise was of great moment, especially if Ulfilas did what is generally attributed to him, namely, create a Gothic alphabet and reduce the spoken language to written form. At any rate, his translation of the Old Testament was a remarkably faithful rendering of the Lucian recension. Although this work was done in the mid-fourth century (*c.* 350), very little remains of his Old Testament.[25] The books of Samuel and Kings were not translated because the translator believed that these books were "too warlike to be transmitted" to the Gothic tribes. Much more remains of the New Testament translation made by Ulfilas, the earliest known literary monument in the Germanic dialect, but it is not found in a single complete extant manuscript. This translation adheres closely, almost literally, to the Greek text of the Byzantine type, and tells little to the textual critic. The value of the Gothic version is in the fact that it is the earliest literary work in the Germanic group, to which English belongs.[26] There are six fragmentary manuscripts of the Gothic version, the most famous of which is the Codex Argenteus, "the silver codex." It was written on purple vellum in silver and some gold letters. All the other manuscripts in Gothic are palimpsests, except a vellum leaf of a bilingual Gothic-Latin codex. Gothic, like Coptic, is a language whose script was expressly devised for the writing of the Scriptures.[27] All six of the manuscripts of the Gothic version date from the fifth and sixth centuries A.D.

ARMENIAN VERSION

As the Syrian churches carried out their work of evangelization in the early centuries, they contributed to several secondary translations of the Bible. These secondary translations are so named because of the fact that they were not translated from the original languages

---

[25]According to Archer, p. 45, only Nehemiah 5-7 remains in Codex Argenteus.
[26]Bruce, p. 216.
[27]Metzger, *The Text* . . . , p. 82.

but from translations of the originals. One of the foremost is the Armenian, although not everyone holds that it is a translation of a translation. There are two basic traditions concerning the origin of the Armenian version. One attributes it to St. Mesrob (d. 439), a soldier turned missionary who created a new alphabet to assist Sahak (Isaac the Great, 390-439) in translating the Bible from the Greek text. The other view claims that Sahak translated it from the Syriac text. While there is merit in both views, the latter best fits the situation, as it stems from the nephew and disciple of Mesrob himself.[28] The earliest Armenian versions were revised prior to the eighth century in accordance with "trustworthy Greek codices" which were brought from Constantinople following the Council at Ephesus (431). This revision gained a dominant position over the Old Armenian by the eighth century, and is still the common Armenian text in use today.[29] It is this revised text which has been preserved, as the oldest manuscript is from the ninth century. Therefore, the Armenian text does not weigh heavily in matters of textual criticism, for its text type is either Caesarean or Byzantine. This matter has not yet been clearly determined, but the Gospels tend toward the Caesarean text.[30] The Armenian Old Testament was first translated in the early fifth century and manifests a marked influence from the Syriac Peshitta, as its rendition of the Hexaplaric recension was revised in accordance with the Peshitta.

Georgian (Iberian) Version

The mountainous area between the Black and Caspian seas (Georgia), north of Armenia, received the Christian message during the fourth century, and had its own Bible translation about the middle of the fifth. The message of Christianity proceeded from Armenia into Georgia, and so did the translation of the Bible. Accordingly, if the Armenian Old Testament were a translation of the LXX or the Syriac Peshitta, and the New Testament were a translation of the Old Syriac, they would themselves be secondary translations, and the Georgian version (translated from the Armenian) would be a tertiary work at best. If the Armenian versions were based on the originals, the Georgian version would still be a secondary translation, that is, a translation of a translation. The great majority of manu-

[28]*Ibid.*, pp. 82-83; also see Bruce, p. 212; Souter, pp. 65-67; Robertson, p. 129, has attributed a Greek translation to Mesrob, and a Syriac translation to Sahak.
[29]Greenlee, p. 51.
[30]Bruce, p. 212; Metzger, *The Text* . . . , p. 83; Souter, pp. 65-67.

scripts of the Georgian Bible indicate that it follows the same textual tradition as the Armenian. Its alphabet, like the Armenian and Gothic, was developed expressly for the purpose of Bible transmission.

NESTORIAN VERSIONS

When the Nestorians were condemned at the Council at Ephesus (431), their founder, Nestorius (d. *c.* 451), was placed in a monastery and a compromise brought many of his supporters into the camp of his opponents. The Persian Nestorians broke away however and became a separate schismatic church. They spread into Central and even East Asia in the succeeding period, and translated the Scriptures into several languages as they went, for example, the so-called Sogdian versions. Their translations were based upon their Syriac Scriptures (as discussed above) rather than the Hebrew and Greek Testaments. There are scant remains of their work, all of which date from the ninth to tenth centuries and later, but this is late and tertiary evidence of the text. The devastating work of Tamerlane, "the Scourge of Asia," almost exterminated the Nestorians toward the close of the fourteenth century.

ARABIC VERSION

Subsequent to the rise of Islam (after the *hejirah,* flight of Muhammad, 622), the Bible was translated into Arabic from the Greek, Syriac, Coptic, Latin, and various combinations of these versions. The earliest of the numerous Arabic translations appears to stem from the Syriac, possibly the Old Syriac, near the time of Islam's emergence as a major force (*c.* 720). Muhammad (570-632), the founder of Islam, knew of the gospel story through the oral tradition only, and this was based on Syriac sources. The Old Testament in Arabic was the result of a translation by the Jewish scholar Saadia Gaon (*c.* 930). Other than this, the Old Testament was not standardized in its Arabic translations. In terms of textual criticism, the Arabic manuscripts, which range from the ninth to the thirteenth centuries, offer little, if any, assistance to the textual critic, since they are secondary translations, except the Old Testament.

SLAVONIC VERSION

In the middle of the ninth century a Moravian empire was formed in east-central Europe. This kingdom espoused Christianity, and its church leaders used Latin in their liturgy. But the natives were not familiar with Latin, and Rostislav, the founder of the kingdom, requested that Slavonic priests be sent to conduct the liturgy in the language of the people. At this time only one native tongue was spoken in the region of eastern Europe, namely Slavonic. In response to Rostislav's request, the Emperor Michael III sent two monks from Byzantium to Moravia. These monks were brothers, Methodius and Constantinus. Constantinus changed his name upon entry into the monastery, and is better known by his assumed name, Cyril. These brothers were natives of Thessalonica, and they devised a new alphabet for their work in translating the Scriptures. This alphabet, known as the Cyrillic alphabet and having thirty-six letters, is still used in the Russian, Ukrainian, Serbo-Croatian, and Bulgarian languages.[31] The Glagolithic alphabet, which was superseded by the Cyrillic in the tenth century, is also attributed to Methodius and Cyril, the "Apostles to the Slavs." Shortly after the mid-ninth century, they began translating the Gospels into Old Slavonic. Their Old Testament was formerly regarded as a translation of the LXX, although recent evidence indicates that it was a translation from the Latin. The New Testament follows the Byzantine text basically, but it has many readings which are of the Western and Caesarean types.[32] Most of the known Slavonic manuscripts are lectionaries, and the first version may itself have been in the form of a lectionary.[33]

Miscellaneous Versions

There are several other translations and versions of the Bible text which need only be mentioned, as their witness is of little or no concern to the recovery of the original text, and they have not all had thorough analysis made of their manuscript witness. The Nubian version has been found in fragmentary form, but not yet analyzed. There is an Anglo-Saxon version which was translated from the Latin Vulgate. These are considered in chapter 28. Two Old Persian versions of the Gospels are known but they are translations of the fourteenth century version based on the Syriac, and from a later version based on the Greek. This latter work has some affinity to the Cae-

---

[31]See Albert C. Baugh, *A History of the English Language,* 2d ed., pp. 32 ff., for a discussion of this and other related topics.

[32]See Metzger, *The Text . . . ,* p. 85. Also see Metzger, *Chapters . . . ,* pp. 73-96, for full treatment of the Slavonic version.

[33]Greenlee, pp. 53-54.

sarean text but is little used in textual criticism.[34] "One fragmentary eighth-century manuscript preserves parts of Matthew in Frankish, a language of west-central Europe, with Frankish and Latin on facing pages."[35] This rounds out the survey of ancient versions and translations containing the Old and New Testaments, except for the Latin Vulgate version and its antecedents, which is the subject of the following chapter.

SUMMARY AND CONCLUSION

The multitude of early versions of the Bible demonstrates not only the universality of Christianity but the antiquity of the biblical text as well. These early versions provide some of the earliest copies of the complete canon of Scripture, and in many cases they outdate the manuscript copies in Greek. The Syrian church, for example, had begun its Peshitta in the second century. Tatian's *Diatessaron* dates back to a time prior to A.D. 170. Soon after that time, in the third century and following, other versions began to appear in Egypt and the area near the Mediterranean Sea. Hence, the early existence of the Ethiopic, Coptic, Sahidic, Bohairic, Gothic, Arabic and other versions provides ample evidence of the presence of the entire Bible during the second, third and fourth centuries. These early versions of the Bible text also provide another valuable link in the work of reconstructing the original text of the Scriptures.

---

[34]See Metzger's chapter in M. M. Parvis and A. P. Wikgren (eds.), *New Testament Manuscript Studies,* pp. 25-68. Also see Metzger, *The Text* . . . , pp. 85-86.
[35]Greenlee, p. 54.

24

LATIN VERSIONS OF THE OLD AND NEW TESTAMENT TEXTS

Western Christianity produced only one great translation of the Scriptures during the Middle Ages, the Latin Vulgate, which was destined to reign unchallenged for a thousand years. There were of course some forerunners to Jerome's great Vulgate which need to be discussed first.

THE FORERUNNERS IN THE LATIN LANGUAGE

The Linguistic Setting in the Roman Empire

Before an accurate picture of the forerunners of the Latin Vulgate version may be traced, it is necessary to note the linguistic setting of the ancient world in general, and the Roman Empire in particular. Since the geographic structure played a major role in the linguistic and cultural aspects of life, it will be well to observe the latter by the former.

The Near East. The fortunes of the Near East have been quite varied in terms of language as well as politics and society. There were several languages which were spoken in the area of Palestine and Asia Minor at any given moment in ancient times, but during various periods the official language of the regions under consideration underwent radical shifts. Most of the important languages of the Semitic family have been considered (see chap. 16), but their periods of dominance need to be presented in order to give a sense of perspective to the overall study of Bible transmission. After the Babylonian captivity, the official language of Palestine became Aramaic. This language was used in the writings of the scribes as early as the time of Ezra (Neh. 8:1-8).[1] It was this language which gave rise to the Targums during the Sopherim period (*c.* 400 B.C.-*c.* A.D. 200) and to the Gemara later on in the Talmudic period (*c.* A.D. 200-

[1]See chap. 16.

500) (See chap. 22.) This Aramaic language was commonly spoken in Palestine during the life of Christ and His disciples, and it supplanted Hebrew among the Jews insofar as their religious life was concerned.

After the campaigns of Alexander the Great (335-323 B.C.), the Greek language became the official language within the confines of his conquests. Much of this territory was later incorporated into that part of the Roman Empire bordering on the eastern part of the Mediterranean Sea. Hellenistic Greek prevailed as the official language in the Near East under the Ptolemaic and Seleucid empires in Egypt and Syria, respectively, and even in Palestine during the Hasmonean independence (142-63 B.C.). Beginning with the death of Attalus III (133 B.C.), when the kingdom of Pergamum was bequeathed to Rome, and ending in 63 B.C., when the East was incorporated into the Roman Republic, the Latin language gradually spread as the "military language" in the Near East.

Greece. The various dialects of Hellenic Greek[2] were related to three waves of immigration into the southern part of the Balkan Peninsula during the second millennium B.C.: the Ionian, Achaean and Dorian. The Ionians were early pushed out and forced to settle across the Aegean Sea.[3] Later, other Greeks immigrated and/or founded colonies in the Near East, North Africa, and even in southern Italy and the islands of the Mediterranean. The Greeks were divided into a series of small states, and their unifying feature was their common language. The Dorians made their dialect well known, but the Attic dialect became the most famous. This Attic dialect came into its own as a result of the one great example of Greek unification, their united effort against the Persians (490-480 B.C.) who were led by Darius I and his son Xerxes. In the fifty years following, the Athenian Empire advanced only to be defeated by the Spartans during the Peloponnesian War (431-404 B.C.). The independent city-states again went their separate ways, only to find Philip of Macedonia (c. 359-336 B.C.) making a bid to reunify them. He was killed, and his young son Alexander (356-323 B.C.) crushed the revolts among the Greek city-states in 335 B.C. With his ascendancy,

---

[2]"Hellenic" is derived from the word "Hellene," the name applied to the Greeks by themselves. "Hellene" is derived from the Greek word for Greece, "Hellas." Hellenic is applied to Greek culture of the Classical Age, whereas Hellenistic refers to Greek culture as it is carried out from Greece following Alexander the Great.

[3]As they came into contact with the Near Eastern peoples they were called Ionians, and this name was used to refer to all Greeks. Hebrew *Javan* (Gen. 10:2, 4; Isa. 66:19; Ezek. 27:13) is equivalent to Greek *Ion*, the ancestor of the Ionians.

the Hellenic period shifts into what is commonly called the Hellenistic Age.[4] This age was characterized by the intentional advancement of Greek culture and civilization into the areas conquered by Alexander. The language used in this Hellenistic society was derived from blending the various dialects of the Greeks into a new "common speech" (*Koine dialektos*), as the individualistic Greek city-states lost their older differences when they were united under Alexander. The philosopher-teacher of Alexander played a major role in developing this new Koine Greek; he is the well-known Aristotle, who is more noted for his work in politics, zoology, metaphysics, and philosophic method than his linguistic efforts. While the Koine Greek was an admixture of various dialects, it was based primarily on the Attic. After the death of Alexander, this new speech became the official language of the Eastern Mediterranean. It was this very dialect that was used in the translation of the Septuagint in Alexandria (*c.* 280-*c.* 150 B.C.). After the rise of Alexander, his *Koine dialektos* (common speech) was the official language of Greece. It remained so even after Rome had made its advances into the Near East and Egypt. Latin was used by military personnel in Greece, and especially after the Battle at Actium (31 B.C.). It was this battle that gained the victory over the forces of Mark Antony and Cleopatra for Octavian. During the years between 31 B.C. and 27 B.C., Octavian was busy consolidating his gains and converting the Roman Republic into the Roman Empire. The Greeks had expended their energies in their independent activity, and were no longer in a role of leadership. Their golden age had truly turned to silver, and their culture was no longer Hellenic, but Hellenistic.

Italy. During the first century B.C., and the centuries following, all roads truly led to Rome. Here was the center of the greatest empire the West had ever seen. Its rise continued to progress from about the tenth century B.C., before the city itself was founded (*c.* 753). About 509 B.C., the Tarquin kings were expelled from the city, and the Republic was born. From this point, the chief city in Latium began to extend its nearly three-hundred-square-mile territory along the Tiber River until it and its allies controlled most of the Italian Peninsula (*c.* 265 B.C.). Hence the language of *Latium* (Latin) became the common speech of the Romans. As the unification

---

[4]Hellenic culture is that culture which belongs to those peoples who spoke Greek as their mother tongue; Hellenistic culture is that which followed the conquests of Alexander the Great and was superimposed upon peoples having another native language.

of the peninsula was completed, Rome came into conflict with Carthage, an African colony of the Phoenicians, in the Punic Wars (264-146 B.C.). Before this series of wars was half over, Rome was involved in the eastern Mediterranean area in the Illyrian and Macedonian wars (c. 229-148 B.C.). By 148 B.C., Macedonia was a Roman province, and in 133 B.C. (when Attalus III of Pergamum died and left his kingdom to Rome) Rome became involved in the Near East. With this intrusion came the military and commercial language of Rome, Latin, but it never actually became the official language in the East.

In Italy, and especially Rome, the people were thoroughly bilingual, including slaves (often Greeks) and freedmen. The literary language of the upper classes was often Greek, and even Latin literature followed the Greek pattern. The language of the military and the market was Latin, and this was the official language, since it was the native tongue. During the early years of the church, the Christians in Rome were largely Greek-speaking, as demonstrated by such works as Romans, by the Apostle Paul, and *Corinthians*, by Clement of Rome. It was later that the Christians in the West took Latin for the language of their writings, and during the late fourth and early fifth centuries A.D., the Germanic tribes used the familiar Latin instead of the more literary Greek. This latter point is easily understood when it is recalled that the Germanic tribes were in more intimate contact with the Roman legions and merchants long before they were with their literature.

Africa. The basic languages of North Africa were Greek and Latin. Greek was in vogue in Egypt under the Ptolemies. It was in Alexandria that the Hebrew Old Testament underwent a Greek translation, and a widespread Greek literature was preserved. Farther to the west, Latin was the basic tongue within the Roman Empire, and this was a result of the military, commercial and administrative contacts of the Romans beginning as early as the Punic Wars. As the Romans became better entrenched in North Africa, their native tongue became the leading official language of that province. It was this language which Tertullian, who actually wrote in both Greek and Latin, Cyprian and others used in writing their message to the Christians of the area. Thus, the earliest church within the whole Roman Empire used Greek as its literary language, and only later did Latin literature become necessary and widespread.

THE OLD LATIN VERSION

Although Latin was the official as well as the market (common) language in the West, Greek retained its position as the literary language of Rome and the West until the third century A.D. By the third century, many Old Latin versions of the Scriptures were already circulating in North Africa and Europe, indicating that local Christians had begun to express a desire for the Scriptures in Latin as early as the second century. One of the earliest known translations was the Old Latin[5] (composed prior to c. 200). This version was actually a translation from the Septuagint which probably arose in North Africa, and it was actually a secondary translation rather than a version, although it did have some Jewish influence on its translation. This version was widely quoted and used in North Africa, and may have been the Old Testament translation quoted by Tertullian (c. 160-c. 220) and Cyprian (c. 200-258). It was apparently the unrevised Apocryphal books of this translation which Jerome reluctantly added to his Vulgate version of the Old Testament. The remainder of the Old Testament fell into disuse after Jerome's translation appeared. Nothing other than citations and fragments remains of the Old Latin text of the Old Testament, and since it was merely a translation of a translation, its value to the textual critic is minimal at best.

The Old Latin version of the New Testament is an entirely different matter, however, for some twenty-seven manuscripts of the Gospels have survived, along with seven of Acts, six of the Pauline Epistles, as well as fragments of the Catholic Epistles and of the book of Revelation.[6] While no codex of the entire New Testament is extant, the manuscript witnesses date from the fourth to the thirteenth centuries, and thus indicate that the Old Latin version continued to be copied long after it had been displaced by the Vulgate in general use. The fact that the Old Latin version was eventually superseded by the Vulgate ultimately led to a scarcity and impurity of the older text. Nevertheless, the Old Latin sources are of an early date, and

---

[5]It is probably a mistake to consider the "Itala" as a precursor of the Vulgate; cf. H. S. Miller, *A General Biblical Introduction*, 7th ed., p. 237, whom Merrill F. Unger apparently follows, *Introductory Guide to the Old Testament*, pp. 170-71. It seems better to consider Augustine's reference to the "Itala" version as simply a reference to the Vulgate New Testament. Cf. Sir Frederic G. Kenyon, *Handbook to the Textual Criticism of the New Testament*, 2d ed., pp. 213-16. See also F. F. Bruce, *The Books and the Parchments*, rev. ed., pp. 203-9; and Bruce M. Metzger, *The Text of the New Testament*, pp. 72-73.

[6]Bruce, p. 203.

represent at least two, and possibly three different texts.[7] The African text was that used by Tertullian and Cyprian, the European text is found in the writings of Irenaeus and Novatian, "while the Italian text appears conspicuously in Augustine (A.D. 354-430)."[8] With the above evidence it is easy to see that the African and European texts of the Old Latin appeared before the beginning of the third century. The Italian version, if it was distinct from the Vulgate, probably appeared about two centuries later, but the variants among the manuscripts make a coherent history of the text all but impossible to determine. Thus the Old Latin versions are among the most valuable evidences pertaining to the condition of the New Testament text from early times. The multiplicity of texts which appeared in the third and fourth centuries led to an intolerable situation in the late fourth century and, as a result, the bishop of Rome, Damasus (366-84), commissioned Jerome to make a revision of the Old Latin in 382. The most important witness to the African text is the Codex Bobiensis, which represents a free and rough translation of the original, and may stem from a second century papyrus.[9] This codex is designated k in the critical apparatus of Matthew and Mark. The European text of the Old Latin is best represented by Codex Vercellensis (a) and Codex Veronensis (b), which represent a more polished and literal translation of the original text. The former is reported to have been written by Eusebius of Vercelli (d. 370 or 371), and the latter represents the same text type as that used by Jerome. Both of these codices contain most of the Gospels; incidentally, the arrangement in b is Matthew, John, Luke and Mark, while a follows the common order.

THE FAMOUS LATIN VULGATE VERSION

As was indicated above, a revision of the Scriptures into Latin became necessary during the last half of the fourth century. In A.D. 382, Jerome was commissioned by the bishop of Rome to revise the Old Latin text.

AUTHOR OF THE TRANSLATION

Sophronius Eusebius Hieronymus (c. 340-420), better known as St. Jerome, was born to Christian parents in Stridon, Dalmatia. He

[7]Sir Frederic G. Kenyon, *Our Bible and the Ancient Manuscripts*, 4th ed., pp. 171-73, discusses this matter at length.
[8]*Ibid.*, p. 171.
[9]Metzger, p. 73.

was trained in the local school until he went to Rome at the age of twelve. He studied Latin, Greek and pagan authors for the next eight years, and became a Christian at the age of nineteen. After his baptism by the bishop of Rome, Jerome devoted himself to a life of rigid abstinence and service to the Lord. He spent several years pursuing a semiascetic and later a hermitic life. In so doing, he traveled to the East, southwest of Antioch, where he employed a Jewish rabbi to teach him Hebrew (374-79). He was ordained a presbyter at Antioch, and went to Constantinople where he studied under Gregory Nazianzen. In 382, Damasus, the bishop of Rome, called Jerome to Rome as his secretary, and commissioned him to undertake a revision of the Latin Bible. He had picked Jerome to do this revision because of the latter's qualifications as an outstanding scholar. Jerome probably accepted the task in order to please the bishop, as he knew of the strong opposition his translation would encounter among the less educated.

DATE OF THE TRANSLATION

Jerome was commissioned for his task in 382 and began his work immediately. He completed his translation of the Old Testament in

23. *Jerome is supposed to have translated the Vulgate while living in a cave under the present Church of the Nativity in Bethlehem. Commemorating this fact, a statue of Je-* rome *has been erected in the courtyard of the church (Howard F. Vos)*

24. *Alcuin's ninth century revision of the Vulgate (British Museum)*

405 and spent the last fifteen years of his life writing, translating, and supervising his monks at Bethlehem. He cared little for the Apocrypha and only reluctantly made a hasty translation of portions of it—Judith, Tobit, the rest of Esther, and the additions to Daniel—before his death. Hence, the Old Latin version of the Apocrypha was only brought into the Vulgate version of the Old Testament in the Middle Ages "over his dead body."

At the request of Damasus, Jerome made a slight revision of the Gospels which he completed in 383. In submitting his work to Damasus, he wrote the following:

> You urge me to revise the old Latin version, and, as it were, to sit in judgment on the copies of the Scriptures which are now scattered throughout the whole world; and, inasmuch as they differ from one another, you would have me decide which of them agree with the Greek original. The labour is one of love, but at the same time both perilous and presumptuous; for in judging others I must be content to be judged by all. . . . Is there a man, learned or unlearned, who will not, when he takes the volume into his hands, and perceives that what he reads does not suit his settled tastes, break out immediately into violent language, and call me a forger and a profane person for having the audacity to add anything to the ancient books, or to make any changes or corrections therein? Now there are two consoling reflections which enable me to bear the odium—in the first place, the command is given by you who are the supreme bishop; and secondly, even on the showing of those who revile us, readings at variance with the early copies cannot be right. . . .[10]

The Latin text used by Jerome for this revision is not known, but it was probably of the European type, and it was corrected in accordance with a Greek manuscript apparently following the Alexandrian text.

Shortly after he had completed the revision of the Gospels, Jerome's patron died (384) and a new bishop was elected. Jerome, who had aspired to the Holy See and had also hastily revised the so-called Roman Psalter, now returned to the East and settled at Bethlehem. Before he left, however, he made an even more cursory revision of the remainder of the New Testament. The exact date of this revision is not known, and some have felt that Jerome did not

---

[10]Jerome, *The Four Gospels*, "Preface," as cited in Philip Schaff and Henry Wace (eds.), *Nicene and Post-Nicene Fathers*, 2d series, VI, 487-88.

even do the work.[11] He soon turned his attention to a more careful revision of the Roman Psalter and completed it in 387. This revision is known as the Gallican Psalter and is the version of Psalms currently employed in the Vulgate version of the Bible. It has also been the version used in Roman Catholic services until very recently.[12] This version of the Psalter was actually based on the fifth column of Origen's *Hexapla*, and was thus only a translation, not a version.

As soon as the Psalter was completed, Jerome began a revision of the Septuagint, but this had not been his original objective. While at Bethlehem, Jerome set about perfecting his knowledge of the Hebrew language so he could make a fresh translation of the Old Testament directly from the original language. While his friends and admirers applauded his endeavor, those more remote to him became suspect that he might be Judaizing, and even became outraged that "he should cast doubts on the divine inspiration of the Septuagint."[13] The first portion of the Hebrew text to be translated was Jerome's Hebrew Psalter, based on the Hebrew text currently in use in Palestine. This translation was never really able to supersede and replace Jerome's earlier Gallican, or even his Roman, Psalter in liturgical use. Jerome persisted in his translation of the Hebrew Old Testament in spite of opposition and even illness. In his many prefaces he would lash out at the opposers of his work for their unreasonableness in the whole matter. Finally, by 405, his Latin translation based upon the Hebrew was completed, but it was not readily received. Nevertheless, his work of revision continued after the completion of his Old Testament translation.

PLACE OF THE TRANSLATION

Jerome had done his revision of the Gospels, the Roman Psalter, and his hurried work on the remainder of the New Testament in Rome. These works were done prior to the election of Damasus' successor, Siricius (384-98), to the Episcopal See at Rome. At this time Jerome left Rome with his brother, a few monks, and his new patroness, Paula, and her daughter Eustochium. He departed from Rome on a pilgrimage "from Babylon to Jerusalem, that not Nebu-

---

[11]Metzger, p. 76, mentions De Bruyne, Cavallera, and B. Fischer, but adds that this is not the common view.

[12]Bruce, p. 205, n. 2, indicates that the earlier revision of Jerome, the Roman Psalter, is employed by the Catholic Church in Rome. In very recent times the vernacular has become the utilized language, though based on the Vulgate.

[13]Philip Schaff, *History of the Christian Church*, 5th ed., rev., Vol. III, p. 974, n.3, states the terms used, "*Falsarius, sacrilegus, et corruptor Scriptura.*"

chadnezzar, but Jesus, should reign over him."[14] In Bethlehem he presided over a monastery, while Paula governed a convent, from 386 to his death in 420. It was during these years that he studied Hebrew, revised the Roman Psalter, translated the Hebrew Old Testament, began revising his work, and started his translation of the Apocrypha. This latter work was done quite reluctantly, as Jerome had a low regard for the Apocrypha, and it was his successors who inserted the Old Latin version of the Apocrypha into his Vulgate Old Testament.

PURPOSE OF THE TRANSLATION

Damasus, bishop of Rome (366-84) demonstrated a keen interest in the Scriptures as well as in scholars whom he befriended and patronized. With this twofold interest in view, it is readily seen that he would be concerned that the diversity of Bible versions, translations, revisions and recensions by the mid-fourth century demanded a new and authoritative edition of the Scriptures. This situation is especially true in light of the fact that the church in the West had, and has, always demonstrated an attitude of outward conformity which was virtually unknown, and certainly uncommon, in the church of the East. Several factors demanding a new and authoritative Bible translation may be observed in passing.

Confusion in the Latin texts. Much confusion existed in the Latin texts of the Bible. This diversity in the Latin language alone was a result of the copying and recopying of the Latin texts by independent and unauthorized, or formal and informal, means. A case in point would be Tertullian, who wrote equally well in both Greek and Latin. He would generally quote the African text of the Old Latin version when writing his many treatises, but not infrequently he would make his own on-the-spot translation of the Greek text into Latin. This practice has caused no end of problems to those who have attempted to trace the text underlying the writings of Tertullian and others.

Many translations existed. Many translations of the Scriptures existed. The situation within the Latin language, which was rapidly becoming the official language of the church, was not the only one demanding a new and authoritative text. Take, for example, the Old Testament. In Jerome's time,

Men read their Old Testament in the recension of Lucian, if

[14]*Ibid.*, p. 212.

they lived in North Syria, Asia Minor, or Greece; in that of Hesychius, if they belonged to the Delta or the valley of the Nile; in Origen's Hexaplaric edition, if they were residents at Jerusalem or Caesarea.[15]

Add to this the two basic Old Latin texts, the African and the European, and it is little wonder that the bishop of Rome desired a new and authoritative translation upon which the official doctrines of the church could be based.

Heresies and disputes. Multiple heresies and disputes with the Jews were springing up in the Empire. Many of the heretical groups which appeared in the second, third and fourth centuries—for example, the Marcionites, the Manichaeans, the Montanists—based their doctrines on their own Bible translation and/or canon. The Arian controversy led to the Council at Nicea (325), and the Council at Contantinople (I) (381) was followed by the Council at Ephesus (431), which met just a decade after Jerome's death. The fact that Jerome met with such marked opposition when he began translating the Hebrew Old Testament supports the view that there were conflicts between the Christians and the Jews. But the most obvious reason for the need of a Hebrew-based Old Testament translation was the error held by many, including Augustine, that the Septuagint was actually the inspired and inerrant Word of God. This view led to the fourth factor demanding a new and authoritative Bible translation.

Need for standard text. Manifold needs in the existing situation demanded a scholarly, authentic and authoritative standard text of the Christian Scriptures to facilitate the church's missionary and teaching activities. Also, in order to defend the doctrinal position of the conciliar movement there needed to be an authoritative text. The transmission of copies of the Scriptures to the churches in the Empire required that a trustworthy (authentic) text be secured. Nevertheless, while Jerome was eminently qualified for his task, his New Testament revision was not nearly so adequate as was his Old Testament revision, for he was less prone to revise the available texts after the initial reactions to his work on the four Gospels.

REACTION TO THE TRANSLATION

When Jerome published his revisions of the four Gospels, there were sharp criticisms made. But, since the bishop of Rome had spon-

[15]Henry Barclay Swete, *An Introduction to the Old Testament in Greek*, p. 85.

sored his work, the opposition was silenced. The fact that Jerome was even less disposed to alter the remainder of the New Testament in his revision indicates that he may have been aware of his patron's imminent death, and he desired that his revision be mild enough to be met with approval by his critics in the event that his benefactor should die. The fact that Jerome left Rome the year after Damasus' death reinforces this view. The Roman Psalter remained the official text in the church at Rome, which indicates where Jerome's translation was first used, and that his scholarship was already apparent. The acceptance of his Gallican Psalter in churches outside Rome shows the influence of those who were critical of his earlier work under Damasus.

When Jerome began to study Hebrew at Bethlehem, and when he had translated his Hebrew Psalter, sharp cries of accusation arose against him. He was accused of presumption, making unlawful innovations, and sacrilege. Not being one to take biting criticism without retaliation, Jerome used his prefaces as the tools of his counter-attack. His accusations and acid rejoinders merely added fuel to the flame of opposition against his version of the Old Testament. Jerome's work was opposed by many of the most outstanding leaders of the church, including Augustine, who was outspoken against Jerome's Old Testament while wholeheartedly favoring his New Testament revision (after c. 398).

Augustine's position gives a candid recapitulation of what actually happened to the Vulgate Old Testament. During the early years of Jerome's translation of the Old Testament, Augustine (and the large majority of influential leaders in the church) opposed the translation on the basis that it was not based on the Septuagint. In fact, Augustine used Jerome's New Testament revision while he urged him to translate the Old Testament from the LXX which the bishop at Hippo believed to be inspired. Philip Schaff aptly states this point as he writes,

> Augustine feared, from the displacement of the Septuagint, which he regarded as apostolically sanctioned, and as inspired, a division between the Greek and Latin church, but yielded afterwards, in part at least, to the correct view of Jerome, and rectified in his Retractions several false translations in his former works. Westcott, in his scholarly article on the Vulgate (in Smith's *Dictionary of the Bible*, iii, 702), makes the remark: "There are few more touching instances of humility than that of the young Au-

gustine bending himself in entire submission before the contemptuous and impatient reproof of the veteran scholar."[16]

Shortly after the great scholar's death in 420, his Old Testament translation gained a complete victory in the field of Bible translations. Whether this fact is attributed to the sheer weight of the translation alone can only be questioned, as the biting criticism and scathing denunciation of all opponents by Jerome would hardly lend to the acceptance of his greatest endeavor. But, while Jerome's Vulgate was unofficially recognized as the standard text of the Bible throughout the Middle Ages, it was not until the mid-sixteenth century Council of Trent (1546-63) that it was officially placed into that position by the Roman Catholic Church. In the interim it was published in parallel columns with other versions as well as by itself. When the Latin tongue became the lingua franca of Europe, the other translations and versions acquiesced and succumbed to the majestic Vulgate.

RESULTS OF THE TRANSLATION

Of primary concern to the modern Bible student is the relative weight of the Latin Vulgate. It is important therefore to consider this version in the light of history. As has been previously demonstrated, the Vulgate New Testament was merely a revision of the Old Latin text, and not too critical a revision at that. In terms of the Apocrypha, the Vulgate is of even less value, as it was simply the Old Latin text attached to Jerome's Old Testament, with minor exceptions. The Old Testament of the Vulgate has a somewhat different character and merit, however, as it was actually a version of the Hebrew text, not a revision or another translation. Thus, the value of the Old Testament is higher than the New. But it was inevitable that the text of the Vulgate would be corrupted in its transmission during the Middle Ages, "sometimes by careless transcription and with copies of the Old Latin"[17] with which it was often published. As a result, several revisions and/or recensions of the Vulgate were made in medieval monasteries, leading to a total of over eight thousand extant Vulgate manuscripts. It is among these manuscripts that the greatest amount of "cross-contamination" of textual types is evident.[18]

[16]Schaff, p. 975, n.1.
[17]Metzger, p. 76.
[18]*Ibid.*

The above information notwithstanding, the Council of Trent issued a "Decree Concerning the Edition, and the Use, of the Sacred Books," which stated:

> Moreover, the same sacred and holy Synod,—considering that no small utility may accrue to the Church of God, if it be made known which out of all the Latin editions, now in circulation, of the sacred books, is to be held as authentic,—ordains and declares, that the said old and Vulgate edition, which, by the lengthened usage of so many ages, has been approved of in the Church, be, in public lectures, disputations, sermons, and expositions, held as authentic; and that no one is to dare, or presume to reject it under any pretext whatever.[19]

However, it might be asked which editions of the Vulgate should be regarded as the ultimate authority. Thus the Council of Trent decided to have an authentic edition of the Latin Scriptures prepared. The work was committed to a papal commission, but it was unable to overcome the difficulties set before it. Finally Pope Sixtus V published an edition of his own in 1590. This was not the first edition of the printed Vulgate, as it had been printed by Johann Gutenberg in Mainz between 1450 and 1455. In 1590, Pope Sixtus V died, just a few months after publication of his Vulgate edition. The Sixtene edition was quite unpopular among scholars, especially the Jesuits, and it was circulated for only a short time. Gregory XIV (1590-91) succeeded to the papal chair and immediately proceeded to make a drastic revision of the Sixtene text. His sudden death would have ended the revision of the Vulgate text had it not been for the sympathies of Clement VIII (1592-1605). In 1592, Pope Clement VIII recalled all of the remaining copies of the Sixtene edition and continued the revision of its text. In 1604 a new authentic Vulgate edition of the Bible appeared, known today as the Sixto-Clementine edition. It differed from the Sixtene edition with some 4,900 variants. Since 1907 the Benedictine order has been making a critical revision of the Vulgate Old Testament. The New Testament has been undergoing a critical revision, with apparatus, under the auspices of a group of Anglican scholars at Oxford. This work was begun by Bishop John Wordsworth and Professor H. J. White between 1877 and 1926, and was completed by H. F. D. Sparks in 1954.

The consistency of the value of the Vulgate text is rather mixed

[19]Philip Schaff (ed.), *The Creeds of Christendom*, II, 82.

after the sixth century, and its overall character is rather faulty. The influence of the Vulgate on the language and thought of Western Christianity has been immense, but its value in textual criticism is not nearly so high. When the text of Jerome is arrived at, by its own textual study, it is valuable in ascertaining rather late manuscript evidence to the Greek and/or Hebrew text. Jerome's New Testament was a late fourth century revision of the Old Latin, and his Old Testament was a late fourth or early fifth century version of the Hebrew text. The Apocrypha witnesses to the disregard which Jerome had for it, as he only worked on four books (and those were reluctantly done), and the inclusion of it is evidence of the popularity it had in the Roman Catholic Church. Only a few voices which supported the Septuagint Old Testament as authoritative and inspired were capable of admitting their error, and acknowledging the accuracy of the Hebrew text underlying Jerome's Vulgate.

SUMMARY AND CONCLUSION

Christianity was born into a Roman world, and it was not long before its Western branch adopted the language of that world, Latin. There is evidence that the Old Latin versions of the Bible were in existence prior to A.D. 200. In the third century Latin versions were circulated freely in North Africa. However, it was Jerome's Latin version, the Vulgate, that endured longest, reigning for nearly a thousand years before it was challenged in the sixteenth century. The Vulgate version of the Bible was not only the Bible of the Middle Ages, it also served as the basis for most of the modern Bible translations made prior to the nineteenth century.

25

PATRISTIC WITNESSES TO THE
TEXT OF SCRIPTURE

THE PURPOSE FOR USING THE CHURCH FATHERS

In addition to possessing the manuscripts, including the miscellaneous items, and versions of the Old and New Testaments, the student of textual criticism has available the patristic citations of these Testaments which aid him in his search for the true text of the Bible. The Fathers lived during the early centuries of the church, and their witness to the original text assists in locating the precise area, date, and type of text used throughout the early church. This evidence assists the textual critic in ascertaining the authentic text of the originals.

WHEN THE FATHERS LIVED

Since the Old Testament canon was closed and recognized prior to the time of Christ, it is only necessary to mention with B. F. Westcott:

> In the direct citation of Scripture the usage of the Apostolic Fathers agrees generally with that of the Apostles. They continued to look upon the Old Testament as a full and lasting record of the revelation of God. In one remarkable particular they carried this belief yet further than it had been carried before. With them the individuality of the several writers falls into the background. They practically regarded the whole Book as one Divine utterance; and, with the exception of Barnabas, no one of them ever makes a distinct reference by name to any book of the Old Testament. . . .[1]

When considering their use of the New Testament, the picture is much more diverse and the role of the Fathers is much more important, for the recognition of the canon by the church was not

[1]Brooke Foss Westcott, *The Bible in the Church*, 2d ed., pp. 83-84.

finally completed until the fourth century.[2] With this in view, it is necessary to trace the historical process of the recognition of the canon in a cursory manner in order to bring the position of the Fathers into sharper focus.[3]

First century. During the last half of the first century, there was already in progress the selecting, sorting (Luke 1:1-4; I Thess. 2:13), reading (I Thess. 5:27), circulating (Col. 4:16), collecting (II Peter 3:15-16), and quoting (I Tim. 5:8) of apostolic literature (see chap. 14). In brief, all twenty-seven books were written, copied, and began to be disseminated among the churches before the end of the first century.

First half of the second century. During this period the apostolic writings became more generally known and more widely circulated, because the apostles had all passed off the scene, and their teachings were carried on through written copies instead of their voices. At this time almost every New Testament book was cited as Scripture explicitly; however, "up to A.D. 150 the quotations in extant ecclesiastical writers, though important in their bearing on questions of the date and acceptance of the New Testament Scriptures, are of little value for purely textual purposes."[4] The writings of the Fathers were read in the churches, and they tell much of the history, doctrine and practices of the church. It was in this period that the writings of the Fathers quoted Scripture with authority in struggles with heretical groups, dialogues with the heathen, and exhortations against vice.

Second half of the second century. During this period the New Testament books were widely recognized as Scripture just as the Old Testament was. This was a time of missionary activity, as the church spread beyond the confines of the Empire, and the Scriptures, Old and New Testaments, were translated into other languages. It was during these years that commentaries began to appear. Among the commentaries were Papias' *Exposition of the Lord's Oracles*, Heracleon's commentary on the Gospels, and Melito's commentary on the Apocalypse of John. This was also the period in which Tatian compiled his *Diatessaron*. The writings of the Fathers make profuse citations of the New Testament as the authoritative Scriptures, and

[2]See chap. 12 on the Old Testament canon and chap. 14 on the New Testament canon.
[3]The following discussion follows G. T. Manley (ed.), *The New Bible Handbook*, 3d ed., pp. 33-38.
[4]Sir Frederic G. Kenyon, *Handbook to the Textual Criticism of the New Testament*, 2d ed., p. 199.

the Muratorian Fragment (*c.* 170) lists all but five of the books of the modern New Testament.[5]

Third century. During this century the New Testament books were collected into a single catalog of "recognized books," and separated from other species of Christian literature. It was this century that evidenced the great rise in intellectual activity within the church, as Origen's *Hexapla* and other works indicate. The recognition of the New Testament's authority, its collection as a valuable unit, its translation as a missionary tool, and its commentaries as teaching aids all combine to illustrate the need for distinguishing between the Christian Scriptures and other religious literature. No longer were there only two classes of Christian literature (Scripture and the writings of the Fathers), there was also a body of Apocryphal and Pseudepigraphical literature emerging. The abundance of religious literature gave rise to the application of sorting and sifting tests to all religious literature in the church. These tests, and others (see chap. 14), led to the ultimate recognition of the canonical New Testament, and the erasure of doubts concerning the Antilegomena books of the New Testament.

Fourth century. By this time the New Testament canon was fully recognized and settled. The writings of the Fathers present the general agreement of all Christians on the canon of the New Testament. It was this period which gave rise to the various classifications of books mentioned in chapters 14-15.

WHAT THE FATHERS DID

It should be pointed out that there are several considerations which must be kept in view when the textual critic attempts to use patristic citations to recover the original texts. While the witness of the Fathers is quite early, actually older than the best codices, it is not always reliable. As a case in point, a patristic writer may have quoted a variant reading from one of the manuscripts which existed at the time. Another factor is that the writing of the particular Father may have been altered or modified during the history of its transmission in a manner similar to the Greek text of the New Testament.[6]

---

[5]No conclusive evidence against the inclusion of the five missing books can be made from this fragment, as it is what its name implies, "incomplete."

[6]Bruce M. Metzger, *The Text of the New Testament,* p. 87, indicates that scribes were tempted to assimilate the reading of the citation into agreement with their New Testament manuscripts, and thus are prone to copy the later ecclesiastical text (Koine, Textus Receptus, or Vulgate).

A third factor to be considered is whether the patristic author was quoting the New Testament verbatim, loosely, as a paraphrase, or possibly in a mere allusion to the original. Again, if it is an attempt to quote verbatim, the question must be asked whether or not the quote was made from memory rather than by consulting a manuscript. Often the writer was a member of a group which held heretical doctrines, and this factor needs to be kept in view as well. Still another consideration appears if a Father cites the same passage more than once, namely, are the quotes identical or divergent?

Finally, as in the case of Origen, an amanuensis would listen to dictation and hunt the passage of Scripture at a later time. His available manuscripts could result in a variety of readings for any given passage. But, the above difficulties notwithstanding, the evidence of the patristic writers "is of such great importance in tracing the history of the transmission of the text that the labour of refining the ore from the dross is well worth the effort."[7] Their importance may be summarized as showing the history of the text of the New Testament, rendering the best evidence as to the canon of the New Testament, providing a means of dating the manuscripts of the New Testament, and assisting in determining just when translations, versions and revisions of the text occur. With this information in hand, the following discussion may be more adequately considered.

THE PRINCIPAL FATHERS OF THE CHURCH AND THEIR WITNESS[8]

THE APOSTOLIC FATHERS (c. 70-c. 150)

The writers of this period all wrote in the Greek language. Their writings, for the most part, have been compiled in two excellent volumes of the Loeb Classical Library.[9] The citations of these Fathers must be weighed in light of the factors cited above, and their precision in quotation is far from modern standards, as some of their quotes would be regarded as mere allusions, and their allusions are often quite remote by modern standards.

The Epistle of Pseudo-Barnabas (c. 70-79). This makes many quotations and allusions to New Testament books. It cites Matthew 22:14, 44-45; and 26:31 (in 4:14; 12:11; and 5:16, respectively), while alluding to Matthew 20:16 in 6:13. In 11:10; 13:7; and 15:4,

[7]*Ibid.*, p. 88.
[8]*Ibid.*, pp. 88-89; Metzger has an alphabetical listing of thirty additional important Church Fathers, covering basically the same period, which may also be consulted.
[9]*The Apostolic Fathers*, Kirsopp Lake (ed.).

this same epistle, falsely ascribed to Paul's associate, quotes John 6:51; Romans 4:11; and II Peter 3:8, respectively. Again, these quotations are rather loose, perhaps from memory rather than from a manuscript copy.

Corinthians, by Clement of Rome (*c.* 95-97). This contains several quotations from the New Testament, including the synoptic gospels. His citations are more precise than those attributed to Barnabas, but they still lack modern precision. Among his many citations from the Gospels are Matthew 5:7; 7:1-2 (in his chap. 13); 13:3 (chap. 24); 18:6; 26:24 (chap. 46). Mark 4:3 or Luke 8:5 may have been in view when Clement cited the Gospels in chapter 24, and Mark 9:42 and 14:21 or Luke 17:1-2 and 22:22 may have been in view in his chapter 46. Acts 20:35 and Titus 3:1 were both cited in Clement's epistle (chap. 2), as were I Corinthians 2:9 (chap. 34); Hebrews 1:3-5, 7, 13 (chap. 36); 3:5 (chaps. 17, 43); I Peter 4:8 (chap. 49); and 5:5 (chap. 30). It is possible that Clement was alluding to Revelation 22:12 when he wrote 34:3-4.

Seven Epistles by Ignatius (*c.* 110-17). Ignatius wrote these while en route to martyrdom in Rome. Although his references to the New Testament are either loose quotations from memory or allusions, they do indicate his wide selection of Bible materials for his own letters, in which he sought to strengthen respect for bishops and presbyters, and protested against the docetic heresy. In his *Ephesians* letter, Ignatius quoted Matthew 12:33 (chap. 14); Romans 6:4 (chap. 19); I Corinthians 1:20 (chap. 18); Galatians 5:21 (chap. 16); Colossians 1:23 (chap. 10); James 4:6 (chap. 5); and I Peter 5:5 (chap. 5). In his letter *Magnesians,* he cited Matthew 27:52 (chap. 9); John 5:19, 30 (chap. 7); and Acts 1:25 (chap. 5). The *Trallians* letter quoted Matthew 15:13 (chap. 11); I Corinthians 4:1 (chap. 2); 9:27 (chap. 12); 15:12 ff. (chap. 9); and Colossians 1:16 (chap. 5). In writing *Romans,* Ignatius used John 4:10; 7:38, 42 (chap. 7); I Corinthians 15:8-9 (chap. 9); I Thessalonians 2:4 (chap. 2); II Thessalonians 3:5 (chap. 10); and II Timothy 2:8 (chap. 7). His *Philippians* epistle cited Matthew 15:13 (chap. 3); John 3:8 (chap. 7); and I Corinthians 2:10 (chap. 7); 6:9-10 (chap. 5); and 10:16-17 (chap. 4). He then wrote *Smyrnaeans* and cited Matthew 3:16 (chap. 1); 19:12 (chap. 6); Luke 24:39 (chap. 3); Acts 10:41 (chap. 3); Romans 1:3 (chap. 1); Ephesians 2:16 (chap. 1); Philippians 3:15 (chap. 11); 4:13 (chap. 4); and II Timothy 1:16 (chap. 10). In his personal letter to *Polycarp,* Ignatius cited several of the same books, for example, Matthew 8:17 (chap. 1); 10:16 (chap. 2); Ephesians 4:2 (chap. 1); 5:25, 29 (chap. 5); I Timothy 6:2 (chap. 4); and II Timothy 2:4 (chap. 6). It is advisable to mention again that quotation technique has changed throughout the course of history, as has the work of translation. This, along with the fact that modern scholars employ different criteria in distinguishing a citation from an allusion, may provide a basis for disagreement on just *what* is a quotation.

Philippians by Polycarp. The disciple of the Apostle John, Polycarp wrote an epistle to the *Philippians* (*c.* 110-35), which contains a large number of citations, as did Clement's *Corinthians.* Among his quotations are the following: Matthew 5:3, 10 (chap. 2); 5:44 (chap. 12); 6:13 (chap. 7); Mark 9:35 (chap. 5); 14:38 (chap. 7); Acts 2:24 (chap. 1); 10:42 (chap. 2); Romans 12:10 (chap. 10); 14:10 ff. (chap. 6); I Corinthians 6:2 (chap. 11); 14:25 (chap. 4); 15:58 (chap. 10); II Corinthians 3:2 (chap. 11); 4:14 (chap. 2); 8:21 (chap. 6); Galatians 1:1 (chap. 12); 4:26 (chap. 3); 5:17; 6:7 (chap. 5); Ephesians 2:8 ff. (chap. 1); 4:26 (chap. 12); 5:21 (chap. 10); 6:18 (chap. 12); Philippians 2:16 (chap. 9); 3:18 (chap. 12); II Thessalonians 1:4; 3:15 (chap. 11); I Timothy 2:1; 4:15 (chap. 12); 6:7, 10 (chap. 4); II Timothy 2:12 (chap. 5); 4:10 (chap. 9); I Peter 1:8 (chap. 1); 1:13, 21 (chap. 2); 2:11 (chap. 5); 2:12, 17 (chap. 10); 2:22, 24 (chap. 8); 3:9 (chap. 2); 4:7 (chap. 7); I John 4:2-3 or II John 7 (chap. 7). His work shows strong apostolic influence, and his prominence is noted in that Ignatius wrote a letter to him, and the church of Smyrna wrote a letter to the church of Philomelium entitled *The Martyrdom of Polycarp.*

The Shepherd of Hermas (*c.* 115-40). "Free" quotations from memory and allusion to the New Testament make themselves more evident in this writing than in the above cited works. Nevertheless, all three portions of the *Shepherd* cite the New Testament. Matthew 26:24 is cited in Vision IV.2.6, although it may be the parallel passage in Mark 14:21. In Mandate IV.6, Matthew 19:9 was quoted, while Mark 5:23-24 was cited in Similitude IX.20.2-3. While many other passages were quoted in the *Shepherd,* only a sampling is listed at this point: I Corinthians 7:40 (Mandate IV.4.2); Hebrews 11:33 (Vision IV.2.4); James 1:21 (Similitude VI.1.1); 2:7 (Similitude VII.6.4); 4:7 (Mandate XII.5.2); 4:12 (Mandate XII.6.3); I Peter 1:7 (Vision IV.3.4); 5:7 (Vision III.11.3); I John 2:27 (Mandate III.1); Revelation 21:14 (Vision III.5.1).

Teaching of the Twelve, or Didache (*c.* 120-50). This was widely used in the early church as a religious handbook. It followed the loose quote and allusion pattern of the *Shepherd* but gave wide variety to its quotations, as the following survey testifies. Matthew 5:5 (chap. 3); 5:26, 39-42, 46 (chap. 1); 6:9-13, 16 (chap. 8); 7:6 (chap. 9); 10:10 (chap. 13); 21:9 (chap. 12); 22:37, 39 (chap. 1); 24:10-13, 24, 30 (chap. 16); 25:13 (chap. 16); 28:19; Mark 11:9 (chap. 12); and Luke 6:27-35 (chap. 1); 9:2-4 (chap. 8); 12:35, 40 (chap. 16); 19:38 (chap. 13); 21:12 (chap. 16) witness to the widespread use of the Gospels. Other portions of the New Testament cited in the *Didache* include Acts 4:32 (chap. 4); Romans 12:9 (chap. 5); I Corinthians 16:22 (chap. 10); Hebrews 8:7 (chap. 4); I John 4:18 (chap. 10); Jude 22 (chap. 2).

Epistle to Diognetus (*c.* 150). This epistle makes a few direct quotations from the New Testament, but it makes loose quotes or allusions mostly. Among the former are I Corinthians 8:1 (chap. 12); I Peter 3:18 (chap. 9); and I John 4:9, 19 (chap. 10). Among the latter are passages in John 1:1 (chap. 11); 3:17 (chap. 7); 17:11, 14 (chap. 6); Acts 17:24-25 (chap. 3); I Corinthians 4:12 (chap. 5); II Corinthians 6:9-10 (chap. 5); Ephesians 4:22-24 (chap. 2); Philippians 3:20 (chap. 5); I Timothy 3:16 (chap. 11); Titus 3:4 (chap. 9); and I John 1:1 (chap. 11).

Exposition of the Lord's Oracles (*c.* 130-40). In this period, Papias, who fits into this period chronologically but not topically, wrote his *Exposition of the Lord's Oracles.* It survives in fragments only. Among the fragments is his reference to Revelation 12:9 (Fragment 9), thus lending support to the quotations of the Apocalypse by other Apostolic Fathers. From the above citations, it may be observed that every book of the New Testament was quoted clearly before A.D. 150, with the possible exception of Philemon and III John.[10]

The Ante-Nicene Fathers (*c.* 150-*c.* 300)

In contrast to the Apostolic Fathers, the Ante-Nicene Fathers wrote in Greek, Syriac and Latin. The writers in this period include such individuals as Marcion (d. *c.* 160), the heretic who mixed Gnosticism and orthodox Christianity into a dualistic and sharply anti-Judaistic sect, and Montanus, a second century convert from

[10]In his *Philippians* 7:1, Polycarp may have used II John 7 as his authority instead of I John 4:2-3. If he did, only two "personal" letters were unquoted; if not, three "personal" letters were omitted as far as this study has revealed.

Cybele worship in Phrygia who fancied himself "the inspired organ of the promised Paraclete or Advocate, the Helper and Comforter in these last times of distress."[11] While heretical groups such as these, including the Donatists and the Novatians, may be appealed to in support of the present thesis, the treatment limits itself to the more notable Fathers of the Ante-Nicene period.

Justin Martyr. Justin lived and worked at Rome, where he confronted Marcion at about 150. He later took a trip to Ephesus, where he wrote *Dialogues with Trypho, a Jew.* Upon his return to Rome (c. 165) he was captured and martyred. But he had written two apologies in which he presented Christianity as the oldest, truest and most divine of all philosophies. He quoted the Scriptures very loosely, especially the Old Testament, and a Western text of the New Testament. In his writings, Justin quoted the Gospels of Matthew (3:17; 7:23; etc.); Luke (3:33; 22:19; etc.); and John (3:3-5; etc.). He alluded to several of Paul's epistles (Romans, I Corinthians, Ephesians, Colossians, etc.), but did not mention Paul by name. Justin also cited the Apocalypse in his free style. There is a total of over 330 citations of the New Testament in Justin's work, with an additional 266 allusions.[12]

Tatian (c. 110-72). Tatian wrote his *Oratio* as a defense of the Christian faith and a condemnation of the pagan philosophies. He is better known, however, for his *Diatessaron.* His work has been considered in chapter 23, and need not be reviewed at this point, especially since he came under the influence of Gnosticism after the death of Justin. His writings were written in Syriac, or translated into it from Greek.

Irenaeus (c. 130-c. 202). Irenaeus wrote in Greek, and was the first Father to make full use of the New Testament in his writings. His greatest work, *Against Heresies,* was written in Gaul (c. 185), and was a defense against Gnosticism and other heresies. He freely quoted the New Testament, and demonstrated its unity with the Old. While there are some differences, "we shall not err greatly in concluding that Irenaeus's copy of the Gospel was practically equivalent to an early ancestor of the Greek side of Codex Bezae, excelling the latter by a greater freedom from corruption."[13] This situation prevails in the Acts as well.[14] In addition to the clarity of Irenaeus' text,

---

[11]Philip Schaff, *History of the Christian Church,* 5th ed., II, 418.
[12]See chart on p. 357 for totals on some of the following writers.
[13]Alexander Souter, *The Text and Canon of the New Testament,* p. 73.
[14]*Ibid.,* pp. 73-74.

there is manifold witness to his use of Scripture, as he makes over eighteen hundred quotations from the New Testament alone. Also interesting is the fact that Irenaeus' writings indicate that the canon of the New Testament was recognized in his day to be practically the same as it is today.

Clement of Alexandria (*c.* 150-*c.* 215). Clement became head of the Catechetical School in Alexandria shortly before A.D. 200. While he was not careful in his citation of Scripture, he had left evidence that his text was also basically related to Codex Bezae.[15] He wrote several works in Greek, which were repetitious and lacking in clarity, and sometimes even permitted error to creep into his theology. His works included an *Exhortation to the Heathen; Pedagogus,* which contains the earliest extant hymn of the church; and the *Stromata,* miscellaneous writings. His quotations were taken from both Testaments, and he cited all of the New Testament books except Philemon, James and II Peter. There are some 2,400 citations of the New Testament, including over 1,000 from the Gospels and over 1,000 from the Pauline Epistles. It is interesting to note that Clement quoted all of the Old Testament books except Song of Solomon and Ruth.

Tertullian (*c.* 160-*c.* 220). A contemporary to Clement of Alexandria, Tertullian is known as the "Father of Latin Christianity," as he was the first Father to write a body of Christian literature in Latin. His writings were in both Greek and Latin, as he served in the vital area of North Africa. His work was apologetical, polemical, practical and pro-Montanist. He was a schismatic adherent to Montanism, and used his powerful pen and pulpit to reprove what he considered to be compromise and worldliness within the Old Catholic Church. His writings were prolific, and his use of Scripture was profuse but not always accurate. Many of his quotations were made from an Old Latin manuscript, basically following b, although he often cited and/or translated a Greek manuscript closely akin to that used by Clement of Alexandria and Origen. This text, the farthest removed from Codex B among the Greek manuscripts, was closely related to D. In his writings, he makes over 7,200 New Testament citations, with over 3,800 arising from the Gospels, while over 2,600 were from the Pauline Epistles.

Hippolytus (*c.* 170-*c.* 236). Hippolytus lived in or near Rome and wrote in Greek, although little of his work has survived in the orig-

15*Ibid.,* pp. 74-75.

inal language. His text type appears to be based upon a good Western copy of the Gospels, but he may have also used Tatian's *Diatessaron* in his writing. In the Pauline Epistles he follows the Western text. "In the Apocalypse his text is particularly important: there he is found to agree with the best authorities."[16] In his writings, over 1,300 New Testament citations appear. Of these, over 700 are from the Gospels, nearly 400 are Pauline, and almost 200 are from the Apocalypse.

Origen (*c*. 185-*c*. 254). Origen succeeded Clement of Alexandria at the Catechetical School. He was by far the most prolific writer in the early church, as he wrote over 6,000 items and books. In his writings he made nearly 18,000 New Testament quotations. Among his outstanding works are the *Hexapla* and *De Principiis*. The former has been treated in chapter 22, and the latter is of importance as well, for it was his great work on the basic doctrines of Christianity. Still another work, *Against Celsus*, is a polemic in eight volumes, which has been preserved in Greek. It is interesting to observe that of Origen's citations of the New Testament, over 95 percent were taken from the Gospels and Pauline Epistles, while only 205 were from the Apocalypse, and a mere 120 were taken from the General Epistles. When his views met with the theological bias of the West during the late fourth century, his writings were almost entirely neglected. This sad situation has resulted in the survival of only a few late and poor manuscripts to the present. The loss is tragic, as Origen had practically every existing text type at his disposal when he wrote. Hence, it is significant that his manuscript basis was closely allied with that of Clement of Alexandria and Tertullian.

Cyprian (*c*. 195 or 200-258). Cyprian of Carthage wrote some eighty-one letters and twelve long treatises in Latin. He was one of the most careful and accurate quoters of the Bible in the early church. In his writings, Cyprian made about 740 Old and 1,030 New Testament quotations. He cited all of the New Testament books except Philemon and II John. The quotations of Cyprian from the Gospels adhere to the Old Latin k type text.

A brief inventory at this point will reveal that there were some 32,000 citations of the New Testament prior to the time of the Council of Nicea (325). These 32,000 quotations are by no means exhaustive, and they do not even include the fourth century writers. Just adding the number of references used by one other writer, Eusebius,

16*Ibid.*, p. 75.

who flourished prior to and contemporary with the Council at Nicea, will bring the total citations of the New Testament to over 36,000. Hence, prior to the period of the Nicene and Post-Nicene Fathers, there is overwhelming evidence in the manifold witness of the outstanding Church Fathers to the text of the New Testament.

The Nicene and Post-Nicene Fathers (c. 300-c. 430)

The Nicene–Post-Nicene period of church history must be discussed at this point, because the New Testament canon had not yet been formally recognized by the entire church in A.D. 325 (see chap. 14). During the period prior to the Council at Nicea, the church had gone through a series of local and imperial persecutions. As late as 302/3, the Emperor Diocletian had decreed that all copies of the Scriptures be destroyed, and those people having them in their possession should be punished (often unto death). Thus, the Fathers of the period under discussion appeared *after* the Edict of Galerius (311) and the Edict of Milan (313), with the exception of Eusebius of Caesarea who bridged the transition from "the persecuted to the patronized Church."

Eusebius of Caesarea (c. 263 or 265-c. 340). Eusebius was the bishop of Caesarea (315-40), and historian of the early church. He wrote, in Greek, such items as *Ecclesiastical History, Chronicles, Life of Constantine* and a tract on *Martyrs of Palestine,* which earned for him the title "Father of Church History." Much of his work has survived to the present, and his role in the copying of the Scriptures is of great importance.[17] The literary value of his writing is not nearly so great as its historical value, and his use of the Scriptures in his writing follows the pattern of his forebears. He cited the New Testament over 5,000 times, and follows the basic text type of Origen's sources. Eusebius was not a satisfactory quoter of Scripture, however, as he rarely cited long passages and, when he did quote, he usually quoted loosely or from memory. His citations from the Gospels number over 3,200, with over 1,500 from the Pauline Epistles. But, it is with Eusebius that a new era opens in the transmission and citation of the biblical text.

Athanasius of Alexandria (c. 295-c. 373). Athanasius is known as the "Father of Orthodoxy" as a result of his role at the Council at Nicea (325) and his opposition to Arius and his followers. The writings of Athanasius were quite varied, as he spent some forty-six

[17]See discussion in chap. 14.

years as bishop of Alexandria and "defender of the faith" against Arianism. He was exiled five times, a total of twenty years, and did much of his writing in Greek during this period. Alexander Souter indicates that the text of Athanasius' New Testament, from which he made a vast number of citations, corresponded almost identically with Westcott and Hort's "Neutral text," as pointed out by Hermann von Soden.[18]

Cyril of Jerusalem (*c*. 315-86). Cyril wrote a series of lectures in Greek, *Twenty-three Catechises*, which he gave to candidates for baptism. He was later elected bishop of Jerusalem (350), but was deposed several times because of his personal prejudices. Each time he was reinstated, and he rose to a position of high esteem in the church because of his knowledge of Scripture and his general education. Cyril died in 386 after having spent sixteen years in exile and being recalled and highly esteemed. He was known for his willingness to suffer for his beliefs, and freely quoted the New Testament in his catechises, which were actually a compendium of the Christian religion. The text of Cyril was basically that of Eusebius of Caesarea.[19]

Basil of Caesarea, "the Great" (c. 329-79), *Gregory of Nazianzus* (330-c. 390), *and Basil's younger brother, Gregory of Nyssa* (d. *c*. 395). These men are called the "Three Cappadocian Fathers." Their works were written in Greek, and their work was widespread, influential and beneficial. They were archdefenders of orthodoxy, and wrote numerous items attacking Arianism. The text type underlying their numerous citations of the New Testament was basically that of "the official ecclesiastical text associated with Constantinople and the regions under her influence."[20] There were, however, more ancient elements still preserved in their text, which they quoted rather carefully.

John Chrysostom (*c*. 347-407). Chrysostom was the first great writer to use the fully ecclesiastical text of the New Testament. He exerted much influence in his role as Metropolitan of Constantinople, and his support of the ecclesiastical text carried much weight. The numerous Greek commentaries written by Chrysostom included Matthew, John, Acts, all of Paul's epistles, and Hebrews. He also wrote over six hundred exegetical homilies. All of these works are saturated with citations of the New Testament text. Other out-

[18]Souter, p. 77.
[19]Cf. Kenyon, p. 366; also Souter, pp. 121-24.
[20]Souter, p. 77.

standing leaders in the East, for example, Theodoret of Cyrrhus, and John of Damascus, used the same basic text as Chrysostom.

Ambrose of Milan (340-97). Ambrose represents the voice of the church in the West during this period. He was born into an aristocratic family and became bishop of Milan. While his works were written in Latin, he based them on Greek sources. Thus, his vast number of quotations in his *Letters* are relatively poor samples of the Latin Bible. His text type followed the Old Latin d and g, as seen in the Latin side of Codex Boernerianus. It may have been this very text type that was used by Jerome in his revision of the Old Latin New Testament. Ambrose left a tremendous impact on the church in the West, as he was the "spiritual father" of the "Medieval Monolith," Augustine.

Jerome (*c.* 340-420). Jerome has been previously considered, and needs only to be mentioned in passing. Even prior to the death of Ambrose, Jerome was translating the Hebrew Old Testament into Latin (see chap. 24). His text type for the Gospels was the Old Latin a, while he turned to other Old Latin manuscripts for the remainder of the New Testament. It was this revision which became the "standard" for the Western Church in the Middle Ages, and especially after the Council at Trent (1546-63).

Augustine of Hippo Regius (*c.* 354-430). Augustine is one of the greatest scholars of this entire period. He wrote many extant Latin works, including *The City of God* and *The Confessions*. In his writings Augustine quoted profusely from both the Old and New Testaments. Prior to about 400, he followed the text of the Old Latin e in the Gospels. After that time he turned to Jerome's Vulgate for his long citations, using memorized portions in shorter quotes. The remainder of his New Testament quotations appear to follow the Old Latin text of h or r. His role in history has been amply seen before, but it should be pointed out that he was not a great philologist. His early opposition to Jerome's Vulgate was later reversed (see chap. 24).

SUMMARY AND CONCLUSION

The patristic citations of Scripture are not primary witnesses to the text of the New Testament, but they do serve two very important secondary roles. First, they give overwhelming support to the existence of the twenty-seven authoritative books of the New Testament canon. It is true that their quotations were often loose, although in the case of some Fathers they were very accurate, but they do at least reproduce the substantial content of the original text. Second, the quotations are so numerous and widespread that if no manuscripts of the New Testament were extant, the New Testament could be reproduced from the writings of the early Fathers alone. Sir David Dalrymple's curiosity was aroused on this subject when once he was asked, "Suppose that the New Testament had been destroyed, and every copy of it lost by the end of the third century, could it have been collected together again from the writings of the Fathers of the second and third centuries?"[21] Having given himself to research on this question, he was later able to report,

> Look at those books. You remember the question about the New Testament and the Fathers? That question roused my curiosity, and as I possessed all the existing works of the Fathers of the second and third centuries, I commenced to search, and up to this time I have found the entire New Testament, except *eleven verses.*[22]

In brief, Greenlee was right when he wrote, "These quotations are so extensive that the New Testament could virtually be reconstructed from them without the use of New Testament Manuscripts."[23] Compare, for example, the numerous quotations from the New Testament given in Burgon's index, in the case of a few of the earlier and more important writers.[24]

EARLY PATRISTIC QUOTATIONS OF THE NEW TESTAMENT

Writer	Gospels	Acts	Pauline Epistles	General Epistles	Revelation	Totals
Justin Martyr	268	10	43	6	3	330 (266 allusions)
Irenaeus	1,038	194	499	23	65	1,819
Clement Alex.	1,017	44	1,127	207	11	2,406
Origen	9,231	349	7,778	399	165	17,922
Tertullian	3,822	502	2,609	120	205	7,258
Hippolytus	734	42	387	27	188	1,378
Eusebius	3,258	211	1,592	88	27	5,176
Grand Totals	19,368	1,352	14,035	870	664	36,289

[21]Charles Leach, *Our Bible: How We Got It*, pp. 35-36.
[22]*Ibid.*
[23]J. Harold Greenlee, *An Introduction to New Testament Textual Criticism*, p. 54.
[24]Cf. also Leach, pp. 35-36; Joseph Angus, *Bible Handbook*, Samuel G. Green (rev.), p. 57; Kenyon, p. 264.

26

RESTORATION OF THE SCRIPTURE TEXT

THE PROBLEM OF TEXTUAL CRITICISM

It has already been stated that there are no known autographs of the New Testament.[1] There are available, however, numerous biblical manuscript copies (chaps. 19, 20), versions (chap. 21), and quotations (chap. 25) by which the text can be restored. This process is known as textual criticism, or lower criticism.

MANUSCRIPT EVIDENCE

A summary of the manuscript evidence will prove beneficial at this point.

Biblical manuscripts. The Old Testament has survived in few complete manuscripts, most of which date from the ninth century A.D. or later. There are, however, abundant reasons for believing that these are *good* copies, as support for this position has been known for years from several lines of evidence: (1) the few variants in the existing Masoretic manuscripts; (2) the almost literal agreement of most of the LXX with the Masoretic Hebrew text; (3) the scrupulous rules of the scribes; (4) similarity of parallel Old Testament passages; (5) archaeological confirmation of historical details of the text; and even (6) the agreement, by and large, of the Samaritan Pentateuch. (7) The most phenomenal confirmation of the fidelity of the Hebrew text, however, is much more direct than any of these witnesses, namely, the discovery of hundreds of Hebrew manuscripts near the Dead Sea, which are a thousand years earlier than those previously possessed. From these Qumran caves have come fragments, sometimes complete copies, of almost every book of the Old Testament, some of which date as far back as the fourth century B.C. (cf. chap. 19).

The manuscripts of the New Testament are much more numerous

[1]See chap. 2 for suggested reasons as to why God has permitted the autographs to perish.

than those of the Old Testament, but so are the variant readings. Consequently, the science of textual criticism is much more necessary in the restoration of the New Testament text. There are over 3,000 Greek manuscripts of the New Testament, dating from the second century and onward. Hence, while the fidelity of the Old Testament is based on relatively *few* but *good* manuscripts, the integrity of the New Testament is derived by a critical comparison of *many* manuscripts which are of *poorer* quality (i.e., they possess more variant readings).

Versions. Other lines of evidence for the biblical text are the ancient and medieval versions. The Old Testament is represented by the Septuagint (LXX), the Samaritan Pentateuch, and the Babylonian Targums, as well as all of the major ancient versions which contain both Old and New Testaments. Into this latter category may be placed the Old Syriac, the Old Latin, the Coptic, Sahidic, Latin Vulgate, and others (see chaps. 23-24). Of these versions, there are some 9,000 manuscript copies available to scholars today.

Quotations. A third line of evidence for the reconstruction of the Bible is derived from the quotations of the Fathers. Rabbinic quotations of the Old Testament are numerous in the Hebrew Talmudic writings. Other Jewish quotations, such as those by Philo the philosopher and Josephus the historian, are also found in proliferation. The patristic citations of the New Testament have survived in even greater abundance, as has been shown in chapter 25. The extant writings of the Fathers of the second and third centuries alone contain over 36,000 citations of the verses of the New Testament. In fact, if there were no biblical manuscripts available today, the entire New Testament could be reconstructed from the writings of the Church Fathers of the first three centuries with the exception of eleven verses.

Lectionaries. One further source of evidence which applies to the reconstruction of the New Testament text is the church service books, known as the lectionaries. Recent counts indicate that there are some 2,000 lectionaries. Revived interest in the lectionaries has demonstrated their value in textual reconstruction and their use in the diacritical apparatus that pertains thereto (see chap. 21). There are, then, a grand total of nearly 14,000 manuscripts containing New Testament texts, to say nothing of the 36,000 patristic quotations containing almost every verse of the New Testament. These are the materials which provide the data by which the textual critic attempts to reconstruct the original New Testament text.

MULTITUDE OF VARIANTS

The multiplicity of manuscripts produces a corresponding number of variant readings, for the more manuscripts that are copied the greater will be the number of copyist's errors. However, as will be seen, what at first seems to be a grave hindrance to the reconstruction of the biblical text actually becomes extremely beneficial.

Old Testament Variants. The variant readings of the Old Testament are relatively few for several reasons: (1) because there are fewer manuscript copies and the grand total of variants is less; (2) because copies were made by an official class of sacred scribes who labored under strict rules; (3) because (it is believed that) the Masoretes systematically destroyed all copies with "mistaken" and/ or variant readings.[2] The Samaritan Pentateuch, however, contains about 6,000 variants from the Hebrew Masoretic Text, but most of these are matters of spelling. Some 1,900 of the variants agree with the LXX (e.g., in the ages given for the patriarchs). The most significant variants are Samaritan sectarian insertions which are used to indicate that the Lord actually chose Mount Gerizim rather than Mount Zion, and Shechem rather than Jerusalem as His sacred sites.[3]

New Testament Variants.[4] Because the New Testament manuscripts are so numerous, and because there were many private and "unofficial" copies made, there is a grand total of more variants than in the Old Testament.

1. *How many variants are there?* The gross number of variants increases with every new manuscript discovery.

    a. In 1707 John Mill estimated about 30,000 variants in the known New Testament manuscripts.[5] Many of the great manuscripts were discovered after this time.[6]

    b. By 1874, F.H.A. Scrivener counted nearly 150,000 variants.[7]

---

[2]Critical study in the Old Testament has not been as necessary or as extensive as in the New. The first collection of evidence was made by Bishop Kennicott (1776-80) who published a critical text at Oxford based on 634 Hebrew manuscripts. Later, in 1784-88, the Italian scholar De Rossi published a collation of 825 more manuscripts. The critical edition of the Hebrew Bible edited by C. D. Ginsberg for the British and Foreign Bible Society (1926) has been superseded by Rudolf Kittel and Paul E. Kahle (eds.), *Biblia Hebraica,* currently in its third edition.

[3]Gleason L. Archer, Jr., *A Survey of Old Testament Introduction,* p. 37.

[4]R. L. Clark, Alfred Goodwin, and W. Sanday (eds.), *The Variorum Edition of the New Testament of Our Lord and Saviour Jesus Christ,* may be consulted for a comprehensive listing of variants. In Greek, see Eberhard Nestle (ed.), *Novum Testamentum Graece,* for a complete critical apparatus.

[5]James Hastings (ed.), *A Dictionary of the Bible,* IV, 735.

[6]The great period of manuscript discovery began about 1650 and continues to the present. Cf. chap. 27.

[7]Hastings, p. 735.

c. To date there are over 200,000 known variants,[8] and this figure will no doubt increase in the future as more manuscripts are discovered.

2. *How are the variants counted?* There is an ambiguity in saying that there are some 200,000 variants in the existing manuscripts of the New Testament, since these represent only 10,000 places in the New Testament. If one single word is misspelled in 3,000 different manuscripts, this is counted as 3,000 variants or readings. Once this counting procedure is understood, and the mechanical (orthographic) variants have been eliminated, the remaining, significant variants are surprisingly few in number.

3. *How did variants occur?* In order to fully understand the significance of variant readings, and to determine which are the correct or original readings, it is necessary to examine first just how these variants came into the text. Careful students of textual criticism have suggested two classes of errors: intentional and unintentional.[9]

a. Unintentional changes of various kinds all arise from the imperfection of some human faculty. These comprise by far the vast majority of all transcriptional errors.

1) *Errors of the eye.*

a) Wrong division of words actually resulted in the formation of new words. Early manuscripts did not separate words by a space, therefore, *HEISNOWHERE* could either mean *HE IS NOW HERE* or *HE IS NOWHERE.* A more amusing example is *DIDYOUEVERSEEABUNDANCEONTHETABLE.*[10]

b) Omissions of letters, words and even whole lines occurred when an astigmatic eye mistook one group of letters or words for another, sometimes located on a different line. This error is known as a homoeoteleuton (similar ending). When only one letter was omitted, it was called a haplography (single writing).

c) Repetitions result in the opposite error to omissions. Hence, when the eye picked up the same letter or word twice and repeated it, it was called a dittography. Such an error may be the reason that some minuscules read, "Whom do you want me to release for you, (Jesus) Barabbas or Jesus?" (Matt. 27:17).

[8]Neil R. Lightfoot, *How We Got the Bible,* p. 53.
[9]See Bruce M. Metzger, *The Text of the New Testament,* pp. 150 ff.
[10]Suggested by Alexander Souter, *The Text and Canon of the New Testament,* C. S. C. Williams (rev.), p. 103.

d) *Transposition* is the reversal of position of two letters or words. This is technically known as metathesis. In II Chronicles 3:4, the transposition of letters would make the measurements of the porch of Solomon's temple out of proportion, for example, 120 cubits instead of 20 cubits as in the LXX.

e) *Other confusions* of spelling, abbreviation or scribal insertion account for the remainder of scribal errors. This is especially true of Hebrew letters, which were used for numbers and could be easily confused. These errors of eye may account for many of the numerical discrepancies in the Old Testament; for example, the reading of 40,000 stalls in I Kings 4:26 rather than 4,000 in II Chronicles 9:25 is undoubtedly an error of this kind, as is the 42 years in II Chronicles 22:2 in contrast to the correct reading of 22 in II Kings 8:26.[11]

2) *Errors of the ear* occurred only when manuscripts were copied by listening to someone read them. This may explain why some manuscripts (fifth century onward) read *kamelos* (a rope) instead of *kamēlos* (a camel) in Matthew 19:24. In I Corinthians 13:3, *kauthasomai* (he burns) was confused with *kauchasomai* (he boasts). This type of confusion occurred sometimes among the manuscripts, and some of them drastically affect the meaning of given passages. Codex D, for example, erroneously writes *mē* instead of *me*, changing the reading in Mark 14:31 from "If I must die . . ." to "If it is *not* necessary to die . . . ." The interchange of personal pronouns in manuscript copying from oral readings was frequent. *Hāmon* (our) and *Humon* (your) are quite similar in sound; hence, it would be difficult to determine whether John wrote "that *your* joy may be complete," or "that *our* joy may be complete." First Peter contains at least seven such confusions (1:3, 12; 2:21 (2); 3:18, 21; 5:10).[12] Anyone who has written "their" for "there," or mistaken "here" for "hear" can readily understand this type of error.

3) *Errors of memory.* These are not so numerous, but occasionally a scribe might forget the precise word in a passage and substitute a synonym. Perhaps he might be unconsciously influenced by a parallel passage or truth. For example, Ephesians 5:9 has "the fruit of the Spirit" in the Byzantine manuscripts and P[46] rather than "the fruit of light," as in all other good manuscripts.

[11]For a brief but good discussion of the types of manuscript errors in the Old Testament, see Archer, chap. 4.
[12]See Metzger, pp. 190-93, for a more detailed treatment.

The confusion is probably with Galatians 5:22. Quite often today popular quotations of Hebrews 9:22 (AV) will add ". . . there is no remission [of sins]." Thus, the memory may almost automatically transcribe a passage in one gospel to conform to another. However, variants of this type have more frequently been found to be intentional emendations.

4) *Errors of judgment.* The most common error of this type is occasioned by dim lighting or poor eyesight. Sometimes marginal notes were incorporated into the text under the misapprehension that they were part of the text. A. T. Robertson suggests that this is the explanation of the angel disturbing the water (John 5:4).[13] B. B. Warfield provides an obvious example of a judgmental error by a sleepy scribe who added to a minuscule copy of II Corinthians 8:4-5, as the scribe interpolated into the text, "it is found thus in many of the copies,"[14] as though it were part of Paul's admonition to the Corinthians instead of a marginal notation. It is difficult to tell whether some variants are due to faulty judgment or intentional doctrinal changes. No doubt I John 5:8, John 7:53—8:11, and Acts 8:37 fall into one of these categories.

5) *Errors of writing.* If a scribe, due to imperfect style or accident, wrote indistinctly or imprecisely, he would set the stage for future error of sight or judgment. Sometimes the scribes would be careless or ignorant, as in I Samuel 13:1 which reads, "Saul was ___ years old when he began to reign." The scribe neglected to put in the number. But rapid copying was no doubt responsible for many errors in writing.

b. Intentional changes. Although most of the variant readings resulted from unintentional errors arising from human limitations, there were also a good number that occurred as a result of scribal intentions. Good intentions, no doubt, but nonetheless deliberate.

1) *Grammatical and linguistical.* The orthographical variations in spelling, euphony and grammatical form are abundantly illustrated in the papyri. Each scribal tradition had its own idiosyncrasies, and a scribe tended to modify his manuscript to conform to them. This included the spelling of proper names, verb forms, the smoothing out of rough grammar, the changing of genders to agree with their referents, and other syntactical altera-

---

[13]Benjamin B. Warfield, *An Introduction to the Textual Criticism of the New Testament,* p. 154.
[14]*Ibid.,* p. 100.

tions. These changes were akin to recent efforts to change the older English "which" to "whom," "I shall" to "I will."

2) *Liturgical changes.* The lectionaries provide abundant examples of these changes. At the beginning of a given section, minor changes were made in order to summarize the context. Some of these changes crept into biblical manuscripts, for example, "Joseph and Mary" in place of "his parents" (Luke 2:41). Outside the lectionaries, minor textual alterations were made in order to conform with ecclesiastical usage. The "doxology" of the "Lord's Prayer" (Matt. 6:13) probably arose in this manner.

3) *Harmonizational changes.* This type of change is frequently encountered in the Gospels. The account of the "Lord's Prayer" in Luke 11:2-4 was made to agree with the more popular version in Matthew 6:9-13. Some manuscripts have made Acts 9:5-6 agree more literally with Acts 26:14-15. In like manner, quotations from the Old Testament were enlarged in some manuscripts to conform to the LXX (cf. Matt. 15:8 with Isa. 29:13; the phrase "this people" is added). To Paul's list of four commandments in Romans 13:9, another, "You shall not bear false witness," is added in some manuscripts.

4) *Historical and factual changes.* Well-meaning scribes sometimes "corrected" manuscripts by changing what they thought was an error. This is no doubt what happened in Revelation 1:5, where a scribe changed *lusanti*, "loosed [us from our sins]," to *lousanti*, "washed [us from our sins]." The change of "sixth hour" to "third hour" in John 19:14 in some manuscripts was probably an attempt to correct what the scribe considered to be an inaccuracy. A similar effort to emend a chronological "error" changed "after three days" to "on the third day" (Mark 8:31). Geographical corrections can be found among the manuscripts. Origen changed "Bethany" to "Bethabara" in order to explain a geographical difficulty.

5) *Conflational changes.* Conflation is the combining of two or more variants into one reading. The clause, "And every sacrifice will be salted with salt" (Mark 9:49), is probably a conflation. The "unto all" and "upon all" of Romans 3:22 (AV) is probably another example of combining two alternate readings (see RSV which reads only "for all").

6) *Doctrinal changes.* Most deliberate doctrinal changes have been in the direction of orthodoxy, as is the reference to the Trin-

ity in I John 5:7-8. The addition of "fasting" to "prayer" in Mark 9:29 and the long ending of Mark (16:9-20),[15] if they were deliberate, may not be so orthodox. In I Corinthians 6:20, the addition of "and in your spirit, which are God's" (AV) and "who walk not after the flesh . . ." (Rom. 8:1) are probably deliberate doctrinal additions to the text. Other passages that may be of this variety are John 1:18, "only begotten son" instead of "only begotten God," and Acts 20:28, "church of the Lord which he obtained with his own blood" (RSV) instead of "church of God, which he [God] hath purchased with his own [God's] blood" (AV). It is well to add Greenlee's observation that "no Christian doctrine, however, hangs upon a debatable text; and the student of the New Testament must beware of wanting his text to be more orthodox or doctrinally stronger than is the inspired original."[16]

4. *How significant are the variants?* It is easy to leave the wrong impression by speaking of 200,000 "errors" which have crept into the text by scribal mistakes and intended corrections. It was already mentioned that there are only 10,000 places where these 200,000 variants occur. The next question is: "How significant are these 10,000 places?" Textual critics have attempted to answer this question by offering the following percentages and comparisons.

   a. Westcott and Hort estimated that only about one-eighth of all the variants had any weight, as most of them are merely mechanical matters such as spelling or style. Of the whole, then, only about one-sixtieth rise above "trivialities," or can in any sense be called "substantial variations."[17] Mathematically this would compute to a text that is 98.33 percent pure.

   b. Ezra Abbot gave similar figures, saying that about 19/20 (95 percent) of the readings are "various" rather than "rival" readings, and 19/20 (95 percent) of the remainder are of so little importance that their adoption or rejection makes no appreciable difference in the sense of the passage.[18]

   c. Philip Schaff surmised that of the 150,000 variations known in his day, only 400 affected the sense; and of these only 50 were

---

[15]"Fasting" is also added in Acts 10:30 and I Cor. 7:5.
[16]J. Harold Greenlee, *An Introduction to New Testament Textual Criticism*, p. 68.
[17]Brooke Foss Westcott and Fenton John Anthony Hort, *The New Testament in the Original Greek*, 2d ed., II, 2.
[18]Cf. Warfield, pp. 13-14.

of real significance; and of this total not one affected "an article of faith or a precept of duty which is not abundantly sustained by other and undoubted passages, or by the whole tenor of Scripture teaching."[19]

d. A. T. Robertson suggested that the real concern of textual criticism is of a "thousandth part of the entire text."[20] This would make the reconstructed text of the New Testament 99.9 percent free from substantial or consequential error. Hence, as Warfield observed, "the great mass of the New Testament, in other words, has been transmitted to us with no, or next to no variations."[21] At first, the great multitude of variants would seem to be a liability to the integrity of the Bible text. But, just the contrary is true, for the larger number of variants supplies at the same time the means of checking on those variants. As strange as it may appear, the corruption of the text provides the means for its own correction.

e. The foregoing discussion cannot be fully appreciated unless it is contrasted with the textual integrity of other books from the ancient world. The first comparison to consider is that of the number or quantity of manuscripts. The Greek manuscripts of the New Testament alone total over 5,000, plus the versions (9,000) and lectionaries (2,000); whereas some of the greatest writings of antiquity have survived in only a handful of manuscripts (see chap. 18). Furthermore, a comparison of the nature or quality of the writings sets the fidelity of the biblical text in bold relief. Bruce M. Metzger, in an excellent study of Homer's *Iliad* and the Hindu *Mahābhārata*, demonstrates that their textual corruption is much greater than that of the New Testament.

1) The *Iliad* is particularly appropriate, since it has the most in common with the New Testament. Next to the New Testament, there are more extant manuscripts of the *Iliad* (643)[22] than any other book. Both it and the Bible were considered "sacred," and both underwent textual changes and criticism of their Greek manuscripts. The New Testament has about 20,000 lines;

[19]Philip Schaff, *Companion to the Greek Testament and the English Version,* 3d ed., rev., p. 177.
[20]Archibald T. Robertson, *An Introduction to the Textual Criticism of the New Testament,* p. 22.
[21]Warfield, p. 14.
[22]Bruce M Metzger, *Chapters in the History of New Testament Textual Criticism,* p. 144, lists 453 papyri, 2 uncials, and 188 minuscules, after the computation of Kurt Aland of Münster, July 11, 1962.

the *Iliad* about 15,600. Only 40 lines (or 400 words) of the New Testament are in doubt, whereas 764 lines of the *Iliad* are questioned. This 5 percent textual corruption compares with one-half of 1 percent of similar emendations in the New Testament.

2) The national epic of India, the *Mahābhārata*, has suffered even more corruption. It is about eight times the size of the *Iliad* and the *Odyssey* together, roughly 250,000 lines. Of these, some 26,000 lines are textual corruptions (10 percent).[23] The New Testament, then, has not only survived in more manuscripts than any other book from antiquity, but it has survived in a purer form than any other great book—a form that is 99.5 percent pure.

THE PRINCIPLES OF TEXTUAL CRITICISM

The full appreciation of the arduous task of reconstructing the New Testament text from thousands of manuscripts containing tens of thousands of variants can be derived, in part, from a study of just how textual scholars proceed. The evidence available for textual criticism is of two kinds: internal and external.

EXTERNAL EVIDENCE

There are three varieties of external evidence.

Chronological. The date of the text type (not necessarily the manuscript) is important. Earlier text types are to be preferred to later ones.

Geographical. A wide distribution of independent witnesses that agree in support of a variant are to be preferred to those having closer proximity or relationship.

Genealogical. Witnesses to variants are to be weighed and not counted. The "weight" of a manuscript is based upon some basic considerations about families and individual manuscripts.

1. *The relative order of families.* Of the four major textual families (see chart), Alexandrian, Caesarean, Western and Byzantine, (1) the Alexandrian is considered to be the most reliable text, although it sometimes shows a "learned" correction.[24] However, (2) readings

---

[23]Even the Koran, which did not originate until the seventh century A.D., has suffered from a large collection of variants that necessitated the Orthmanic revision. In fact, there are still seven ways to read the text (vocalization and punctuation), all based on Orthman's recension, which was made about twenty years after the death of Muhammad. Cf. Arthur Jeffery, *Materials for the History of the Quran Text*, and the more recent work of Richard Bell, *Introduction to the Qur'an*.

[24]The discussion here follows Greenlee, pp. 115 f.

supported by good representatives of two or more text types are to be preferred to single text types. (3) The Byzantine text is generally considered to be the poorest.

2. *Consideration of individual manuscripts.* When the manuscripts within an individual text type are divided in their support of a variant, the true reading is probably (1) the reading of the manuscripts which are generally the most faithful to their own text type, (2) the reading which differs from that of the other text types, (3) the reading which is different from the Byzantine textual family, and/or (4) the reading which is most characteristic of that textual type to which the manuscripts in question belong.

Internal Evidence

There are also two varieties of internal evidence—transcriptional (depending on the habits of the *scribes*), and intrinsic (depending on the characteristics of the *author*).

Transcriptional evidence. This renders four general assertions.

1. *The more difficult reading* (for the scribe) is to be preferred, particularly if it is sensible. The tendency of scribal emendations is to produce a superficially improved reading by combining "the appearance of improvement with the absence of its reality."[25]

2. *The shorter reading* is to be preferred unless it arose from an accidental omission of lines due to similar ends (*parablepsis*), or an intentional deletion of material on grammatical, liturgical or doctrinal grounds.

3. *The more verbally dissonant readings* of parallel passages, whether they involve Old Testament quotations or different accounts of the same events (as in the Gospels), are to be preferred. There was a scribal tendency to harmonize divergent accounts of a given event recorded in Scripture.

4. *The less refined grammatical construction*, expression, word, etc., is preferred, because scribes tended to smooth out the rough grammar and improve the expression of Scripture.

Intrinsic evidence. This depends upon the probability of what the author is more likely to have written, and is determined by considering the following: (1) the style of the author throughout the book (and elsewhere), (2) the immediate context of the passage, (3) the

[25]Westcott and Hort, p. 27.

harmony of a reading with the author's teaching elsewhere (as well as with other canonical writings),[26] and (4) the influence of the author's background, for example, Aramaic background of Jesus' teaching.[27]

As may be well imagined, the consideration of all the internal and external factors involved in the process of textual criticism is not only a technical science but it is also a delicate art. This is especially true when there is conflict in the evidence. A few observations, however, may assist the beginner in getting acquainted with the process of textual criticism. (1) In general, external evidence is more important than internal evidence, because it is more objective than the latter. (2) Nevertheless, decisions must take both lines of evidence into account and carefully evaluate them. In other words,

> If the two are apparently contradictory, a satisfactory solution must be sought. To disregard external evidence and depend too completely upon internal evidence may lead to unduly subjective decisions. At the same time, one must not depend upon external evidence without proper regard to internal considerations, since no manuscript or text-type is perfectly trustworthy.[28]

(3) "Since textual criticism is an art as well as a science, it is understandable that in some cases different scholars will come to different evaluations of the significance of the evidence,"[29] just as they do over other matters where both subjective and objective factors are involved. (4) Gleason L. Archer, Jr., summarizes the factors of external and internal evidence into the following rules or canons, and cautiously suggests that *priority* should be given in the following order should a conflict occur.[30]

1. The older reading is to be preferred.
2. The more difficult reading is to be preferred.
3. The shorter reading is to be preferred.
4. The reading which best explains the variants is to be preferred.
5. The reading with the widest geographical support is to be preferred.

[26]Harmony with other biblical teaching is only a secondary consideration, unless the passage has an ideological contradiction with other biblical teaching instead of a mere verbal difference.
[27]Metzger, *The Text* . . . , p. 210, also adds two other considerations: (1) the priority of the gospel of Mark, and (2) the influence of the Christian community on the formulation and transmission of a given passage.
[28]Greenlee, p. 119.
[29]Metzger, *The Text* . . . , p. 211.
[30]Archer, pp. 51-52.

6. The reading which most conforms to the style and diction of the author is to be preferred.

7. The reading which reflects no doctrinal bias is to be preferred.

THE PRACTICE (PRAXIS) OF TEXTUAL CRITICISM

The most practical way to observe the results of the principles of textual criticism is to compare the differences between the Authorized Version (King James, 1611), which is based on the "Received Text," and the American Standard Version (1901) or the Revised Standard Version (1946, 1952), which are based on the "Critical Text."[31] A survey of several passages will serve to illustrate the procedure of reconstructing the true text when significant variants are involved.

NEW TESTAMENT EXAMPLES

I John 5:7 (AV). This reads, "For there are three that bear record in heaven, the Father, the Word, and the Holy Ghost: and these three are one." The American Standard Version and Revised Standard Version omit the entire verse with no explanation. There is an explanation, however, and it provides an interested scene in the history of textual criticism. There is virtually no textual support for the Authorized Version reading in any Greek manuscript, although there is ample support in the Vulgate. Therefore, when Erasmus was challenged as to why he did not include the reading in his Greek text edition of 1516 and 1519, he hastily replied that if anyone could produce even one Greek manuscript with the reading, he would include it in his next edition. One sixteenth century Greek minuscule (the 1520 manuscript of the Franciscan friar Froy, or Roy) was found, and Erasmus complied with his promise in his 1522 edition. The King James Version followed Erasmus' Greek text, and on the basis of a single testimony from an insignificant and late manuscript all of the weight and authority of some 5,000 Greek manuscripts were disregarded in favor of this text. In fact, the acceptance of this verse as genuine breaks almost every major canon of textual criticism.

Luke 11:2 (AV). This reads, "Our Father which art in heaven, Hallowed be thy name," whereas the American Standard Version relegates this reading to a footnote, and the Revised Standard Version omits it altogether, and reads, "Father, hallowed be thy name."

[31]Those familiar with Hebrew and Greek will of course make reference to *Biblia Hebraica* and *Novum Testamentum Graece*, or *The Greek New Testament*.

A consideration of several of the "canons" listed above is relevant here. In favor of the Revised Standard Version is canon No. 1 (the oldest reading is the best). Codices Aleph and B omit the longer phrase. By the same token canon No. 3 supports the Revised Standard Version, in that it is the shorter reading. Likewise, the longer reading shows a clear harmonistic attempt to bring the passage in line with the parallel passage in Matthew 6:9 (canon No. 4, the reading which best explains the variants). Furthermore, the shorter reading is supported by the chief representatives of the purest textual family (Alexandrian), as well as the leading manuscripts in the Caesarean (f¹ and 700), and the Western family (SYˢ and Tertullian).

John 7:53—8:11 (AV). The story of the woman taken in adultery is put in brackets by the American Standard Version with a note that most ancient authorities omit it. It is also put in a footnote in the Revised Standard Version with a note that other ancient authorities place it there, at the end of John's gospel, or after Luke 21:38. The evidence that this passage is part of John's gospel is decidedly lacking.

1. It is not in the oldest and best Greek manuscripts, including P⁶⁶, א, B, L, N, T, W, X, Δ, Θ, Ψ, 33, 157, 565, 892, 1241, family 1424, etc.[32]

2. Neither Tatian nor the Old Syriac betrays any knowledge of it, nor do the best manuscripts of the Peshitta. Likewise, it is omitted by the Coptic (Sahidic and Bohairic), and several Gothic and Old Latin manuscripts.

3. No Greek writer refers to it until the twelfth century.

4. Its style and interruption do not fit the fourth gospel.

5. The earliest known Greek manuscript to contain it is Bezae (*c.* A.D. 550).

6. Scribes placed it in several other locations: some after John 7:36 (manuscript 225); after John 21:24 (family 1, 1076, 1570, 1582); after John 7:44 (eleventh century revision of Old Georgian Version); or after Luke 21:38 (family 13). Many of the manuscripts which included it marked it with an obelus, indicating their doubts about it.

While it is possible that the passage preserves a true story, it seems

[32]Listed in Metzger, *The Text* . . . , p. 223.

best to conclude with Metzger and the New English Bible, from the standpoint of textual criticism, that it should be included as an appendix to John with a note that it has no fixed place in the ancient witnesses.[33]

Mark 16:9-20 (AV). This is one of the most perplexing of all textual problems.

1. These verses are lacking in many of the oldest and best Greek manuscripts (Aleph, B, Old Latin manuscript k, the Sinaitic Syriac, many Old Armenian manuscripts and a number of Ethiopic manuscripts). Many of the ancient Fathers show no knowledge of it (e.g., Clement, Origen, Eusebius, *et al.*). Jerome admitted that "almost all Greek copies do not have this concluding portion."[34] Among some of the witnesses that have these verses, there is also an asterisk or obelus to indicate it is a spurious addition.

2. There is also another ending which occurs in several uncials (L, Ψ, 099, 0112), a few minuscules (274[mg], 579), and several manuscript copies of ancient versions (k, Syr[h mg], Coptic[pt], Eth[codd]).[35] This passage reads, "But they reported briefly to Peter and those with him all that they had been told. And after this Jesus himself sent out by means of them, from east to west, the sacred and imperishable proclamation of eternal salvation."

3. The familiar long ending (AV) of the Received Text is found in a vast number of uncial manuscripts (C, D, L, W, Θ), most minuscules, most Old Latin manuscripts, the Vulgate, and in some Syriac and Coptic manuscripts.

4. The long ending is expanded in Codex W after verse 14 (see chap. 21).

Which reading is the original ending? Metzger concludes that "none of these four endings commends itself as original,"[36] because of limited textual evidence, the Apocryphal flavor, and the non-Marcan style (e.g., it contains seventeen non-Marcan words). On the other hand, if none of these is genuine, it is difficult to believe with Metzger that Mark 16:8 does not represent the original ending. Defense of the Received Text (vv. 9-20) has been made by John W.

[33]*Ibid.*, p. 224.
[34]*Ibid.*, p. 226.
[35]*Ibid.*
[36]*Ibid.*, p. 227.

Burgon,[37] and more recently by M. van der Valk.[38] It is admittedly difficult to arrive at the conclusion that any of these endings is the original. But, on the basis of the known manuscript evidence, it seems more likely that either Mark ended in verse 8, or the real ending is not extant. Of these two views the former is more compatible with the concept of a complete canon.[39]

Acts 20:28 (AV). This is rendered "feed the church of God, which he [God] hath purchased with his own [God's] blood." The American Standard Version and Revised Standard Version follow the reading, ". . . church of the Lord." However, on the basis of textual rules, the Authorized Version reading is to be preferred.

1. The earliest and best manuscripts (Aleph, B., etc.) render the variant "God" as opposed to P[74], A, D, etc., which read, "Lord."

2. "God" is the more difficult reading, because it raises the question: Does God have blood?

3. Furthermore, "God" is Alexandrian, the purest tradition, as opposed to Western reading for "Lord."

4. In the light of the Arian controversy over the deity of Christ, it is easy to see how "God" could have been toned down to "Lord."[40] It is apparently for the same reason that the committee of the Revised Standard Version chose (wrongly) to consider the *weaker subjective* evidence of more weight than the *external objective* evidence plus *internal* transcriptional factors.

OLD TESTAMENT EXAMPLES

Zechariah 12:10. This illustrates the same point. The Masoretic text (followed by the Authorized Version and American Standard Version) reads, "They shall look upon me [Jehovah speaking] whom they have pierced." The Revised Standard Version follows the Theodotion version (*c.* A.D. 180) in rendering it, "When they look on him whom they have pierced." It should be observed that the Masoretic text, followed by the Authorized Version and American Standard Version, preserves the preferred reading, because:

---

[37]John W. Burgon, *The Last Twelve Verses of the Gospel According to St. Mark.*
[38]M. van der Valk, "Observations on Mark 16:9-20 in Relation to St. Mark's Gospel," *Humanitas,* as cited in Metzger, *The Text . . . ,* p. 229.
[39]Ned B. Stonehouse argues convincingly from internal evidence that Mark intended to end his gospel at v. 8, *The Witness of Matthew and Mark to Christ,* pp. 86-114.
[40]Henry Alford, "Prolegomena," *The Greek Testament,* new ed., Vol. I, pp. 83, n. 1, argues for this position.

1. It is based on the earlier and better manuscripts.

2. It is the more difficult reading.

3. It can explain the other reading, namely, (1) theological prejudice against the deity of Christ, and/or (2) the influence of the New Testament which, when quoting this passage, changes the personal pronoun from the first person (me) to the third person (him) in order to apply it to Christ (cf. John 19:37).

Exodus 1:5. In the Masoretic text this reads that "seventy" descended to Egypt. This has been a perplexing problem because the New Testament (Acts 7:14) and the LXX read "seventy-five souls." This problem has occasioned many ingenious attempts at harmonization, including the counting of five grandsons, alleging that Stephen was wrong (his sermon is not inerrant, but the record of it is). Nevertheless, a much simpler explanation is now possible. A fragment of Exodus from Qumran reads "seventy-five souls." It is possible that the LXX and Dead Sea fragment preserve the true text. This explanation cannot be considered harmonistic, since it still faces the problem of Genesis 46:27, which says the number was "seventy." At least there is now a Hebrew manuscript to support the rendering of Exodus 1:5 as "seventy-five souls."

Deuteronomy 32:8. This provides another interesting exercise in Old Testament criticism. The Masoretic text (followed by the AV and ASV) reads, "The Most High gave to the nations their inheritance. . . . He set the bounds of the peoples according to the number of the children of Israel." The Revised Standard Version followed the LXX in reading, "According to the number of the sons [or angels] of God." A fragment from Qumran now supports this latter reading. Notice:

1. It is the more difficult reading.

2. It is supported now by the earliest manuscript.

3. It is in harmony with the patriarchal description of angels as "sons of God" (cf. Job 1:6; 2:1; 38:7 and possibly even Gen. 6:4).

4. It explains the origin of the other variant. It seems most likely, then, that the Revised Standard Version has preserved the correct rendition of the text.[41]

[41]For a more detailed study of the variants, see chap. 19, and Millar Burrows, *The Dead Sea Scrolls.*

SUMMARY AND CONCLUSION

Textual criticism is the art and science of reconstructing the original text from the multitude of variants contained in the manuscripts. It is significant that the Bible has not only been preserved in the largest number of manuscripts of any book from the ancient world, but that it also contains fewer errors in transmission. Actually, the variant readings which significantly affect the sense of a passage are less than one-half of 1 percent of the New Testament, and none of these affect any basic doctrine of the Christian faith. The textual critic has given a studied judgment on many of these significant variants, so that for all practical purposes the modern critical editions of the Hebrew and Greek texts of the Bible represent, with their footnotes, exactly what the autographs contained—line for line, word for word, and even letter for letter.

27

DEVELOPMENT OF TEXTUAL
CRITICISM

TEXTUAL AND HIGHER CRITICISM DISTINGUISHED

There has been much confusion and controversy over the matter of "higher" and "lower" criticism of the Bible. Much of this misunderstanding is a result of the semantic difficulty involved. "Criticism" in its grammatical sense is merely the exercise of judgment. When criticism is applied to the Bible, it is used in the sense of exercising judgment about the Bible itself. But, there are two basic types of criticism, and two basic attitudes toward each type. The titles ascribed to these types of criticism have nothing whatsoever to do with their importance, as the following discussion illustrates.

HIGHER (HISTORICAL) CRITICISM

When scholarly judgment is applied to the *genuineness* of the biblical text, it is classified as "higher" or "historical" criticism. This judgment is applied to the date of the text, its literary style and structure, its historicity, and its authorship. As a result, higher criticism is not actually an integral part of "General Introduction" to the Bible, but is rather the essence of "Special Introduction." The outcome of higher critical approaches to the Old Testament by those who were heirs to the "destructive theology" of the late eighteenth century has been a kind of "destructive criticism."

The Old Testament. Late dating of the Old Testament documents led some scholars to attribute its supernatural elements to legend or myth. This in turn resulted in a denial of the historicity and genuineness of much of the Old Testament. As a case in point, the "documentary theory" of Julius Wellhausen and his followers, actually an attempt at mediation between Traditionalism and skepticism, was an attempt to date the Old Testament books in a less supernaturalistic manner.[1] Hence, they developed the JEDP theory.

[1]See chap. 8.

This theory was based largely upon the argument that Israel had no writing prior to the monarchy,[2] and that an Elohist (E) Code and a Yahwist (J) Code were based on two oral traditions about God ("E" being the tradition using the name Elohim, and "J" being the Jehovah [Yahweh] tradition). To these were added the Deuteronomic (D) Code (documents ascribed to the time of Josiah), and the so-called Priestly (P) documents (allied to Judaism from the post-exilic period). These views were not palatable to orthodox scholars, and a wave of opposition arose. This opposition was forthcoming only after a considerable period of time, and the scholarly world at large followed Wellhausen, W. Robertson Smith and Samuel R. Driver. When the opposition finally raised its voice against "destructive criticism," it was generally written off as an insignificant minority and ignored. Among the opposition (proponents of "constructive criticism") were such scholars as William Henry Green, A. H. Sayce, Franz Delitzsch, James Orr, Wilhelm Möller, Eduard Naville and Robert Dick Wilson.

The New Testament. Application of similar principles to the New Testament writings appeared in the Tübingen school, following the views of Heinrich Paulus, Wilhelm De Wette and others. These principles were used to challenge the authorship, structure and style, and date of the New Testament books. The "destructive criticism" of Modernism led to the "form criticism"[3] in the Gospels and to a denial of the Pauline authorship of most of the Pauline Epistles, as the "Big Four" (Romans, Galatians, and I and II Corinthians) alone were regarded as *genuinely* Pauline.[4] Toward the close of the nineteenth century, capable orthodox scholars began to challenge the "destructive criticism" of many higher critics. Among these orthodox scholars were George Salmon, Theodor von Zahn and R. H. Lightfoot, and their work in higher criticism must assuredly be considered "constructive criticism." Much of the recent work in the area of higher criticism has revealed itself as rationalistic in theology, while advocating that it is claiming to uphold Christian doctrine. This recent criticism manifests itself most openly when it considers such

---

[2] See chap. 17.

[3] See chap. 9, and pp. 58-61.

[4] A recent study has come to the same conclusion, viz., A. Q. Morton and James McLeman, *Christianity in the Computer Age.* For a critique of the fallacious presuppositions of this new work, see Reinier Schipper's article, "Paul and the Computer," *Christianity Today* (Dec. 4, 1964). Dr. John W. Ellison is reported to have "subjected Morton's own writing to a similar computer analysis and found it indicated multiple authorship." Cf. *Christianity Today* (Feb. 26, 1965), p. 48.

matters as miracles, the virgin birth of Jesus, and the bodily resurrection of Christ.

Lower (Textual) Criticism

When scholarly judgment is applied to the *authenticity* of the biblical text, it is classified as "lower" or "textual" criticism. Lower criticism is applied to the form or text of the Bible in an attempt to restore the original text, the autograph. It is not to be confused with higher criticism. Instead of studying the value of a document (higher criticism), the lower critic studies the form of the words of a document. Many examples of lower criticism may be seen in the history of the transmission of the Bible text: some of these examples were done by staunch supporters of orthodox Christianity, while others were done by sharp opponents.[5] Those who are interested in obtaining the original text by applying certain criteria or standards of quality are textual critics; their work is basically constructive, and their attitude basically positive. Some of these individuals follow the example of B. F. Westcott, Sir Frederic G. Kenyon, Bruce M. Metzger and others. Those who use these criteria in order to undermine the text are faultfinders; their work is basically destructive, and their attitude basically negative.

Since many of the adherents of higher criticism have also spent considerable time and energy in the study of textual criticism, there has been a tendency to classify all textual critics as "modernists," destructive critics, or higher critics. In so doing, some Christians have virtually "thrown the baby out with the bath water." To avoid textual criticism just because certain higher critics have used its method in their work is hardly a justifiable reason, as Sir Frederic Kenyon has so aptly observed: "The question of importance is not whether the criticism is 'higher,' but whether it is sound; and that is a question of evidence and argument, not of *a priori* assumptions or of impeaching the motives of those whose views we find unpalatable or consider to be unsound."[6]

TEXTUAL CRITICISM IN THE ANCIENT PERIOD OF CHURCH HISTORY (to *c.* 325)

From as early as the third century b.c., scholars in Alexandria attempted to restore the texts of the Greek poets and writers of prose.

[5]See discussion in chap. 8.
[6]Sir Frederic G. Kenyon, *Our Bible and the Ancient Manuscripts,* 4th ed., rev., p. 30.

It will be recalled that this center also produced the Septuagint version of the Old Testament at about 280-150 B.C. In addition to these facts, Alexandria was also a center of Christianity during the early centuries of the church. The city retained its position of scholarly leadership until the rise of Islam. As a result, it is understandable that it would be a center of activity during attempts at restoring the biblical text prior to about A.D. 325. Basically, however, there was no real textual criticism of the New Testament books in this period; it was a "period of reduplication" of the manuscripts rather than one of evaluation of them. On the other hand, there was diligent textual work done in Palestine by the rabbis on the Old Testament between A.D. 70-100.

COPIES OF THE AUTOGRAPHS (to c. 150)

During the second half of the first century most of the New Testament books were written. These manuscripts were written under the direction of the Holy Spirit and were inerrant. They were undoubtedly written on papyrus and have all subsequently been lost, since papyrus survives for long periods of time only under exceptional conditions. Nevertheless, the autographs of the New Testament were providentially copied and circulated before they became illegible or lost. These copies were made as early as A.D. 95; if it had not begun very soon after the autographs were written, there would be no Bible today. Just as the autographs were written on papyrus rolls, so the earliest copies were probably written on papyrus rolls. Soon, however, papyrus codices were written, and parchment and vellum were employed still later. Very few, if any, of the early copies are extant today, for basically the same reasons as indicated with regard to the autographs.

But while there were many early copies of the autographs, they are not all of the same quality, for as soon as a manuscript was copied misprints began to creep into the text. Some of the early copies were highly accurate and quite expensive, as they were copied by professional scribes. Manuscript copies made by less capable scribes were less expensive, but they were of a generally poorer quality and wider distribution. Still other copies made in this early period were quite poor in quality, as they were often copied by nonprofessionals, and were often all that an individual or group could afford to have copied.

COPIES OF THE COPIES (*c*. 150-*c*. 325)

After the period of the Apostolic and Subapostolic Fathers, copies were made of the copies of the New Testament autographs. During these years there were widespread local persecutions of Christians, as well as two imperial persecutions (under Decius and Diocletian). During these persecutions Christians were confronted with intense persecution, suffering and even death. In addition, their sacred writings were often confiscated and destroyed. As a result of their widespread destruction, the Scriptures were in danger of being lost to the church. Therefore, Christians often made copies of the manuscripts to take the place of those which had been destroyed. Many of these copies were made hastily, as the scribes were in danger of persecution if apprehended, and quite often they were copied "unprofessionally," or in an amateur fashion, by members of a given church. Thus, the possibility of errors within the copies was multiplied while the number of manuscripts and older copies were systematically destroyed. All of this was going on during the time when the church was progressively collecting, sifting, sorting and recognizing the canonical books of the New Testament.[7]

During this period of persecution of the church on the local level, the church in Alexandria began to do pioneer work in the comparison and publication of the texts (*c*. 200-*c*. 250). This leadership was extended to other areas of the Empire as well, and some basic work in textual criticism was done by the time of persecution under the Emperor Decius (249-51). Work on the Old Testament was done by Origen in Alexandria. His *Hexapla* was never published in its entirety, but it was a masterful attempt at textual criticism of the Old Testament.[8] In addition to his Old Testament work, Origen also wrote many New Testament commentaries in which he functioned as one of the first New Testament critics.[9] Other examples of early textual criticism would also include such works as the *Lucian Recension*, Julius Africanus' work on *Susanna*, and the *Song of Songs* by Theodore of Mopsuestia, who represents the school of theology having its center in Caesarea. The work of these early textual critics notwithstanding, the early church witnessed a period of casual, unsystematic and largely unintentional creation of variants in the text of the New Testament. It also witnessed a conscious, though often

[7]See discussion in chap. 14.
[8]See chap. 22.
[9]The choice of manuscripts at his disposal made his selection of a text guide significant, cf. chap. 25.

elementary, selection and editorial revision of the text materials. It was this period which, according to Kenyon, "may be summarily characterised as the period when the textual problems came into being, which we have to try to solve with the help of the evidence afforded by the later periods."[10]

TEXTUAL CRITICISM IN THE MEDIEVAL PERIOD
(c. 325-c. 1500)

When the church was released from the threat of persecution, after the Edict of Milan (313), the influence was soon felt on the copying of the manuscripts of the Bible. This period was marked by the introduction of parchment and vellum codices, and paper books toward the close of the Middle Ages. During the medieval period, the Greek uncials gave way to minuscules, and printing gave way to cursive writing. Throughout the entire period, critical revisions of the texts of the Bible were relatively rare, except for the efforts of such scholars as Jerome (c. 340-420) and Alcuin of York (735-804). Nevertheless, the period from about 500 to 1000 witnessed scholars who were revising the Old Testament and adding finer points to the Hebrew text. These scholars, the Masoretes, produced the Masoretic text, which is still the authoritative text of the Hebrew Scriptures.[11]

The letter of Constantine to Eusebius, instructing him to make fifty copies of the Christian Scriptures,[12] marked a new direction in the history of textual criticism, the period of standardization of the text. The New Testament began to be carefully and faithfully copied from existing manuscripts. The text of a given area was copied by the copyists in that area. Hence, when Constantine moved the seat of the Empire to the city named after him (Constantinople), and that city became the dominant city in the Greek-speaking world, it was only reasonable that the ecclesiastical text of that imperial city would become the dominant text of the church. This is especially true in light of the emperor's patronage in producing careful copies of the New Testament text. It is undoubtedly true that other great cities of the Empire must have followed this same pattern.

As a result of the precedent established by Constantine, great numbers of carefully copied manuscripts were produced in the Mid-

---

[10]Sir Frederic G. Kenyon, *Handbook to the Criticism of the New Testament*, 2d ed., p. 40.
[11]See chap. 19.
[12]See chap. 14 for the text of this letter to Eusebius, written during the first third of the fourth century.

dle Ages. But, official critical comparison and careful, planned revision of the text were relatively rare in this manifold transmission.
J. Harold Greenlee correctly observes this point as he writes,

> The evidence of the mss. indicates that the processes of stan-
> dardization of the text and consequent displacement of the older
> text-types continued from the fourth century until the eighth, by
> the end of which time the standardized or "Byzantine" text had
> become the accepted form of the text.
>
> Approximately 95 percent of the existing mss. of the N.T. are
> from the eighth and later centuries, and very few of these differ
> appreciably from the Byzantine text. This means that the wit-
> nesses from the pre-Byzantine text of the N.T. consist of a rela-
> tively small percentage of the mss., mostly from the period earlier
> than the eighth century.[13]

Since a standardized text was developed, there was little need for
classification and critical evaluation of the earlier manuscripts of the
text. As a result, the text remained relatively unchanged throughout
the entire period, for the standardization had been the result of a
comparison and mixing of these earlier manuscripts. Again, Greenlee states the situation with insight, as he writes,

> There was apparently some comparison of this text with other
> texts, resulting in something of a mixed type of text. The text
> seems to have been subjected to some editing, with parallel ac-
> counts tending to become harmonized, grammatical irregularities
> corrected, and abrupt transitions modified, producing a generally
> smooth text.[14]

Toward the end of the period a completely standardized text with
an unlimited number of more-or-less identical copies became possible with the introduction of cheap paper and the printing press.
Paper copies of the text had begun to appear in abundance after the
twelfth century, and then in about 1454 Johann Gutenberg introduced movable type into the printing process. Thus, the door was
open for the efforts of more careful textual criticism during the Reformation era.

TEXTUAL CRITICISM IN THE REFORMATION PERIOD
(c. 1500-c. 1648)

In the Reformation era, the Bible text entered into a "period of

---

[13]J. Harold Greenlee, *An Introduction to New Testament Textual Criticism*, p. 62.
[14]*Ibid.*

crystallization" in printed rather than manuscript form. Often attempts were made at revising and editing existing manuscripts in order to publish printed texts of the Bible as accurately as possible. Frequently these Bibles were published in polyglot (multilingual) form, including such titles as the Complutensian Polyglot (1514-17), the Antwerp Polyglot (1569-72), the Paris Polyglot (1629-45), and the London Polyglot (1657-69). During this time, a standard edition of the Masoretic text was published. It was printed under the editorship of Jacob Ben Chayyim, a Hebrew Christian, at about 1525, and was based on manuscripts dating from the fourteenth century. This text was essentially a recension of the Masorete Ben Asher (fl. c. A.D. 920), and it became the basis for all subsequent copies of the Hebrew Bible, whether in manuscript or printed editions. Work on the New Testament text in particular was more varied in this era, as well as being more sweeping in its outreach, as the results of Gutenberg's invention were felt.

CARDINAL FRANCISCO XIMENES DE CISNEROS (1437-1517)

Cardinal Francisco Ximenes de Cisneros of Spain planned the first printed Greek New Testament to come off the press. It was planned in 1502 as a part of the Complutensian Polyglot, consisting of the Hebrew, Aramaic, Greek and Latin texts. It was printed in the university town of Alcalá (*Complutum* in Latin), after which the polyglot was named, and printed in 1514 (Old Testament in 1517). While this was the first printed New Testament, it was not the first to be placed on the market. Pope Leo X did not give his sanction for publication until March, 1520. The Greek manuscripts underlying the Complutensian Polyglot have never been adequately determined, and there is some question about Ximenes' statements in his dedication about the manuscripts used in the polyglot.[15]

DESIDERIUS ERASMUS (1466-1536)

Desiderius Erasmus of Rotterdam, the Dutch scholar and humanist, had the honor of editing the first Greek New Testament actually to be published. As early as 1514, Erasmus had discussed such a work with the printer Johann Froben of Basle. In July of 1515, Erasmus journeyed to Basle looking for Greek manuscripts which would be usable as copy to set up in type along with his own Latin translation. He could only find manuscripts which required editing

[15]See the discussion of this point in Bruce M. Metzger, *The Text of the New Testament,* p. 98, and the references listed therein.

before use, but he proceeded with his task. On October 2, 1515, printing was begun; on March 1, 1516, the first edition was completed. This edition contained numerous errors, including such things as hundreds of typographical and mechanical errors. Some of the problems which Erasmus bypassed in his hasty work have been summarized by Bruce M. Metzger:

> Since Erasmus could not find a manuscript which contained the entire Greek Testament, he utilized several for various parts of the New Testament. For most of the text he relied on two rather inferior manuscripts in the university library at Basle, one of the Gospels and one of the Acts and Epistles, both dating from about the twelfth century. Erasmus compared them with two or three others of the same books and entered occasional corrections for the printer in the margins or between the lines of the Greek script. For the Book of Revelation he had but one manuscript, dating from the twelfth century, which he borrowed from his friend Reuchlin. Unfortunately, this manuscript lacked the final leaf, which had contained the last six verses of the book. For these verses, as well as at numerous passages throughout the book where the Greek text of the Apocalypse and the adjoining Greek commentary with which the manuscript was supplied are so mixed up as to be almost indistinguishable, Erasmus depended upon the Latin Vulgate, translating this into Greek. As would be expected from such a procedure, here and there in Erasmus' self-made Greek text are readings which have never been found in any known Greek manuscript but which are still perpetuated today in printings of the so-called Textus Receptus of the Greek New Testament.[16]

This evidence demonstrates that Erasmus' text, which was later the basis for the so-called Textus Receptus, was not based on early manuscripts, not reliably edited, and consequently not trustworthy.

The reception of Erasmus' edition of the Greek New Testament was quite mixed, but a new edition was necessary by 1519. This second edition was probably the basis of Martin Luther's German translation. One additional manuscript was used in the preparation of this edition. In 1522, Erasmus produced his third edition, in which he reluctantly inserted I John 5:7.[17] In 1527, Erasmus employed many of the readings of the Complutensian Polyglot, which he saw just after publishing his third edition. It was this edition which be-

[16]*Ibid.*, pp. 99-100.
[17]See discussion of this passage in chap. 26.

came the basis for the Textus Receptus. In 1535, a fifth and final edition of Erasmus' text was published. It was still based on the Byzantine text type, contained readings from very late manuscripts, and included the spurious readings of I John 5:7-8 and his translations back into Greek of verses in Revelation.

ROBERT ESTIENNE (STEPHANUS)

The royal printer of Paris, Robert Estienne, published the Greek New Testament in 1546, 1549, 1550 and 1551. The third edition (1550) was the earliest edition to contain a critical apparatus, based on fifteen manuscripts. It was based on the text of Erasmus' fourth and fifth editions, and became the basis of the Textus Receptus. The fourth edition in 1557 stated Estienne's conversion to Protestantism, and demonstrated for the first time the modern verse divisions of the New Testament, which he produced. Estienne's third edition of the New Testament was the dominant text used in England after its 1550 publication.

THEODORE DE BEZE (BEZA) (1519-1605)

Théodore de Bezè was the successor to John Calvin at Geneva. He published nine editions of the New Testament after the death of his famous predecessor (1564), plus a posthumous tenth edition in 1611. The most outstanding edition to come from Beza was published in 1582, in which he included a few of the readings of the Codex Beza (D) and the Codex Claromontanus (D²). The sparse use of these manuscripts may be attributed to the fact that they departed too radically from the Erasmusan and Complutensian texts. Thus, Beza's Greek New Testament editions were in general agreement with the 1550 edition of Robert Estienne, and their influence lies in the fact that they tended to popularize and stereotype the Textus Receptus. The translators of the King James Version made widespread use of Beza's 1588/89 edition.

THE TEXTUS RECEPTUS

While the text of Robert Estienne held sway over England, the Elzevir brothers, Bonaventure and Abraham, produced the most popular editions to appear on the Continent. They were quite enterprising as publishers, and their company in Leiden published seven editions between 1624 and 1787. The 1624 edition was drawn basically from Beza's 1565 edition, and their second edition (1633) is the source of the title given to their text, as their preface reads, *"Textum ergo habes, nunc ab omnibus receptum: in quo nihil immutatum aut corruptum damus."[18]* Thus, the publisher's "blurb" became the catchword (Textus Receptus, "Received Text") to designate the Greek text which they had incorporated from the editions of Stephanus, Beza and Ximenes. Their Greek text was almost identical to that of Stephanus, which lay as the basis of the King James Version because it was regarded as "the only true text" of the New Testament. However, the textual basis was actually very late, from only a handful of manuscripts, and several passages were inserted which had no actual authority supporting them. Only new manuscript discoveries, classification and comparison could remedy this state of affairs.

TEXTUAL CRITICISM IN THE POST-REFORMATION PERIOD (*c.* 1648-Present)

With the close of the Reformation period, the Bible entered into a "period of criticism and revision." This period actually revolves around three shorter periods, each of which is characterized by an important phase of criticism and revision, namely, preparation, progression and purification. It is important to remember that "constructive" rather than "destructive" criticism is in view in this discussion.

The Period of Preparation (*c.* 1648-*c.* 1831)

This period was characterized by the gathering of textual materials and their systematic collection.[19] Thus, when Brian Walton (1600-61) edited the London Polyglot in 1655-57, he included the variant readings of Estienne's 1550 edition. This polyglot contained the New Testament in Greek, Latin, Syriac, Ethiopic, Arabic and Persian (in the Gospels). In its footnotes appeared the variant readings of the recently discovered (1627) Codex Alexandrinus, as well as a critical apparatus prepared by Archbishop Ussher. In 1675 an anonymous edition of the Greek New Testament appeared at Oxford. This work was done by John Fell (1625-86), who first presented evidence from the Gothic and Bohairic versions. In 1707 John Mill (1645-1707) reprinted Estienne's text of 1550, with the addition of some 30,000 variants from nearly 100 manuscripts. This provided

[18]"The reader has the text which is now received by all, in which we give nothing changed or corrupted." Cf. Metzger, p. 106.
[19]The following discussion follows Metzger, pp. 107-24.

all subsequent scholars with a broad basis of established textual evidence. Mill published his epochal work just two weeks before his death.

Richard Bentley (1662-1742) had established himself as an outstanding scholar in the classics before he began to work on the New Testament. In 1720 he issued a prospectus for his work, which he never completed. He did, however, produce a specimen of his proposed text from the last chapter of Revelation. In this manuscript, he forsook the Textus Receptus over forty times. While he did not complete his work, he did challenge other scholars to take up the task.

One of the scholars so challenged was Johann Albrecht Bengel (1687-1752). He was disturbed by the 30,000 variants of Mill's text, and began to study the transmission of the text. He gathered all the available editions, manuscripts, and early translations available to him for study. Having done this, he developed a canon of textual criticism which has been approved by almost all textual critics since his day in one form or another. This canon is that "the difficult reading is to be preferred to the easy," as scribes were more likely to make a reading easier than more difficult.

One of Bentley's collators had been Johann Jakob Wettstein (1693-1754). He showed an early disposition for textual criticism, and was the first to publish an apparatus with the uncials indicated by capital Roman letters and minuscules by Arabic numerals. He also advocated the sound principle that "manuscripts must be evaluated by their weight, not by their number."[20] He published the fruits of forty years' work in 1751-52 at Amsterdam. A reprint of Wettstein's *Prolegomena* was made in 1764 by Johann Salomo Semler (1725-91), known as the "Father of German Rationalism." He followed Bengel's pattern of classifying manuscripts by groups, but carried the process farther. He is also the first to apply the term "recension" to groups of New Testament witnesses, as he indicated three: Alexandrian, Eastern and Western. All later materials were regarded as mixtures of these three recensions.[21]

The individual who actually carried Bengel's and Semler's principles into their fruition was Johann Jakob Griesbach (1745-1812). He classified the New Testament manuscripts into three groups (Alexandrian, Western, Byzantine), and laid the foundations for all

---

[20]*Ibid.*, p. 114, "*codices autem pondere, non numero estimandi sunt.*"
[21]*Ibid.*, p. 115.

subsequent work on the Greek text of the New Testament. He showed great skill in evaluating the evidence of variant readings, and developed fifteen canons of criticism. Shortly after Griesbach published the first edition of his New Testament (1775-77), several other scholars published collations which greatly increased the availability of New Testament textual evidence from the Church Fathers, early versions, and the Greek text.

Christian Friedrich Matthaei (1744-1811) published a valuable critical apparatus in his Greek and Latin New Testament, which otherwise was of little value. He added evidence, which appeared for the first time, from the Slavic version of the New Testament. Frary Karl Alter (1749-1804), a Jesuit scholar in Vienna, added evidence from Slavic manuscripts, from twenty additional Greek manuscripts, and from other manuscripts as well. Andrew Birch (1758-1829) published the results of the textual work done by a group of Danish scholars in four volumes (1788-1801). This work presented readings from the Codex Vaticanus (B), which appeared for the first time in print.

Meanwhile, two Roman Catholic scholars were intense in their work of textual criticism. Johann Leonhard Hug (1765-1846) and his pupil Johannes Martin Augustinus Scholz (1794-1852) developed the theory that a "common edition" (*Koine ekdosis*) appeared after the degeneration of the New Testament text in the third century. Scholz added 616 new manuscripts to the body of materials available, and stressed for the first time the importance of ascertaining the geographical provenance represented by several manuscripts. This last point was elaborated in 1924 by B. H. Streeter in his theory of "local texts." After some time Scholz adopted Bengel's classification of manuscripts, and published a New Testament in 1830-36 which marked a retrogression toward the Textus Receptus, as he followed the Byzantine text rather than the Alexandrian. Only in 1845 did he retract this view in favor of the Alexandrian readings.

THE PERIOD OF PROGRESSION (*c.* 1831-*c.* 1881)

While some progress had been made earlier, it was this period which brought the constructive critics to the fore in their grouping of textual materials. It was this period that witnessed the first complete break with the Textus Receptus, by such outstanding men as Karl Lachmann (1793-1851), who published the first Greek New Testament edition to rest wholly on the application of textual criticism and variant reading evaluation, Lobegott Friedrich Constantin von Tischendorf (1815-74), the man to whom modern textual critics owe most,[22] Samuel Prideaux Tregelles (1813-75), who was chiefly instrumental in leading England away from the Textus Receptus during the mid-nineteenth century, and Henry Alford (1810-71), who is well known for his commentaries as well as his efforts to bring about the "demolition of the unworthy and pedantic reverence for the received text, which stood in the way of all chance of discovering the genuine word of God."[23]

Several other great scholars must be mentioned at this point, as they have played key roles in the development of textual criticism. Caspar René Gregory finished the last edition of Tischendorf's Greek Testament with a prolegomenon (1894). This work "provided the chief magazine of textual materials on which scholars still depend; and his catalogue of manuscripts . . . is, with the continuations of von Dobschütz and Lietzmann, the universally accepted official list."[24] Two Cambridge scholars, Brooke Foss Westcott (1825-1901) and Fenton John Anthony Hort (1828-92), rank with Tischendorf as making outstanding contributions to the study of the New Testament text. In 1881-82 they published *The New Testament in the Original Greek* in two volumes. The text of this work had been made available to the revision committee which produced the English Revised New Testament in 1881. Their views were not original but were based on the work of Lachmann, Tregelles, Griesbach, Tischendorf and others. The use of their text in the English Revised Version and the thoroughness of the explanation of their views in their introduction added to the acceptance of their critical text. However, the Textus Receptus had some scholarly advocates who spared no efforts in arguing against the Westcott and Hort text. Three of these scholars were John W. Burgon (1813-88), who was vehement in his denunciation of the critical text; F. H. A. Scrivener (1813-91), who was milder than Burgon in his criticism; and George Salmon (1819-1904), who decried the lack of weight Westcott and Hort ascribed to purely "Western" readings.

The "genealogical theory" of Westcott and Hort divided the textual materials into four text types: the Syrian, Western, Neutral and

[22]In addition to purchasing manuscripts and producing more critical editions of the New Testament than anyone else, Tischendorf was instrumental in seeking out many valuable manuscripts; cf. chap. 20.

[23]Henry Alford, "Prolegomena," *The Greek Testament*, new ed., I, 76.

[24]Kenyon, *Our Bible* . . . , p. 122.

Alexandrian. The Syrian text type included the Syrian, Antiochian and Byzantine texts. Some of the manuscripts in the Syrian text were A, E, F, G, H, S, V, Z, and most of the minuscules. The Western text of Westcott and Hort had its roots in the Syrian church but was carried farther west. Some of the Western manuscripts included Delta (Δ), Old Latin, Syriac^c, and the Theta (Θ) family so far as it was known. The Neutral text was supposedly of Egyptian origin, and included the codices B and Aleph (א). The fourth text type, the Alexandrian, was made up of a small number of witnesses in Egypt which were not of the Neutral type. This family included C, L, family 33, the Sahidic, and the Bohairic texts. According to Westcott and Hort there was a common ancestor (X) to both the Neutral and Alexandrian families, and it was quite early and pure. The accompanying chart illustrates these family (text type) relationships to each other and to the autographs of the New Testament.

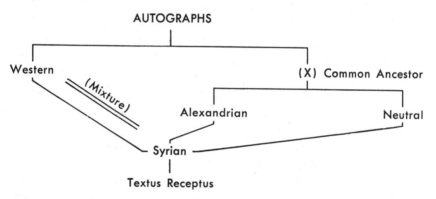

THE PERIOD OF PURIFICATION (*c.* 1881-Present)

This period witnessed the reaction against the Westcott and Hort theory, which had all but dethroned the Textus Receptus, as well as the growth of material for textual criticism. The chief opponents to the Westcott-Hort theory were Burgon and Scrivener, while its proponents included Bernhard Weiss (1827-1918), Alexander Souter and others. After the death of Burgon and Scrivener, the opposition to the critical text had fallen from serious consideration.[25] Their arguments against the critical text may be summarized as follows: (1) the traditional text of the church for fifteen hundred years must be cor-

---

[25]Greenlee, p. 82, cites a recent scholarly work favoring the Textus Receptus, but mentions that it is hardly more than a scholarly curiosity. This work is by Edward F. Hills, *The King James Version Defended.*

rect because of its duration; (2) the traditional text had hundreds of manuscripts in its favor, whereas the critical text had only a few early ones; and (3) the traditional text is actually superior because it is older. Hermann Freiherr von Soden (1852-1914), another opposer (or critic) of Westcott and Hort, began his work on a different basis than Westcott and Hort, but confirmed many of their findings in his work on the New Testament. His work, while boasting of tremendous financial assistance, was quite disappointing, however, and is referred to as "a magnificent failure." The opponents of Westcott and Hort pointed out that the view of these two scholars concerning a Syrian recension was not acceptable, and that the Syrian text possibly represented an earlier and better lost text.

This situation resulted in a reinvestigation of the textual materials and theory of Westcott and Hort. The results of this scholarly and constructive criticism may be seen in the current status of the Westcott-Hort theory. The text types have been reclassified as a result of the work of von Soden and others. The Syrian family has been renamed Byzantine or Antiochian because of the possibility of confusion with the Old Syriac version. There is now a general recognition that more intermixture took place between the Alexandrian and Neutral text types, and both of these texts are actually slightly different variations of the same family. Hence, the Alexandrian designation now includes the Neutral text. In the re-evaluation of the Western text type, scholars have determined that there are actually three subgroups (Codex D, Old Latin, Old Syriac), and that the text is not generally reliable when its readings stand alone. Since the deaths of Westcott, Hort, and von Soden, a new text type has been discovered, the Caesarean. This family lies midway between the Alexandrian and Western texts, or possibly closer to the Western. The most recent collations of these text types are available in Eberhard Nestle's *Novum Testamentum Graece* and in *The Greek New Testament* of the United Bible Societies, edited by K. Aland and others.[26] They generally rank the manuscript evidence in the following descending order of importance: Alexandrian, Caesarean, Western, Byzantine. Since the Textus Receptus follows the Byzantine text basically, it is almost redundant to indicate that its authority is not highly regarded. The accompanying chart indicates the distribution of textual materials among the various text types.[27]

[26]Both books are available through the American Bible Society.
[27]This chart is from Greenlee, pp. 117-18.

SUMMARY AND CONCLUSION

The history of the New Testament text may be divided into several basic periods: (1) the period of reduplication (to *c.* 325), (2) the period of standardization of the text (*c.* 325-*c.* 1500), (3) the period of crystallization (*c.* 1500-*c.* 1648), and (4) the period of criticism and revision (*c.* 1648-present). During the period of criticism and revision, the struggle between the "Received Text" and a "critical text" has been waged, with the latter emerging as the victor. While scarcely a modern scholar seriously defends the superiority of the Received Text, it should be pointed out that there is no substantial difference between it and the critical text. Their differences are merely technical, not doctrinal, for the variants are doctrinally inconsequential. Nevertheless, the "critical" readings are often exegetically helpful to Bible students. Thus, for all practical

	GOSPELS	ACTS	CATHOLIC EPISTLES	PAUL, HEBREWS	REVELATION
Alexandrian	P1 P3 P4 P5 P7 P22 P34 P39 (P66) P75 א B C L Q T (W-Luke 1– John 8:12) Z Δ Ξ Ψ 054 059 060 0162 220 33 164 215 376 579 718 850 892 1241 (1342 Mark) Boh (Sah) Ath Cyr-Alex (Or)	P8 (P50) א A B C Ψ 048 076 096 6 33 81 104 326 1175 Boh (Sah) Ath Cyr-Alex Clem-Alex? (Or)	P20 P23 P72 א A B C P Ψ 048 056 0142 0156 33 81 104 323 326 424c 1175 1739 2298 Boh (Sah) Ath Cyr-Alex Clem-Alex? (Or)	P10 P13 P15 P16 P27 P32 P40 P65 א A B C H I M P Psi 048 081 088 0220 6 33 81 104 326 424c 1175 1739 1908 Boh (Sah)	P18 P2 P47 א A C P 0207 0169 61 59 94 241 254 1006 1175 1611 1841 1852 2040 2053 2344 2351
Caesarean	P37 P45 Θ (W-Mark 5 ff.) N O Σ Φ Fam 1 Fam 13 28 565 700 7071 1604 Geo Arm Pal-Syr Eus Cyr-Jer (Or)	P45? I? I? (Text type not determined in the remainder of the New Testament) Cyr-Jer?			
Western	P25 D (W-Mark 1–5?) 0171 It, especially k e Sin-Syr Cur-Syr Tert Ir Clem-Alex Cyp (Aug)	P38 P41 P48 D E 066 257 440 614 913 1108 1245 1518 1611 1739 2138 2298 It Hark-Syr mg	P38 D E It Hark-Syr mg Ir Tert Cyp Aug Eph	D E F G 88 181 915 917 1836 1898 1912 It	F? It?
Byzantine	A E F G H K M S U V (W-Matt., Luke 8:12 ff.) Y Γ Λ Π Ω Most minuscules Goth Later versions Later Fathers	H L S P Most minuscules Goth Later versions Later Fathers	H K L S 42 398 Most other minuscules Goth Later versions Later Fathers	K L Most other minuscules Goth Later versions Later Fathers	046 82 93 429 469 808 920 2048 Most other minuscules Goth Later versions Later Fathers

From J. Harold Greenlee, *Introduction to New Testament Textual Criticism,* pp. 117-18. Used by permission.

purposes, both texts convey the *content* of the autographs, even though they are separately garnished with their own minor scribal and technical differences.

28

THE BIBLE IN ENGLISH

The chain "from God to us" takes on a new dimension at this point, as the general transmission of the text in the original languages and early translations gives way to the particular transmission of the text in the English language. Before this may be traced, however, it is necessary to sketch the background of the English language and the biblical text therein.

THE BACKGROUND OF THE ENGLISH LANGUAGE

The Languages and Nations of the Indo-European Family

While the Old Testament was originally recorded in languages belonging to the Semitic family, and the New Testament was written in the Indo-European family (with influence from the Semitic), the Bible was transmitted to the Western world via the Indo-European family. And, just as the Semitic family was subdivided into several divisions, so the Indo-European languages, the languages of the Japhetic peoples of Genesis 10, quickly formed two basic divisions, with their subfamilies. These divisions are characterized by their dialectic and geographic similarities.

The Eastern Division (satem). The Eastern division of the Indo-European family is observed in the similarities of pronunciation in the satem dialects. While these similarities may sound strange to the modern ear, they probably stem from a common source. The Indo-European languages which reflect an *s* sibilant in the word for "hundred" are classified as satem dialects. The subdivisions of the satem branch include four basic groups.

1. The Indo-Iranian (Aryan) group includes the Indic and Iranian branches, and was represented by ancient Sanskrit (from *c.* 1500 B.C.) and Persian.

2. The Thraco-Phrygian group was trapped in the mountain valley region of Trans-Caucasia, and has Armenian as its repre-

sentative. Whatever written records may have been extant before Christianity and the Bible were introduced (in the fifth century A.D.), were destroyed, and the earliest records in this language are of the Bible text.

3. The Thraco-Illyrian group settled in the Balkan Peninsula, and is represented by Albanian. The earliest texts in Albanian date from the seventeenth century.

4. The Balto-Slavic group fills in the satem division of the Indo-European languages. This group is distributed over the region around the Baltic Sea and down to the area of Bulgaria and Yugoslavia. It is further divided into the Baltic branch, including Latvian (Lettish), Lithuanian, and Prussian; and the Slavic branch, including Great Russian (Russian), Ukranian, White Russian, Polish, Czechoslovak, Serbian (Wendish), Bulgarian, Serbo-Croatian, and Slovenian. The Baltic branch is very old and some of it is even extinct, for example, Prussian was replaced by German in the seventeenth century. On the other hand, no Slavic language was written prior to the ninth century, but Old Church Slavic has much in common with Old Bulgarian. One of the interesting features of the Slavic languages is their use of the Cyrillic alphabet, which was developed especially for the Slavic languages by the monks Cyril and Methodius in the ninth century.[1]

The Western Division (centum). The Western division of the Indo-European family is also observed in the similarities of pronunciation in the centum dialects. While the *s* sibilant is reflected in the satem words for "hundred," the centum dialects reflect either a *c* or an *h* sibilant sound. There are, of course, other differences, but these are common characteristics. Just as the satem division has four groups, so has the centum.

1. The Hellenic group has been sketched in chapter 24, and is represented by the various dialects of Greek.

2. The Italic group is represented by several unimportant ancient languages (Oscan, Umbrian, Sabine and Volscian), and one important one, namely, Latin. The modern representatives are called Romance languages, as they are derived from Latin, the

[1]See chap. 23 where the background factors to the development of this alphabet are presented.

language of the Roman Empire. These languages include such notables as Spanish, French, Italian, Portuguese, Rhaeto-Romanic and Romanian.

3. The Celtic group is divided into two branches: Continental, represented by Gallic, the language of ancient Gaul, and Insular represented by Cornish, Welsh, Breton, Irish, Gaelic and Manx.

4. The Teutonic (Germanic) group is divided into three branches, and is of special interest to the English-speaking individual.

　　a. East Teutonic is represented by the Gothic language. Its earliest records date from the fourth century A.D., when Ulfilas (311-81) introduced Christianity to the ancient Germans.[2]

　　b. North Teutonic (Scandinavian) is closely related to the Eastern branch. Its earliest records are inscriptions dating from the third century A.D., written in the Rhunic alphabet. Scandinavian is divided into the Old Norse, Icelandic, Swedish, Danish and Norwegian languages.

　　c. West Teutonic is subdivided on the basis of a shift in consonants known as the High German sound shift, which began at about A.D. 600 in south Germany and moved north. The impulse of this consonant shift died out as it reached the lowlands. Thus, the languages to the north are called "Low German," and to the south, "High German."[3] "High German" is represented by Old High German, Bavarian, Middle High German, and German. "Low German" includes Old Saxon, Low German, Dutch, Flemish, Frisian, Anglo-Saxon, Middle English and English.

THE LATE DEVELOPMENT OF THE ENGLISH LANGUAGE

English is a sort of tag end dialect of "Low German," which has developed into a predominant world language. Just how this development took place is not known with certainty, but the most scholarly estimates, based on the available evidence, generally agree with the traditional account as presented by the Venerable Bede (*c.* 673-735) in his *Ecclesiastical History of the Saxons.*[4] But, this account begins with the landing of Henga and Horsa and the Germans in A.D. 449, who had been invited by the Britons to help withstand the

[2]See chap. 23 for a discussion of the spread of Christianity to the Goths.
[3]It should be noted that these designations have nothing to do with cultural levels, as "Low German" is *Plattdeutsch*, from the lowlands, while "High German" is from the highlands (so to speak), and is the textbook variety.
[4]This text was written in Latin, and completed in 731; it was later translated into Old English by Alfred the Great (849-901).

Picts and Scots. The Celts were the earliest Indo-Europeans to settle in Britain, and their invasion occurred prior to about 1000 B.C. Their language was the first one recorded in Britain and their widespread culture was related to that of the Gauls on the Continent. When the Romans expanded their empire under Julius Caesar, they attempted an invasion of Britain (55 B.C.); however, they were not able to conquer it until the reign of the Emperor Claudius (A.D. 43). It was at this time that the Druid religion of the Britons was abolished, and the religion of Rome introduced. Between this time and A.D. 410, the year when the last of the Roman armies were officially withdrawn from the island, the Britons underwent a period of Romanization. Their culture and language were affected, and both went into a state of decline after the Roman withdrawal.

When the Romans withdrew, Saxon pirates and the unconquered Picts and Scots, who had been pushed into the northern part of the island during the Roman period, began to make attacks on the Britons. The Britons had relied on the Romans for protection, but the Romans had now been forced to return to protect their tottering empire. As a result, the Britons had to appeal to their "continental cousins" for assistance. Subsequently, the Jutes and the Saxons answered the call, but for a price. The former were very capable warriors, and their contact with the Romans had not made them less savage in battle. They were fully the match for the Picts and the Scots, but they decided to settle in their newly found home. In 447, the *Anglo-Saxon Chronicle* records the founding of the first settlement of Saxons. They settled in the south (Sussex), and later groups settled in the west (Wessex, 495), east (Essex), and central areas north of the Thames River (Middlesex). The Angles followed in 547 and settled in the area north of the Humber River, establishing an Anglican kingdom. All three of these peoples were of Teutonic stock, as were the Britons. They drove their predecessors out of the heartland, into Cornwall, Wales, France and Brittany. Since the Angles were the predominant group to settle in Britain at this time, the name of the whole country became known as Angle-land (hence, England). Their culture borrowed little or no vocabulary from its predecessors, and this at least implies a drastic and sudden conquest. All of this took place prior to the end of the sixth century A.D., before the missionary expedition under a St. Augustine (not the bishop of Hippo, c. A.D. 400) arrived in England in 597. An account of the landing of this missionary group sent by the first medieval Pope (Gregory I, 590-604) is extant in Bede's ecclesiastical history.

But Christianity was introduced to Britain long before 597. It may have been introduced during the late first century or early second century, and was most assuredly there during the third century. There were enough Christians in Britain to send three bishops to the Council (synod) at Arles in 314. Pelagius (c. 370-450), the archopponent of Augustine of Hippo, and the author of Pelagianism, was from Britain. In fact, St. Patrick (c. 389-c. 461), whose date and place of birth are quite uncertain, was the son of a deacon in the Celtic Christian Church, and a grandson to a priest.

Thus, by the time Gregory's missionary force arrived in England, a variety of Christianity was certainly known to the Angles, Saxons and Jutes. This expedition, however, injected another period of Latinization into the language with its influence on the speech. Nevertheless, the language of the Angles, Saxons and Jutes, in its various dialects, has come to be known as Old English or Old Saxon. Its period of dominance extends from about 450 to about 1100, at which time the influence of the Normans, following their conquest at Hastings in 1066, came to the fore. Prior to the Norman invasion, however, Scandinavians had settled in large numbers in England, as evidenced by the institution of the ancient law they observed and imposed on the northeastern part of England at the Treaty of Wedmore in 878 (called the Danelaw).

The second period, Middle English, extends from about 1100 to about 1500. The language of this period was again influenced by the Scandinavians, as the Normans were actually a transplanted group of sea-roving Northmen from Scandinavia and Denmark. Their exploits during the eighth and ninth centuries made Europe tremble. Some of the great literature in English arose during the Middle English period, including the works of Geoffrey Chaucer (c. 1340-1400). It was during this period that John Wycliffe (c. 1330-84) was associated with the first complete translation of the Bible into English.

The third period, Modern English, had its beginning shortly after Johann Gutenberg's invention of movable type (c. 1454). But, it was not related to that invention. Instead, it was related to a "great vowel shift" which took place within the fifteenth century. This event is strictly an English language phenomenon, and it occurred primarily in the south of England. External forces only exerted an influence on this change but did not cause it, as no satisfactory answer has been discovered to explain its cause.[5] Before 1400, there was no indication of the shift in vowel sounds (Middle English), but after 1500, the sounds had completed their shift and Modern English was born. With this background in view, the history of the translations of the Bible into English should be more meaningful.

THE BEGINNINGS OF THE BIBLE IN OLD AND MIDDLE ENGLISH (PARTIAL VERSIONS)

OLD ENGLISH PARTIAL VERSIONS (c. 450-c. 1100)

At first only pictures, preaching, poems and paraphrases were used to communicate the message of Scripture to the Britons. These early translations of portions of Scripture were based upon the Old Latin and Vulgate versions of the Bible. None of these translations included the entire Bible, but they do illustrate the way that the Bible entered into the English tongue.[6] Several individuals and their translations made contributions in this direction.

Caedmon (d. c. 680). Caedmon was a laborer at the monastery at Whitby in Yorkshire (Northumbria). His story, recorded in Bede's ecclesiastical history (IV. 24), indicates that he was completely ungifted in poetry until one night when he slipped away from a party. He left the party for fear that he would be called upon to sing. That night he dreamed that he was commanded to sing by an angel. When he asked what he should sing, he was told to sing how all things were first created. Hence, he began to sing praises unto God in words he had never before heard:

> Now we must praise the Maker of the Celestial Kingdom, the power and counsel of the Creator, the deeds of the Father of Glory, how he, since he is the Eternal God, was the beginning of all wonders, who first, Omnipotent Guardian of the human kind, made for the sons of men Heaven for their roof, and then the earth.[7]

[5] It is beyond the province of this study to go into this subject, but further information and discussion may be seen in works similar to and including Albert C. Baugh, *A History of the English Language*, 2d ed., pp. 287 ff.; Margaret M. Bryant, *Modern English and Its Heritage*; Otto Jespersen, *Growth and Structure of the English Language*.

[6] It should be pointed out at this juncture that Old English (Anglo-Saxon) is so different from Middle and Modern English as to be for all practical purposes a foreign language. But, the transition was not radical, and thus there is a close relationship between the Bible in Old, Middle, and Modern English.

[7] Caedmon, as cited by H. W. Hoare, *The Evolution of the English Bible*, 2d ed., p. 27.

Other paraphrases and poems sung by Caedmon included the full story of Genesis, the story of Israel's exodus, the incarnation, passion, resurrection and ascension of the Lord, the coming of the Holy Spirit, the apostles' teaching, etc.[8] His work became the basis for other poets, writers and translators, as well as the popularized people's Bible of the day, for his songs were memorized and disseminated throughout the land. F. F. Bruce adds that Caedmon "may very reasonably be credited with the ultimate authorship of a metrical version of the narratives of Genesis, Exodus, and Daniel."[9]

Aldhelm (640-709). Aldhelm made the first straightforward translation of portions of the Bible into English. Aldhelm was the first bishop of Sherborne in Dorset, southern England, and he translated the Psalter into Old English shortly after A.D. 700.

Egbert (fl. *c.* 700). Egbert of Northumbria became the archbishop of York shortly before the death of Bede. He was also the teacher of Alcuin of York, who was later called by Charlemagne to establish a school at the court of Aachen (Aix-la-Chapelle). Egbert was the first to translate the Gospels into English (*c.* 705).

The Venerable Bede (674-735). The Venerable Bede was one of the greatest scholars of all Europe, and undoubtedly the greatest in England. He was situated at Jarrow-on-the-Tyne in Northumbria, where he wrote his ecclesiastical history and other works. He also translated the fourth gospel, probably to supplement the other three which were done by Egbert.[10] He was able to finish translating the gospel of John in the very hour of his death. Tradition relates that he was suffering much in his final days, but that he compelled his scribe to take dictation until the very last verse was translated. Then, he is reported to have chanted a "Gloria" as he passed on to the great Master.

Alfred the Great (849-901). Alfred the Great was king of England (870-901), and a scholar of first rank. It was during his reign that the Danelaw was established under the Treaty of Wedmore (878), with only two basic stipulations: Christian baptism and loyalty to king. Along with his translation of Bede's ecclesiastical history from Latin into Anglo-Saxon, Alfred translated the Ten Commandments, extracts from Exodus 21-23, Acts 15:23-29, and a neg-

[8]Bede, *Ecclesiastical History of the English Nation*, IV, 24.
[9]F. F. Bruce, *The English Bible*: *A History of Translations*, p. 3.
[10]Whether the actual translation by Egbert is extant is a moot question; but the inference is that he only did three of the Gospels, as Bede corresponded with him during the translation process, and it is doubtful that he would retranslate a gospel with other books still untranslated.

ative form of the golden rule. It was largely a result of his efforts that the religious life of Britain, which had nearly become extinct, experienced a revival.

Aldred (fl. *c.* 950). Aldred introduced a new element in the history of the English Bible as he wrote an interlinear "gloss" in the Northumbrian dialect between the lines of a late seventh century Latin copy of the Gospels. The Latin copy was the work of Eadfrid, bishop of Lindisfarne (698-721) and from that individual the interlinear work of Aldred receives its name, the Lindisfarne Gospels. About a generation later, an Irish scribe, Mac Regol, made another Anglo-Saxon gloss known as the Rushworth Gospels.[11]

Aelfric (fl. *c.* 100). Aelfric, abbot of Eynsham, Oxfordshire (Wessex), translated portions of the first seven books of the Old Testament from the Latin, in addition to other Old Testament portions which he cited in his homilies. Before his time, the Wessex Gospels had also been translated into that dialect. The Wessex Gospels constitute the first extant independent Old English version of the Gospels.

MIDDLE ENGLISH PARTIAL VERSIONS (*c.* 1100-*c.* 1400)

A dispute over the throne of Edward the Confessor (1042-66) erupted after his death. It was between Harold, the eldest son and successor to Godwin, the adviser of Edward, and William, the duke of Normandy and second cousin to the late king. At the Battle of Hastings (1066), William defeated Harold, who was slain in the battle, and became king. This ended the Saxon period of domination in Britain, and began the period of domination by the Northmen, rather than a time of their mere influence. The Norman Conquest brought a tremendous Norman-French influence into the language of the people, and after a time the language itself was transformed into Middle English. In this period, several other partial translations of the Scriptures were made, as well as some complete versions toward the end of the period.

Orm, or Ormin (fl. *c.* 1200). Orm was an Augustinian monk who wrote a poetical paraphrase of the Gospels and Acts, which was accompanied by a commentary. This work, called the *Ormulum,* is preserved in only one manuscript, possibly the autograph, of some 20,000 lines. While the vocabulary is purely Teutonic, the cadence

[11]The Rushworth Gospels are almost transcriptions of the Lindisfarne Gospels, except that the gospel of Matthew is in the Mercian dialect rather than the Northumbrian.

and syntax show evidence of Norman influence. He states his own justification of his version as he writes, "If any one wants to know why I have done this deed, I have done it so that all young Christian folk may depend upon the Gospel only, and may follow with all their might its holy teaching, in thought, in word and deed."[12]

William of Shoreham. William of Shoreham has often been credited with producing the first prose translation of a Bible portion into a southern dialect of English (*c.* 1320). Prior to the fourteenth century no complete book of Scripture had been literally translated into English. While the Psalter ascribed to Shoreham was translated in the dialect of the West Midlands, from the Vulgate, William is known to have written his poetry in Kentish. Thus, the actual author of one of the literal translations of a Bible book into English is still unknown.

Richard Rolle. "The Hermit of Hampole," Richard Rolle was responsible for the second of these literal translations into English. He lived near Doncaster, Yorkshire, and made his literal translations into the North English dialect from the Latin Vulgate (*c.* 1320-40). This literal translation of the Psalter was widely circulated, but even more important is the fact that it reflects the history of the English Bible to the time of John Wycliffe, who was born at about 1320.

THE BIBLE IN COMPLETE VERSIONS IN MIDDLE AND EARLY MODERN ENGLISH

While there were no complete Bibles in the English language prior to the fourteenth century, there were several indications that such an enterprise would be forthcoming. Among these indications were the attempts at translating the Psalter literally, the wide circulation of these early translations, the fact that the language of the rulers and the ruled was rapidly becoming fused, the recently completed Crusades, the rebirth of learning, and, perhaps the most important, the conflict between the leading princes of the church, which resulted in the "Babylonian Captivity" (1309-77). During this period, the papal court was moved from Rome to Avignon and back to Rome.

JOHN WYCLIFFE (*c.* 1320-84)

"The Morning Star of the Reformation," John Wycliffe lived contemporaneously with the "Babylonian Captivity," Geoffrey Chaucer, and John of Gaunt. In his recoil from the spiritual apathy and moral

[12]As cited in Hoare, p. 40, with the note that the author (Hoare) has rendered "his words in modern English."

degeneracy of the clergy, Wycliffe was thrust into the limelight as an opponent to the Papacy.

> The readiest key to Wycliffe's career is to be found in the conviction,—a conviction which grew deeper as life went on,—that the Papal claims are incompatible with what he felt to be the moral truth of things, incompatible with his instinct of patriotism, and finally, with the paramount authority of the inspired Book which was his spiritual Great Charter.[13]

He seems to have become one of the king's chaplains about 1366, and became a doctor of theology in 1372, before being sent to France in 1374 to negotiate peace and meet with papal authorities in the matter of filling ecclesiastical appointments in England. Upon his return to England he began to speak as a religious reformer and issued nineteen articles in 1377 which resulted in the issuance of five bulls against him. In 1382 he denied the doctrine of transsubstantiation and was relieved of his teaching duties at Oxford, but he was permitted to retire to his parsonage at Lutterworth, where he died on December 31, 1384, in communion with the church.

Wycliffe cast aside his dry scholastic Latin to appeal to the English people at large in their common language. This appeal was primarily through the Lollards, an order of itinerant preachers, "poor priests," who went throughout the countryside preaching, reading and teaching the English Bible.

Toward the close of the fourteenth century the great Wycliffite translations of the Bible were made. The New Testament (1380) and Old Testament (1388) translations associated with him formed a new epoch in the history of the Bible in England. They were translated from contemporary manuscripts of the Latin Vulgate, with the probability that the translator(s) followed the principles of translation set forth in *The English Hexapla*, which makes the following observation:

> In translating from the Vulgate, Wycliffe has most faithfully adhered to that version; he seems to have adopted Hampole's principle: "In this work y seke no straunge englishe, bot esieste and communeste, and siche that is moost luche to the latyne, so that thei that knoweth not the latyne by the englishe may come to many latyne words."[14]

---

[13]Hoarse, p. 71. For further study see William E. Nix, "Theological Presuppositions and Sixteenth Century English Bible Translations," *Bibliotheca Sacra*, Vol. CXXIV, Nos. 493-94 (Jan.-Mar., Apr.-June, 1967).
[14]*The English Hexapla in Parallel Columns*, p. 8, col. 2.

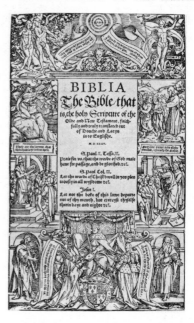

25. *A page from the Wycliffe Bible (British Museum)*

26. *Title page of the Coverdale translation, the first printed English Bible (British Museum)*

He adhered to this principle to such an extent that "the earlier Wycliffite version is an extremely literal rendering of the Latin original. Latin constructions and Latin word-order are preserved even where they conflict with English idiom."[15] Although this Wycliffite version is attributed to John Wycliffe, it must be noted that the work was completed after his death by Nicholas of Hereford. The translation was based on poor Latin manuscripts, and was circulated by the Lollards, who were the followers of Wycliffe and the anticlerical party in the church.

John Purvey (*c.* 1354-1428)

John Purvey, who had served as Wycliffe's secretary, is credited with a revision of the earlier Wycliffite translation at about 1395. This work replaced many of the Latinate constructions by the native English idiom, as well as removing the prefaces of Jerome in favor of an extensive prologue. The result of this revision was a weakening of papal influence over the English people, as this revision tended to

[15]Bruce, p. 15.

drift away from the liturgical Latin of the church. This work, known as the Later Wycliffite version, was published prior to the invention of Johann Gutenberg, which caused a dampening effect on the spread of these particular vernacular versions. Nevertheless, the first complete English Bible was published, revised, and in circulation prior to the work of John Hus (c. 1369-1415) in Bohemia. It was the close identity with the work of Hus which resulted in the exhumation of Wycliffe's body; it was burned and the ashes were scattered on the River Swift in 1428, still before Gutenberg's invention.

WILLIAM TYNDALE (c. 1492-1536)

William Tyndale came onto the English scene at one of the most opportune moments in history. In the wake of the Renaissance, he brought with him one of the major contributions to the transmission of the English Bible. This contribution was the first printed edition of any part of the English Bible, although not the first complete Bible printed in the English language. Coverdale had that honor in 1535.

The transformation of England, and all Europe for that matter, followed the Renaissance and the features accompanying it: the rise of nationalism, the spirit of exploration and discovery, and the literary revival. The resurgence of the classics followed the fall of Constantinople in 1453; then, Johann Gutenberg (1396-1468) invented movable type for the printing press, the Mazarin Bible was published in 1456, and cheap paper was introduced into Europe. In 1458 Greek began to be studied publicly at the University of Paris, the first Greek grammar appeared in 1476, and the first Greek lexicon was published in 1492. The first Hebrew Bible was published in 1488, the first Hebrew grammar in 1503, and a Hebrew lexicon followed in 1506. Over eighty editions of the Latin Bible appeared in Europe before 1500, only a generation after the new printing method was introduced into England by William Caxton (1476). The situation in Europe has been aptly stated by Basel Hall, as he writes,

> There was a *preparatio evangelico* in the first quarter of the sixteenth century, for it was then, and not before, that there appeared in combination the achievements of the humanist scholar-printers; the fruits of intensive study in grammar and syntax of all three languages; and the energy provided by the economic development and regional patriotism of the cities where *bonae*

litterae flourished—Basle, Wittenberg, Zurich, Paris, Strassburg, Geneva.[16]

But, an English printed version of the Bible was yet to come. The galling knowledge that vernacular versions were circulating, sometimes with the consent of the church, in many European countries merely stiffened the determination of Christians in England for an English Bible. A scholarly man was needed for the enterprise of fashioning the Hebrew and Greek originals into a fitting English idiom, as no mere rendering of the Vulgate would suffice.

William Tyndale was the man who could do what was wanted, for he was "a man of sufficient scholarship to work from Hebrew and Greek, with genius to fashion a fitting English idiom and faith and courage to persist whatever it cost him."[17] Before Tyndale finished his revision work, he became involved in a dispute where a man charged that Englishmen were "better without God's law than without the Pope's." He replied with his now famous statement, "I defy the Pope and all his laws; if God spares my life, ere many years I will cause a boy that driveth the plough shall know more of the Scriptures than thou dost."

After his unsuccessful attempts to do his translation in England, he sailed for the Continent in 1524. Further difficulties ensued, and he finally had his New Testament printed in Cologne toward the end of February, 1526. This was the first such achievement to be accomplished, and it was followed by a translation of the Pentateuch, at Marburg (1530), and Jonah, from Antwerp (1531). Tyndale worked under constant threat of being exposed. Lutheran and Wycliffite influence was clearly observable in his work, and his version had to be smuggled into England. Once it was there it was greeted with sharp opposition by Cuthbert Tunstall, bishop of London, who purchased copies of it to be burned at St. Paul's Cross. Sir Thomas More issued a *Dialogue* in which he attacked Tyndale's version as belonging to the same "pestilent sect" as Martin Luther's translation. Nevertheless, the first English version of the Pentateuch, Jonah and the New Testament was published and began circulating in England.

In 1534, Tyndale published a revision of Genesis, and began to revise his New Testament. It was during this time that the Catholic lord chancellor Sir Thomas More was removed from office, sent to

---

[16]S. L. Greenslade (ed.), *The Cambridge History of the Bible*, II, 61.
[17]*Ibid.*, p. 141.

the Tower of London, and executed in 1535. More, who was succeeded by Thomas Cromwell as lord chancellor, successfully
spearheaded Henry VIII's Reformation movement between 1534
and 1540, when he too fell from royal favor. Shortly after the completion of his revision, Tyndale was kidnapped, conveyed out of
Antwerp, imprisoned in the fortress at Vilvorde in Flanders where
he continued his translation of the Old Testament (Proverbs, Prophets, etc.) before he was found guilty of heresy in August, 1536. He
was then "degraded from his priestly office, handed over to the
secular power for execution, which was carried out on October 6 . . .
crying thus at the stake with the fervent zeal and a loud voice:
'Lord, open the King of England's eyes.' "[18]

Tyndale's version of the New Testament provided the basis for
all the successive revisions between his day and ours. The Authorized Version is practically a fifth revision of Tyndale's revision; and
where it departs from his, the revision committee of 1881, 1885 and
1901 return to it with regularity.

MILES COVERDALE (1488-1569)

Paralleling the death prayer of Tyndale, much was happening to
bring an answer to his request, including more versions "by the Protestants, fresh proposals from the conservatives, royal proclamations,
and the publication of the first complete English Bible."[19] The key
individual in the publication of this first complete English Bible in
printed form was Miles Coverdale, Tyndale's assistant and proof-
reader at Antwerp in 1534. While he did not translate directly from
the Hebrew and Greek, he was

> . . . lowly and faithfully following his interpreters, five in number,
> according to the *Dedication to the King*. They were the Vulgate,
> Pagnini's Latin version of 1528 (very literal in rendering the Old
> Testament), Luther's German, the Zurich Bible in 1531 and 1534
> editions, and Tyndale, or, if Tyndale was not counted; Erasmus's
> Latin version. . . .[20]

His translation was basically Tyndale's version revised in the light of
the German versions, and not noticeably improved thereby.[21] He
introduced chapter summaries, separated the Apocrypha from the

---

[18]Bruce, p. 52.
[19]Greenslade, p. 147.
[20]*Ibid.*, p. 148.
[21]Bruce, p. 52.

other Old Testament books (a precedent generally followed by English Protestant Bibles ever since), and introduced some new expressions into the text. Although the Coverdale Bible, first published in 1535, was reprinted twice in 1537, once in 1550, and once again in 1553, the true successor to the first edition was the Great Bible of 1539. This may be due to the fact that Anne Boleyn favored Coverdale's Bible, and her execution in 1536 probably brought disfavor upon his work.

THOMAS MATTHEW

Thomas Matthew was the pen name of John Rogers (c. 1500-55), the first martyr of the Marian Persecution. He too had been an assistant to Tyndale, and merely combined the Tyndale and Coverdale Old Testaments with the 1535 revision of Tyndale's New Testament to make another version. He would not associate his name with the work which was done by others, but he used his pen name and added copious notes and references to his edition. He borrowed heavily from the French versions of Lefèvre (1534) and Olivétan (1535), and secured the consent of the crown for his version.

Thus, within one year of the death of Tyndale at Vilvorde, two of his assistants had secured separate licenses for the publication of their printed English Bibles. With these two licensed Bibles, the widespread circulation of the Scriptures in English was inevitable. But Coverdale's Bible was not based on the original languages, thus alienating the scholars in the church, and Matthew's Bible offended the conservatives in the church because of its notes and its origin. Hence, a new revision was necessary.

RICHARD TAVERNER (1505-75)

Richard Taverner, a layman who knew his Greek quite well, used his talent to revise Matthew's Bible in 1539. He improved the translation, especially in more accurately rendering the Greek article. But, this revision was soon followed by another revision of Matthew's Bible, known as the Great Bible, under the leadership of Miles Coverdale and with the approval of Thomas Cranmer (1489-1556), the first Protestant archbishop of Canterbury, and Thomas Cromwell (c. 1485-1540), Protestant Lord Chancellor under Henry VIII. The Great Bible soon eclipsed Taverner's work, and the latter has had little influence on subsequent English Bible translations.

THE GREAT BIBLE (1539)

The Great Bible was done under the direction of Coverdale, with the approval of Cranmer and Cromwell. It received its name because of its size, and was offered as a means of easing the tense situation stemming from John Rogers' work; which brought about the fact that "Royal injunctions of November 1538 forbade printing or importation of English Bibles with notes or prologues unless authorized by the king."[22] The Great Bible was authorized for use in the churches in 1538, but it was not able to solve the problem either, as it was actually a revision of Rogers' revision of Tyndale's Bible, so far as Tyndale's version went. Not only was the Great Bible not a version, nor a revision of a version, but it had the Apocryphal books removed from the remainder of the Old Testament and had the title Hagiographa (holy writings) attached to them, and the bishops of the church were still predominantly Roman Catholic. Thus, when the second edition of the Great Bible appeared (1540), it had a preface by Cranmer (hence, Cranmer's Bible) which was included in all subsequent editions of the Great Bible. One interesting feature of this preface is the note at the bottom of the page which reads, "This is the Byble apoynted to the use of the churches." Five other editions of this Bible followed in 1540 and 1541, and even the edicts of Henry VIII in 1543, which forbade unlicensed persons to read the Bible aloud in the churches, and 1546, which forbade anyone of any "estate, condition, or degree . . . to receive, have, take, or keep, Tyndale's or Coverdale's New Testament,"[23] were not sufficient to keep the Great Bible from maintaining its prominent position in the churches. Thus, when Henry VIII died on January 28, 1547, the Great Bible was still appointed to be read in the Church of England. Edward VI ascended to the throne and the Great Bible was reprinted twice, in 1549 and 1553. It was this Bible which was the authoritative text of *The Booke of the Common Prayer and Administration of the Sacraments,* published in 1549 and 1552. The prestige of the Great Bible was able to withstand the onslaughts of the brief but violent reign of Mary Tudor (1553-58), as the order of 1538 was not revoked.

THE GENEVA BIBLE (1557, 1560)

The Geneva Bible was produced during the reign of Mary Tudor.

[22]Greenslade, p. 151, n. 1, makes reference to Alfred W. Pollard, *Records of the English Bible.*
[23]Bruce, p. 79.

When persecution in England resulted in the death of such men as John Rogers and Thomas Cranmer, others fled to the Continent, including Miles Coverdale. That faith is strengthened in persecution is among the commonest lessons of history, yet these lessons are rarely learned. Thus, while England was offering persecution, Geneva was offering refuge, and there John Knox was leading a group of Protestant exiles in the preparation of an English version of the Bible to meet their religious needs. In 1557 they produced an edition of the New Testament, which was merely a stopgap measure. It is interesting to note:

> The New Testament of 1557 was the work principally of William Whittingham, later Dean of Durham, who took as his basic text not the Great Bible but Tyndale, perhaps in Jugge's edition of 1552, and revised it "by the most approved Greek examples and conference of translations in other tongues."[24]

In addition, the Geneva Bible introduced italicized words into the text where English idiom required additional words; chapters were divided into verses; and the latest textual evidence was utilized, including the *editio regia* of Stephanus (Paris, 1550) with its collection of variants, and Beza's Latin version of 1556. The Old Testament and a revised translation of the New Testament were completed by 1560, and the Geneva Bible began its long and eventful history. It went through at least 140 editions prior to 1644, and retained its popularity against the Bishops' Bible (1568) and the first generation of the Authorized Version (1611). Although the notes were too Calvinistic for Elizabeth and James I, they were much milder than those of Tyndale. The Puritans in England used this Bible extensively, and its influence permeated the pages of Shakespeare as well as the households of English-speaking Protestants. Even the address from "The Translators to the Reader," which is prefaced to the Authorized Version of 1611, took its quotations of Scripture from the Geneva Bible.[25] Still another innovation made by the translators of the Geneva Bible exhibited itself in that "the distinguishing method of the Geneva Committee had been a system of careful and methodical collaboration, as contrasted with the isolated labours of the pioneers of translation."[26]

[24]Greenslade, p. 156.
[25]Bruce, p. 92.
[26]Hoare, p. 227.

THE BISHOPS' BIBLE (1568)

The Bishops' Bible was a revision of the Great Bible, as the immediate success of the Geneva Bible among the common people and the Puritans made it impossible for the Anglican Church leaders to continue using the Great Bible in the churches. Their revision was called the Bishops' Bible, because most of the translators were bishops, and their work was "a compromise—a dignified and 'safe' version for public reading, a sign that the bishops were not unmindful of their responsibilities, in scholarship an improvement upon the Great Bible, less radical than Geneva but willing to learn from it."[27] The scholars involved were better equipped in Hebrew and Greek, and many of their innovations were carried over into the Rheims and the Authorized versions.

Had the Bishops' Bible appeared prior to 1557, it would have been the best translation to date. However, even with the strong support given it by the Convocation of Canterbury in 1571, it could not overcome its insurmountable disadvantage of being introduced after there had already been a better translation in circulation, the Geneva Bible. And although the "Bishops' Bible was that generally found in churches from 1568 to 1611, the Geneva Bible was still the home Bible, and no copies of the Bishops' Bible were printed after 1602 [sic]."[28] While the Bishops' Bible was not a work of high merit in itself, it was the official basis for the revision of 1611.

SUMMARY AND CONCLUSION

Although the English language is only a sort of tag end dialect of Low German, it has nevertheless become the most significant vehicle of the biblical text in modern times. From Caedmon's paraphrases (late seventh century) to the first complete book of the Bible (Psalms) in Shoreham's day (fourteenth century), then to the pioneer works of Wycliffe, Tyndale, and the publication of the first complete English Bible under the direction of Miles Coverdale (1535), and on to the Great Bible and the Geneva Bible which soon followed, there proceeded a continual parade of translations which linked their Latin predecessors to the monumental King James Version and its English successors. In a real sense, then, the long chain of transmission "from God" has been brought "to us" in the English-speaking world by the events recorded in this chapter.

[27]Greenslade, p. 160.
[28]Margaret T. Hillis, A Ready-Reference History of the English Bible, rev. ed., p. 19. The date here should be 1606 instead of 1602, cf. Hoare, Bruce, Greenslade, Nix, et al.

29

MODERN ENGLISH VERSIONS AND TRANSLATIONS OF SCRIPTURE

THE ENGLISH BIBLE FOR ROMAN CATHOLICS

While the Protestants were busy making vernacular translations of the Bible for use in England, their Roman Catholic counterparts were beginning to sense a similar desire. After the death of Mary Tudor (1558), Elizabeth I (1558-1603) ascended to the throne, and the Roman Catholic exiles of her reign undertook a task similar to that of the Protestant exiles at Geneva during her predecessor's reign.

THE RHEIMS-DOUAY (RHEMES-DOUAY) VERSION OF THE BIBLE

During the first decade of Elizabeth's reign, a group of English Roman Catholics moved to and settled in Spanish Flanders, easily accessible to England and under Roman Catholic rulers. While there they founded the English College at Douay (1568), for the training of priests and the maintenance of their Catholic faith. William Allen (1532-94), Oxford canon under Mary Stuart, led in the founding of the college and its move to Rheims in France (1578) when political troubles arose. At Rheims the English College came under the direction of another Oxford scholar, Richard Bristow (1538-81), who had gone to Douay in 1569. Meanwhile, Allen was called to Rome, where he founded another English College and was later made a cardinal. In 1593 the college at Rheims returned to Douay.

In a letter written to a professor at the college in Douay in 1578, Allen expressed the feeling of the Roman hierarchy toward an English translation of the Vulgate, as he wrote,

> Catholics educated in the academies and schools have hardly any knowledge of the Scriptures except in Latin. When they are preaching to the unlearned and are obliged on the spur of the moment to translate some passage into the vernacular, they often

do it inaccurately and with unpleasant hesitation because either there is no vernacular version of the words, or it does not occur to them at the moment. Our adversaries, however, have at their finger tips from some heretical version all those passages of Scripture which seem to make for them, and by a certain deceptive adaptation and alteration of the second words produce the effect of appearing to say nothing but what comes from the Bible. This evil might be remedied if we too had some Catholic version of the Bible, for all the English versions are most corrupt. . . . If his Holiness shall judge it expedient, we ourselves will endeavor to have the Bible faithfully, purely and genuinely translated according to the edition approved by the Church, for we already have men most fitted for the work.[1]

Only four years later the translation which he had projected was completed by Gregory Martin (d. 1582). This Oxford scholar received his M.A. in 1564. He then renounced his Protestantism and went to Douay to study, becoming lecturer in Hebrew and Holy Scripture in 1570. In 1578 he first began to translate the Old Testament, usually doing about two chapters a day over three and a half years. Just before his death the New Testament was published, with many notes. These notes were the work of Bristow and Allen. Another Protestant-turned-Catholic who had a part in the publication of the Rheims New Testament (1582) was William Reynolds, but his role in the project is uncertain.

While the Rheims translation of the New Testament was designed to act as an antidote to the existing Protestant versions in English, it had some serious defects. In the first place, it was a poor rendition of the English language. It was based on the Latin Vulgate, and as such was actually a translation of a translation. Again, the principles of translation explained in the preface indicate that the translators guarded themselves "against the idea that the Scriptures should always be in our mother tongue, or that they ought, or were ordained by God, to be read indifferently by all."[2] In addition, the Rheims New Testament was vitiated by its self-imposed limitation of being avowedly polemic in nature, a purpose often clearly stated in its copious notes. The New Testament was republished in 1600, but this time from Douay, as the political climate reversed itself and the

[1]*Letters and Memorials of Cardinal Allen*, with introduction by T. F. Knox, pp. 64 f., as cited by Geddes MacGregor, *The Bible in the Making*, pp. 248-49.
[2]William E. Nix, "Theological Presuppositions and Sixteenth Century English Bible Translations," *Bibliotheca Sacra*, Vol. CXXIV, No. 494 (Apr.-June, 1967), pp. 120-21. Also see Clyde L. Manschreck, *A History of Christianity*, II, 131(a)-139(b).

English College moved back to its place of origin in 1593. The new edition was published under Thomas Worthington, another Oxford scholar, alumnus of the college at Douay, and recipient of a D.D. from the Jesuit University of Trier in 1588. Worthington became the third president of the college at Douay in 1599, and was himself active in mission work.

Meanwhile the Old Testament, which had actually been translated before the New, was delayed in its publication. The reason for this delay is actually twofold: primarily, there was a lack of funds available to finance the project; then there was the contributory fact that between 1582 and 1609 there were several new editions of the Vulgate text which needed to be taken into consideration by the translators and revisers. At length the Douay Old Testament was published (1609/10), but it was greeted with criticisms similar to those made of the two editions of the New Testament. It followed the Latin Vulgate exclusively, introduced excessive Latinisms into the text (especially the Psalms), followed the principle of guarding against the idea of translating the Scriptures into the vernacular, and added polemical notes to the translation (although not so extensive as in the New Testament). Since the Old Latin and Vulgate versions generally contained the Old Testament Apocrypha, the Douay translation followed the example and placed them within the Old Testament.[3] Actually there were only seven full books added to the other thirty-nine: Judith, Tobit, Wisdom of Solomon, Ecclesiasticus, Baruch (with the Epistle of Jeremiah attached), I Maccabees, and II Maccabees. In addition to these full books, four parts of books were added to the English translation: added to Daniel were the portions about Bel and the Dragon, the Song of the Three Hebrew Children, and Susanna, while Esther was expanded.

The Old Testament translation was begun by Martin and probably completed by Allen and Bristow, although little exact evidence is available to determine this matter with certainty, and the notes were apparently furnished by Worthington. "The version had been based on the unofficial Louvain Vulgate (1547, ed. Henten), but was 'conformed to the most perfect Latin edition', the Sixtine-Clementine of 1592."[4] The annotations were basically designed to bring the interpretation of the text into harmony with the decrees of the Council

---

[3]See discussion of the Old Latin and Vulgate versions in chap. 24; see chap. 13 for the treatment of the Old Testament Apocrypha.
[4]Stanley L. Greenslade (ed.), *The Cambridge History of the Bible*, II, 163.

of Trent (1546-63). The translation was uniform throughout including the over-literal Latinizations.

While the New Testament was reprinted in 1600, 1621 and 1633, it was not until 1635 that the second edition of the Old Testament was published. The New Testament had been in circulation long enough to have an important influence on the translators of the Authorized Version, as may be seen in the reentry of several ecclesiastical terms, the increased number of Latinisms, etc. The Authorized Version of the Old Testament, however, was probably set for printing by the time the Douay Old Testament was published, and the lack of its influence on the Authorized Version is manifest. Nonetheless, with a Protestant queen on the throne, and then a Protestant king, the Rheims-Douay Bible had little possibility of succeeding the Protestant Bibles in the religious life in England. The paucity of reprint editions has led some to observe, in contrast to the Protestants, that the Catholics should have "no fear that the few available copies would be found in the hand of every husbandman."[5]

The Rheims-Douay-Challoner Version

Although several reissues of the Rheims-Douay appeared after 1635, it was not until 1749/50 that Richard Challoner, bishop of London, published the second revised edition. This publication was little short of a new translation. In the meantime, a New Testament translation based on the Latin Vulgate appeared in Dublin (1718) as the work of Cornelius Nary. In 1730, Robert Whitham, president of the college at Douay, published a revision of the Rheims New Testament. In 1738, a fifth edition of the Rheims New Testament was published, with some revisions generally attributed to Challoner, who had been associated with Whitman at Douay.[6] Challoner published his revision of the Douay Old Testament in 1750 and 1763, and his revised Rheims New Testament in 1749, 1750, 1752, 1763 and 1772. Since that time, further revisions of the Rheims-Douay Bible have been made, but they are practically all based on the Challoner revision of 1749/50.[7] Therefore, the verdict of Father Hugh Pope, in his *English Versions of the Bible* (1952) still stands, namely, "English-speaking Catholics the world over owe Dr. Challoner an immense debt of gratitude, for he provided them for the first time with a port-

[5]*Ibid.*
[6]While the 1738 Rheims New Testament is called the "fifth edition," it should be noted that the fourth edition was the 1633 issue, not the 1730 edition of Whitman.
[7]For a fuller development of this topic see MacGregor, pp. 256-62.

able, cheap, and readable version which in spite of a few inevitable defects has stood the test of two hundred years of use."[8]

THE CONFRATERNITY OF CHRISTIAN DOCTRINE VERSION

While the Confraternity edition of the New Testament was not the first English translation of the Catholic Bible in the United States, it is the official one. The first Catholic Bible published in the United States (1790) was a large quarto edition of the Douay Old Testament, with admixtures of several of the Challoner revisions and the third Rheims-Challoner revision of 1752. This Bible was actually "the first *quarto* Bible of any kind *in English* to be published in the United States."[9] Francis Patrick Kenrick then made a new revision of the Rheims-Douay-Challoner Bible in six volumes (1849-60), although he claimed that it was "translated from the Latin Vulgate, diligently compared with the Hebrew and Greek."[10] After this time, other editions appeared on both sides of the Atlantic.

In 1936 a new revision of the Rheims-Challoner New Testament was begun under the auspices of the Episcopal Committee of the Confraternity of Christian Doctrine. A committee of the twenty-eight scholars of the Catholic Biblical Association began the revision under the direction of Edward P. Arbez. While the Vulgate text was still used as its basis, the new translation took advantage of the most recent developments in biblical scholarship. It removed many of the archaic expressions of the Rheims-Challoner version, incorporated paragraphs, used American spelling, and removed many of the prolific notes of its forebears. The Confraternity New Testament was published by the St. Anthony Guild Press in 1941, and became widely used by English-speaking Catholics around the world as a by-product of the Second World War (1939-45).

In 1943 Pope Pius published the papal encyclical *Divino Afflante Spiritu,* in which he indicated that translations of the Bible could be based on the original Greek and Hebrew texts rather than only on the Latin Vulgate. After wartime restrictions were lifted, the Confraternity began to publish a new version of the Old Testament based on the original texts. This version is nearing completion, and consists of four volumes: (1) Genesis to Ruth (1952); (2) Samuel to Maccabees (1967); (3) Job to Sirach (Ecclesiasticus) (1955); (4) Isaia to Malachia (1961).[11] As soon as the Old Testament version

[8]Cf. citation in Greenslade, p. 357.
[9]MacGregor, p. 258.
[10]*Ibid.,* p. 269.
[11]Margaret T. Hills, *A Ready-Reference History of the English Bible,* rev. ed., p. 29.

is completed, the Episcopal Committee, now working under the chairmanship of Louis F. Hartman, plans to make a new translation of the New Testament based on the original Greek.

The Ronald A. Knox Version

Just as the Confraternity Version is the official American edition of the Roman Catholic Bible, the Knox Version is the official Catholic Bible in Great Britain. After the papal encyclical of 1943, a new edition of the Latin Vulgate was published (1945). This Vulgate text was not the basis of Monsignor Knox's New Testament translation. In 1949 Knox's Old Testament was published, but this was based on the new Vulgate, actually a revision of the 1592 Sixto-Clementine Vulgate. In 1955, hierarchical approval was given to Knox's translation, some sixteen years after the English hierarchy had asked the convert to Roman Catholicism to undertake the work (1939). It should be pointed out at this juncture that the Confraternity edition of the Roman Catholic Bible in English is based on older and more reliable Latin texts, and on original texts throughout most of the Old Testament. Hence, the Confraternity Version is based on a much firmer foundation than Knox's.

THE ENGLISH BIBLE FOR PROTESTANTS

Turning now to the Protestant versions of the Bible in English, it becomes quite apparent that the diversity and multiplicity of translations which appeared during the early Reformation period began to take on a more unified front as the various groups used the same translations. Thus, when James VI of Scotland became James I of England (1603-25), he summoned a conference of churchmen and theologians to discuss things "amiss in the Church." It was at this conference that the wheels were set in motion for the most influential single translation of the English Bible that the Protestants were to produce.

King James Version (1611)

In January, 1604, James I called the Hampton Court Conference in response to the Millenary Petition, which had been presented to him while he was traveling from Edinburgh to London. The Millenary Petition, so called because it contained about a thousand signatures, set forth the grievances of the Puritan party in the English church. The Puritans were a force to be reckoned with in James' new domain, and James was obliged to hear their petitions. While James, who regarded himself above all religious parties and principles, treated the Puritans with rudeness at the conference, it was there that John Reynolds, the Puritan president of Corpus Christi College, Oxford, raised the question of the advisability and desirability of having an authorized version of the English Bible that would be acceptable to all parties in the church. James I voiced his wholehearted support of such a venture, as it gave him the opportunity to act as peacemaker in his newly acquired realm. It also provided him with the occasion to replace the two most popular versions of the English Bible: the Bishops' Bible, used in the churches, and the Geneva Bible, the home Bible which he regarded as the worst of the existing translations. This was due largely to his distaste for the accessories which accompanied the translation rather than the translation itself. James had been brought up to believe that kings were appointed by God and had a divine right to rule their people. As a result, his view of "no bishop no king" led him to call for a version "which would embody the best in the existing versions and which could be read both in the public services of the Church and in homes by private individuals."[12]

The first order of business was to select a committee of revisers, a precedent established by the translators of the Geneva Bible.[13] This was done, and six companies were assigned, totaling fifty-four men, though only forty-seven actually did the work of revision.[14] Two companies met at Cambridge to revise I Chronicles through Ecclesiastes, and the Apocrypha; at Oxford two other companies met to revise Isaiah through Malachi, the four Gospels, Acts, and the Apocalypse; and the two remaining companies met at Westminster, where they revised Genesis through II Kings and Romans through Jude. Each company was given a set of instructions, which included the English translations to be used when they agreed better with the text than the Bishops' Bible: Tyndale's, Matthew's, Coverdale's, Whitchurche's, Geneva.[15] Using the Bishops' Bible as the basis for the revision, the committees retained many old ecclesiastical words, undoubtedly the influence of the Rheims New Testament, which had

[12]Kenneth Scott Latourette, A History of Christianity, p. 817.
[13]Nix, pp. 122 ff.; also see chap. 28.
[14]See Hills, pp. 21-22; MacGregor, pp. 164-78; F. F. Bruce, The English Bible: A History of Translations, pp. 96-112; H. W. Hoare, The Evolution of the English Bible, 2d ed., pp. 241-70; et al.
[15]Hoare, pp. 252-54, lists fifteen rules, number fourteen is cited here. Whitchurche's translation was the 1549 folio edition of the Great Bible.

recently been published. No marginal notes were affixed, except for the explanation of the Hebrew and Greek words which would require them. Many Latinisms were reintroduced, but the Geneva Bible influenced the precision of expression and contributed to the clarity of the revision. Frequently the new revision departed from Tyndale's version, as did the Great Bible, only to have the revisers of 1881 and 1885 return to the earlier rendering.

Strictly speaking, the Authorized Version was never authorized. It replaced the Bishops' Bible in public use, as the latter was last printed in 1606 and no other large, folio-size Bible was printed after 1611. In competition among the laymen of England, the Authorized Version ran headlong into the popular Geneva Bible of the Puritans, but the grandeur of its translation ultimately swept all opposition aside. But, there is one fact that has often been overlooked by the adherents to the Authorized Version, namely, the Authorized Version is not really a version at all. Even the original title page of 1611 indicates that it is a translation, as it reads,

THE HOLY BIBLE, Conteyning the Old Testament, and the New:
Newly Translated out of the Originall Tongues:
and with the former Translations diligently compared and revised,
by his Majesties speciall Commandement.

Appointed to be read in Churches.

IMPRINTED at London by Robert Barker,
Printer to the Kings most Excellent Maiestie
Anno Dom. 1611
Cum Privilegio.[16]

While the familiar expression "Appointed to be read in Churches" occurs on the title page, there is no evidence that any formal appointment as to its liturgical use by either the king, Parliament, Privy Council, or Convocation was actually made. What really happened was that this Bible was the third so-called "Authorized Bible" rather than "The Authorized Bible," keeping in mind that "authorized" was used as a synonym for "recognized by various churches as accepted for use in public worship."[17] The actual purpose of the translators of the Authorized Version was set forth in a lengthy preface written by Myles Smith. In it he illustrates how the translation being

[16]*The Holy Bible, an Exact Reprint Page for Page of the Authorized Version Published in the Year MDCXI.*
[17]Edgar J. Goodspeed, "The Versions of the New Testament," *Tools for Bible Study,* Palmer H. Kelly and Donald G. Miller (eds.), p. 118.

done by the six committees actually rested on the immediate prede-
cessors rather than being a new translation from the original tongues.
In following this reasoning, the message from "the translators to the
Reader" indicates their purpose:

> But it is high time to issue them, and to shew in briefe what was
> proposed to our selues, and what course we held in this our
> perusall and suruay of the Bible. Truly (good Christian Reader)
> wee neuer thought from the beginning, that we should needs to
> make a new Translation, nor yet to make a bad one a good one,
> (for then the imputation of Sixtus had bene true in some sort,
> that our people had bene fed with gall of Dragons in stead of
> wine, with whey in stead of milke:) but to make a good one bet-
> ter, or out of many good ones one principall good one, not iustly
> to be excepted against; that hath bene our indeauour, that our
> marke. . . .[18]

The Authorized Version text was based on little if any of the superior
texts of the twelfth to the fifteenth centuries, as it followed the 1516
and 1522 editions of Erasmus' Greek text, including the interpolation
of I John 5:7.

The reasons for the gradual but overwhelming success of the
Authorized Version have been well stated by several writers and
may be briefly summarized as follows:[19]

1. the personal qualifications of the revisers, who were the choice
   scholars and linguists of their day as well as men of profound and
   unaffected piety
2. the almost universal sense of the work as a national effort, supported wholeheartedly by the king, and with the full concurrence
   and approval of both church and state
3. the availability and accessibility of the results of nearly a century
   of diligent and unintermittent labor in the field of biblical study,
   beginning with Tyndale and Purvey rather than Wycliffe, and
   their efforts to "make a good translation better"
4. the congeniality of the religious climate of the day with the sympathies and enthusiasm of the translators, as the predominant
   interest of their age was theology and religion
5. the organized system of cooperative work which followed the
   precedent of the Geneva translators, while it may have been im-

---

[18]Myles Smith, "The Translators to the Reader," *The Holy Bible*. . . .
[19]After Hoare, pp. 257-70.

proved, resulted in a unity of tone in the Authorized Version which surpassed all its predecessors

6. the literary atmosphere of the late sixteenth and early seventeenth centuries paralleled the lofty sense of style and artistic touch of the translators

The publishers added their contribution to the success of the Authorized Version by ceasing the publication of the Bishops' Bible in 1606, and by issuing the Authorized Version with the same format as the Geneva Bible. Nevertheless, the quality of the work needs no commendation at this late date. It reigns supreme as the "intrinsically" authorized version of English-speaking Protestantism. This, following on the thousand-year reign of the Latin Vulgate, is surely a notable achievement.

Three editions of the Authorized Version appeared during its first year of publication. These folio editions (16 by 10½ inches) were succeeded by quarto and octavo editions in 1612. As the early editions continued to be published, many various readings and misspellings appeared, some of which are quite humorous: for example, in 1631 the word "not" was omitted from the seventh of the Ten Commandments, hence, it was called the "Wicked Bible"; the 1717 edition printed at Oxford was called the "Vinegar Bible" because of the chapter heading of Luke 20, which reads "vinegar" instead of "vineyard"; in 1795 the Oxford edition misspelled "filled" (writing "killed") in Mark 7:27, and was called the "Murderers' Bible." In the course of time, the spelling of the earliest editions of the Authorized Version was modernized and modified. In 1701 the dates of Archbishop Ussher were inserted into the margin at the insistence of Bishop Lloyd and have remained there since. This item has resulted in much inappropriate and unfair criticism of Christians, as well as argument and discussion by them, for it is this system of dates that marks creation at 4004 B.C.

During the reign of Charles I (1625-49) the Long Parliament (1640-60) set up a commission to consider revising the Authorized Version or producing a new translation, but nothing further was done in the matter. Only minor revisions of the Authorized Version actually took place, but they were begun quite early and were well scattered over a long period of time; for example, in 1629 and 1638, then the efforts of Long Parliament in 1653, again in 1701, and finally by Dr. Paris of Cambridge in 1762, and by Dr. Blayney of Oxford in 1769. In the latter two revisions,

> . . . efforts were made to "correct and harmonize its spelling, and to rid it of some antique words like 'sith.'" Some points escaped these professors, but Blayney's edition has remained the standard form of the version ever since, unto this day. His edition probably differs from that of 1611 in at least 75,000 details.[20]

THE ENGLISH REVISED VERSION OF THE BIBLE

Antecedents to the revision of 1881-85. All of the revisions of the Authorized Version mentioned above were made without ecclesiastical or royal authority. In fact, no "official" revision of the Authorized Version was forthcoming for over one hundred years after the revision of Dr. Blayney (1769). Many of the revisions were ill-advised, such as Ussher's chronology, and the exclusion of the Apocryphal books brought a penalty of imprisonment decreed by the archbishop of Canterbury, George Abbot, shortly thereafter. There were, however, some excellent revisions made in an "unofficial" manner, as in the case of an anonymous edition of *The Holy Bible Containing the Authorized Version of the Old and New Testaments, with Many Emendations.* The preface of this work states:

> The history of the English Bible records the great alarm that has always been excited by attempts to improve the translation, or to correct its acknowledged defects; and never did these apprehensions exist in a greater degree than when our present version was issued: but the result has proved groundless; for nothing, perhaps, has contributed more to establish the truth of revelation, or to refute the sophistry of scepticism, than these corrections."[21]

He states further:

> Since the publication of the authorized version, scholars of preeminent piety and profound learning, of untiring industry, and inflexible integrity, have expended more time and talent on the Bible than any other book in existence; and their combined labours have brought it nearer to a state of perfection than any ancient work. And, surely, if this blessed volume, . . . be the most precious boon conferred on the heirs of immortality; if it be the common property of all the children of Adam, . . . as well for such as are of comparatively feeble attainments, as for those of

---

[20]Goodspeed, pp. 117-18.
[21]*The Holy Bible Containing the Authorized Version of the Old and New Testaments, with Many Emendations,* p. iv.

powerful intellect, and of cultivated minds; it should be presented to the church and to the world with the results of those labours which have shed so much light on its obscure and difficult passages; light—which has hitherto been scattered through publication so numerous, rare, or costly, as to be inaccessible to the great mass of mankind.[22]

In his "unofficial" revision of the Authorized Version (published in 1841), the author mentions his use of manuscripts which were not available in 1611.[23]

With the advances in nineteenth century scholarship, the accumulation of earlier and better manuscript materials, the archaeological discoveries in the ancient world in general, and the actual changes in English society and its literary style, the revision of the Authorized Version on a more "official" basis was mandatory. Even before the "official" revision took place, a group of outstanding scholars published *The Variorum Edition of the New Testament of Our Lord and Saviour Jesus Christ* (1880). This work was edited by R. L. Clark, Alfred Goodwin and W. Sanday, and was translated from the original Greek, with diligent comparison and revision in light of former translations, "by his majesty's special command."[24] The Variorum Bible was merely a revision of the Authorized Version, in light of the various readings from the best authorities. The variations appeared in the notes and margin, and were "designed not merely to correct some of the more important mistranslations, but to supply the means of estimating the authority by which the proposed corrections are supported."[25] Thus, while following in the tradition of the Tyndale, Coverdale, Great, Geneva, Bishops', and various editions of the Authorized Version, the Variorum Bible prepared the way for the English Revised Version, which was published in 1881 and 1885, and which had access to the renderings and critical apparatus of the Variorum Bible.

Actual Revision of the Authorized Version. The desire for a full revision of the Authorized Version was so widespread among Protestant scholars after the mid-nineteenth century that a Convocation of the Province of Canterbury was called in 1870, for the proposal

---

[22]*Ibid.*, p. v.
[23]See chap. 20 on the discoveries and contents of the New Testament manuscripts. One of the manuscripts used by this author was "the *Codex Vaticanus* and other rare and valuable manuscripts in the Vatican library at Rome." *Ibid.*, p. ix.
[24]Cf. title page of *The Variorum Edition of the New Testament of Our Lord and Saviour Jesus Christ.*
[25]*Ibid.*, "Editors' Preface."

of a revision of the text where the Hebrew and Greek texts had been inaccurately or wrongly translated. Samuel Wilberforce, bishop of Winchester, made the resolution to revise the New Testament, and Bishop Ollivant enlarged it to include the Old Testament. Two companies were appointed, originally having twenty-four members each, but later including some sixty-five revisers of various denominations. The actual process of revision was begun in 1871, and in 1872 a group of American scholars was asked to join the work.[26]

The general principles of procedure for the revisers were as follows:

1. To introduce as few alterations as possible into the Text of the Authorized Version consistently with faithfulness.
2. To limit, as far as possible, the expression of such alterations to the language of the Authorized and earlier English versions.
3. Each Company to go twice over the portion to be revised, once provisionally, the second time finally, and on principles of voting as hereinafter is provided.
4. That the Text to be adopted be that for which the evidence is decidedly preponderating; and that when the Text so adopted differs from that from which the Authorized Version was made, the alteration be indicated in the margin.
5. To make or retain no change in the Text on the second final revision by each company, except *two-thirds* of those present approve of the same, but on the first revision to decide by simple majorities.
6. In every case of proposed alteration that may have given rise to discussion, to defer the voting thereupon till the next Meeting, whensoever the same shall be required by one-third of those present at the Meeting, such intended vote to be announced in the notice of the next Meeting.
7. To revise the headings of chapters, pages, paragraphs, italics, and punctuation.
8. To refer, on the part of each Company, when considered desirable, to Divines, Scholars, and Literary Men, whether at home or abroad, for their opinions.[27]

Oxford and Cambridge university presses absorbed the costs for the translation, with the proviso that they would have exclusive copyrights to the finished product. After six years the first revision was

[26]Hills, pp. 25-26, names the English and American committee members.
[27]Bruce, p. 137.

completed, and another two and a half years were spent in consideration of the suggestions of the American committee. Finally, on May 17, 1881, the *English Revised Version of the New Testament* was published in paragraph form. In less than a year after publication nearly three million copies were sold in England and America, with 365,000 copies sold in New York and 110,000 in Philadelphia. Most of these were sold in the first few weeks.

The Revised Version appeared in the United States in New York and Philadelphia on May 20, 1881, and on May 22 the entire New Testament was published in the *Chicago Times* and the *Chicago Tribune*. The response to the English Revised Version was generally disappointing, as the old familiar phrases were often replaced by new ones, and old words were removed in favor of new ones. The paragraph arrangement satisfied those who tended to dislike the arrangement of the Authorized Version verses, but they were not satisfied with the "minor changes" in the English. While the text was much more accurate, it would take several generations for acceptance of the altered words and rhythms. In 1885 the Old Testament was published, and the Apocrypha appeared in 1896 (1898 in the United States), and the entire Bible was published in 1898.

The American Standard Version

Some of the renderings of the English Revised Version were not completely favored by the American revision committee, but they had agreed to give for fourteen years "no sanction to the publication of any other editions of the Revised Version than those issued by the University Presses of England."[28] But, in 1901 *The American Standard Edition of the Revised Version* (American Standard Version, ASV), was published. The title indicates that several "unauthorized" editions of the Revised Version had been published in the United States, and this was indeed true. Further revisions were made in the American Standard Version, namely, some antiquated terms were replaced by more modern ones, for example, "Jehovah" instead of "Lord," and "Holy Spirit" replaced "Holy Ghost." The paragraph structures were revised and shortened, and short page headings were added. The version slowly won its way into American churches, and copies were imported into England, as many favored the Americanisms in the American Standard Version. While the American Standard Version lacks the beauty of the Authorized Version, its more accurate readings made it acceptable for teachers and students

[28]Hills, p. 27.

alike. In 1929 the copyright passed to the International Council of Religious Education, and they later revised its text again. The American Standard Version, based on the English Revised Version of 1881, 1885, "was the work of many hands and of several generations. The foundation was laid by William Tyndale . . . ."[29]

THE REVISED STANDARD VERSION

Half a century after the English Revised Version was published, the International Council of Religious Education expressed its desire to utilize the great advances in biblical scholarship. The Westcott-Hort text of the New Testament, the basis underlying the English and American revised versions, had been modified sharply by the light cast upon it by papyrus discoveries, older manuscripts coming to light, etc. In addition, the literary style and taste of English had continued to change, and a new revision was considered necessary. Hence, in 1937, the International Council authorized a committee to proceed with a revision which would

> . . . embody the best results of modern scholarship as to the meaning of the Scriptures, and express this meaning in English diction which is designed for use in public and private worship and preserves those qualities which have given to the King James Version a supreme place in English literature.[30]

The revision committee consisted of some twenty-two outstanding scholars who were to follow the meaning of the American Standard Version in the elegance of the Authorized Version, and change the readings only if two-thirds of the committee agreed.[31] It uses simpler, more current forms of pronouns such as "you" and "yours," except in reference to God, and more direct word order. *The Revised Standard Version: The New Testament* (RSV) was published in 1946, delayed because of World War II (1939-45), the Old Testament in 1952, and the Apocrypha in 1957.

The publication of the Revised Standard Version was launched with a grand publicity campaign, and certain reactions were sure to be set in motion. While the American Standard Version was charged with its over-literalization of the Old Testament, the Revised Standard Version was criticized for going to the opposite extreme, for example, the blurring of traditional "Messianic" passages raised sharp

[29]"Preface," *The Revised Version of the New Testament.*
[30]"Preface," *The Revised Standard Version.*
[31]Hills, pp. 27-28.

cries of criticism, such as the substitution of "young woman" for the traditional "virgin" of Isaiah 7:14. The criticisms of the New Testament were not nearly so vitriolic, but they were sharp enough. In fact, F. F. Bruce indicates that

> . . . when the whole Bible was published in 1952, the criticism which greeted it from some quarters was remarkably reminiscent of criticism voiced in earlier days against the Greek Septuagint and the Latin Vulgate, against the versions of Luther and Tyndale, against the AV and RV. . . .[32]

All the criticism notwithstanding, the Revised Standard Version has provided the English-speaking church with an up-to-date revision of the Scripture text based on the "critical text."

The New English Bible

Not satisfied that the Revised Standard Version was a continuation of the long-established tradition of the earlier English versions, the General Assembly of the Church of Scotland met in 1946 to consider a completely new translation. A joint committee was appointed in 1947, and three panels were chosen: for the Old Testament, New Testament, and Apocrypha. C. H. Dodd was appointed chairman of the New Testament panel, and in 1949, director of the whole translation.[33] In March, 1960, the New Testament portion was accepted by the committee; and it was published in 1961. The principles of the translation were set forth in a memorandum by C. H. Dodd:

> It is to be genuinely English in idiom, such as will not awaken a sense of strangeness or remoteness. Ideally, we aim at a "timeless" English, avoiding equally both archaisms and transient modernisms. The version should be plain enough to convey its meaning to any reasonably intelligent person (so far as verbal expression goes), yet not bald or pedestrian. It should not aim at preserving "hallowed" associations; it should aim at conveying a sense of reality. It should be as accurate as may be without pedantry. It is to be hoped that, at least occasionally, it may produce arresting and memorable renderings. It should have sufficient dignity to be read aloud . . . We should like to produce a translation which may receive general recognition as an authoritative second version alongside the A.V. for certain public purposes as well as for private reading, and above all a translation which may in some measure remove a real barrier

<hr/>

[32]Bruce, p. 195.
[33]*Ibid.*, pp. 225-26, gives the names and details of the members of the committee.

between a large proportion of our fellow-countrymen and the truth of the Holy Scriptures.[34]

Over four million copies were sold in Britain and America during the first year. It was quite different from the American Standard Version and Revised Standard Version, and quite often departed from the literal renderings in footnote form where the translators felt that two interpretations are permitted by the Greek text. This New Testament was dedicated to Queen Elizabeth II, and is a valuable work in its own right. Still, there has been some sharp criticism of this new translation, but it is too soon to tell what its lasting results will be, although some of its "Anglicanisms" sound strange to the American ear (e.g., "cudgels" for "staves" [AV] or "clubs" [RSV] in Matt. 26:47, and "put to rout" instead of "scattered" in Luke 1:51, as well as "mealtub" for "bushel" in Matt. 5:15). The overruling principle of "intelligibility" rather than "literalness" of meaning certainly indicates the influence of contemporary theology on the translation via its translators, but this has been the case with all of its English forebears.

SUMMARY AND CONCLUSION

Protestants were not alone in the production of English translations of the Bible. Their enterprise was paralleled by a Roman Catholic desire for the same. This Roman Catholic desire culminated in the publication of the Rheims-Douay Bible (1582, 1609), the Challoner revision (1750), the Confraternity of Christian Doctrine edition in America (1941), and the version of Monsignor Ronald A. Knox in England (1949). Although the Rheims-Douay was published by the Roman Catholic Church almost two years before the Protestants published the King James Version, the latter was destined to take precedence over the former in both popularity and style. After almost three hundred years the first attempt at an official replacement for the King James Version resulted in the production of the English Revised Version (1881, 1885) and the American Standard Version (1901). Following this have come the attempts of the Revised Standard Version (1946, 1952) and the New English Bible (1961) to update the translation. However, despite these official revisions, the King James Version, with all its archaism, remains one of the most widely circulated books in the world today.

[34]As cited by T. H. Robinson, "A New Translation of the English Bible," *The Bible Translator* 2 (Oct., 1951): 168.

30

MODERN SPEECH VERSIONS AND
TRANSLATIONS OF SCRIPTURE

One of the strongest evidences of the universality of the Bible is
the multiplicity of translations and the variety of languages into
which it has been translated. According to figures from the British
and Foreign Bible Society, the entire Bible has been translated into
over two hundred languages, and biblical portions into over a thousand languages and dialects.[1] A sample selection of these will serve
to illustrate this final link in the chain of transmission that connects
the Hebrew and Greek autographs to the languages of the twentieth
century.

FOREIGN LANGUAGE VERSIONS AND TRANSLATIONS

After the invention of movable type in printing, and the rise of
the Reformation in the first part of the sixteenth century, the first
group of Bible translations in the vernacular were printed.

LATIN VERSIONS IN THE REFORMATION PERIOD

On the very eve of the Reformation the Roman Catholic Church
was producing translations of the Bible into Latin. Among these
Latin versions were the works of Desiderius Erasmus (1466-1536)
in 1516, Santi Pagninus (1466-1541) in 1528, Cardinal Cajetan
(1469-1534) in 1530, and Arius Montanus (1527-98) in 1571. Meanwhile, the early Protestants were busy publishing their own Latin
versions of the Bible. Noteworthy in this area are the works of Sebastian Münster (1489-1552) in 1543/44, Théodore de Bèze (1519-
1605) in 1556/57, and Tremellius (1510-80) who worked with

[1]The British and Foreign Bible Society alone has translated Bible portions into
some 782 languages in recent times. For a complete listing of these see *Historical
Catalogue of the Printed Editions of Holy Scripture in the Library of the British and
Foreign Bible Society*, compiled by T. H. Darlow and H. F. Moule.

Junius to produce the last Latin version of the Old Testament by
Protestants to receive widespread fame (1575-79).[2]

German Versions in the Reformation Period

Prior to the fifteenth century there were some 230 manuscript
copies of the Bible in German. After that time 128 more were made.
The first printed German version of the Bible appeared in 1466, and
eighteen others were published before 1521. In 1521/22 Martin
Luther published his German version of the New Testament. It was
the most common version to circulate in Germany, as Martin Luther
took every precaution to see that his work became the official German version. This was especially true after he completed his Old
Testament translation in 1534. By the year 1580, there were seventy-
two editions of the German New Testament, and thirty-eight of the
Old. The multiplication of German versions has continued to the
present.[3]

French Versions in the Reformation Period

After the twelfth century, several French translations of the Latin
Vulgate were made in manuscript form. Unlike the German and
English counterparts, there is no authorized version of the French
Bible. The first printed edition of a French Bible appeared in Lyons
in 1477/78, and a better edition appeared in Paris in 1487. It was
not until the translation of the Vulgate by the humanist Catholic
Jacques Lefèvre d'Etaples was published at Paris in 1523-30 that an
important French version came into being. By 1535 the first important Protestant version was published. This was the work of
Pierre Robert Olivétan, John Calvin's cousin. His French version
was published at Serrières, with the Waldenses agreeing to contribute to the cost. In 1540 a second edition was published, and in
1545 and 1551, John Calvin revised this first Protestant version of
the French Bible.

Dutch Versions of the Bible

Before the Reformation, Dutch translations of the Bible tended
to be incomplete, and were based on earlier metrical paraphrases and

[2]For a fuller treatment of this subject see S. L. Greenslade (ed.), *The Cambridge
History of the Bible*, II, 38-93.
[3]Space would not permit listing the more recent translations in even the major
foreign languages. The British and Foreign Bible Society has compiled three volumes
(1,849 pp.) with some 10,000 entries of Bibles published in 628 languages between
1400 and the early 1900's in its *Historical Catalogue of the Printed Editions of Holy
Scripture*.

translations. With the change in climate following the Reformation came an increased interest in Bible translation in the vernacular. The Roman Catholics published Dutch translations of the Bible based on Erasmus' Latin text in 1516. In 1522 another translation began to be published in parts; in 1523 the New Testament was finished, and the Old Testament followed in 1527. Other Roman Catholic editions were published in 1539 and 1548. Meanwhile, the Protestants began publishing their own translations of the Bible into Dutch. In 1525 a Dutch translation of Luther's New Testament appeared in Antwerp, while his Old Testament was translated and published in 1526. It was not until 1637 that a Dutch version based on the original texts and authorized by the States General was published. This work was revised in 1866-97.

Italian Versions of the Bible

From the fourteenth century onward, devotional paraphrases of Scripture in Italian were published. The first vernacular version of the New Testament was not published until 1530, by a layman suspected of heresy, Antonio Brucioli (c. 1495-1566). In 1531 he published the Psalms, and the remainder of the Old Testament in 1532. This latter work appears to have drawn heavily on Santi Pagnini's interlinear version of 1528. In 1538 the first complete Italian Bible to receive papal sanction was published by Santi Marmochini. It claims to have been based on the Greek and Hebrew, but it was undoubtedly based on an existing version. The Protestants did not actually publish an Italian version until 1607, when Giovanni Diodati (1576-1649) published the first edition of his Bible in Geneva. The second edition appeared in 1641, with enlarged notes and introductions, and a revised text. It too was published in Geneva. This work is of very high quality, and was later circulated by the British and Foreign Bible Society. It remained the basic Protestant version of the Italian Bible into the present century.

Spanish Versions of the Bible

The first printed Index of the Spanish Inquisition (Toledo, 1551) prohibited the use of vernacular versions of the Bible in Spain. Thus, the Roman Catholics did not actually have a Spanish Bible with papal sanction until Pius VI authorized A. Martini's Italian translation, and Anselmo Petite's Spanish New Testament (1785) was permitted by the Inquisition's Index of 1790. Until this time, verse translations and "outlaw" versions were used. The Protestants provided some of these items as early as 1543, when the New Testament in Spanish was published by Francis of Emzinas in Antwerp. In 1553 a literal Spanish translation of the Old Testament was published by the Jewish press at Ferrara. In 1569 the first complete translation of the Bible into Spanish was published at Basle. This translation included the Apocrypha, and was reissued at Frankfurt in 1602 and 1622. The Spanish Bible, the work of Cassiodoro de Reyna revised in 1602 by Cipriano de Valera, is still a basic edition, and it has been the basis of many Spanish Protestant Bibles published by the British and Foreign Bible Society since 1861.

OTHER VERSIONS AND TRANSLATIONS OF THE BIBLE

In addition to the above languages into which the Bible has been translated, there are over eight hundred other modern languages into which portions of the Bible have been translated.[4] But some of the major translations and versions are worthy of note.

Portuguese. A Roman Catholic missionary turned Protestant, Ferreira d'Almeida published his New Testament translation in 1681, and it went into a second edition in 1712. He began an Old Testament translation which was completed by others in 1751. The Roman Catholics did not produce a Portuguese Bible until 1784.

Danish. The earliest Danish translation was a fourteenth or fifteenth century manuscript now housed in Copenhagen. In 1524 the first printed New Testament was published in Leipsig by J. D. Michaelis. The first complete Bible appeared in 1550.

Norwegian. Until 1814 the Danish version was used in Norway. Then a revision of the 1647 edition was begun in 1842 and finally completed in 1890.

Swedish. In 1523 Sweden and Denmark separated, and in 1526 a New Testament based on Luther's 1522 German edition was published. In 1541 a complete Bible was translated into Swedish, based on Luther's 1534 edition.

Polish. There were many early partial versions in Polish, but the first complete New Testament was published in 1551 at Königsberg. This work was translated by Jan Seklucjan, and was based on the Greek and Latin texts. The whole Bible was translated from the Vulgate at Kraków, and published in 1561.

[4]MacGregor, *The Bible in the Making,* pp. 331-83, has an excellent summary of the editions, languages, Bibles, New Testaments, and portions of Scripture, based on the records of the British and Foreign Bible Society.

Russian. Acts and the Pauline and General Epistles were published in 1554 from Moscow. The publishers were forced to flee to Lithuania, and in 1584 the whole Bible was published in Slavonic from there. This Bible is known as the Ostrog Bible, and it was revised in 1751, almost forty years after Peter the Great (1672-1725) ordered it (1712). It was not until about 1815/18 that the first Russian New Testament was actually published.

Hungarian. Manuscript fragments from the tenth through the fifteenth centuries have been discovered. After several antecedents, the Visoly Bible 1589/90 was published, based on Greek and Hebrew manuscripts. This occurred over a hundred years after the printing press was introduced into Hungary (1473).

Bohemian. Many portions of the Scriptures appeared in Bohemia between the tenth and fifteenth centuries. During the fourteenth century John Hus (1373-1415) was actively involved in placing the Scriptures into the vernacular, as were the United Brethren, who published the New Testament in 1518.

Icelandic. The New Testament translation of Oddur Gottskalksson was completed in 1539/40. It was based on the Vulgate and corrected by Luther's German Bible. In 1584, the Gudgrand Bible was translated into Icelandic from the German and Vulgate versions.

27. *A group of participants in the Zambia Translators Institute studying problems of the Chibemba translation (American Bible Society)*

Far Eastern translations and versions. These began to appear after William Carey went to India. Between 1793 and 1834 over thirty-four Asian languages had translations of portions of the Scriptures. Among these was the work of Robert Morrison, who began his Chinese New Testament in 1809 and completed it in 1814.

The above survey is only a sample selection, as indicated in Geddes MacGregor's "Appendix III."[5] Yet, even his work is provincial, in that it follows the British and Foreign Bible Society. S. L. Greenslade attempts to trace the history of the Bible in the West, from the Reformation period to the present day.[6] His work is also limited, but it is only a portion of a projected work. One other older work is that by Robert Kilgour, in which the author attempts to trace the total picture of Scripture translations.[7] This work is out of date, having been written in 1939. The work of such organizations as the Wycliffe Bible Translators makes it difficult to keep abreast with the widening scope of Bible translations.[8] But the basic direction of the present discussion is the English Bible, and to that the subject returns.

MODERN ENGLISH TRANSLATIONS AND VERSIONS

Besides the major versions of the English Bible discussed in chapters 28-29, there are numerous independent translations of the Bible or the New Testament, called "modern speech translations."[9]

ROMAN CATHOLIC TRANSLATIONS AND VERSIONS

The initial attitude of the Roman Catholic Church toward publishing the Scriptures for laymen was far from enthusiastic. The British and Foreign Bible Society was founded in 1804, and sixty years later Pope Pius IX in his famous *Syllabus of Errors*—once thought to be infallible, though now discounted by Roman Catholic theologians—condemned Bible societies as "pests." However, as early as 1813, a group of enthusiastic churchmen, including some Roman Catholics, founded the Roman Catholic Bible Society. The enterprise evoked the ire of Bishop Milner, who objected to the society's publication of the Rheims-Douay Version without notes.

[5]*Ibid.*
[6]Greenslade, 38-39.
[7]R. Kilgour, *The Bible Throughout the World: A Survey of Scripture Translations.*
[8]Cf. such works on their efforts as Ethel Emily Wallis and Mary Angela Bennett, *Two Thousand Tongues to Go.*
[9]Further reading on the English Bible will be found in Brooke Foss Westcott, *History of the English Bible,* and Hugh Pope, *English Versions of the Bible.*

Another Roman Catholic Bishop, William Poynter, accepted the presidency of the organization, and it published an improved edition of the Rheims-Douay Version in 1815.

Meanwhile, a host of editions of the Bible for use by Roman Catholics appeared, including *Coyne's Bible* (1811), *Haydock's Bible* (1811-14), the *Newcastle New Testament* (1812), *Syer's Bible* (1813-14), *MacNamara's Bible* (1813-14), *Bregan's New Testament* (1814), *Gibson's Bible* (1816-17).[10] In 1836, John Lingard of England published (anonymously) a lively Roman Catholic translation of the Bible which regularly replaced "do pennance" with "repent," an innovation which the Confraternity edition was to pick up a century later (1936), instead of following the Rheims-Douay. In the United States, a Roman Catholic scholar, Francis Patrick Kenrick, pioneered a translation of the entire Bible which was published in sections between 1849 and 1860. Like most of his Roman Catholic precursors, his work is best described as "a revised and corrected edition of the Douay Version."[11] Many other versions of the Bible continued to pour forth, but few of them were notable, except as they perpetuated old errors or created new ones. In 1901, however, a remarkable version of the Gospels appeared by a Dominican Father. Francis Spencer completed his New Testament before his death in 1913, and it was eventually published in New York in 1937.

The *Laymen's New Testament*, first published in London in 1928, was designed as a Bible for zealous Roman Catholic apologists in squelching "Hyde Park hecklers." This work simply set forth the Challoner text on the left page, and provided ammunition for the militant laymen to fire at the skeptics on the right. The Westminster Version was a more scholarly attempt at translation. Cuthbert Lattey, a Jesuit scholar, began it between 1914 and 1918. Contributions came from both sides of the Atlantic until, by 1935, the New Testament was completed. Although parts of the Old Testament have been published, it is still incomplete.

A fully "Americanized" edition of the New Testament was published in the United States in 1941. This widely known Confraternity edition surpassed all previous versions for its innovations. It was arranged in paragraph form, was rendered into modern speech, and

[10]Listed by MacGregor, p. 266.
[11]*Ibid.*, p. 269.
[12]*The Holy Bible: a Translation from the Latin Vulgate in the Light of the Hebrew and Greek Originals*, John Knox (trans.).

the text was accompanied by notes. Monsignor Ronald Knox undertook a translation of the Bible;[12] the New Testament was completed in 1944, the Old Testament in 1948. Although Knox was an Oxford scholar and literary wit, he incorporated few changes into his translation, which has been officially sanctioned by the church. A much more independent translation was made in America by James A. Kleist and Joseph L. Lilly in 1956, under the title *The New Testament Rendered from the Original Greek with Explanatory Notes.*

Probably the most significant recent translation by Roman Catholic Scholars is the *Jerusalem Bible,* produced under the direction of the Dominican scholar, Père Roland de Vaux. As the title page admits, "the English text of the Bible itself, though translated from the ancient texts, owes a large debt to the work of the many scholars who collaborated to produce *La Bible de Jerusalem. . . .*" In fact, the introduction and notes of this Bible are taken, without substantial variation, directly from the French edition published by Les Editions du Cerf, Paris (1961). These very extensive notes represent the work of the "liberal" wing of Catholic biblical scholars. Characteristic of the translation is the use of "Yahwey" for the usual "Lord" in the Old Testament. Its translation is basically literal, although it avoids the King James style and attempts to use a "contemporary" English.

Jewish Translations and Versions

Although Jews have attempted to preserve the study of Scripture in its "sacred" language (Hebrew), it has been their experience, like that of the Roman Catholics with the Latin,[13] that this is not always possible. The very existence of the Greek Septuagint (LXX) bears a witness to the fact that as early as the third century B.C. the Jews found it necessary to translate their sacred Scriptures into another language. Conditions under which Jews lived during the Middle Ages were not conducive to scholarship. Nevertheless, by about 1400, Jewish translations of the Old Testament began to appear in various languages. But it was not until some four centuries later that English versions of the Old Testament were published by the Jews. In 1789, the year of the French Revolution, a version of the Pentateuch appeared, claiming to be an emendation of the King James Version. This work was dedicated to Dr. Barrington, bishop

---

[13]Not only have Roman Catholics found it necessary to translate the Latin Scriptures into local language, but, in a historic stride, Vatican Council II approved the use of the local language for the Mass in 1965.

of Salisbury. In 1839 Salid Neuman published a similar work. Between 1851 and 1856 Rabbi Benisch produced a complete Bible for English-speaking Jewry. One final attempt to amend the Authorized Version for use by Jews was made by Michael Frieländer in 1884.

Isaac Leeser made a version of the Hebrew Bible (1853), a longtime favorite of British and American synagogues which shows a more marked departure from the Authorized Version. Before the close of the century, the inadequacy of Leeser's work was felt in the United States, as Jewry had greatly increased. Thus, in 1892, at its second biennial convention, the Jewish Publication Society of America decided to thoroughly revise Leeser's Bible. As the work proceeded, it became obvious that an entirely new translation would result. After considerable time and reorganization, the Jewish Publication Society's version of the Hebrew Bible in English was published (1917). It seems to follow closely the text of the American Standard Version.

In 1962 this same society published a new translation: *The Torah: A New Translation of the Holy Scriptures according to the Masoretic text.* According to its preface, its purpose was "to improve substantially on earlier versions in rendering both the shades of meaning of words and expressions and the force of grammatical forms and constructions" and this improvement was sought by "the help of neglected insight of ancient and medieval Jewish scholarship and partly by utilizing the new knowledge of the . . . Near East."

PROTESTANT TRANSLATIONS AND VERSIONS

In keeping with their Reformation principle of "private interpretation," Protestants have produced a greater multiplicity of private translations of the Bible than have the Roman Catholics.[14] Some of the earliest attempts at private translations grew out of the discovery of better manuscripts. None of the great manuscripts had been discovered when the Authorized Version was translated, except Codex Bezae (D), and it was used very little in that version.

Eighteenth and nineteenth century translations and versions. In 1703 Daniel Whitby edited a *Paraphrase and Commentary on the New Testament*, which included explanations and expansions of the Authorized Version with a postmillennial emphasis. Edward Wells followed with a revised text of the Authorized Version, which he called *The Common Translations Corrected* (1718-24). A few years

[14]Unless otherwise noted, this section follows the treatment found in the excellent work of F. F. Bruce, *The English Bible: A History of Translations*, pp. 127 ff.

later, Daniel Mace published (anonymously) a critical Greek text of the New Testament with a corrected Authorized Version text alongside. In 1745, William Whiston, best known today for his translations of Josephus, published his *Primitive New Testament.* He leaned heavily on a Western text, and particularly on Codex Bezae in the Gospels and Acts. Other eighteenth century versions continued to make alterations of the Authorized Version, for example, John Wesley's edition contained some 12,000 changes in all. Edward Horwood's *Liberal Translation of the New Testament: Being an attempt to translate the Sacred Writings with the same Freedom, Spirit, and Elegance, with which other English Translations from the Greek Classics have lately been executed* (1768), aroused little more than literary curiosity. In 1808, Charles Thompson, one of the founding fathers of the United States, published an English translation of the Old Testament from the Greek Septuagint,[15] while another translation from the LXX was produced by Lancelot Brenton in 1844.[16] Samuel Sharpe, a Unitarian scholar, issued his *New Testament, translated from the Greek of J. J. Griesbach* in 1840, and the Old Testament in 1865. Meanwhile, Robert Young, best known for his analytical concordance, published his *Literal Translation of the Bible* (1862) in order "to put the English reader as far as possible on a level with the reader of the Hebrew and Greek texts."[17] Dean Alford, who also published a famous Greek New Testament, issued a revision of the King James Version in 1869. His hope had been to provide a work which would serve only as an "interim report" until an authoritative revision could replace it, which was fulfilled in 1881 and 1885 when the English Revised Version appeared.

On the eve of the publication of the English Revised Version, John Nelson Darby, the leader of the "Plymouth Brethren," published his *New Translation of the Bible* (1871, 1890). This translation was equipped with a full critical apparatus of variant readings, but it "falls short in regard to English style."[18] Another fairly literal translation was Joseph Bryant Rotherham's *The Emphasized Bible* (1872, Old Testament, 1897-1902). The first two editions were based on Tregelles' text, while the third followed Westcott and Hort. This version was one of the first to render the ineffable name of God in

---

[15]This work, *The Septuagint Bible,* has been reprinted by Falcon Wing Press.
[16]This translation was reprinted by Bagster, *The Septuagint Version of the Old Testament.*
[17]Bruce, pp. 127 ff.
[18]*Ibid.,* p. 132.

the Old Testament as Yahweh. Thomas Newberry's *The English-man's Bible*, edited in the 1890's, contained the text of the Authorized Version arranged by means of dots, dashes and other notes to aid the English reader instead of actually being a new version.

There were other nineteenth century translations of portions of the Bible which were included in commentaries. One of the best known examples of such a work was *The Life and Epistles of St. Paul* by W. J. Conybeare and J. S. Howson (1864). Their example, as well as others, has led F. F. Bruce to remind the Bible student that "it must be borne in mind that much excellent Bible translation is to be found, down to the present day, embedded in commentaries on various books of the Bible."[19]

Twentieth century translations and versions. The great profusion of speech translations did not occur until the twentieth century for a number of reasons. First of all, the great biblical manuscripts which prompted such attempts at translation were not discovered until the late nineteenth century. Although the committees of the English Revised Version (1881, 1885) and the American Standard Version (1901) incorporated the findings of these newly discovered manuscripts into their texts, the public was not entirely satisfied with their translations. Then too there was the discovery of the nonliterary papyri[20] (see chap. 21) which had shown the New Testament to be written in the colloquial (Koine) language of the first century. This not only prompted a desire to reproduce the New Testament into a similar colloquial, modern speech translation, but the papyri cast new light on the meanings of words, and they needed a fuller expression and clarification in their English translation. Arthur S. Way, a classical scholar, published his translation, *The Letters of St. Paul*, in 1901. The very next year, *The Twentieth Century New Testament: A New Translation into Modern English Made from the Original Greek* (based on the text of Westcott and Hort) appeared (1902). It was appropriately named, but strangely conceived, as it was not until about fifty years later[21] that the identity of the twenty pastors and laymen (none were linguists or textual critics) who had produced this work was revealed. Their desire was to "mediate the word of God in a plainer English idiom."[22] It

---

[19]*Ibid.*, p. 134.

[20]It was not until 1895 that Adolf Deissmann drew attention to the papyri.

[21]Kenneth W. Clark disclosed the real translators from their secretarial records deposited in the John Rylands Library, Manchester. See his article, "The Making of the Twentieth Century New Testament," *Bulletin of the John Rylands Library* (1955).

[22]*Ibid.*, p. 66.

is a remarkable fact that as nonexperts they were so successful in their endeavor. As Kenneth W. Clark has observed, "Somewhere along the line, some transforming miracle seems to have occurred. We are forced to conclude that their devotion to their task has made of them better scholars than they were at first."[23]

Richard Francis Weymouth, a consultee of the *Twentieth Century New Testament*, translated his own version of the New Testament. It was published posthumously in 1903, and was based on his own critical Greek text, *The Resultant Greek Testament*. Weymouth's New Testament was thoroughly revised in 1924 by James A. Robertson of Aberdeen.[24] Weymouth himself had envisioned his effort as a "succinct and compressed running commentary (not doctrinal) to be used side by side with its elder compeers the AV and RV."

Perhaps the most pretentious translation of the twentieth century was Ferrar Fenton's *The Holy Bible in Modern English, containing the complete sacred scriptures of the Old and New Testament, translated into English direct from the original Hebrew, Chaldee and Greek* (1895, Old Testament, 1903). In the preface to the 1910 edition, the author states, "I contend that I am the only man who has ever applied real mental and literary criticism to the Sacred Scriptures." As F. F. Bruce adroitly observes, "On this the best comment is perhaps that of Proverbs 27:2, in Ferrar Fenton's own translation: 'Let a stranger praise you, not your mouth, another, and not your own lips.' "[25] Unique features of the translation include the following: the Authorized Version "Lord" was translated "The Life," or "The ever-Living"; Old Testament names were retransliterated (e.g., Elisha to Alisha), the order of books in the Old Testament followed the Hebrew Bible, and the gospel of John was placed first in the New Testament. The work as a whole was forceful and unique, but not too significant.

Another of the early twentieth century translations was that of an Oxford scholar, James Moffatt, *The New Testament: A New Translation* (1913), and *The Old Testament: A New Translation* (1924). Later the entire work appeared in a single volume as *A New Translation of the Bible* (1928). This translation, which at times reflects a Scottish tone, was characterized by freedom of style

---

[23]*Ibid.*, p. 81.
[24]In this revision the rendering "life of the ages" (which reflected the unorthodox views on eternal life) was corrected to read "eternal life."
[25]Bruce, p. 162.

and idiom. It was based primarily on von Soden's Greek text. Moffatt was more expert in the New Testament than the Old, as is evident in his translation, where his liberal theology was not concealed (cf. John 1:1: "*Logos* was divine"). He also regularly translated the name of God in the Old Testament as "The Eternal" rather than "Lord" or "Jehovah" (ASV).

The American counterpart to Moffatt was *The Complete Bible: An American Translation* (1927). Edgar J. Goodspeed, in the first installment which appeared in 1923, pointed out that "for American readers . . . who have had to depend so long upon versions made in Great Britain, there is room for a New Testament free from expressions which, however familiar in England or Scotland, are strange in American ears."[26] The translation was made with dignity and readability, and had a minimum of "Americanisms." In 1938 he completed his translation of the Apocrypha.

G. W. Wade's *The Documents of the New Testament* (1934) "is a fresh translation of the New Testament documents, arranged in what the translator believed to be their chronological order."[27] The translation was expanded by means of italicized words, which were added for the purpose of clarification. *The Concordant Version of the Sacred Scriptures* (1926 and following years) was based on the principle that "every word in the original should have its own English equivalent." Despite this mechanical word-for-word translation, and the tacit assumption that Hebrew was the original and pure language of the human race, the attempt reflects a dedicated effort. In 1937, Charles B. Williams, an American Greek scholar, issued *The New Testament in the Language of the People*. In it the author aimed to convey the exact shade of meaning of the Greek verb tenses. Although some scholars take issue with particular renderings,[28] Williams did accomplish his goal, although not always in "the language of the people." His renderings were sometimes unique (cf. Heb. 12:2: "who instead of the joy") and often powerful (cf. II Cor. 4:9: "always getting a knock-down, but never a knockout"). *St. Paul from the Trenches* by Gerald Warre Cornish, a Cambridge graduate, was published posthumously in 1937. He died in action during World War I (1916), and among his possessions was a muddy but legible copy of I and II Corinthians and part of Ephesians. It was an expanded-type translation. Archbishop W. C. Wand pro-

26Edgar J. Goodspeed, "Preface," *The Complete Bible: An American Translation.*
27Bruce, p. 173.
28Based on the *Interim Report on Vocabulary Selection* (London, 1936).

duced *The New Testament Letters* (1943) in an attempt, as he put it, "to put the Epistles into the kind of language a Bishop might use in writing a monthly letter for his diocesan magazine." The result reflects a somewhat ecclesiastical and formal style of the cleric.

The Basic English Bible (1940-49) was an attempt by a committee (J. H. Hooke, chairman), using only one thousand "basic" English words to convey all the biblical truth. Considering the vocabulary limitations, the authors did produce a text of marked simplicity while retaining much of the variety of the original Greek. Another simplified form of English, called "plain English," was comprised of fifteen hundred "fundamental and common words that make up ordinary English speech."[29] *The New Testament: A New Translation in Plain English* (1952) was the work of Charles Kingsley Williams, who, with the underlying Greek text of Souter, and a broader vocabulary than "basic" English by some 160 or 170 words—including more verbs—achieved a more expressive translation than did *The Basic English Bible*.

The Berkeley Version in Modern English (1945), Old Testament (1959), has been described "as a more conservative counterpart to the RSV."[30] The New Testament was translated, and the Old Testament edited, by Gerrit Verkuyl of Berkeley, California. There was a concerted attempt to render Messianic prophecies more clearly. Divine Persons were addressed as "Thou," and God's words were not set off in quotes, as the whole Bible was considered the Word of God. The Old Testament in particular shows some editorial inconsistencies and inaccuracies;[31] nevertheless, the effort as a whole is praiseworthy.

One of the most popular of all the modern speech translations has been that of J. B. Phillips, whose *Letters to Young Churches* (1947) was followed by *The Gospels in Modern English* (1952), *The Young Church in Action* (1955), *The Book of Revelation* (1957), and finally the one-volume edition of the completed work entitled *The New Testament in Modern English* (1958). The work was more properly a paraphrase, a "meaning-for-meaning" translation rather than a "word-for-word" translation. The former involves more interpretation than the latter, and this may be regarded as the only real weakness in Phillips' translation. Nevertheless, the strength and freshness of this work have recaptured the spirit and heart of the first century

[29]Bruce, p. 220.
[30]*Ibid.*, pp. 222-23.
[31]*Ibid.*

writers for twentieth century readers in a unique manner. In quite a different vein is *The New World Translation of the Christian Greek Scriptures* (1950), and *The New World Translation of the Hebrew Scriptures* (1953), published by the Watchtower Bible and Tract Society, Inc. (Jehovah's Witnesses). Some of the translations reflected the distinctive theological interpretations of the Jehovah's Witnesses (e.g., "the word was a god," John 1:1), others are colloquial (e.g., "Excuse me, Jehovah," Exodus 4:10), and some few were suggestive (e.g., "a jealous God" is one "exacting exclusive devotion").

The Authentic New Testament (1955) was an attempt by a distinguished Jewish scholar, Hugh J. Schonfield, who said in his preface that he approached the New Testament documents "as if they had recently been recovered from a cave in Palestine or from beneath the sands of Egypt, and had never previously been given to the public." The work, which was of good quality, attempted to reconstruct the "authentic" New Testament Jewish atmosphere for Gentile readers. George M. Lamsa's *The Holy Bible from Ancient Eastern Manuscripts* is unlike most other modern translations, as it was translated from the Peshitta, the authorized Bible of the church of the East. The Gospels, the whole New Testament, and Psalms were published earlier (1933, 1939, 1940) and the remainder of the Old Testament was added in 1957. The use of the Aramaic textual tradition has provided some interesting materials for comparisons, as the New Testament was based on a fifth century manuscript (Mortimer-McCawler manuscript, Ambrosian Library, Milan). This manuscript contains many interesting variants. For example, Matthew 19:24 reads, "It is easier for a rope [*gamla*, same Aramaic word for "camel"] to go through the eye of a needle." In Matthew 27:46, the manuscript records, "My God, My God, for this I was spared!"

Kenneth S. Wuest, in his *Expanded Translation of the New Testament* (1956-59), endeavored to do for all parts of speech what Charles B. Williams had done for the Greek verb, namely, to indicate the philological and theological nuances with greater precision. Since such a translation was intended for study, the stylistic inferiority cannot be pressed. The tendency to interpret is more obvious in an "expanded" translation of this variety than in others, a fact which sometimes necessitates a "reading into" before the interpretation can be "read out" of the text.

The Amplified New Testament (1958), produced by the Lockman

Foundation, shows an even more marked tendency to "add to" the biblical text while "expanding" upon it. By the use of parentheses, brackets, dashes and italics, it attempts to give a full expression to the various shades of thought and meaning in the original text. As F. F. Bruce observes, "The work includes several of the features of a commentary as well as a translation." More recently *The Amplified Old Testament* has been produced in the same style (1962, 1964).

In 1961, Olaf M. Norlie, an American Lutheran scholar, published *The Simplified New Testament in Plain English—for Today's Readers*, along with *The Psalms for Today: A New Translation in Current English*, by R. K. Harrison. According to the preface, "Norlie's *Simplified New Testament* is a new translation from the original Greek designed to make the language of the New Testament more interesting and intelligible, especially for today's young people." The authors have hopefully attempted to make the translation "readable" and "meaningful" in its appeal "to teen-agers, young people and young adults, for whom it will 'make the rough places plain.'"

Living Letters: The Paraphrased Epistles (1962) is one of the most popular of the recent translations. Its purpose was set forth in the preface by the translator, Kenneth Taylor.

> This book is a paraphrase of the New Testament letters. Its purpose is to say as exactly as possible what Paul, James, Peter, John, and Jude meant, and to say it simply, expanding where necessary for a clear understanding by the modern reader.

The author recognized the implicit danger of the paraphrastic method of translating, as he added,

> . . . whenever the author's exact words are not translated from the Greek there is the possibility that the translator, however honest, may be giving the English reader something that the original writer did not mean to say.

However true that statement may be, the author further acknowledges that "the theological lodestar in this book has been a rigid evangelical position." Taylor has also produced *Living Prophecies* (1965), *Living Gospels* (1966) and *Living Psalms and Proverbs* (1967) in the same style.

More recently, the Lockman Foundation has endeavored to revive and revise the American Standard Version (1901) in its translation of *The New American Standard Bible, New Testament* (1963). In the preface, the committee wrote, "It has been the purpose of the

Editorial Board to present the modern reader a revision of the American Standard Version in clear and contemporary language." This they did in the conviction that the American Standard Version was a standard, monumental product, internationally conceived and universally endorsed as a trustworthy translation. The preface also indicates that "the producers of this translation were imbued with the conviction that interest in the American Standard Version should be renewed and increased." Again it admits that "perhaps the most weighty impetus for this undertaking can be attributed to a disturbing awareness that the American Standard Version of 1901 was fast disappearing from the scene."

An even more recent addition to the long list of modern speech translations is *The Letters of Paul: An Expanded Paraphrase* by F. F. Bruce, 1965. It is designed, according to the author, "to make the course of Paul's argument as clear as possible." Bruce confesses frankly of his work, "Well, this one *is* a paraphrase," which according to his own acknowledgment is often an interpretation rather than a mere translation. Paul's epistles are arranged in chronological order, which according to Bruce is Galatians through II Timothy. The translation itself is a kind of amplified version of the English Revised Version (1881) which he considers the most accurate translation of the Greek ever made. The English Revised Version is printed in parallel for comparison. Although it is much too early for evaluation, the tentative observation may be ventured that it is probably more precise than Phillip's paraphrase but will lack some of the popular punch of Taylor's *Living Letters*.

The most recent addition to this never ending list of translations is the work of the American Bible Society called *Good News for Modern Man: The New Testament in Today's English* (1966). According to its brief preface, it "does not conform to traditional vocabulary or style, but seeks to express the meaning of the Greek text in words and forms accepted as standard by people everywhere who employ English as a means of communication." It attempts to avoid outdated and technical words and present the New Testament in a kind of newspaper English, based on a new Greek text prepared by an international committee of scholars sponsored by the United Bible Societies and published in 1966. The broad sponsorship, low cost, and clear presentation of the Greek New Testament insured in advance the success of this translation. By April 10, 1968, the ten millionth copy was put into circulation.

With the great profusion of Protestant, Roman Catholic and Jewish Bibles being published, it was inevitable that in an "ecumenical age" there should be produced some ecumenical Bibles.

The New Testament: Revised Standard Version Catholic Edition (1965) falls into this class. Although it is really the text of the Revised Standard Version with about twenty-four basic changes (also listed in an appendix) and notes added, it has been officially approved for Roman Catholics and, hence, falls into a kind of ecumenical category. The textual changes include such things as translating Jesus' "brothers" (RSV) to "brethren" (Matt. 12:46, 48); "divorce her [Mary]" to "send her away" (Matt. 1:19); adding "and fasting" to "prayer" (Mark 9:29); and restoring the long ending to Mark (16:9-20) as well as the passage on the woman taken in adultery (John 7:53—8:11).

The first attempt of a joint ecumenical committee to produce a common Bible is *The Anchor Bible*. Under the general editors of William F. Albright and David Noel Freedman, it claims to be "a project of international and interfaith scope: Protestant, Catholic, and Jewish scholars from many countries contribute individual volumes." It is "an effort to make available all the significant historical and linguistic knowledge which bears on the interpretation of the biblical record." It is being produced in separate volumes, each of which is accompanied by complete introduction and notes. Although it is much too early to appraise its value as a translation or its success as an "ecumenical" venture, it is difficult to see how it can maintain unity, since individual volumes are being produced separately by different scholars.

Even a glance at this endless procession of modern translations is sufficient evidence to indicate that the twentieth century, as no century before it in human history, possesses the greatest proliferation of translations of the Bible. And with this great diversity and multiplicity of translations, there comes to this century, as to no century before it, a greater responsibility to understand and to communicate the "whole counsel of God" contained in this inspired Book.

CONCLUSION

The general purpose of this book has been twofold: historical and theological. Historically and critically, it has been an attempt to answer the question as to whether the Bible of the twentieth century, based as it is on the critical Hebrew and Greek texts, is a faithful reproduction of the books produced by its original authors. The answer is by now obvious, and it is this: no book from antiquity comes to the modern world with greater evidence for its authenticity than does the Bible. Both the kind and the amount of evidence that supports the fidelity of the present critical text are greater than for any other book from the ancient world.

Directly related to this historical conclusion is a theological one. For if there is overwhelming evidence that the biblical documents are genuine and authentic—that they stem from alleged periods and authors—then one must face seriously their persistent claim to divine inspiration. When these claims are thoroughly examined and honestly faced, one can but conclude that the Bible as a whole claims to be the Word of God and the evidence confirms that claim.

Along with the question as to *whether* the books of the Bible are divinely inspired, it has been necessary to address the kindred question as to *which* books of the Bible are inspired, that is, the question of canonicity. One statement will suffice as a summary for both this and the foregoing question. The sixty-six books of the Protestant Bible known today are the entire and complete canon of inspired Scripture, handed down through the centuries without substantial change or any doctrinal variation.

GLOSSARY

ACCOMMODATION THEORY—The view of the German rationalists and others that Christ and the apostles accommodated their teaching to the current (but false) Jewish traditions about authorship, inspiration, etc., of the Old Testament without thereby either asserting or approving those beliefs.

AMANUENSIS—A scribal secretary or one employed to take dictation.

ANTILEGOMENA—Literally, the books "spoken against," that is, the books of the New Testament canon whose inspiration has been disputed, usually meaning Hebrews, James, II Peter, II and III John, Jude and Revelation.

APOCALYPSE—The English transliteration of the Greek word *apocalypsis* (revelation), this term used as the title for the last book of the Bible in English Roman Catholic versions.

APOCALYPTIC LITERATURE—A designation sometimes applied to the pseudepigraphal books because their contents are largely "revelations" and "visions"; it is also used to describe the canonical books of Ezekiel, Daniel, Zechariah and Revelation.

APOCRYPHA—The Protestant designation for the fourteen or fifteen books of doubtful authenticity and authority which are not found in the Hebrew Old Testament but are in manuscripts of the LXX; most of these books were declared canonical by the Roman Catholic Church at the Council of Trent in 1546.

APOSTOLICITY—In the narrow sense, it refers to that which comes directly from an apostle; but in a broader sense, it may refer to that which was produced under apostolic or prophetic ministry.

AUTHENTICITY—A word describing the truthfulness of the contents of a given text or composition; it is sometimes incorrectly used interchangeably with *genuineness* (see below).

AUTOGRAPHS or AUTOGRAPHA—Sometimes inaccurately defined as the original writings from the hand of an apostle or prophet, but it is more precisely a writing produced under the authority of an apostle or prophet, whether or not it was through a scribe or in several editions.

CANONICITY—The character of a biblical book which marks it as a part of the canon of Scripture, namely, the divine inspiration and authority which designate a book as part of the rule or standard of faith and practice.

CODEX—A manuscript in book form, that is, with sheets bound together rather than in the form of a roll or scroll.

CONSERVATIVE—The theological position which affirms the basic, fundamental doctrines of Christianity as the virgin birth, the deity, substitutionary atonement, and resurrection of Christ, and the inspiration of the Bible. In this sense, Conservative is used interchangeably with Fundamental, Evangelical and Orthodox, and it is to be contrasted with Liberal or Modernistic (see below).

COVENANT—An agreement or compact between two parties, such as the Mosaic Covenant.

CREDIBILITY—As applied to the Scriptures, it is their right to be believed and received as the truth of God.

CRITICAL TEXT—An edited text of the Bible which attempts, by critical comparison and evaluation of all of the manuscript evidence, to most closely approximate what was in the autographs; the Westcott and Hort text of the Greek New Testament is an example of a critical text.

CURSIVE MANUSCRIPTS—Usually the equivalent of minuscule or small lettered manuscripts written in a "running hand," hence "cursive," it is akin to handwriting rather than printing.

DECALOGUE—Literally, "ten words," that is, the Ten Commandments as recorded in Exodus 20 or Deuteronomy 5.

DEISM—The belief that there is a Creator who operates in His creation only through natural law which He has ordained from the beginning, and who never intervenes in the world by miracles; hence, it is anti-supernaturalistic in outlook.

DEMYTHOLOGY—A modern critical method of biblical interpretation espoused by Rudolph Bultmann and others which attempts to divest biblical stories of the *religious myth* of their day in order to arrive at their *real message*, and to see through the *historical* to their *supra-historical* truth; hence, this view does not accept the historicity and inerrancy of the Bible.

DESTRUCTIVE CRITICISM—A term used by conservative theologians to describe the harmful result of certain liberal forms of higher criticism of the Bible (see below).

EXISTENTIALISM—Religious existentialism holds, among other things, that revelation is not *propositional* but that it is *personal*. That is, it is not found in objective statements but only in a subjective and personal encounter.

FATHERS OF THE CHURCH—The writing theologians and teachers of the first seven or eight centuries of the Christian church, usually, the great bishops and leaders noted for sound judgment and holy living, whose writings preserve the doctrines, history and traditions of the early church.

FOLIO—A book made of full-sized leaves or sheets, each folded once to form four pages (twelve by nineteen inches, scale of American Library Association), or a book of the largest size.

FORMER PROPHETS—Designation for the first subdivision of the section of the Hebrew Scriptures known as the Prophets, including Joshua, Judges, I and II Samuel, and I and II Kings.

GENUINENESS—The character of a composition which guarantees its alleged authorship; genuineness is sometimes erroneously used interchangeably with authenticity, which concerns the truthfulness of the contents of a composition or text.

GERMAN RATIONALISM—A movement among eighteenth and nineteenth century German biblical scholars which, while attempting to defend Christianity on rational grounds, actually undercut the authority and inerrancy of the Scriptures, and subsequently the other fundamental doctrines arising therefrom. "Destructive criticism" and the "accommodation theory" are two examples of the teachings of this movement.

GRAPHE—The Greek word for "writings" (Scriptures), which are inspired of God, according to II Timothy 3:16.

HAGIOGRAPHA—The English equivalent of the Greek word for "holy writings" designating the same section of the Old Testament canon as does the Hebrew word Kethubhim (see below). In the Middle Ages this term was applied to writings about the saints and saints' lives. This latter sense is not in view throughout the present work.

HEXAPLA—A manuscript with six parallel columns arranged for comparative and critical study, such as Origen's Hexapla which contained various Hebrew and Greek translations of the Old Testament.

HEXATEUCH—the first six books of the Old Testament, namely, the Pentateuch plus Joshua.

HIGHER CRITICISM—The scholarly discipline dealing with the genuineness of the text including questions of authorship, date of composition, destination, etc. It is often called "historical criticism" but in its more radical expressions, it has been labeled "destructive criticism."

HOMOLOGOUMENA—Literally, "to speak the same," that is, those books of the New Testament which have been universally acclaimed as canonical, or all of the twenty-seven books of the New Testament except the Antilegomena (see above).

ILLUMINATION—The process by which God enlightens man's mind so that the objective disclosure of God (revelation) is subjectively understood by man.

INERRANCY—Meaning "without error" and referring generally to the historical and scientific accuracy of the Scriptures.

INFALLIBLE—Literally, "not fallible or breakable"; it refers to the divine character of Scripture which necessitates its truthfulness (cf. John 10:35).

INSPIRATION—Meaning literally "God-breathed" (from II Tim. 3:16), and referring to the process by which God superintended the writing of the sacred Scriptures so that, without destroying the individual styles of the writers, He nevertheless produced an errorless and authoritative book.

KETHUBHIM—The English equivalent for this Hebrew word is "Writings"; the title of the third division of the Hebrew Old Testament.

KOINE GREEK—The common trade language, the "language of the market place" of the first century Western world; the New Testament was originally written in the Koine Greek.

LATTER PROPHETS—The second subdivision of the Hebrew Prophets, including all of the prophets following II Kings.

LECTIONARIES—Early church service books containing selected Scripture readings usually from the Gospels and sometimes from Acts or the Epistles.

LIBERAL—The theological position which denies many of the fundamental doctrines of historic Christianity, such as the deity of Christ, the inspiration of the Bible, and not asserting that the Bible *is* the Word of God but that it merely *contains* the Word of God.

LITERAL TRANSLATION—A word-for-word translation from one language to another as opposed to an idiomatic, thought-for-thought translation or paraphrase.

LOWER CRITICISM—The scholarly discipline dealing with the authenticity of the biblical text and which seeks to discover the original words of the autographs. It is also called "textual criticism."

LXX—Symbol for the Septuagint, meaning "The Seventy," which is the Greek translation of the Old Testament alleged to have been translated by some seventy scribes at Alexandria, Egypt, at about 250 B.C.

MAJUSCULE—See "Uncial."

MANUSCRIPT—A handwritten literary composition rather than a printed copy.

MASORETES—Jewish textual scribes of the fifth through ninth centuries A.D. who standardized the Hebrew text of the Old Testament, which is therefore called the Masoretic text.

MEGILLOTH—The transliteration into English of the Hebrew word meaning "rolls"; it is used to designate the Five Rolls, the group of books from the third division of the Hebrew canon (the Writings) which were read at the festal ceremonies.

MINUSCULE MANUSCRIPT—A manuscript written in rather small letters, commonly in a cursive or free-flowing hand.

NEBHIIM—The transliteration into English of the Hebrew word for "prophets"; it designates the second division of the Hebrew Old Testament (the Prophets).

NEOORTHODOXY—A modern theological view which, while reacting against Liberalism, never quite returned to the orthodox position in general, and which does not accept the verbal inspiration of the Scriptures in particular; it asserts that the Bible becomes the Word of God only when it speaks to an individual personally.

PALIMPSEST—A manuscript which has been "rubbed again," erased for reuse as a rescriptus (see below).

PAPYRUS (papyri)—A kind of ancient paper or writing material made from the pith of a plant by that name, which grew in the marshes of Egypt.

PARCHMENT—An ancient writing material usually prepared from goat or sheep skin.

PENTATEUCH—Literally, a fivefold book; used specifically with reference to the first five books of the Old Testament.

PIETISM—A religious movement in late seventeenth century Germany stressing the subjective and personal aspects of Christianity. This movement often tended to neglect the theological and technical side of Christian truth, and consequently opened the door for skepticism, rationalism, etc.

PLENARY INSPIRATION—The doctrine that the inspiration and divine authority of the Bible are full and complete, meaning that they extend (equally) to every part of the Scriptures.

POLYGLOT—Literally, "many tongues." A multiple-columned edition of a particular writing or composition, usually containing the original and various other versions or translations in the several columns for means of comparison.

PROGRESSIVE REVELATION—The view that the divine disclosure of doctrine did not come in a single deposit, but that at divers times in its historical development later revelation built upon and superseded the former disclosures.

PSEUDEPIGRAPHA—A word meaning "false writings" used to designate those spurious and unauthentic books of the late centuries B.C. and early centuries A.D. These books contain religious folklore and have never been considered canonical by the Christian church.

QUARTO—Literally, "one quarter," referring to manuscripts or books having four leaves (eight pages) to the sheet, that is 9½ by 12 inches (scale of American Library Association).

RECENSION—The systematic and critical revision of a text or composition.

RESCRIPTUS—A manuscript which has been rewritten over lettering that had been erased; it is a palimpsest which has been rescripted.

REVELATION—An objective disclosure of truth by God, and used in contrast to illumination, which is the subjective understanding of a revelation.

REVISION—A text or composition which has been reviewed and has undergone some necessary changes or corrections.

SEPTUAGINT—Literally, "The Seventy"; the Greek translation of the Old Testament allegedly translated by some seventy scribes in Alexandria, Egypt, at about 250 B.C. and symbolized LXX.

TESTAMENT—Loosely the equivalent of "covenant," but technically a testament does not require a two-way agreement, as it needs only the action of the testator with or without the assent of the heir.

TEXTUAL CRITICISM—Synonymous with "lower criticism" (see above).

TEXTUS RECEPTUS—The Greek text presumed to underlie the Authorized Version of 1611 (King James Version). This text is basically that of Erasmus' fifth edition (1535), Stephen's third edition (1550), and named the Received Text in the introduction of the Elzevir Brothers' second edition (1633). It is based on few early manuscripts and is opposed by Westcott, Hort, and all those who accept a "critical text" (see above).

THEOPNEUSTOS—The English equivalent of this Greek word is "inspiration," which literally means "God-breathed."

TORAH—The English transliteration of the Hebrew word for "law"; it often refers to the first five books of the Old Testament.

TRANSLATION—The rendering of a composition or piece of literature from one language to another, as contrasted with a version, which is a translation from the original language of a manuscript into another language.

TRANSLITERATION—A letter-for-letter transposition of a word from one language to another.

TRANSMISSION—The process by which the biblical manuscripts have been copied and recopied down through the ages; it deals with the history of the text from the autographs to the present printed Hebrew and Greek Testaments.

UNCIAL MANUSCRIPT (or majuscule)—Literally, "inch high," referring to a manuscript written in formally printed large letters similar in size to capital letters.

VELLUM—A fine quality writing material in ancient times, usually prepared from calf or antelope skin.

VERBAL INSPIRATION—The doctrine holding that the very words of the Bible are vested with divine authority and not merely the thoughts or ideas.

VERSION—A literary composition which has been translated from its original language into another tongue.

VULGATE—Literally, "common" or "usual"; generally the designation for the Latin translation of the Bible made by Jerome in the fourth century A.D.

BIBLIOGRAPHY

SOURCES

Aland, K.; Black, M.; Metzger, B.; and Wikgren, A. (eds.). *The Greek New Testament.* New York: United Bible Societies, 1966.

Alford, Henry. *The Greek Testament.* 5th ed. London: Rivingtons, 1871.

Ambrose. *Letters* in *Library of Christian Classics.* Vol. V. Trans. and ed. S. L. Greenslade. Philadelphia: Westminster, 1956.

Apocrypha. Revised Standard Version of the Old Testament. New York: Nelson, 1957.

The Apostolic Fathers. 2 vols. Loeb Classical Library Series. Ed. Kirsopp Lake. New York: Putnam, 1930.

Aquinas, Thomas. *Summa Theologiae.* Ed. Thomas Gilby. New York: McGraw-Hill, 1964.

Athanasius. *Letters* in *Nicene and Post-Nicene Fathers.* Vol. IV, 2d series. Trans. Archibald Robertson. Eds. Philip Schaff and Henry Wace. Grand Rapids: Eerdmans, 1953.

Augustine, Aurelius. *The City of God.* Trans. Marcus Dods, introduction by Thomas Merton. New York: Random, 1949.

———. *Expositions on the Book of Psalms* in *Nicene and Post-Nicene Fathers.* Vol. VIII, 1st series. Trans. A. Cleveland Coxe. Ed. Philip Schaff. Grand Rapids: Eerdmans, 1956.

———. *On Christian Doctrine* in *Nicene and Post-Nicene Fathers.* Vol. II, 1st series. Trans. J. F. Shaw. Ed. Philip Schaff. Grand Rapids: Eerdmans, 1956.

Bede, Venerable. *Ecclesiastical History of the English Nation.* Cambridge: U. Press, 1881.

Calvin, John. *Institutes of the Christian Religion.* Trans. Henry Beveridge. Grand Rapids: Eerdmans, 1957.

Clement of Alexandria. *Stromata* in *Ante-Nicene Fathers.* Vol. II. Eds. Alexander Roberts and James Donaldson. Grand Rapids: Eerdmans, 1951.

Cyprian. "Epistle About Cornelius and Novatian." *Ante-Nicene Fathers.* Vol. V. Grand Rapids: Eerdmans, 1951.

———. *The Unity of the Catholic Church* in *Library of Christian Classics.* Vol. V. Trans. and ed. S. L. Greenslade. Philadelphia: Westminster, 1956.

Cyril of Jerusalem. *Catechetical Lectures* in *Nicene and Post-Nicene Fathers.* Vol. VII, 2d series. Rev. trans. Edwin H. Gifford. Ed. Philip Schaff. Grand Rapids: Eerdmans, 1955.

The Dead Sea Scrolls in English. Trans. Geza Vermes. New York: Heritage, 1962.

The English Hexapla in Parallel Columns. London: S. Bagster, n.d.

Eusebius. *Ecclesiastical History.* Loeb ed. Vol. I. Trans. Kirsopp Lake, 1926. Vol. II. Trans. J. E. L. Oulton, 1932. London: Heinemann.

The Glorious Koran. An explanatory translation by Mohammed Marmaduke Pickthall. New York: New Amer. Lib. of World Lit., 1953.

Gregory the Great. *The Commentary of Job* in *Library of Christian Classics.* Vol. IX. Trans. and ed. George McCracken. Philadelphia: Westminster, 1957.

The Holy Bible. Newly edited by the American Revision Committee. New York: Nelson, 1901.

————. Authorized Version. New York: Oxford U., n.d.

————. English Revised Version. Cambridge: U. Press, 1881, 1885.

————. Revised Standard Version. New York: Nelson, 1945, 1952.

The Holy Bible Containing the Authorized Version of the Old and New Testaments With Many Emendations. London: Bartlett, 1841.

The Holy Bible, an Exact Reprint Page for Page of the Authorized Version Published in the Year MDCXI. Oxford: U. Press, 1833.

The Holy Bible: a Translation from the Latin Vulgate in the Light of the Hebrew and Greek Originals. Trans. John Knox. New York: Sheed & Ward, 1948.

The Holy Scriptures According to the Masoretic Text. Philadelphia: Jewish Pubn. Soc. of Amer., 1917.

Irenaeus. *Against Heresies* in *Library of Christian Classics.* Vol. I. Ed. and trans. Edward Rochie Hardy. Philadelphia: Westminster, 1953.

Jerome. *The Four Gospels* in *Nicene and Post-Nicene Fathers.* Vol. VI, 2d series. Eds. Philip Schaff and Henry Wace. Grand Rapids: Eerdmans, 1954.

————. *Letters* in *Library of Christian Classics.* Vol. V. Trans. and ed. Stanley L. Greenslade. Philadelphia: Westminster, 1956.

————. *Lives of Illustrious Men* in *Nicene and Post-Nicene Fathers.* Vol. III, 2d series. Eds. Philip Schaff and Henry Wace. Grand Rapids: Eerdmans, 1952.

The Jerusalem Bible. Garden City, N.Y.: Doubleday, 1966.

Josephus, Flavius. *The Life and Works of Flavius Josephus.* Trans. William Whiston. Philadelphia: Winston, 1936.

Justin Martyr. *Apology* in *Ante-Nicene Fathers.* Vol. I. Eds. Alexander Roberts and James Donaldson. Grand Rapids: Eerdmans, 1954.

Kahle, Paul E. *The Cairo Geniza.* 2d ed. London: British Academy, 1959.

Kittel, Rudolf, and Kahle, Paul E. (eds.). *Biblia Hebraica.* 3d ed. New York: Amer. Bible Soc., 1937.

Living Talmud. Selected and trans. Judah Goldin. Chicago: U. of Chicago, 1957.

The Massorah. 4 vols. Compiled from manuscripts by C. D. Ginsberg. London: British & Foreign Bible Soc., 1926.

The Mishnah. Trans. Herbert Danby. Oxford: U. Press, 1958.

Novum Testamentum Graece. Editio vicesima tertia. Ed. Eberhard Nestle. New York: Amer. Bible Soc., 1957.

Origen. *De Principiis* in *Ante-Nicene Fathers.* Vol. IV. Ed. Philip Schaff. Grand Rapids: Eerdmans, 1951.

Petry, Ray C., and Manschreck, Clyde L. (eds.). *A History of Christianity.* 2 vols. Englewood Cliffs, N. J.: Prentice-Hall, 1962, 1964.

Philo. Trans. F. H. Colson. Vol. IX. Cambridge, Mass.: Harvard U., 1941.

Rodkinson, Michael L. *The Babylonian Talmud.* N.p., 1916.

Schaff, Philip, and Wace, Henry (eds.). *Nicene and Post-Nicene Fathers.* Vols. I, VI, XIV, 2d series. Grand Rapids: Eerdmans, 1952.

Schaff, Philip (ed.). *The Creeds of Christendom.* 3 vols. 6th ed., rev. and enlarged. New York: Harper, 1919.

The Septuagint Version of the Old Testament. London: S. Bagster, n.d.

The Seven Ecumenical Councils in *Nicene and Post-Nicene Fathers.* Vol. XIV, 2d series. Trans. Henry R. Percival. Eds. Philip Schaff and Henry Wace. Grand Rapids: Eerdmans, 1956.

Tertullian. "On the Apparel of Women." *Ante-Nicene Fathers.* Vol. IV. Eds. Alexander Roberts and James Donaldson. Grand Rapids: Eerdmans, 1951.

The Variorum Edition of the New Testament of Our Lord and Saviour Jesus Christ. Eds. R. L. Clarke, Alfred Goodwin, and W. Sanday. London: Eyre & Spottiswoode, 1881.

Westcott, Brooke Foss, and Hort, Fenton Anthony. *The New Testament in the Original Greek.* Vol. II, 2d ed. Cambridge: n.p., 1896.

PERIODICAL ARTICLES

Albright, William F. "The Elimination of King 'So'," *Bulletin of the American Schools of Oriental Research,* No. 171 (Oct., 1963).

Carnell, Edward John. "The Problem of Religious Authority," *His* magazine (Feb., 1950).

Clark, Kenneth W. "The Making of the Twentieth Century New Testament," *Bulletin of the John Rylands Library* (1955).

Culver, Robert D. "The Old Testament as Messianic Prophecy," *Bulletin of the Evangelical Theological Society,* Vol. VII, No. 3 (1964).

Foster, Lewis. "The Earliest Collection of Paul's Epistles," *Bulletin of the Evangelical Theological Society,* Vol. X, No. 1 (Winter, 1967).

Goedicke, Hans. "The End of 'So,' King of Egypt," *Bulletin of the American Schools of Oriental Research,* No. 171 (Oct., 1963).

Grounds, Vernon. "Postulate of Paradox," *Bulletin of the Evangelical Theological Society*, Vol. VII, No. 1 (1964).

Harris, R. Laird. "Was the Law and the Prophets Two-Thirds of the Old Testament Canon?" *Bulletin of Evangelical Theological Society*, Vol. IX, No. 4 (Fall, 1966).

Hatch, W. H. P. "The Origin and Meaning of the Term 'Uncial'," *Classical Philology*, Vol. XXX (1935).

Hoskier, H. C. "Evan. 157 (Rome Vat. Urb. 2)," *Journal of Theological Studies*, Vol. XIV (1913).

King, Marchant A. "Notes on the Bodmer Manuscript of Jude and 1 and 2 Peter," *Bibliotheca Sacra*, Vol. CXXI, No. 481 (1964).

———. "The Text of I Peter in Papyrus 72," *Journal of Biblical Literature*, Vol. LXXXX (Sept., 1961).

Lyon, Robert W. "Re-examination of Codex Ephraemi Rescriptus," *New Testament Studies*, Vol. V (1959).

Nix, William E. "Theological Presuppositions and Sixteenth Century English Bible Translations," *Bibliotheca Sacra*, Vol. CXXIV, Nos. 493-94 (Jan.-Mar., Apr.-June, 1967).

Rowley, H. H. "The Interpretation of the Song of Songs," *Journal of Theological Studies*, Vol. XXXVIII (1937).

Schipper, Reinier. "Paul and the Computer," *Christianity Today* (Dec. 4, 1964).

Streeter, B. H. "Codices 157, 1071, and the Caesarean Text," *Quantualacumque, Studies Presented to Kirsopp Lake* (1937).

Trever, J. C. "The Discovery of the Scrolls," *Biblical Archaeologist*, Vol. XI (Sept., 1948).

Van der Valk, M. "Observations on Mark 16:9-20 in Relation to St. Mark's Gospel," *Humanitas* (1958).

Witmer, John A. "The Biblical Evidence for the Verbal-Plenary Inspiration of the Bible," *Bibliotheca Sacra*, Vol. CXXI, No. 483 (1964).

REFERENCE WORKS

Bauer, Walter. *Griechisch-Deutsches Wörterbuch zu den Schriften des Neuen Testaments und der übrigen urchristlichen Literatur*. 4th rev. and augmented ed., 1952. Trans. William F. Arndt and F. Wilbur Gingrich, *A Greek-English Lexicon of the New Testament and Other Early Christian Literature*. Chicago: U. of Chicago, 1957.

The Catholic Encyclopedia. New York: Appleton, 1908.

Cross, F. L. (ed.). *The Oxford Dictionary of the Christian Church*. London: Oxford U., 1957.

Douglas, J. D. (ed.). *The New Bible Dictionary*. Grand Rapids: Eerdmans, 1962.

Edwards, Tryon. *A Dictionary of Thoughts*. Detroit: Dickerson, 1904.

Ellicott, Charles John (ed.). *Ellicott's Commentary*. Vol. IV. Introduction by Stanley Leaves. Grand Rapids: Zondervan, 1954.

Englishman's Greek Concordance. 9th ed. London: S. Bagster, 1903.

Gore, Philip Babcock (ed.). *Webster's Third International Dictionary*. Springfield, Mass.: Merriam, 1961.

Harrison, Everett F. (ed.). *Baker's Dictionary of Theology*. Grand Rapids: Baker, 1960.

Hastings, James (ed.). *A Dictionary of the Bible*. 4 vols. plus one extra volume. New York: Scribner, 1909.

Historical Catalogue of the Printed Editions of Holy Scripture in the Library of the British and Foreign Bible Society. 2 vols. Compiled by T. H. Darlow and H. F. Moule. New York: Kraus Reprint, 1963. Originally Published London, 1903.

The Jewish Encyclopedia. New York: Funk & Wagnalls, 1906.

Kraeling, Emil G. (ed.). *The Rand-McNally Bible Atlas*. New York: Rand-McNally, 1956.

Lange, John Peter. *Commentary on the Holy Scriptures, Revelation*. Trans. from the German and ed. with additions by Philip Schaff. Grand Rapids: Zondervan, n.d.

Orr, James (ed.). *International Standard Bible Encyclopaedia*. Rev. ed., 5 vols. Grand Rapids: Eerdmans, 1943.

Strong, Augustus H. *Systematic Theology*. Grand Rapids: Revell, 1907.

Thayer, Joseph Henry. *A Greek-English Lexicon of the New Testament*. New York: Amer. Bk. Co., 1889.

The Twentieth-Century Encyclopedia of Religious Knowledge. 2 vols. Grand Rapids: Baker, 1955.

Yust, Walter (ed.). *Encyclopaedia Britannica*. Chicago: Encyclopaedia Britannica, 1954.

BOOKS

Albright, William F. *From the Stone Age to Christianity*. 2d ed. Garden City, N.Y.: Doubleday, 1957.

———. "Recent Discoveries in Palestine and the Gospel of St. John" in *The Background of the New Testament and Its Eschatology*. Eds. William D. Davies and D. Daube. Cambridge: U. Press, 1956.

———. *Recent Discoveries in Bible Lands*. New York: Funk & Wagnalls, 1956.

Allegro, John M. *The Treasure of the Copper Scroll*. 2d rev. ed. Garden City, N.Y.: Doubleday, 1965.

Allen, Cardinal. *Letters and Memorials of Cardinal Allen*. Introduction by T. F. Knox. London: n.p., 1882.

Andrews, Herbert T. *An Introduction to the Apocryphal Books of the Old and New Testaments.* Rev. and ed. Charles F. Pfeiffer. Grand Rapids: Baker, 1964.

Angus, Joseph. *The Bible Handbook.* Rev. by Samuel G. Green. Grand Rapids: Zondervan, 1952.

Archer, Gleason L., Jr. *A Survey of Old Testament Introduction.* Chicago: Moody, 1964.

Bachmann, E. Theodore (ed.). *Luther's Works.* Vol. XXXV. Philadelphia: Muhlenberg, 1960.

Barth, Karl. *Church Dogmatics* in *The Doctrine of the Word of God.* Vol. I. Trans. G. T. Thompson. Edinburgh: T. & T. Clark, 1936.

Barthélemy, D., and Milik, J. T. *Discoveries in the Judaean Desert.* London: Oxford U., 1955.

Baugh, Albert C. *A History of the English Language.* 2d ed. New York: Appleton-Century-Crofts, 1957.

Beegle, Dewey M. *The Inspiration of Scripture.* Philadelphia: Westminster, 1963.

Bell, Richard. *Introduction to the Qur'an.* Edinburgh: U. Press, 1953.

Berkhof, Louis. *The History of Christian Doctrines.* Grand Rapids: Eerdmans, 1937.

Brownlee, William Hugh. *The Meaning of the Qumran Scrolls for the Bible.* New York: Oxford U., 1964.

Bruce, F. F. *The Books and the Parchments.* Rev. ed. Westwood, N.J.: Revell, 1963.

———. *The English Bible: A History of Translations.* New York: Oxford U., 1961.

———. *The New Testament Documents: Are They Reliable?* Grand Rapids: Eerdmans, 1965.

———. *Second Thoughts on the Dead Sea Scrolls.* Grand Rapids: Eerdmans, 1956.

Bruce, F. F., and Simpson, Edmund Kidley. *Commentary on the Epistles to the Ephesians and Colossians.* Grand Rapids: Eerdmans, 1957.

Brunner, Heinrich Emil. *Theology of Crisis.* New York: Scribner, 1929.

Bryant, Margaret M. *Modern English and Its Heritage.* New York: Macmillan, 1948.

Buhl, Franz. *The Canon and Text of the Old Testament.* N.p., 1892.

Bultmann, Rudolf K. *Jesus Christ and Mythology.* New York: Scribner, 1958.

Burgon, John W. *The Last Twelve Verses of the Gospel According to St. Mark.* Marshallton, Del.: Sovereign Grace, 1959.

Burrows, Millar. *The Dead Sea Scrolls.* New York: Viking, 1955.

———. *More Light on the Dead Sea Scrolls.* New York: Viking, 1958.

––––. *What Mean These Stones?* New Haven, Conn.: Amer. Schools of Oriental Research, 1941.

Burtner, Robert W., and Chiles, Robert E. *A Compend of Wesley's Theology*. Nashville: Abingdon, 1954.

Carnell, Edward John. *The Case for Orthodox Theology*. Philadelphia: Westminster, 1959.

Charles, Robert Henry (ed.). *The Apocrypha and Pseudepigrapha of the Old Testament in English*. 2 vols. Oxford: Clarendon, 1913.

Chase, Mary Ellen. *Life and Language in the Old Testament*. New York: Norton, 1955.

Clark, Gordon H., *et al. Can I Trust My Bible?* Chicago: Moody, 1963.

Collett, Sidney. *All About the Bible*. Westwood, N. J.: Revell, 1959.

Coss, Thurman L. *Secrets from the Caves*. Nashville: Abingdon, 1963.

Cross, Frank Moore, Jr. *The Ancient Library of Qumran and Modern Biblical Studies*. Garden City, N.Y.: Doubleday, 1958.

Cumont, Franz. *Textes et Monuments figurés relatifs aux Mystères de Mithra*. 2 vols. Bruxelles: n.p., 1896, 1899; English trans. T. J. McCormick. London: n.p., 1903.

Danby, Herbert. *The Mishnah*. Oxford: U. Press, 1933.

Davidson, Samuel. *Introduction to the Old Testament*. London: n.p., 1862.

––––. *The Hebrew Text of the Old Testament*. London: n.p., 1856.

––––. *The Canon of the Bible*. 2d ed. London: n.p., 1877.

Davis, G. T. B. *Bible Prophecies Fulfilled Today*. Philadelphia: Million Testaments Campaigns, 1955.

Dāwūd, Ibn Abi. *Materials for the History of the Text of the Qur'an*. Ed. Arthur Jeffery. Leiden: Brill, 1937.

The Dead Sea Manual of Discipline. Trans. P. Wernberg-Moller. Grand Rapids: Eerdmans, 1957.

Deissmann, Gustav Adolf. *Light from the Ancient East*. Trans. L. R. M. Strachan. New York: Harper, 1923.

DeWolf, L. Harold. *The Case for Theology in Liberal Perspective*. Philadelphia: Westminster, 1959.

Dietrich, Karl. *Untersuchungen zur Geschichte der griechischen Sprache von der hellenistichen Zeit bis zum 10. Jahrhundert nach Christus* (*Researches on the History of the Greek Language from the Hellenistic Period to the Tenth Century A.D.*). Leipzig: Teubner, 1898.

Dupont-Sommer, Andre. *The Essene Writings from Qumran*. Trans. G. Vermes. Cleveland: World, 1962.

Enslin, Morton S. *Christian Beginnings*. New York: Harper, 1938.

Estep, W. R. *The Anabaptist Story*. Nashville: Broadman, 1963.

Evans, William. *The Great Doctrines of the Bible*. Chicago: Moody, 1949.

Ferm, Robert O. *The Psychology of Christian Conversion*. Westwood, N.J.: Revell, 1959.

Finegan, Jack. *Light from the Ancient Past*. 2d ed. Princeton, N.J.: Princeton U., 1959.

Free, Joseph P. *Archaeology and Bible History*. 5th ed. rev. Wheaton, Ill.: Scripture Press, 1956.

Gaussen, F. S. R. Louis. *Theopneustia*. Rev. ed. Trans. David Scott. Chicago: Bible Inst. Colportage, n.d.

Geisler, Norman L. *Christ: The Theme of the Bible*. Chicago: Moody, 1968.

Glueck, Nelson, *Rivers in the Desert*. New York: Farrar, Strauss & Cudahy, 1959.

Goodspeed, Edgar J. *The Complete Bible: An American Translation*. Chicago: U. of Chicago, 1923.

Grant, Robert M. *The Secret Sayings of Jesus*. Garden City, N.Y.: Doubleday, 1960.

Green, William H. *General Introduction to the Old Testament: The Canon*. New York: Scribner, 1899.

Greenlee, J. Harold. *An Introduction to New Testament Textual Criticism*. Grand Rapids: Eerdmans, 1964.

Greenslade, Stanley L. (ed.). *The Cambridge History of the Bible*. Vol. II. Cambridge: U. Press, 1963.

Gregory, Caspar René. *Canon and Text of the New Testament*. New York: Scribner, 1912.

Hackett, Stuart Cornelius. *The Resurrection of Theism*. Chicago: Moody, 1957.

Haley, John W. *An Examination of the Alleged Discrepancies of the Bible*. Grand Rapids: Baker, 1951.

Harris, R. Laird. *Inspiration and Canonicity of the Bible*. Grand Rapids: Zondervan, 1957.

Harrison, Everett F. *Introduction to the New Testament*. Grand Rapids: Eerdmans, 1964.

Heidel, Alexander. *The Babylonian Genesis*. 2d ed. Chicago: U. of Chicago, 1954.

Hennecke, Edgar, and Schneemelcher, Wilhelm (eds.). *New Testament Apocrypha*. Vol. I. Philadelphia: Westminster, 1963.

Henry, Carl F. H. (ed.). *Revelation and the Bible*. Grand Rapids: Baker, 1958.

Herklots, Hugh G. G. *How Our Bible Came to Us*. New York: Oxford U., 1954.

Hills, Edward F. *The King James Version Defended*. Des Moines: Chr. Research, 1956.

Hills, Margaret T. *A Ready-Reference History of the English Bible*. Rev. ed. New York: Amer. Bible Soc., 1962.

Hoare, H. W. *The Evolution of the English Bible.* 2d ed. London: Murray, 1902.

Hodge, Charles. *Systematic Theology.* 3 vols. Grand Rapids: Eerdmans, 1940.

Hordern, William. *The Case for a New Reformation Theology.* Philadelphia: Westminster, 1959.

Horne, Thomas. *An Introduction to the Critical Study and Knowledge of the Holy Scriptures.* 8th ed. London: n.p., 1856.

Husselman, Elinor M. *The Gospel of John in Fayumic Coptic* (P. Mich. inv. 3521). Ann Arbor: U. of Michigan, 1962.

Jauncey, James H. *Science Returns to God.* Grand Rapids: Zondervan, 1961.

Jespersen, Otto. *Growth and Structure of the English Language.* 9th ed. Garden City, N.Y.: Doubleday, 1955.

Kelly, J. N. D. *Early Christian Doctrines.* New York: Harper, 1958.

Kelly, Palmer H., and Miller, Donald G. (eds.). *Tools for Bible Study.* Richmond: Knox, 1956.

Kenyon, Sir Frederic G. *Handbook to the Textual Criticism of the New Testament.* 2d ed. Grand Rapids: Eerdmans, 1912.

———. *Our Bible and the Ancient Manuscripts.* 4th ed., rev. by A. W. Adams. New York: Harper, 1958.

Khayyám, Omar. *Rubaiyat.* Trans. Edward FitzGerald. New York: Black, 1942.

Kilgour, R. *The Bible Throughout the World: A Survey of Scripture Translations.* London: World Dominion, 1939.

Kramer, Samuel Noah. *History Begins at Sumer.* New York: Doubleday, 1959.

Latourette, Kenneth Scott. *A History of Christianity.* New York: Harper, 1953.

Leach, Charles. *Our Bible: How We Got It.* Chicago: Moody, 1897.

Leupold, Herbert Carl. *Exposition of Ecclesiastes.* Columbus, Ohio: Wartburg, 1952.

Lightfoot, J. B. *Saint Paul's Epistles to the Colossians and to Philemon.* Grand Rapids: Zondervan, 1965.

Lightfoot, Neil R. *How We Got the Bible.* Grand Rapids: Baker, 1963.

MacGregor, Geddes. *The Bible in the Making.* Philadelphia: Lippincott, 1959.

Machen, J. Gresham. *Christianity and Liberalism.* Grand Rapids: Eerdmans, 1956.

Manley, G. T. (ed.). *The New Bible Handbook.* 3d ed. London: Inter-Varsity, 1950.

Mansoor, Menahem. *The Dead Sea Scrolls.* Grand Rapids: Eerdmans, 1964.

Markwardt, Albert. *Introduction to the English Language.* New York: Oxford U., 1942.

Metzger, Bruce M. *Chapters in the History of New Testament Textual Criticism.* Grand Rapids: Eerdmans, 1963.

———. *An Introduction to the Apocrypha.* New York: Oxford U., 1957.

———. *The Text of the New Testament.* New York: Oxford U., 1964.

Miller, H. S. *A General Biblical Introduction.* 7th ed., rev. Houghton, N.Y.: Word-Bearer, 1952.

Morton, A. Q., and McLeman, James. *Christianity in the Computer Age.* New York: Harper & Row, 1964.

Mould, Elmer W. K. *Essentials of Bible History,* rev. ed. New York: Ronald, 1951.

Nash, Ronald. *The New Evangelicalism.* Grand Rapids: Zondervan, 1963.

Oesterley, W. O. E., and Robinson, Theodore H. *An Introduction to the Books of the Old Testament.* London: Soc. for Promoting Chr. Knowledge, 1934.

Orlinsky, Harry M. *Ancient Israel.* Rev. ed. Ithaca, N.Y.: Cornell U., 1960.

Orr, James. *The Problem of the Old Testament.* London: Nisbet, 1906.

———. *Revelation and Inspiration.* Grand Rapids: Eerdmans, 1952.

Parvis, M. M., and Wikgren, A. P. (eds.). *New Testament Manuscript Studies.* Chicago: U. of Chicago, 1950.

Pei, Mario A. *The World's Chief Languages.* 4th ed. New York: Vanni, 1955.

Petry, Ray C., and Manschreck, Clyde L. (eds.). *A History of Christianity.* 2 vols. Englewood Cliffs, N.J.: Prentice-Hall, 1962.

Pickering, Hy. *One Thousand Wonderful Things About the Bible.* London: Pickering & Inglis, n.d.

Plummer, Alfred. *International Critical Commentary: II Corinthians.* New York: Scribner, 1915.

Pollard, Alfred W. *Records of the English Bible.* London: Oxford U., 1911.

Pope, Hugh. *English Versions of the Bible.* Rev. and amplified by Sebastian Bullough. St. Louis: Herder, 1952.

Preus, Robert. *Inspiration of Scripture.* Edinburgh: Oliver & Boyd, 1955.

Pyles, Thomas. *Origins and Development of the English Language.* New York: Harcourt, Brace & World, 1964.

Ramm, Bernard. *Protestant Biblical Interpretation.* Rev. ed. Boston: Wilde, 1956.

Ramsay, W. M. *St. Paul the Traveller and the Roman Citizen.* 3d ed. Grand Rapids: Baker, 1949.

Rice, John R. *Twelve Tremendous Themes.* Wheaton, Ill.: Sword of the Lord, 1943.

Roberts, B. J. *The Old Testament Text and Versions.* Cardiff: U. of Wales, 1951.

Robertson, Archibald T. *A Harmony of the Gospels for Students.* Nashville, Tenn.: Broadman, 1922.

———. *An Introduction to the Textual Criticism of the New Testament.* Nashville: Broadman, 1925.

Robinson, G. L. *Where Did We Get Our Bible?* New York: Doubleday, Doran, 1928.

Rodkinson, Michael L. *Babylonian Talmud.* Boston: Talmud Soc., 1918.

Ryrie, Charles C. *Biblical Theology of the New Testament.* Chicago: Moody, 1959.

Saphir, Adolph. *Christ and the Scriptures.* Kilmarnock, Scotland: Ritchie, n.d.

Sauer, Erich. *The Dawn of World Redemption.* Trans. G. H. Lang. London: Paternoster, 1951.

———. *The Triumph of the Crucified.* Trans. G. H. Lang. London: Paternoster, 1951.

Schaff, Philip. *Companion to the Greek Testament and the English Version.* 3d ed., rev. New York: Harper, 1883.

———. *History of the Christian Church.* 7 vols. 5th ed., rev. New York: Scribner, 1910.

Scrivener, F. H. A. *A Plain Introduction to the Criticism of the New Testament.* 2 vols. 4th ed. Ed. Edward Miller. London: Bell, 1894.

Scroggie, W. Graham. *Know Your Bible.* 2 vols. London: Pickering & Inglis, n.d.

Souter, Alexander. *The Text and Canon of the New Testament.* London: Duckworth, 1913.

Stonehouse, Ned B. *The Witness of Matthew and Mark to Christ.* 2d ed. Grand Rapids: Eerdmans, 1958.

Stonehouse, Ned B., and Woolley, Paul (eds.). *The Infallible Word.* Philadelphia: Presb. Guardian, 1946.

Sundberg, Albert C., Jr. *The Old Testament of the Early Church.* Cambridge, Mass.: Harvard U., 1964.

Swete, Henry Barclay. *An Introduction to the Old Testament in Greek.* 2d ed. Cambridge: U. Press, 1902.

Tenney, Merrill C. *New Testament Survey.* Rev. ed. Grand Rapids: Eerdmans, 1961.

———(ed.). *The Word for This Century.* New York: Oxford U., 1960.

Terry, Milton S. *Biblical Hermeneutics.* Grand Rapids: Zondervan, 1950.

Thomas, W. H. Griffith. *Christianity Is Christ.* Chicago: Moody, 1965.

Torrey, C. C. *The Four Gospels.* New York: Harper, 1933.

Unger, Merrill F. *Archaeology and the New Testament.* Grand Rapids: Zondervan, 1962.

———. *Archaeology and the Old Testament.* Grand Rapids: Zondervan, 1954.

———. *Commentary on Zechariah.* Grand Rapids: Zondervan, 1963.

———. *Introductory Guide to the Old Testament.* 2d ed. Grand Rapids: Zondervan, 1956.

Van Loon, Henrik W. *The Story of the Bible.* Garden City, N.Y.: Garden City, 1941.

Voobus, Arthur. *Early Versions of the New Testament.* Stockholm: Estonian Theol. Soc. in Exile, 1954.

Walker, Williston. *A History of the Christian Church.* Rev. Cyril C. Richardson, *et al.* New York: Scribner, 1959.

Wallis, Ethel Emily, and Bennett, Mary Angela. *Two Thousand Tongues to Go.* New York: Harper, 1959.

Warfield, Benjamin B. *The Inspiration and Authority of the Bible.* Philadelphia: Presb. & Ref., 1948.

———. *An Introduction to the Textual Criticism of the New Testament.* London: n.p., 1886.

Westcott, Brooke Foss. *The Bible in the Church.* 2d ed. New York: Macmillan, 1887.

———. *A General Survey of the History of the Canon of the New Testament.* 7th ed. New York: Macmillan, 1896.

———. *History of the English Bible.* New York: Macmillan, 1905.

———. *An Introduction to the Study of the Gospels.* 7th ed. London: Macmillan, 1888.

Westcott, Brooke Foss, and Hort, Fenton John Anthony (eds.). *The New Testament in the Original Greek.* 2d ed. New York: Macmillan, 1928.

Wikgren, Allen P. *The Text, Canon and Principal Versions of the Bible, an Extract from the Twentieth Century Encyclopedia of Religious Knowledge.* Grand Rapids: Baker, 1955.

Williams, Charles B. *Interim Report on Vocabulary Selection.* London: n.p., 1936.

Winer, George Benedict. *A Grammar of the Idiom of the New Testament Greek.* 8th English ed. Trans. W. F. Moulton, from 2d ed. Edinburgh: T. & T. Clark, 1877.

Wolfson, Harry Austryn. *Philo: Foundations of Religious Philosophy in Judaism, Christianity, and Islam.* Vol. II. Cambridge, Mass.: Harvard U., 1962.

Wright, G. E. (ed). *The Bible and the Ancient Near East.* Garden City, N.Y.: Doubleday, 1961.

Wuest, Kenneth S. *Wuest's Expanded Translation of the Greek New Testament.* Grand Rapids: Eerdmans, 1961.

Young, Edward J. *An Introduction to the Old Testament.* Grand Rapids: Eerdmans, 1958.

———. *My Servants the Prophets.* Grand Rapids: Eerdmans, 1952.

Young, Robert. *A Literal Translation of the Holy Bible.* 3d ed. Grand Rapids: Baker, 1956 reprint.

Young, Robert. *Young's Literal Translation of the Holy Bible.* 3d ed. Grand Rapids: Baker, 1898.

Zeitlin, Solomon. *The Dead Sea Scrolls and Modern Scholarship.* Philadelphia: Dropsie Col., 1956.

AUTHOR INDEX

SUBJECT INDEX

SCRIPTURE INDEX